CW01262653

FLYING LIGHT HELICOPTERS WITH THE ROYAL MARINES

To all Royal Marines, Army and Navy personnel who served with
3 Commando Brigade Air Squadron Royal Marines all over the world and
to their long-suffering wives, partners and girlfriends, so often separated
for months on end.

FLYING LIGHT HELICOPTERS WITH THE ROYAL MARINES

COLLECTIVE TALES FROM
MARINE AIR 489

ROBERT WILSEY

AIR WORLD

FLYING LIGHT HELICOPTERS WITH THE ROYAL MARINES COLLECTIVE TALES FROM MARINE AIR 489

First published in Great Britain in 2021 by
Air World
An imprint of
Pen & Sword Books Ltd
Yorkshire – Philadelphia

Copyright © Robert Wilsey, 2021

ISBN 978 1 39900 250 9

The right of Robert Wilsey to be identified as Author of this work has been asserted by him in accordance with the Copyright, Designs and Patents Act 1988.

A CIP catalogue record for this book is available from the British Library.

All rights reserved. No part of this book may be reproduced or transmitted in any form or by any means, electronic or mechanical including photocopying, recording or by any information storage and retrieval system, without permission from the Publisher in writing.

Typeset by SJmagic DESIGN SERVICES, India.

Printed and bound in the UK by CPI Group (UK) Ltd, Croydon, CR0 4YY.

Pen & Sword Books Limited incorporates the imprints of Atlas, Archaeology, Aviation, Discovery, Family History, Fiction, History, Maritime, Military, Military Classics, Politics, Select, Transport, True Crime, Air World, Frontline Publishing, Leo Cooper, Remember When, Seaforth Publishing, The Praetorian Press, Wharncliffe Local History, Wharncliffe Transport, Wharncliffe True Crime and White Owl.

For a complete list of Pen & Sword titles please contact

PEN & SWORD BOOKS LIMITED
47 Church Street, Barnsley, South Yorkshire, S70 2AS, England
E-mail: enquiries@pen-and-sword.co.uk
Website: www.pen-and-sword.co.uk

Or
PEN AND SWORD BOOKS
1950 Lawrence Rd, Havertown, PA 19083, USA
E-mail: Uspen-and-sword@casematepublishers.com
Website: www.penandswordbooks.com

Contents

Preface vii

Introduction x

Chapter 1   Basic Training   1
Chapter 2   Advanced Training   12
Chapter 3   Gazelle Conversion   27
Chapter 4   All at Sea   35
Chapter 5   Malta   46
Chapter 6   Malta – Towards Withdrawal   55
Chapter 7   Brunei – The Jungle   66
Chapter 8   Northern Ireland – Trouble at t'Mill   77
Chapter 9   Central Flying School (H) – RAF Shawbury   86
Chapter 10 Instructing on Gazelle – Early Days and BAOR   95
Chapter 11 Instructing on Gazelle – Flight Commander   105
Chapter 12 Crash, Bang, Wallop   113
Chapter 13 You Need Eyes in the Back of Your Head   118
Chapter 14 Instructing on Lynx   125
Chapter 15 Display Flying   139
Chapter 16 Senior Pilot – Arctic Training   151
Chapter 17 Senior Pilot – The Mountains   162

Chapter 18	Senior Pilot – St Kilda	172
Chapter 19	Squadron Command	183
Chapter 20	Air Combat Manoeuvring – Tally One, Visual One, Fight's On	191
Chapter 21	Op HAVEN – Deployment	198
Chapter 22	Op HAVEN – Establishing the Safe Haven	206
Chapter 23	Op HAVEN – Life in the Field	214
Chapter 24	Op HAVEN – Withdrawal	219
Chapter 25	In the Back	224
Chapter 26	Private Flying	232
Chapter 27	Envoi	238

Glossary	241
Bibliography and References	245
Endnotes	248
Index	273

Maps

Map of Europe	35
Plan of Middle Wallop Airfield	95
Map of Op HAVEN	198

Preface

It was my training and career in the Royal Marines that enabled me to travel and work in some far-flung places as well as undergo some of the best military rotary flying training in the world. Now retired, it is the comradeship, sense of purpose and, particularly, the sense of humour of the marines that I miss today. The harder the conditions, the blacker the humour became and my memories of any physical hardship are mixed with those of laughter, often connected with an unrepeatable and witty aside. It is a difficult thing to explain to anyone who has not experienced it but perhaps these elements were best portrayed in the media in the excellent TV series *Band of Brothers* which gave a real feel for the spirit in a rifle company. Especially important was the overriding ethos of 'not letting your oppo down' which is the cement that binds infantrymen together and helps them act in a way that, in the cold light of day, no civilian would normally contemplate. This story, however, is about aviation because, firstly, that was my specialisation as a Royal Marines infantry officer; secondly because aviation tends to breed its own fair share of adventure stories; and lastly because I have never grown out of it. Everyone makes mistakes but in aviation lapses can be unforgiving. Despite modern technology there is still something elemental about defying gravity and the end result of a miscalculation has not changed since the days of Icarus. The ground is still as solid as it has always been and this is perhaps why balloonists, free-fall parachutists and climbers all have their special tales to tell, along with aviators. I am conscious that this story contains a surprising amount of peacetime death and disaster. That is how it was; it never put any of us off flying and the accident records of my era were a huge improvement over those of the 1950s and 1960s. It is sobering to recall that the United Kingdom lost more aircraft due to flying accidents in the Second World War than to enemy action.

To my great regret I missed the Falklands War. There is, however, plenty written separately about aviation in this conflict. Also for those who wish to read the full history of Royal Marines aviation they can do no better than Michael Reece's excellent book *Flying Royal Marines*.

Memory is fallible but I have relied on my diaries, notebooks and aircrew log book which compulsorily recorded all flights, dates, times and crew members and which is such a useful prop to the memory of ageing aircrew (I am sure this is why the memoirs of so many Second World War pilots are often so precise and fresh). I also asked many friends and colleagues to check the events that they shared with me, in order to try and retain accuracy and balance. This also gives me the opportunity to correct some myths about the Scout engine-off landing collision at Middle Wallop that have grown with passing years. Some events, such as the Airfix model kit of the Scout helicopter, certainly stretch the imagination but I have recorded the tales as they happened, or as they were reported to me at first-hand, and leave the reader to make up their own mind.

The reader may notice all the references to pilots are in the masculine gender. This is not sexism, just a fact about UK military flying in the 1970s and 80s. Since then of course female military pilots have more than proved their worth on various operations.

Why *Collective Tales from Marine Air 489*? Well, it's difficult to find an aviation title that has not already been used. My first thoughts of *Keeping in Balance* or *Maintaining Balance* are already in use with publications on either religion or mental health ... perhaps not entirely irrelevant subjects.

'Marine Air 489' was the callsign I was allocated when I first joined the Royal Marines Air Squadron and, despite later being offered the Senior Pilot's callsign and then the CO's callsign, I opted to retain '489' throughout my RM flying career. My salutations to anyone who used that callsign before I arrived or for the few years after I left.

I would like to thank all my colleagues and friends who checked my text for inaccuracies and proof-read relevant sections. The stories and dialogue in this book reflect my recollection of events. Although I have been faithful to my memory, aided by my notes and logbooks, I recognise that some others may remember events differently. In a few cases some names, locations and identifying characteristics have been changed to protect the privacy of those depicted. Pseudonyms are asterisked when first used. Dialogue has been re-created from memory.

Details of helicopter accidents of the 1970s and 80s have been confirmed or corrected by reference to some useful websites, notably the 'Aviation Safety Network' database, 'helis.com', 'Aviafora.com', 'demobbed.org.uk' and 'ukserials.com'.

PREFACE

My special thanks to Paul Bancroft, Alastair Rogers and David Storrie who read large portions of my text and offered valuable suggestions. My grateful thanks also to the following who also contributed, checked my memories or allowed me to use their photographs: Patrick Allen, Todd Ashcraft, Robert Atac, Simon Bailey, Oliver Barnham, Alan Barnwell, Colin Baulf, Séan Bonner, Julian Bourne, Jim Browne, Peter Cameron, Eddy Candlish, Brian Carter, Geoff Carvell, Tony Collins, Bryan Cox, Nigel Culliford, Kevin Dale, Dick Eastment, Ken Edgington, Robert Eckhoff, Tim Gedge, John Gilbert, Mike Goodfellow, Nicholas Hall, Tony Hancke, Graham Hancock, Virginia Harkin, Chris Ions, Damian Irving, Rowan Jackson, Wayne Kubek, Anthony Lawrence, Denis Lewis, Neil Macaulay, Tony Markham, John Menghini, David Minords, Greg Morris, Paul Morris, Terry Murphy, Jeff Niblett, Mike Nixon, Pete O'Connor, Victoria Parkes, Rick Peacock-Edwards, Keith Reid, Charles Sharland, Barrie Shepherd, John Sherly, Jon Spencer, Nicholas Steele, David Stewart, Keith Sturgess, Guy Vander Linden, Mike Wawn, Jacky Webby, Adrian Went, Robert Wilde, Katherine Wilsey, Simon Wilsey, David Woods, Adrian Wray and Jerry Young.

Also my gratitude to my publishers, the 'Pen & Sword, Frontline' team, who were receptive to my ideas and guided me around the pitfalls of publishing, especially Martin Mace, Amy Jordan and my editor Richard Doherty, who patiently gave me such sound advice and polished my manuscript, and to Jon Wilkinson who designed the cover. Without them this book would not have seen the light of day.

My enduring thanks also to those who taught me to fly; the late Charles Cuthill, Tony Collins, Mike Wawn and his QHIs at ARW, the CFS(H) team and all those instructors who converted me onto other types. Finally I remain eternally grateful to my wife Jane for her patience and unfailing support to me during my military service, despite so many months of my absence on deployment.

Knighton 2020
RPWW

Every effort has been made to trace the copyright holders of the images used and we apologise in advance for any unintentional omissions. We would be pleased to insert the appropriate acknowledgement in any subsequent edition of this publication.

Introduction

I have always nurtured a desire to fly. Why, I do not know because there was no great history of interest in my family and none of my relatives had been aviators. My first flight was in a Vickers Viking 1 of Hunting Clan Airways in 1952 when I flew from Stansted to Malta via Nice and Rome, an eight-hour journey. I was sick at Nice Airport, having just eaten an expensive and rare post-war banana. I have striking memories of being entranced looking at rows of Avro Yorks at Blackbushe in 1954. My next flight was in a polished-aluminium BEA Airspeed Ambassador (the stylish Elizabethans, named after Elizabethan knights, soon to be replaced by the Vickers Viscount) from Heathrow to Luqa via Nice in 1956, sitting in a window seat under the port wing next to the Bristol Centaurus nacelle and undercarriage. At RAF Luqa in 1957 I often watched Shackletons, Varsities, Hastings, Hermes, Elizabethans and Blackburn Beverleys and remember especially the first Bristol Britannia, the 'whispering giant', landing in Malta from a vantage point 100 metres from the threshold of runway 24 (now runway 23) next to the Schinas Reservoir. It was near to here in May 1953 that my father, then a Captain in the Royal Marines, was waiting with men of 40 Commando RM to emplane in a line of Vickers Valetta C.1 transports for the Canal Zone. He and his stick of marines watched as one of the Valettas failed to get airborne, crashed in the runway overshoot and caught fire.[1] All of this aircraft viewing at close quarters would, of course, be impossible in these days of security fences and no-stopping zones.

Battle of Britain Day at RAF Ta Kali in Malta in 1957 also remains impressed on my mind as we drove in our Hillman Minx to see a long line of Gloster Meteor FR.9s lined up precisely in dispersal, their polished-aluminium finish and coloured squadron stripes glinting in the harsh white sunlight.[2] These were the last days of the Meteor and by 1958 all had been replaced by the camouflaged Hawker Hunter. Later, as a prep-school boy, I went to Farnborough during my summer holidays in 1958 where a far-off

INTRODUCTION

roar heralded the approach of the un-environmentally friendly Fairey Rotodyne, an engineering feat which perhaps is only being equalled by the Bell V-22 Osprey tilt-rotor fifty years later. At that same Farnborough Roland Beamont flashed low overhead at just about sonic speed in the English Electric Lightning P1B and six Supermarine Scimitars of 803 Naval Air Squadron conducted a simulated bombing raid on the trees to the north side of the runway. What 9-year old boy could fail to be thrilled by this!

My first flight in a light aircraft took place at Roborough Airport, Plymouth, in 1962, aged 13, when I saved up my pocket and birthday money for a trip in Auster J/1N Alpha G-AGVF of the Plymouth Aero Club. It was silver with red trim and I was flown by the airport manager W.H.W. Lucas.[3] I remember him well, dressed as a 1930s era flying instructor with heavy sheepskin jacket, black flying boots and a large RAF moustache. I enjoyed it so much I saved up for a second flight. At prep school in Upper Deal, Kent, one day in autumn 1961, whilst playing soccer, we heard the multiple drone of heavy engines. Over the boundary trees came three four-engined aircraft in vic formation at about 900 feet. This was a change from the usual Bristol Freighters operated by Silver City. Everyone stopped playing and looked skywards. 'B-17 Flying Fortresses,' I excitedly yelled. 'Don't be silly boy,' said a master. Much later I realised they were almost certainly filming the '*The War Lover*' starring Steve McQueen and Shirley Anne Field out of RAF Manston. The film was released in 1962.[4]

Only a year later during the school holidays I saw three Mosquitos flying over our house at Amersham on a number of consecutive days. Knowing that they probably came from RAF Bovingdon, a few miles away, I hopped on my bike with sandwiches and spent a happy day watching *633 Squadron* being filmed from the lane which passed the threshold of runway 02.[5] I would never have dreamed that eighteen years later I would be flying at an air show where one of those Mosquitos was being displayed. My first experience of aerobatics was aged 14 in a light blue Chipmunk T.22 G-AOSO of the London School of Flying at Denham when the instructor said 'let's see how you like a little G' before pulling into a loop and then a roll.[6] If nothing else this demonstrated what an exciting impression of aviation these instructors imparted to me in what must for them been a chore of a thirty-minute jolly for a young boy.

At Shrewsbury School I was in the RAF Combined Cadet Force (CCF) section and enjoyed more Chipmunk aerobatics from RAF Shawbury. Our CCF camp in Easter 1964 was at RAF Lossiemouth operating Avro Shackletons. This was a first introduction to service discipline. When my turn came to be duty cadet of our accommodation hut, Flight Lieutenant Potts, who was duty officer, came to inspect it. 'Is it clean?' he enquired. 'More or less,' I replied. 'What does that mean?' 'More clean than less clean' was my cheeky but honest reply ... and you can imagine his reaction. I had a ninety-minute ride in the back of a Shackleton T.4 WB832 'U' of the Maritime Operational Training Unit during night circuits.[7] The T.4s were originally Shackleton MR.1s dating from 1951, seventeen of which were converted to trainers in the mid-1950s, still fitted with blanked-out rear gun turrets and much more 'Lancaster-like' than the later well-known operational Shackletons. My overall impression of the sortie was noise. The roar from the four Griffons at maximum power and the popping as the throttles were retarded in the flare, the hiss of compressed air and the squeal of brakes. I sat braced with my back against the main spar looking at the Air Engineer's panel with a myriad of luminous engine instruments. I also remember the deep red glow from the Griffons' exhaust shrouds. This was the nearest thing to a night flight in a Lancaster that you could get.

During my time at Shrewsbury School CCF the RAF section was assigned a Slingsby T.38 Grasshopper primary glider or, as the RAF termed them, the Grasshopper TX1. It was assembled by we cadets under the watchful eye of an RAF flight sergeant from Shawbury and launched by a V-shaped elastic rope pulled by two teams, each of five or six cadets. When at full stretch the 'pilot' released the hold-back, the glider skidded across the grass and occasionally leapt ten feet or so into the air before landing on its fixed skid. With a stall speed of 26 knots it was difficult to come to any harm, especially when the flight sergeant had access to spoilers and a method of limiting the elevator control range with pip pins. After some slides I was one of the lucky ones given a much fuller control range and from then on managed longer and higher hops which was far more interesting for my cadet muckers on the ropes always hoping for a spectacular prang. I once got to about twenty-five feet and had to bank slightly to avoid goalposts on my longer than expected touch-down. This simple glider gave us a useful basic understanding of rigging, construction and the effects of flying controls.[8]

My godfather's wife, Freydis (Fay) Sharland, also played a part in my aviation enthusiasm. As Freydis Leaf she was a wartime Air Transport Auxiliary (ATA) delivery pilot and flew thirty-eight different single- and twin-engine types to and from maintenance units and operational squadrons (she never took a four-engine heavy conversion). She showed me her copy of *Ferry Pilot's Notes* which contained a single page of key checks and limitations for each aircraft type in alphabetical order. Fay would literally

INTRODUCTION

jump into a Hurricane, followed by a Typhoon and then a Mosquito and return to White Waltham in an Anson or Oxford 'taxi' ready for the next day's deliveries. The ATA pilots were always required to deliver unarmed aircraft but Fay told me that the Polish squadrons usually gave her an aircraft loaded with some belts of ammunition and told her to 'have a go at a Hun if she met one'. This caused consternation on arrival at the civilian Castle Bromwich aircraft factory where they complained about not having the staff and facilities to de-arm aircraft. A friend of Hawker test pilot Neville Duke, in March 1949 she delivered a refurbished Hawker Tempest FBII from Manston to Pakistan, carrying out all the daily servicing on the Centaurus engine en route herself.[9] On arrival at Karachi Fay was refused entry to the base officers' mess after eight days of flying. She also flew in the King's Cup Air Races and in 1954 became the British Air Racing Champion in her Miles Hawk,[10] receiving the trophy from John Profumo.[11] I was fortunate enough to meet some of her former ATA colleagues and particularly remember Joan Hughes, an instructor at the British Airways Flying Club at Booker. Joan was diminutive at 5 foot 2 inches but with a calm air of professionalism; there is a famous wartime photograph of her standing dwarfed beside the main wheel of a Short Stirling bomber she had just delivered.[12] Fay Sharland died aged 93 in 2014 and I wish she had told me more but she was always somewhat diffident about her achievements. I once asked her which her favourite aircraft was and, without hesitation, she replied, 'the light blue Spitfire PR XI'. Ironically, after years of being overlooked, the last few of the Spitfire girls achieved public interest and recognition in their 80s and 90s and Fay and her few surviving colleagues were often interviewed on TV.

I took an RAF flying aptitude test at sixteen, which in retrospect was a mistake. I failed it and this set my confidence back considerably and I assumed for some years thereafter that I was unsuited to be a pilot. During school holidays in Singapore I was fortunate that my father was great friends with the station commander at RAF Tengah, Group Captain Teddy Hawkins.[13] I was also a chum of his son and we were both kindly allowed into the Gloster Javelin simulator when there was a gap between training slots. This was the final year of the Javelin FAW.9 with 60 and 64 Squadrons in the Far East. The simulator was a first-generation affair, static with an opaque white canopy and a pen-and-map trace at the instructor's station. The cockpit was a typical 1950s' ergonomic jumble of instruments. We took turns in front and rear seats and it was a good introduction for me to learn a scan and to struggle with trim whilst totally IMC 'over' southern Malaya.

FLYING LIGHT HELICOPTERS WITH THE ROYAL MARINES

Whilst on holiday in Singapore I sometimes crewed in dinghy sailing races for Colonel Wallace Pryke from HQ FARELF. Although I only heard Wally mention it once in passing, I was told that he had had a miraculous escape as a major whilst sitting in the back of a Valetta C.1 containing a jeep when they were in collision with a de Havilland Venom at 2,000 feet in the circuit at Boscombe Down. Both aircraft crashed in fields one-and-a-half miles west of the airfield and, amazingly, the Valetta occupants all survived, albeit with injuries.[14]

After leaving school I went into merchant banking for two years, having a ball after hours in 1960s London, and then, although it sounds a cliché, yearning for some action and adventure, I applied for a commission in the Royal Marines. When I was selected and underwent officer training at Lympstone (then the Infantry Training Centre Royal Marines now the Commando Training Centre Royal Marines) one of our directing staff was Captain Tim Donkin, a Wessex and Sioux pilot who had been the first OC of 3 Commando Brigade Air Squadron, formed in 1968 from the various air troops supporting RM units in Singapore.

Light aviation training for the Royal Marines at that time was a convoluted business. The first RM officer helicopter pilots in 1961 underwent basic rotary training with Bristow Helicopters at Redhill on the Hiller 12C but this was soon switched to the Royal Navy Hiller HT.2 at 705 NAS Culdrose.[15] They graduated with naval wings and went on to fly the Wessex HAS.1 (assault version), the Whirlwind Mk 7 and in later years the twin-engined Wessex HU.5. Those who were earmarked for unit light aircraft underwent a short Sioux conversion at Middle Wallop and then 'picked up' Army aviation helicopter skills 'on the job'. Since the Navy did not accept non-commissioned pilots, our SNCO pilots were all trained by the Army at Middle Wallop and wore Army wings.[16] Lieutenant Peter Cameron was the first RM officer to gain his Army wings in 1965 and thereafter an increasing proportion of RM officer pilots were trained by the Army at Middle Wallop.

Following officer training, I joined 42 Commando in Singapore where my first company commander, Major T.J.P. (Terence) Murphy was a pilot, a QHI and the first RM pilot to have flown jets, having qualified on the Hawker Sea Hawk FGA.6. I remember him telling me that his first deck landing was flown from RNAS Hal Far in Malta to join HMS *Albion* which was steaming east of the island heading for Port Said. He and his contemporary tossed a coin to see who would go first. Terence lost and his colleague took off into a hazy Mediterranean day. An hour later he was back. 'How did it go?' 'Not well – I couldn't find the ship.' After some time flying a heading

INTRODUCTION

in poor visibility, Terence was vectored to the ship by a Fighter Direction Officer and conducted three rollers followed by an arrested landing. After a tough initial few months of indoctrination, and being referred to as 'Mister Fricking Wilsey' by my company commander, I made the grade as far as he was concerned and thereafter thoroughly enjoyed my two and a half years with M Company. The company sergeant major was Derek Blevins, also a QHI, and thus my interest in aviation was kept alive. Coincidentally, Terence was posted on to command 3 Commando Brigade Air Squadron in Plymouth and was replaced as OC M Company by Captain David Storrie, who had brought the newly-formed Air Squadron home from Singapore. He was also a QHI, who had demonstrated the Westland Scout at the Paris Air Show at le Bourget in 1967. He was another company commander we would have followed anywhere, albeit with quite a different style from Terence Murphy.

Whilst serving in Singapore I cadged a flight in a Lightning T.5 of 74 Squadron at RAF Tengah and went supersonic over the east coast of Malaya whilst conducting a simulated head-on interception of another Lightning F.6. When off-duty I regularly went on water-skiing trips in the Straits of Johore opposite Pungoll with friends. We used to base ourselves on a small sandy beach on Pulau Ketam island amongst the mangrove inlets with a few Tiger beers and a packed lunch. It was usually mirror-calm in the mangrove swamps and ideal for water skiing. A colleague, hearing the distinctive noise of an approaching Sioux at low level, was reportedly dumbstruck to see a Sioux come around the corner at about twenty feet and 25 knots, slightly yawed as it pulled a water skier by a tow-rope attached to a rear skid post. If true, the tail rotor clearance from the rope doesn't bear thinking about, especially if the skier ever came off.

During my time as a rifle troop commander, my batch officer during training, Lieutenant Peter Seymour RM, underwent Army flying training, qualified and joined the Squadron in Plymouth. In February 1972 his Sioux crashed in bad weather in Leicestershire, killing both himself and Sergeant Hodson who were both newly qualified.[17] This narrative may give the impression that half the Royal Marines were pilots. This was far from true; the Royal Marines was a small Corps with perhaps at that time 600 officers, thirty-five of whom might have been unit light helicopter or RN Wessex pilots. For five years my mind was concentrated on Commando infantry soldiering and it was an unusual coincidence that led me to serve with so many RM pilots. It seemed inevitable therefore that I should volunteer for flying.

FLYING LIGHT HELICOPTERS WITH THE ROYAL MARINES

After leaving 42 Commando, having trained as a Forward Air Controller, I had a number of flights in Hunter T.7s from RAF Chivenor with 229 OCU. On one sortie, after carrying out some close air support runs, my pilot suggested that we see how high we could get in a zoom climb. Near Holsworthy, we reached over 520 knots at 200 feet and then pulled up into a near vertical climb, stalling at just over 17,000 feet. It was whilst on course there that I heard the strange story of the overseas student who, after landing long, engaged the barrier and ran into the overshoot. When the crash crews arrived they found the canopy open and the ejection seat empty. After a protracted search the pilot was found in the officers' mess ante-room wearing working dress reading the paper and denied being the pilot of the aircraft or of flying that morning. An odd ruse, considering there was an authorisation sheet and Form 700 that presumably said otherwise. I also flew in a Canberra TT.18 (silver with black and yellow diagonal undersurfaces) of 7 Squadron from RAF St Mawgan acting as a simulated low-level Rapier target for the Royal Artillery on the Salisbury Plain Training Area. I sat in the navigator's position in the rear, watching the airspeed indicator for the critical single-engine safety speed after take-off and, after a safe climb was achieved,[18] inserted the seat pins, unstrapped from the seat and lay prone in the plexiglass nose as we flew low over the Plain.

By 1974 I had volunteered for loan-service duty with the Sultan of Oman's Armed Forces and when I went to see the Assistant Military Secretary in London to confirm the details and timings of this posting, whilst leafing through his files, he suddenly remarked, 'I see from your documents that you were a volunteer for flying. We happen to be desperately short of pilots at present. Are you still interested? If so, you can attend aircrew selection in a fortnight's time.' There were plenty of other volunteers for Oman loan service, but his priority at that time was to find suitable student pilots so, ten years after my first visit, I returned to RAF Biggin Hill, passed the flying aptitude test without any problem, illustrating how one's mind and reactions can mature in those critical years between boyhood and manhood, and went on to RNH Haslar for my aircrew medical. On being assessed fit to fly, I was told to report to the Army Air Corps Centre at Middle Wallop for Army Pilots Course 238 on 1 July 1974 instead of flying out to Muscat.

Chapter 1

Basic Training

Royal Marines helicopter pilots had undergone flying training both with the Fleet Air Arm and the Army but, in the early 1970s, with a few exceptions who were trained by the Royal Navy for support helicopter flying with the Wessex HU.5, most Royal Marines were trained by the Army. At that time the Army Pilots Course was ten months long and included three phases, totalling 215 hours flying, divided up as follows:

Basic Fixed Wing on Chipmunk T.10	40 hours
Basic Rotary Wing on Bell 47G-4A	75 hours
Advanced Rotary Wing Squadron on Sioux AH.1	100 hours

Middle Wallop, the Army Air Corps Centre, was, and still is, a virtually unspoilt Second World War era grass airfield covering about 2,200 by 1,600 metres. Constructed on a hard chalk base, the grass provided a firm surface and had even by used by a Lockheed Constellation in summer months. This large expanse of grass allowed for two opposing circuits, fixed-wing to the west of the field and rotary in the centre of the field, both of which were marked out by dayglo runway-edge cones. A red-and-white chequered ex-RAF air traffic control (ATC) caravan was positioned near the threshold of the fixed-wing runway. At the extreme east of the airfield near 'Knock Wood' was an engine-off landing area. The runway directions were 26/08, 35/17 and 22/04 and all three circuits would be altered by ATC Land Rovers in about five minutes after a wind change by re-arrangement of the coloured runway marker cones. Thus on runway 26 the Chipmunks used a left-hand circuit whilst the rotary-wing aircraft used a right-hand circuit with helicopters in the engine-off circuit doing a tight right-hand orbital circuit within the rotary-wing circuit. Hidden in the grass were two surviving Pickett-Hamilton forts – circular concrete retractable two-man Bren-gun positions which were raised just thirty inches or lowered to ground level by a hand-operated hydraulic pump in order to defend the airfield against German airborne attack. Now protected, they are among the few surviving examples from the Battle of Britain era. There was even a small semi-derelict house, Holmlea Bungalow, on the edge of the airfield, in which the CO of 609 Auxiliary Squadron RAF lived with his wife during the Battle of Britain. He and his pilots could sit in deckchairs in the garden on stand-by and run through a gap in the hedge to their Spitfire dispersal.[1] On the northern edge of the airfield were five type-C aircraft hangars, behind which was the camp. The disused airfield bomb dump to the south east was used for storage and fire-fighting practice.

Despite many studies and changes to the syllabus of the Army Flying Course, the failure rate of students arriving at Middle Wallop remained at a mean average of approximately 33 per cent during the 1970s and early 1980s. The well-tried and tested system was that the student would be allocated a colour code completed by his flying instructor for each sortie. A green box indicated satisfactory progress, brown meant little or no progress and red signalled unsatisfactory lack of progress. An occasional brown was not unusual but a row of browns indicated a problem. Two or more reds led to being put on 'review' which involved an instructor change and five extra flying hours devoted to sorting out the particular problem in question. At any time during those five hours the student could be taken off review if the problem had been solved, but if this were not the case he had a final review sortie, or 'chop ride' as it was known to the students, with the Chief Flying Instructor or with Standards Flight which either resulted in removal from review or suspension from flying training. Well aware of this, I elected to spend the first eight weeks of basic fixed-wing training living in the Officers' Mess at Middle Wallop without moving my wife, Jane, from Plymouth. There were fourteen of us students who assembled for the 238 Army Pilots Course group photograph on 1 July 1974. Eight were sergeants in the Army from the infantry, cavalry, artillery, RAOC and REME and the remaining six officers comprised myself and Lieutenant Les Thresh from the Royal Marines, a captain from 6th Gurkha Rifles, a Royal Pioneer Corps lieutenant, an RCT lieutenant and the first direct entry Army Air Corps second lieutenant. After drawing and signing for our flying clothing, a helmet and a navigation bag, containing a useful wooden pencil box lined with green baize to prevent the contents rattling, a ruler, Dalton computer and a mass of text books, the course kicked straight off with ground school for half the day and flying for the remainder. Ground school consisted of classroom instruction in navigation, airmanship, principles of flight,

BASIC TRAINING

meteorology and engines and was conducted mostly by retired ex-service aviators or engineers. Some of their humour and sound advice remains with me today and I can still hear us being exhorted not to abandon a Chipmunk unless the ground ahead and below was clear of all habitation as it was 'unfair to drag other people into your own personal disasters'. Despite the tension of wondering whether one would make the grade, I found it hard to believe I was being paid to do something which was so enjoyable. My Basic Fixed Wing instructor, whom I shared with Sergeant Michael Taylor RA, was Charlie Cuthill, a civilian instructor employed by Airwork Services, who had been a Lancaster pilot in the Second World War. Wearing an old tweed sports jacket, he had a kindly and somewhat vague and forgetful air on the ground and I can remember him changing his mind a couple of times about which of we two was to fly first. I don't know if this was an act or not but once in the air his skill and judgement were immediately apparent and I realised how lucky I had been to be allocated to him. He never raised his voice despite the frustration of watching our basic errors and it was years later that I discovered he had a DFC and AFC.[2]

The de Havilland Chipmunk T.10 had been in service as a basic trainer with the RAF since 1951 but was a simple, tough, reliable workhorse which, nevertheless, as a tail dragger, requiring a degree of co-ordination to handle, thereby fulfilling a role as an inexpensive way of eliminating those who would not make the grade onto helicopters. The cockpit smelt of that distinctive, but hard to define, tang of leather, fuel, vomit and sweat common to all military aircraft which has a strange appeal to any ex-pilot. My eight weeks of learning to master the Chipmunk passed without any great problems although I can remember my surprise at the vigorous and deft footwork required to keep the aircraft straight on the take-off run and on landing. In the air every slight power change meant a corresponding rudder input in order to keep the aircraft in balance. The engine was a Gipsy Major Mk 8 with four in-line inverted air-cooled cylinders. It was started by a Coffman starter which was a six-shot revolver mechanism firing large brass blank cartridges. The gas from the cartridge impinged on a starter piston which spun the crankshaft and started the engine. Once the engine had been primed by the ground handler and with magneto switches 'On', the front-seat pilot pulled a ring on the end of a spring-retained cable on the right of the instrument panel which turned the cylinder, cocked and then fired one cartridge. A further pull turned the cylinder and repeated the process with the next-to-fire cartridge. In my experience the engine always fired on the first cartridge with a loud bang and cloud of black smoke, leaving a further five cartridges for the sortie in case of the requirement for in-flight starting. Although the wind-milling prop would normally re-start the Gipsy. Like every other student, before and since, I vividly remember my first solo flight after 8.6 hours dual with Charlie clambering out of the rear cockpit behind me and leaning back in, braced against the prop wash, as he secured his five-point harness before clapping me on the shoulder, closing the hood and waddling away from the trailing edge of the wing with his seat parachute banging against the back of his legs. The aircraft leapt into the air on take-off without the extra weight in the rear and the circuit went smoothly as I talked myself through all the checks and remembered his advice.[3] Later, during my first night-flying sortie in the circuit when I tensed up and started over-controlling, Charlie raised my confidence and relaxed me by taking over control, turning off the navigation lights so that we were briefly invisible from the Tower, and rolling the aircraft whilst we were downwind in the circuit. One bright morning, we climbed through some scattered fair-weather cumulus which whipped past the windshield and, as we ascended into the clear blue above, a strange object appeared suddenly 20 metres directly ahead of us. I instinctively ducked as it shot just over the top of our canopy. Charlie grabbed the controls and turned hard so we could identify it. It turned out that we had nearly run into a radiosonde package under a drogue descending from high altitude after a balloon launch and, in forty-five years of flying, this was a new experience for Charlie, as well as for me. We followed it as it descended under its tiny parachute into a field near the village of West Tytherley where we saw a group of children running out to recover it. The Kew Mk 2 MO radiosonde had probably been launched from Aughton or Larkhill under a balloon and measured temperature, pressure and humidity as it rose through the atmosphere, the readings, controlled by a little windmill-operated multiplex switch, being transmitted to a ground station. When the balloon burst at altitude the sonde descended under a parachute together with a postcard offering a small reward (originally 5 shillings) if it was posted back to the Met Office by the finder. It was designed to be light enough at 1.7 kilos not to do serious damage in collision with an aircraft or habitation on the ground but it was a million-to-one chance to have had such a close encounter.

Since we were to be trained as Army pilots specialising in low level, nap-of-the-earth flying we were introduced to low flying in the Chipmunk phase, initially at 200 feet above ground or obstacle level. It immediately became apparent that the horizon had foreshortened to the next mile or so rather than the vast vistas visible from 3,000 feet and above. We also had to fly in accordance with the contours of the ground, descending into the Test Valley and climbing as we approached Stockbridge Downs to remain at our 200 feet, all the while avoiding built-up areas, masts, pylons and the sensitive areas such as stables marked on our maps. The 90 knots of the Chipmunk seemed much faster at low level and map reading and navigation became more demanding.

We were all introduced to spinning on the Chipmunk. After a climb to above 5,000 feet and a HASEL (height, airframe, security, engine, and lookout) check, the throttle was closed whilst maintaining height and, at about 50 knots, just before the stall occurred, full rudder was applied in the desired direction of spin as the stick was pulled back to the stomach. There was a banging and rattling as the aircraft pitched up and then rotated as the nose dropped below the horizon and the green fields of Hampshire revolved in front of the nose. It was reputed that the Chipmunk spin was vicious, but I never found it so and the aircraft recovered quickly once recovery action was taken. We were only permitted to spin dual but, later in my flying career after only a short refresher, I was cleared to spin solo. It was a great confidence booster and I was somewhat horrified to discover many years later when private flying that many PPL aeroplane holders not only had never experienced spinning but often declared that they were scared stiff of the idea of having a spin demonstrated to them. I couldn't help wondering why they were pilots. I don't like the idea of being piloted by someone who has not experienced positive and negative G, unusual attitudes and spinning.

We lost one of our number during the Chipmunk phase but we were all in for a surprise as we joined Basic Rotary Flight. The Flight was run by Bristow Helicopters under contract to the MoD, using Bell 47G-4As painted light blue with dayglo orange lettering. This was a three-seat helicopter powered by a normally-aspirated Lycoming horizontally-opposed six-cylinder engine mounted vertically under the rotor mast. The Bristow aircraft were not equipped with an artificial horizon and were suitable for flying under visual flight rules (VFR) only. Forty-eight gallons of AVGAS were carried in two flexible bubble tanks mounted high above the engine, designed to break-off in the event of a crash. Les Thresh and I were allocated to Tony Collins as our instructor. Most of the instructors had come from flying on the North Sea oil rig operations or from overseas. Tony was an ex-RAF and Fleet Air Arm pilot, who had undergone flying training with the NATO Air Training Plan in Canada,[4] followed by a wide experience of various rotary operations including underslinging timber in Canada. A perfectionist, who required high standards, he gave us the most detailed and neat briefings before each sortie. Anything we did not understand was patiently explained with the aid of precise blackboard drawings. Overnight, from being confident Chipmunk pilots, we were starting once again from scratch and the initial disheartening aspect was that helicopter flying was quite different to fixed wing. From being 'Ace of the Base' we had reverted once again to being hamfisted incompetents. Helicopters are basically unstable. Any change made to the position of the yaw pedals, the collective pitch lever with its incorporated twist-grip throttle, or the cyclic stick required a corresponding input to all the other controls to keep the aircraft doing what you wanted it to do. Raising the collective lever, for instance, increased the pitch on the main rotor blades, increasing the lift and the drag. The drag would slow the blades, so a small increase in throttle was required to counteract the drag by twisting the throttle grip at the end of the collective lever (away from the pilot) in order to keep the rotor revs within the permitted band. An increase in engine torque meant that the aircraft would yaw to the right, so more left pedal was required to keep the aircraft straight and in balance. The process has been described as like patting your head at the same time as rubbing your tummy whilst balancing on a tightrope. We also became initially mesmerised by the rotor rpm tachometer and the magic band of 300 to 320 revs inside which it was necessary to keep the main rotor blades turning by means of the twist-grip throttle. In time I became used to rolling the throttle away from me as I raised the lever and closing it towards me whenever lowering the lever and even now, nearly fifty years later, that synchronised movement is second nature to me. Even on the ground the controls had to be monitored. The cyclic stick had to be held in the central position so as not to endanger the tail boom at low revs (although there were centrifugally-operated bumper stops to help prevent this), to ensure that passengers entering or leaving underneath the disc were safe and that both skids remained firmly on the ground. Only a few years earlier at Aldergrove a Sioux was running on dispersal for a night sortie when the pilot dropped his torch. It fell behind the instrument pack between the pedals. The pilot borrowed the marshaller's lighted wand to illuminate the front of the cockpit whilst he reached forward to feel for the torch. In doing so he displaced the cyclic and inadvertently raised the collective. The left skid lifted until the main rotor blades hit the concrete but the badly damaged aircraft remained upright and was written off.[5] We were all told this story, the effectiveness of which is proven by my recollection of it forty-five years later.

After four hours of flying in the G-4 I remember wondering if I would ever get the hang of it. Our first attempts to hover, being given initially one control, then two and finally all three controls (four if you count the throttle), ended with aching wrists and arms, evidence of over-controlling and the vice-like grip we were exerting on the controls, which is the enemy of the would-be rotary wing pilot. Eventually hover work, climbing, descending, turning and transitions to and from the hover all came together in circuit work and after 10.7 flying hours Tony Collins finally unstrapped, stepped out and, feigning unconcern, walked away to discreetly watch my first helicopter solo circuit from the dispersal.

Before going solo we had been introduced to autorotation, the rotary equivalent of a glide forced landing in an aeroplane. This is often misunderstood by the public but, if a helicopter's engine stops, by pushing the collective lever all the way down to the bottom stop a negative pitch is applied to the blades and the descent provides an 'autorotative force' which keeps the blades spinning within the rotor revs band. The helicopter does descend at a much steeper angle than a Chipmunk in a glide and basically the pilot is free to manoeuvre and land somewhere in the area underneath his knees. In the last 150 feet a lot of things happen quite quickly; the helicopter must be flared to reduce the forward speed and the rate of descent; a check up on the collective to further reduce the descent as the helicopter is levelled with the cyclic and then kept straight with the pedals as the remaining collective is used to cushion the touchdown and allow the skids to run gently across the landing area as the blades slow down. The two key things are to lower the collective immediately the engine fails as, once the blades slow down beyond a certain point, it is impossible to recover the revs, and the judgement required to know when to raise the collective prior to touchdown as the revs on the main rotor blades will very rapidly decay during the cushioning process. It soon becomes second nature to any competent military pilot of a single-engine helicopter to dump the lever at the first sign of trouble. After solo we were taught to turn 180 and 360 degrees in autorotation, how to lengthen the autorotation for range and to reduce it to 'zero speed' if the only suitable landing area happened to be right underneath the helicopter. All this added significantly to our flying skills, judgement and confidence.

Navigation and low-level map reading were next covered and we learned how to hold a carefully pre-folded map between finger and thumb of the right hand on the cyclic, whilst still being able to operate the press-to-transmit button on the top of the cyclic stick. Because all helicopters are inherently dynamically unstable, and the Bell 47 was not equipped with any form of stabilisation, you could only remove your hand from the controls momentarily. We did try letting go of the cyclic at altitude by way of a demonstration of trying to control the aircraft by throwing our weight from one side of the cabin to the other but the aircraft normally would settle into an undamped phugoid, describing an ever-increasing switchback through the sky until we had to grab the controls. The workload at low level in these simple but demanding little helicopters was high and the concept of two-pilot operation or flying with a crewman had not yet been introduced within Army aviation. Avoiding habitation and livestock, watching for wires and other aircraft, keeping the rotor rpm at 320 (10 extra revs at low level), remembering the wind direction in case of low-level engine failure, flying a heading, checking your wrist watch (it is hard to believe today that the Bell 47 was not fitted with a clock), glancing at the map, keeping in balance and listening to the radio all seemed at times like some sort of co-ordination challenge. Add the pressure of being uncertain of your position or the complications of low cloud and rain and it amazes me that a much higher proportion of students did not fail the course or crash. The layman often asks that if it all becomes too much to handle, why not simply slow the helicopter down or stop it? Theoretically the pilot can, except that the transition to any speed below 40 knots significantly increases the workload rather than decreases it as the aircraft becomes increasingly less stable and demands more power, and such a manoeuvre would lead to disaster unless it is carried out in a planned and organised fashion well before getting into trouble. In retrospect the Bell 47 was an excellent training machine and required the aspiring pilot to understand fundamental helicopter characteristics such as overpitching, inflow roll, flap back and vortex ring which can be masked on more advanced and powerful turbine-engined training helicopters.

One of the flying exercises that Tony Collins taught Les and me was what he called a 'Precision Transition'. This involved finding a field, preferably flat, with about half a mile of clear area into wind. After coming to the low hover the exercise started and it was important that every segment was flown with the utmost precision. From a three-foot hover a vertical ascent was made to an estimated 30 feet where a 360-degree spot turn was made at a constant rate and height whilst checking the rear. The aircraft was then accelerated smoothly to 60 knots whilst maintaining height, balance and heading and once the target speed was achieved the aircraft was decelerated again smoothly back to the 30-foot hover where another 360-degree turn was made and the aircraft descended vertically to a three-foot hover. If the ground was not absolutely flat the exercise could be still flown maintaining a height of 30 feet above mean ground level. No one else ever asked me to fly this manoeuvre but I taught it to my Gazelle students later in my career as a QHI. It was a clever exercise which demonstrated the ability to control power, yaw, keep in balance, control translational lift and the loss of it, whilst maintaining heading and, like a circuit, was very difficult to achieve absolutely accurately. If completed competently, a precision transition indicated that you could fly a helicopter.

Our first introduction to helicopter night flying was an eye opener. We were in a totally different environment and all our recently acquired visual cues of attitude, horizon and familiar geographic markers had vanished. We were learning to fly all over again. It was vital to know where all the switches were as the cockpit took on a different appearance with instruments and indicators backlit with luminescent indications. Many of the levers and switches were, however, unlit and it was important to know where they were by feel.[6]

Although the cockpit was equipped with a wander light on a retractable coiled lead, it was good practice to turn the cockpit lighting levels right down in order to reduce internal reflections and preserve our night vision. Even though we were flying under the nocturnal equivalent of VFR, night flying required a constant scan of instruments although it was important to look outside.[7] We learned to recognise from our map the shapes of towns and villages so that the lights of Andover could be differentiated from Whitchurch by the overall outline of the lighted areas. Dark black holes we recognised as woods and strings of lights as main roads. The occasional headlight indicated minor roads. Near London the flashes from the electrical pick-ups of tube trains were surprisingly spectacular from the air, like lightning. Our airfield pundit beacon situated on the airfield boundary flashed the code 'MW' in Morse every few seconds and could be seen from many miles away on a clear night. Lights on the horizon dimming and disappearing were indicators of a lowering cloud base or patches of low stratus. It was a diametric world and required different skills to day flying.

Because the G-4s were civil-registered aircraft they were required to be fitted with two Schermuly parachute flares during night flying, which were attached to a bracket on the skids, angled upwards and outwards to clear the rotor disc.[8] In the event of engine failure, and whilst in autorotation, the pilot fired these flares in order to illuminate the forced landing area below and which gave about a minute's illumination. The first was fired if above 1,000 feet and the second at 1,000 feet above ground level (AGL) to ensure illumination throughout the drama. This we practised (without actually firing the flares) over the airfield using our landing light to illuminate our landing area before re-joining the tacho needles at 200 feet and climbing away, and on a few occasions, recovering to the hover; something that today might be regarded as 'sporty'.

We were also introduced to landing and taking off from confined areas in the local woods on the Salisbury Plain military training area and in the surrounding farmland of Hampshire where permission had been obtained from landowners. At first, entering these clearings, where rotor-tip clearance seemed to be alarmingly tight, the white knuckle, vice-like grip on the controls became apparent once again whilst the perspiring student over-controlled and wasted valuable rotor thrust in unnecessary control inputs. We learned to protect our vulnerable tail rotor by never swinging the tail around but, instead, by turning the cockpit round the tail rotor. Apocryphal tales of previous disasters were handed down delectably from course to course. A few years before us, a young cavalry officer had crashed whilst manoeuvring his Sioux in the Pennings clearings near Tidworth and, carrying his helmet, walked unhurt from his burning aircraft to the A338 main Tidworth to Salisbury road 400 yards away. When he reached the roadside verge, another cavalry officer of his acquaintance just happened to be driving past and stopped to give him a lift. 'How's your flying course going?' he was asked. 'Not too well actually. You see that column of smoke behind those trees?' History recorded that he walked back into the crew room at Middle Wallop twenty minutes later to be greeted by his instructor, 'Back already. How did it all go?' A part of his Sioux ended up as trophy on the wall of the Officers' Mess bar.[9]

At first it was remarkably easy to lose sight of your clearing as you orbited around the tree tops conducting a reconnaissance of its suitability (size, shape, surface, slope, surrounds), carrying out a full power check and pre-landing checks whilst all the time keeping an eye out for other aircraft popping out of nearby clearings. It was not surprising that, on completion of all these preparations at low level, the embarrassed student could occasionally lose sight of the clearing and had to search again for the small landing area in the trees that was the focus of all this fuss.

Learning to land on sloping ground was yet another skill which initially caused tenseness on the controls. A delicate and relaxed touch is necessary to balance the aircraft on the uphill skid and then lower the aircraft onto the downhill skid whilst keeping the rotor disc parallel to the horizon and at the same time keeping the helicopter straight by countering the changes in torque and wind velocity with the yaw pedals. A suitable series of grassy mounds was thoughtfully provided at the edge of the airfield where one could practise nose up the slope, left skid up and right skid up (note: never nose down the slope.) in any wind direction before tackling natural slopes in the countryside. This was also a difficult time for the instructor because he could not allow matters to get out of hand so close to the ground, which could occur within a second. Dynamic rollover was a possibility if gross mishandling occurred with one skid balanced on the slope and, like a chair tipped too far backwards on two legs, a point could be reached where recovery was impossible and the helicopter could roll around the skid in contact with the slope until the main rotor blades hit the ground. However, it was important that the instructor did not allow his close interest in the proceedings to be transmitted to the sweating and tense student or handling was liable to go from bad to worse. It was also important for the student to learn to recover from his own mistakes.

Gradually all these sorties, good, indifferent and occasionally bad, came together so that after eight weeks and seventy-five hours I was ready to take a final handling test on the G-4. Just before this, however, I had a Flight Commander's check from the chief Bristow pilot at Middle Wallop, Arthur Sharples. After experiencing hours of conscientious attention to detail, it was something of a surprise when this bluff Yorkshireman grabbed the controls and took off without, apparently, carrying out any checks at all. I was amazed to see the rotor rpm vary randomly between 290 and 320 whilst he chatted animatedly as we left the circuit, again apparently without watching what he was doing. After observing my flying for thirty minutes or so we returned to Middle Wallop for a couple of autorotative engine-off landings. Whilst I was hover-taxiing back to dispersal he suddenly announced 'I'll show you how to get the sand out of your boots when you are in the desert, lad.' Without further ado he took the controls and accelerated the G-4 backwards across the airfield at low level at what seemed to me to be a disastrously high speed, all the while talking and gesticulating to me. The demo over, he unstrapped himself whilst I was still carefully hover-taxiing back to the dispersal and, as he got out, stated, 'You'll probably be all right on the day.' In retrospect, of course, this highly experienced pilot and instructor, having assessed my flying as somewhat over-pedestrian, was showing me 'what you could make a helicopter do' without catastrophe, and trying to get me to chill-out and relax a bit.[10]

Chapter 2

Advanced Training

The final and most important phase of the course was with the Advanced Rotary Wing Squadron where we were to convert to the Sioux AH.1, or Westland Agusta-Bell 47G-3B1[1] to give it its full title, and learn to use the aircraft tactically. The atmosphere at Advanced Rotary Wing Squadron was more brusque and more unforgiving now that we were firmly back in the military. Our flying instructors were all young serving sergeants, warrant officers, lieutenants and captains and the pace hotted up. My instructor was Captain Mike Wawn, the Flight Commander, who was then an infantry officer in the KOSB (King's Own Scottish Borderers) as well as being a patient, experienced and practical instructor; he subsequently transferred to the Army Air Corps. After the initial few weeks, however, we flew with any instructor who was available and this was a useful insight into different attitudes, personalities and varying methods of approaching the task in the cockpit. The real test was now in tactical flying and learning how to *use* the aircraft, not just to fly it. The syllabus covered nap-of-the-earth flying, low-level map reading, observation, acting as an artillery air observation post directing gunfire, forward air control techniques with ground attack aircraft, crossing under pylons, underslung loads and more advanced night flying. The Agusta-Bell Sioux AH.1 was externally similar to the G-4 but was now equipped for military use and had an increased maximum all up weight of 2,950lb. The slightly smaller capacity six-cylinder Lycoming TVO-435-BIA engine (TVO for Turbocharged, Vertically mounted, horizontally Opposed) was fitted with a turbocharger to give a rated 270 brake horsepower (bhp) up to 12,400-feet pressure altitude. The British Army used the Sioux operationally in Aden, Borneo, Malaya, Cyprus and Hong Kong, so the hot and high performance was necessary. It was a surprise during our first Sioux night-flying exercises to walk out to the aircraft for a running change to see the whole turbocharger unit glowing cherry red – not so surprising when one considered that the turbine was driven by the Lycoming's exhaust

ADVANCED TRAINING

gasses. The Sioux was also fitted with external litters attached by clips to the top of the skid posts in order to carry casualties or light stores such as jerry cans, bergen rucksacks or rations. Three radios were fitted: an STR 37E VHF AM radio for civilian air traffic control; a PTR 170 UHF radio and an ARC 44 military VHF radio together with homing aerials for military tactical communications. An external hook was fitted on a load beam, suspended from cables under the base of the engine, for underslinging and a vacuum-powered and very basic blind-flying instrument pack was fitted to the left-hand side of the instrument console.[2] It was a straightforward conversion from the G-4 and I soloed in the Sioux after three hours dual.

It was now a particularly cold spell in March and we sat in the Second World War vintage crew room, attached to the side of the hangar, being given a lecture on centre of gravity (C of G) calculations by an infantry captain instructor. Outside, the course ahead of us, who were almost at graduation stage, were departing for solo tactical sorties. On one particular Sioux the electrical starter irritatingly ground on and on without the engine catching, having probably been flooded, interrupting the lecture with interminable urrrrr….urrrrr….urrrrr noises. The QHI suddenly flung down his chalk exclaiming 'For fuck's sake', pulled open the door and ran out to the Sioux whilst we watched entranced from the windows. Reaching the aircraft, he ordered the hapless student out and, leaping into the left seat, primed the carburettor a couple of times by sharply rolling the twist-grip throttle between his palms. He then pressed the starter button on the end of the collective, the Lycoming coughed and then caught with a roar. The roar turned to scream, which could be heard all over the airfield, as the engine suddenly accelerated uncontrollably to what sounded like 3,000 rpm, presumably due to pooled fuel and the fact that the throttle may have been fully open. There were other expensive noises as the main rotor centrifugal clutch suffered a snatch engagement and various other rotating components were shock-loaded. As he hurriedly selected the cut-out and switched off the mags, the silence was palpable, except for the swishing from the rudely-treated slowing blades. I cannot remember much of the C of G lecture but this spectacle was another memorable lesson for all of us.

There was an exception to the serving military flying instructors. Captain Hugh Colquhoun was an ex-Army pilot with great experience and, in his mid-40s, older than his colleagues. Nicknamed Huge Balloon by his friends, he was a character and had a reputation for the unexpected. My first flight with him was memorable as we departed for the Salisbury Plain training areas along the low-level routes. At 150 feet AGL just past

Shipton Bellinger Hugh suddenly exclaimed, 'Did you see that?' Adrenaline pumping, thinking we might have just missed another aircraft, I replied in the negative. Without further ado Hugh grabbed the controls, turned hard and decelerated, landing in a ploughed field with the curt explanation, 'Those sheep have got into the winter wheat. You have control.' He unstrapped and ran across the field to an amazed tractor driver a few hundred yards away who had come to a standstill, presumably wondering what the hell was going on. After climbing alongside the tractor's cab gesticulating and shouting above the combined Sioux and tractor noise to the farmhand Hugh returned. When he reconnected his mic/tel lead, he said, 'Keep your bloody eyes open. How do you expect to be an operational recce pilot if you can't notice something like that?' Somewhat confused, I completed the sortie. My second sortie with Hugh (we of course called him Sir) was also memorable as I had planned a 200-foot low-level navex to eight turning points, such as a dew pond in the corner of a field, a bridge over a stream etc. As I descended to low-level after clearing the Middle Wallop MATZ, Hugh asked for my map and planning card and, folding them away, invited me to fly the sortie from memory. I told him that there wasn't much point as I could only remember the heading, distance and timing to the first turning point. Eventually, I was given the map back but had a critical debrief and was told that I had to start 'switching-on'. I left the debrief thoroughly perplexed. I soon learned, however, that it was no bad thing to think laterally and to be challenged, even if it was unsettling, and I always remembered his technique of checking the shadow of the aircraft during a constant angle approach. I should mention that the tough RA sergeant who was Hugh's allocated student engaged in a number of shouting matches with him but this did not upset the student/instructor relationship and they often had a beer together. During the foot-and-mouth disease precautions a year or so earlier, because of landing in fields and clearings, all Wallop based aircraft had to touch down in a large shallow metal tray of disinfectant to clean the skids before hover-taxiing to dispersal. The story I was told was that just prior to airfield closing time, Hugh and his student arrived at 700 feet overhead Wallop, entered autorotation and carried out a constant attitude engine-off, accurately landing with a great 'splat' of disinfectant in the centre of the tray. Many years later I was saddened to hear that Hugh was killed flying a Jet Ranger during a night take-off from a confined area in 1996.[3] He had amassed 13,700 hours; a huge amount of flying for a helicopter pilot in single-engine aircraft often at low level – quite unlike airline or North Sea flying time.

ADVANCED TRAINING

During night flying on Chipmunk and basic rotary we had used battery-operated Glim lights[4] (which had replaced the wartime goose-neck flares) placed in two rows to illuminate our landing area but, on advanced rotary, our approaches to a landing point were guided by picking up the beam on a portable angle-of-approach indicator (AAI) which shone a red light down a narrow path when the approach angle was too low and amber when too high.[5] The trick was to descend in the 2-degree-wide green beam of the AAI down to the hover 10 metres short of the indicator. The AAI was set up by students, under close supervision, so the beam was clear of all obstacles and was usually adjusted for a 3-degree glidepath. Later we progressed to tactical landing aids such as the crossed headlights of two Land Rovers or a simple 'T' laid out with torches.

One of the highlights of navigation was a sortie through the low-level VFR helicopter lanes across central London. On 17 March I was due to fly this sortie with Staff Sergeant Brian Backhouse as my instructor and I planned the route to Farnborough, joining the VFR low-level helicopter route along the Thames at Barnes and then following the river down to the Westland Heliport at Battersea for a refuel. Clutching my maps and navigation cards I pre-flighted the Sioux and started up. As I waited for Staff Backhouse to join me in the cockpit, I heard on the Wallop Tower UHF frequency a Scout being diverted to pick up the doctor and take him to the scene of an accident. As the six-figure grid was passed over the air I copied it down on my kneepad and checked my map. The accident grid was at the disused airfield at Chilbolton, which just happened to be my starting point to set heading for Farnborough, well outside the airfield boundary. When Staff Backhouse joined me I passed on this information and we left the circuit as normal. As we approached the satellite dish at Chilbolton from 1,500 feet we could see below us the Scout departing from some wreckage spread liberally over a ploughed field. Looking directly down, we realised with a shock from the dayglo patches on the fuel tanks and tail, now re-arranged dramatically from their originally designed positions, that it was one of our Sioux. Staff Backhouse glanced down, agreed with me that it looked serious and commented, 'These things happen. Put it out of your mind and get on with the sortie.' It was a strange feeling wondering which of my classmates had been involved. The complexities of talking to Heathrow Approach and navigating over London for the first time cleared my mind of the event. On our return to Middle Wallop, two and a half hours later, I immediately saw Mike Schofield, our Royal Pioneer Corps student, outside the crewroom with a sticking plaster rather dramatically placed on his face. It turned out that both he and his instructor were only cut and bruise after a downwind quick-stop that they were practising had gone 'a bit wrong'.[6] Seven years later, when I was an instructor at Middle Wallop, after the ploughing season I could still see the evidence from the air of slight oil and fuel stains in the field at Chilbolton where Mike had crashed.

The very next day after this incident the whole course moved to Snowdonia for a three-day introduction to mountain flying. Only half the students could fly, so the other half was sent by train whilst our heavier baggage and flight stores went by truck. It was only possible to put a small case or grip in each litter on the Sioux, which then had to be tightly secured with canvas webbing straps. If the weather was uncertain it was sensible to also wrap your belongings in waterproof material and many of the Sioux litters carried polythene covered packages. One instructor I flew with later insisted on strapping his plastic suit bag in the litter and I well remember him opening the right-hand door in the cruise over Devon whilst he leaned out, attempting to re-secure the rapidly disintegrating and violently flapping remains of his natty suit cover before we landed at Exeter. I am still uncertain as to whether his primary concern was for his suit or our tail rotor.

On arrival at RAE Llanbedr, in a typical violent rain squall, we parked the aircraft and tied them firmly down in the blustery dusk and departed for the warmth of the Victoria Inn. We shared the windswept expanse of Llanbedr airfield with Jindivik pilotless drones and some radio-controlled Meteors, which were sent out over Cardigan Bay as targets for RAF Lightnings and Phantoms. We discovered the next day that flying any light helicopter, and especially the Sioux, in the mountains gave the pilot a very firm impression of who was in charge – and it was definitely nature. The turbulence was alarming and judging height, distance and attitude in the mountains was difficult. All our normal perspectives had vanished and full climbing power had little effect on the downdraughts in the Llanberis Pass. I was to have my confidence in the mountains severely dented for a number of years by an incident that happened on the second day. My experienced instructor was demonstrating an approach to a razor-backed ridgeline near Carnedd Llewellyn. As I followed him through on the controls in the final stages of the approach over a yawning drop, I noticed that his running commentary started to dry up and that the control inputs became more energetic. There was a muted curse from the right-hand seat and I saw that we were pulling full power and the vibrating aircraft was still descending, now under only partial control, the last few feet to the ridge. We hit just below the stony path that wound along the summit of the ridge with a bang and rocked backwards with our tail rotor seemingly hanging over space. I had an alarming feeling that we were about to somersault backwards down the near vertical slope and involuntarily leaned hard forward against my straps, but we were firmly on the ground, albeit right on the limits for nose-up-the-slope and with the cyclic fully forward. To my alarm my instructor said 'You have control' and got out, but only to inspect the aircraft. I later learned that the transverse skid tubes were slightly bowed but there was no other damage. At this stage I would have been a willing volunteer to get out of the aircraft in order to lighten the load for the take-off attempt and to walk back down the mountainside. However, Mike got back in and, at the third try, we lifted off into a low hover, inched up the slope to the path and threw ourselves off the other side into the abyss to gain airspeed. We quietly returned home to Llanbedr and I have always had a profound respect for the mountains and the need to have a planned escape route ever since.

As part of our Sioux flying skills we were given a brief introduction to instrument flying. The Sioux was fitted with a suction-driven instrument pack consisting of an artificial horizon and turn-and-bank indicator which was designed purely to 'get you out of trouble' for a minute or so if you inadvertently entered cloud. It was perhaps sufficient to do a rate-one level turn through 180 degrees, although the admonition with the Sioux was always 'never enter IMC (instrument meteorological conditions)'. Because of the widespread low stratus prevalent in UK this inevitably led to a number of controlled flight-into-terrain (CFIT) accidents and wire strikes as pilots tried to grope their way home at very low level in weather below minima. This sadly had been the pattern since the First World War. Between 1939 and 1945 the RAF lost more aircraft in training accidents (often CFIT) than they did to enemy action and even the more recent advent of properly IFR-equipped light aircraft has not eliminated this cause of accident.

A story of low-level disorientation, which happily ended without disaster, occurred when an officer from Netheravon was tasked to fly a general and his wife from an official visit back to the Tidworth area in bad weather in a Scout. On the way home the weather further deteriorated, still just within minima, but the general then asked if he could be dropped at his residence rather than the garrison HLS and offered to direct the pilot. The aircraft inadvertently went IMC near their destination and, after a few minutes of intense disorientation during which the AI toppled, the altimeter at one stage indicated 2,000 feet and they experienced a 4,000 fpm rate of descent, the pilot centralised the controls. The aircraft suddenly broke out of the cloud base at 100 feet in a steep descent over married quarters but the pilot noticed a clear green patch between the houses and amazingly put the aircraft down in a heavy zero-speed landing, hitting a street lamp standard as he did so. The main rotor blades severed the tail rotor drive shaft but everyone was unhurt.[7] Reportedly the general's wife uttered the legendary words, 'You've saved our lives' to the pilot as she stepped from the intact cabin.

Walking out to my allocated aircraft for a dual sortie one morning at Middle Wallop, I was dumbfounded when I leaned inside to turn on the power and check the gauges before doing my external checks to find a completely different shaped instrument panel and layout. Instead of the stark upright pedestal there was a more substantial panel surmounted by a glare shield. When I returned to the 700 office and mentioned this to the duty instructor he told me to 'Just get on with it'. It turned out that the Army Air Corps Centre had received one or two ex-RAF Sioux HT.2s with a more conventional instrument layout and pedestal used for training at RAF Tern Hill.[8] The instructor's advice had been sound. It took only ten minutes or so to adjust to the different layout; the drills and checks were the same (we only used the Sioux AH.1 Flight Reference Cards), and once again it was good experience. Although probably not an acceptable approach to flying training today, in the mid-1970s it was very much a matter of 'stop talking and just get on with it', which did breed a self-reliant pilot with sound captaincy and airmanship if he survived training.

Only occasionally did I fly with Paul Bancroft, the Royal Marine QHI on Advanced Rotary Wing. An embarrassing incident which stayed with me for years occurred when I had started up the aircraft on dispersal and was waiting for him to join me before taking off. Paul climbed into the right seat, attached his helmet lead, did up his straps and reached across me, flicking on number 2 magneto saying 'I think for this sortie we will use both magnetos.' Nothing else was said (until forty-three years later at a reunion) but I was mortified. When doing my mag drop checks I had for some reason failed to reset the switch, slightly shielded by the magneto guard. I never ever made that mistake again in either piston rotary or subsequent fixed-wing flying.

One of the tactical skills we were made to master was artillery direction from the air or Air OP (Air Observation Post) as it was called. It was Air OP or Direction of Fire which was one of the fundamental roles of the Army Air Corps and dated back to the Second World War when Army officers (usually Royal Artillery) flew Taylorcraft Austers at the front to direct a wide range of artillery, including 25-pounders, 4.5-inch, 5.5-inch, 7.2-inch howitzers and naval gunfire, in support of troops. This was a dangerous job in the face of enemy fire and fighters such as Bf 109 and FW190 but the techniques used were directly applicable to helicopters. We spent many days on Salisbury Plain ranges where we would land at one of the designated OPs (observation posts) and take turns to fly well forward of the gunline, under the trajectory, directing fire onto targets designated to us by our Royal Artillery IG (Instructor of Gunnery) officer. When we were not flying we were working with the gunners or observing and learning from the efforts of our fellow students airborne. The section of three guns were usually 105mm pack howitzers, but sometimes we used Second World War-era 25 pounders and on one occasion a section of elderly 5.5-inch medium guns. There were two flying techniques used to direct fire. The hover behind cover, popping up to observe the fall of shot (the splash) just before the rounds impacted and then dropping back out of sight to relay the correction for the adjustment. The second technique was to adopt a racetrack circuit in dead ground to the enemy and porpoise up to observe the splash before diving back into dead ground. It was not easy at first to identify the target from the air, work out a grid reference and altitude, give the direction to the target that the pilot would give corrections in relation to, and pop up at the right moment to observe the shot which was a distant puff of grey smoke. The gun position would always give us the time of flight of the shell in seconds so that having ordered 'fire' we had some warning as to when the splash would occur and could plan when to pop up out of cover. The radio chatter to the gunners would sound something like this (gun position transmissions in italics):

> 'Hello Golf 3 this is Hawkeye, fire mission three guns over. *G3 fire mission three guns out.*
> Grid SJ 234798, altitude 390 feet, direction 210 degrees, over. *(Gun position repeats back).*
> Infantry company, troops digging in, at my command adjust fire, over. *(Gun position repeats back).*
> *Ready over.* Ready fire over.
> *Fire, Shot 20 over.* Shot 20 out.
> *Splash over.* Splash out.
> Right 200 repeat over. *Right 200 repeat out.*
> *Ready over.* Ready, fire over.
> *Fire, Shot 20 over.* Shot 20 out.
> *Splash over.* Splash out.

> Add 100 repeat, over. *Add 100 repeat out.*
> *Ready over.* Ready, fire over.
> *Shot 20 over.* Shot 20 out.
> *Splash over.* Splash out.
> Three rounds fire for effect over. *Three rounds fire for effect out.*
> *Ready over.* Ready, fire over.
> *Fire, Shot 20 over.* Shot 20 out.
> *Splash over.* Splash out. *Rounds complete over.* Rounds complete out.
> Target neutralised, end of mission over. *End of mission out.*

It was satisfying when the technique was at last mastered and it was usually a more complex and prolonged procedure than the much-sanitised example above. I personally liked to combine my azimuth and range corrections in my transmission such as 'Right two hundred, add one hundred' to get a quicker result. This was frowned upon by the purists in training but the RA gunnery instructors were practical men who judged by results and my odd short cuts were tolerated. We also did some basic airborne forward air controller training with the unique Middle Wallop camouflaged 'Spitmunk'[9] simulating a fast jet. We were now really using the aircraft for military purposes and flying had to become second nature whilst we considered wind, terrain, inter-visibility from the enemy, map reading, radio procedure frequencies and call-signs and fire corrections. Of course, we all knew that the purpose of these skills was in support of NATO deterrence and to prevent the Soviet hordes from invading West Germany, or in the case of we Royal Marines, northern Norway or the southern flank of the Mediterranean.

At a similar stage in training, a year or so before us, a previous student had come unstuck whilst out solo on a tactical sortie. The Commandant of the Army Air Corps Centre had been reportedly returning from a meeting in the back of his staff car and was stuck in a holiday traffic jam on Salisbury Plain on a hot summer afternoon. Just ahead of his stationary car was a lay-by where an ice cream van was doing brisk business in the heat wave. The Commandant's attention was naturally drawn to the distinctive sound of a low-flying Sioux and he watched the aircraft correctly climb to clear the main road and then conduct an orbit before landing in an adjacent field. The Commandant was now all attention as he watched the solo student throttle back to ground idle, apply the frictions and unstrap from the idling aircraft. Clambering over the fence bordering the lay-by, the student approached the van, purchased an ice cream and, happily licking his cornet, strolled back to his aircraft while the astounded Commandant watched transfixed.

At about the same time another recently married student had decided that he could not resist the temptation of giving his wife a flight in a Sioux. This, of course, was absolutely forbidden and, even after gaining our wings, we were not qualified to carry service passengers until we had gained our 'passenger qualification' in an operational squadron. He decided that the safest way to carry out this evolution was to pick up his wife from a small clearing in Harewood Forest whilst on a solo training sortie, give her a ten-minute flight and return her to the clearing. Harewood Forest is a large wood about seven miles north-east of Middle Wallop in which there were a number of clearings that we were permitted to use for training. He carefully briefed her and showed her where to park the car and the path to the clearing during a weekend walk. He decided to equip her with a set of DPM combat dress in case his passenger could be seen through the bubble as he flew at low level. All went exactly according to plan except that, as he hover-taxied into dispersal at the end of his sortie, his Flight Commander was waiting for him and told him to report immediately to the Chief Flying Instructor's office, where he was directly asked why he had flown his wife. The dumbfounded student confessed all and was immediately suspended from training. It transpired that the evolution had been witnessed by a forester whose attention had been drawn to a camouflaged female figure hiding in the bushes near a clearing. He had remained concealed watching as the Sioux landed, she furtively embarked and flew away. With his imagination, not unreasonably, running along the lines of an 007 novel, this worthy citizen had reported the possible pick-up of an agent to the local police who had passed it immediately to Middle Wallop who, in turn, had put two and two together.

Army aviation at that time deployed tactically in flight locations in the field, moving at least every twenty-four hours or so to avoid enemy detection and place the aircraft in the right location to give maximum support to the brigade or division that they were supporting. We therefore practised setting up our FOBs (Forward Operating Bases) in the Hampshire and Wiltshire countryside and moving once or twice per day without interrupting our tasking. Thus, having taken off for a casualty evacuation task followed by a reconnaissance for a night approach, the student might well find himself returning 'home' to a completely new grid reference. All approaches in and out of a FOB were conducted as a CATO (concealed approach and take-off) which meant approaching a designated spot perhaps 700 metres from the

FOB and then fast hover taxiing at about ten feet along a concealed route to the FOB. The departure was a route in the opposite direction and the CATO direction was passed to the pilot by radio for his first approach. The FOB tasking was organised by the duty pilot from a 9x9-foot tent attached to the back of a radio-equipped Land Rover. The next-to fly pilots were in an adjacent 9x9 and a few yards away were the REME tent and vehicles with aircraft spares and Forms 700 for each aircraft. Nearby were the ground handlers responsible for marshalling aircraft, refuelling and defence of the FOB together with a Bedford fuel bowser. The aircraft were dispersed amongst convenient bushes, trees or barns and camouflaged with a green military parachute thrown over the canopy, fuselage and blades.

Many of our training sorties involved observation of a point on the ground without being observed by the enemy. This involved carefully planning an approach on the map and moving in dead ground to a place where one could safely observe the target from behind cover. We moved cautiously from tactical bound to tactical bound, coming to the hover to assess the situation before moving forward, in the same way that infantrymen or armour advances but of course speeded up. One solo exercise which I will not forget involved me crossing a cornfield to come to a hover behind a stand of fir trees. I crossed the open ground at about fifteen feet and 60 knots and, as I approached the trees, slowed down to transition to the hover in a gentle quick-stop manoeuvre. However the trees steadily grew nearer. To my consternation, I realised that I was downwind and was now too low and slow for a 'downwind quick-stop'. By climbing a few feet to ensure my tail rotor remained clear of the corn, I increased the flare and came to a wobbly downwind hover with my rotor blades twenty feet or so from the tree line. Whenever I drive on the A303 and see that wood in the distance I remember this embarrassing but private close call.

Towards the end of our training the whole squadron moved down to North Devon for Exercise JASON'S QUEST, a one-week exercise designed to put all we had learned into practice and to be finally assessed by our instructors before returning to Wallop for our final handling tests. The week in Devon went well. We flew a wide variety of sorties under some pressure, we were shown potentially very dangerous hidden high-tension wires slung across the Taw valley[10] and experienced being flown strapped into the external Stokes casualty litter of the Sioux. This was a particularly interesting experience as the casualty was strapped securely on his back, head forwards and looking up at the rotor head. By raising one's head slightly you could look aft to see your boots, the horizontal stabiliser and the tail rotor beyond.

ADVANCED TRAINING

I well remember my concern as to the extent that the tail rotor gearbox vibrated during flight at the end of the Sioux's welded steel lattice-work tail boom, a factor I had been blissfully unaware of whilst flying seated in the goldfish-bowl-like bubble facing forward. Whilst my head and torso froze in the 65-knot April slipstream, the toecap of my right flying boot was being cooked by the Lycoming exhaust. A Royal Marines sergeant instructor, 'Hookey' Walker, was determined that I should experience the whole gambit of being a 'MASH' casualty and thus he climbed up to 3,000 feet and then carried out an autorotative engine-off landing onto Fremington Camp playing fields. He was greatly amused to be able to look out of the bubble at the various expressions on my upturned face during this exercise.

On the return from Fremington to Middle Wallop an entertaining misunderstanding took place. I remember that we moved to RAF Chivenor for a refuel (48 gallons of AVGAS per aircraft) and a briefing. There were six Sioux with six instructors and students with the remainder of the course returning to Middle Wallop by road. It was decided that we should fly back in two separate formations of three aircraft. The flying course syllabus contained only a very few sorties of formation flying and so, once clear of the Chivenor Military Air Traffic Zone, we would take the opportunity to practise some basic formation work of echelon, vic, and line astern en route. The two vics were to be separated by ten minutes and were each allocated a different pre-selected stud on the PTR 170 UHF radio for formation work whilst the VHF STR 37E AM radio would be used to monitor air traffic control frequencies. Mike was to be the leader of Blue Section which was to follow ten minutes behind Red Section.

Once briefed, we all walked out to our aircraft, which were lined up on dispersal and the students got on with the pre-flight inspections. It was a cold unstable day with good visibility, some towering cumulus over Exmoor producing occasional sleet showers and a brisk cold wind. Having completed the walk round, it was only natural to hurriedly climb into the aircraft, the sun having warmed the greenhouse-like bubble, and with plenty of time to spare, to start running through the pre-start up checks. Mike joined me as soon as I had the engine running at ground idle and was watching the oil temperature rise to above 40 degrees C. All six aircraft were running and, as soon as Mike was strapped in, he called Two and Three on Stud 4 of UHF for a radio check. A minute or so later we heard Red Section ask the Tower for take-off clearance from the dispersal on VHF and watched the three Sioux transition away to the east. We checked for mag drop, dead cut and freewheel and then, eager to get on, Mike indicated to me to call for taxi and take-off on the STR 37E. With no conflicting Hunters in the circuit we were cleared to take-off from our present position to depart direct on track. I increased the revs to 3,200, raised the collective, checked the yaw with pedal, countered the drift with a touch of cyclic and raised the aircraft to a low hover. After completing the post take-off checks we departed in loose vic, as briefed, probably only seven minutes behind Red Section and climbed to 3,000 feet at 45 knots over the rising ground of Exmoor. Looking over my left shoulder I could see Two in my 8 o'clock in loose vic rising and falling relative to us in the clear air. Once we were ten miles to the east of Chivenor we cleared to the London Information frequency and were ready to start some basic formation change practices.

'Line astern, line astern, go', Mike transmitted on UHF. 'Two,' 'Three,' came the acknowledgements. A pause ensued while we waited for the formation change to be completed and acknowledged by Three's call of 'Three on board' but no such call came. Glancing over my shoulder I could still see Two in his original vic position. 'Line astern, line astern, go,' repeated Mike. 'Two,' 'Three,' came the acknowledgements. Still no 'Three on board' call was made and over my left shoulder Two was still maintaining his original position. Mike started muttering about it being time that people started to switch on whilst I remained thoroughly perplexed. 'Two get into line astern,' transmitted Mike. 'Two is in line astern but I don't know what Three is playing at,' came the response. 'Is Two still in vic?' Mike asked me. He was. 'Echelon port, echelon port, go,' from Mike. 'Two, Three,' came the acknowledgements. A pause and then 'Three on board' and there over my left shoulder were two Sioux rising and falling in echelon as their students struggled to keep the briefed references in line. 'Thank God for that,' from Mike to me on intercom, but life was not that simple. 'Hello leader this is Two, Three is not on board, what the hell is going on?' Inexperienced, trying to fly a compass heading in balance whilst listening to London Information and map reading, and wondering whether we would have to fly round precipitation from a threatening cumulus cloud well ahead on track, I had little capacity to try and work out what exactly was going awry in our formation. It appeared everyone except us had lost their heads.

Somehow Mike got our formation back into a loose vic and, as we approached Taunton, we abandoned any formation changes and continued in comparative radio silence to Middle Wallop. For some time, however, Two seemed to have a mind of his own, drifting into line astern and then back to vic. Wisely Three kept well clear of him. Back outside the debriefing room at Middle Wallop it was clear from the raised voices that Red Section was being 'debriefed without coffee', and had clearly suffered from a similar degree of chaos to us. It then sunk in. Blue Two had departed Chivenor as part of Red Section (believing he was in company with Blue Section) whilst coincidentally Red Two had joined in with our Blue Section some seven minutes later. The service serial number of each aircraft was painted in black on the camouflaged dark green dorsal fin of the Sioux and was not easy to read at any distance. A Middle Wallop dayglo code letter (A through to Z) was also painted on the lower centre of each bubble but could only be read from ahead and thus considerable care was required to identify a particular aircraft. Blue Two, being on our UHF stud frequency, had been complying with Mike's formation changes but flying some five miles ahead of our formation, whilst our Two was complying with calls originating from five miles ahead on a different frequency. It was an unlikely combination of occurrences but a lesson in Murphy's Law that if anything can possibly go wrong, then it will.

There were two other examples of Murphy's Law that were impressed on us. The right-hand cyclic of the Sioux could be simply removed by undoing a pip pin. This left the hemispherical cyclic base cover on the floor and it was important that passengers did not foul this with their feet. On one occasion in Germany we heard that a Sioux picked up an officer in the Black Watch with a *cromach* (a Scots walking stick with a curved handle). After take-off, the pilot felt a restriction in the cyclic followed by some uncommanded control movements. Thoroughly concerned, he looked for a suitable location for a precautionary landing when he suddenly noticed the officer with both hands resting on the top of his *cromach* with the ferrule neatly inserted in the bush of the cyclic base. The other was an incident a few years earlier in BAOR when an Alouette II had lifted into the hover and promptly crashed onto the dispersal, flinging debris around. It was found that a technician had cross-connected the cyclic control cables. This was despite colour coding and clear differences which were believed to ensure that this error was impossible to make; but a technician, convinced that this was the correct rigging, somehow managed to forcibly join the connections. The pilot was faced with an impossible control conundrum once he lifted off.[11]

Each student had now amassed a total of about 215 flying hours during the ten-month training period and, at the end of April 1975, at long last I underwent my final handling test lasting eighty minutes with Major Heath from the Army Air Corps Standards Flight. I do not remember much about the sortie except hovering in an observation position near pylons behind Watership Down and trying to identify a farm building amongst trees in the low ground to the north, but I passed the test and qualified for the Army Flying Badge. At a wings parade a few days later on 2 May 1975 Major General D.G. House CBE MC, the Director of Infantry, presented us with our Army Flying Badges. Another photograph was taken of 238 Army Pilots Course with our new wings up, but this time there were only eleven of the original fourteen of us who had started training. Statistically, so far, it had been a successful course. During our subsequent flying careers the number would further drop to nine.

Chapter 3

Gazelle Conversion

Just prior to our Wings parade at Middle Wallop, the two Royal Marines on the course, Les Thresh and I, had been told that we were to undergo conversion to the new Aérospatiale Gazelle AH.1. This was because the Royal Marines were one of first-in-line Squadrons in Army Aviation to receive the production issue of the aircraft which was to replace the Agusta Westland Sioux on a one-for-one basis. I was thus allocated a place on Army Gazelle Conversion Course number 11 but there was no vacancy on this course for Les so it was arranged that he would undergo a similar course with 705 Naval Air Squadron of the Fleet Air Arm at the Royal Naval Air Station Culdrose. The Royal Navy was just introducing a very similar brand new Royal Naval version of the Gazelle, the HT.2, painted in high visibility gloss red and white. Also due to attend the same Army conversion course as myself were my future flight commander, Captain Dick Middleton RA, who was on attachment to 3 Commando Brigade Air Squadron RM, and Sergeant John 'Sticks' Cowie RM who was reputed to have originally joined the Corps as a drummer boy. Both of them were experienced Sioux pilots.

One interesting change from the Sioux and most other helicopters was that the Gazelle main rotor blades rotated clockwise when viewed from above. This was a peculiarly French and Russian quirk and meant feeding in right pedal to counter the torque reaction when taking off; the opposite from all other helicopters.[1] The Gazelle was also the first helicopter that the British Army operated using metric units so horsepower was replaced by kilowatts, pounds by kilograms and gallons by litres although in British aircraft the cockpit airspeed indications remained calibrated in knots and the altitude in feet.

It is easy to forget now what a quantum leap in technology the advent of a gas-turbine helicopter represented. As I sat in the brand-new cockpit of one of the first Gazelle AH.1s I stared at an array of miniaturised instruments and coloured lights which looked extremely high tech after the 'alarm clock' sized instruments of the Sioux. There was a properly designed blind-flying panel powered by an alternator, together with a set of standby flight instruments. There was a fuel gauge (calibrated in kilogrammes) which at long last gave an accurate indication of fuel consumption; there was effective heating from engine bleed air, cooling from a nose vent; a baggage compartment; room for two passengers in the back and one in the front and even a clock. The two front bucket seats were slightly reclined and contoured with faux white sheepskin seat cushion covers and looked modern and comfortable compared with the sit-up-and-beg Sioux seats (however, appearances are not everything and years later many pilots had to be treated for 'Gazelle back').[2] A modern American lightweight five-point harness was fitted which was later to be changed for the heavy-duty UK service specification harness. The biggest change was from the Lycoming piston engine of the Sioux to the gas-turbine Turbomeca Astazou engine. Here was an engine which was both smaller and lighter than the piston engine and the IIIN2 version used by the British Army produced 592 shaft horsepower, over twice the power of the Lycoming. It was seemingly unaffected by cold temperatures and did not require being warmed up on start-up, nor run at idle before shut-down. The governed compressor speed was an amazing 43,700 rpm and the engine could also be run at ground idle with the rotors stationary. The governor took care of maintaining throttle settings with changes of collective pitch, so there was no longer any requirement for a twist-grip throttle on the end of the collective lever, but a manual throttle was located in the roof for advancing from ground idle to flight idle governed range and vice versa. Extensive use had been made of plastics and glass fibre in the airframe and we watched a cautionary demonstration where a technician dropped a screwdriver point first onto a section of cabin flooring, manufactured from a 'nida' construction of honeycomb light aluminium foil corrugation. The screwdriver pierced the structure up to its handle and, as this floor was primary aircraft structure, the lesson went home. Later we installed plywood freight floors to protect the honeycomb structure from point loads. Instead of a tail rotor there was a thirteen-blade fenestron ducted fan at the rear of the tail boom enclosed in a fin. The fin had an aerofoil cross section so that, in the cruise, it provided lift, helping to offset the torque reaction and so offloading the fenestron blades. This allowed more power to be available for the main rotor in the cruise but you never 'get something for nothing' and the downside was the amount of power the fenestron could absorb in the hover. Particular care had to be taken in feeding in right pedal whilst hovering as the torque limits could be exceeded if the pilot was too heavy with his right boot, especially with a wind from the left. The flying controls were all hydraulically powered by a reservoir and pump at the front of the main rotor gearbox but the aircraft could be flown in 'manual', although pedal pressures to control the fenestron in the hover were high. But, above all, was the amazing difference in speed and power. The 590 hp Astazou turbine gave a cruise of 125-130 knots instead of the 65 knots we were used to. During my first sortie south of Salisbury I felt I was flying a jet and the feeling was heightened by the technique of flying at an intermediate pitch stop (IPS). There was a sprung indent at a collective pitch level of 13.1 degrees on the collective pitch quadrant and, with the lever raised to the indent, we were taught to fly at whatever torque level that setting gave, controlling the aircraft's attitude, including climb and descent, with the cyclic alone in the same way as a fixed-wing aircraft. At the maximum pitch stop (MPS) of 14.5 degrees of pitch we cruised at about 140 knots and as part of the conversion we were also required to dive the aircraft to the limiting speed (VL) of 168 knots. This went against all one's instincts as a steep dive was required at high power to achieve VL and, as the vibration and noise levels increased, the aircraft was clearly telling the pilot that this was not sensible. In the event of an engine failure the pilot could pull through the MPS indent to cushion an autorotative touch down. These were brand new aircraft, sleek, light and streamlined without the mass of subsequent limitations and modifications which were, in due course, to include homing aerials, heavy duty five-point harness, wooden freight floor, Mini TANS Doppler, SSR, radalt, flotation gear, jettisonable rear doors, armoured seats, windscreen wipers, HF radio and aerials, Stabilisation Augmentation System and observation sight to be incorporated over the next twenty-five years. In fixed-wing terms this rotary-wing advance was the equivalent of moving from the Gloster Gladiator directly to the Gloster Meteor overnight.

My instructor was Sergeant Major Don Fraser AAC, a member of the original Gazelle Intensive Flying Trials Unit and an expert on Gazelle. There was a phenomenon known as jack stall, or servo-transparency in the USA, which was also demonstrated to us. If the aircraft was violently manoeuvred at high speed, the G caused feedback from the blades to the servo-jacks which could result in the jacks being unable to move the pitch-change rods. This was felt as a slight kick aft and to the right on the cyclic followed by freezing of the controls and the aircraft rolling right. By relaxing on the controls, which was second nature, the jack stall ceased as quickly as it had occurred and total control was instantly regained. Sadly, early on in the

FLYING LIGHT HELICOPTERS WITH THE ROYAL MARINES

IFTU there had been a serious accident when a RN engineer had been killed and three others injured in a Gazelle manoeuvring at max all-up weight at very low level in a turn.[3] In squadron service this was only likely to be a problem when manoeuvring the aircraft violently when close to the ground (i.e. mishandling or perhaps taking violent evasive action). Each student was demonstrated jackstall and recovery in the dive and in a descending tight turn to the left (a choice of right turn might give you the unwelcome experience of brief inverted flight) and then was invited to perform the same manoeuvre himself. I know from my later instructing experience that the average student was very cautious of mishandling the aircraft in this way and it went against the natural survival instincts of most pilots.

By the end of May I had progressed to low-level map navigation sorties at IPS setting. I had spoken to Les Thresh on the telephone regularly and found that he was also thoroughly enjoying his course and was at exactly the same stage as me. During the eight-week course they had decided that his wife, Susie, would stay in their quarter at Middle Wallop and that Les would commute home from Cornwall whenever possible. On return from my solo low-level trip at about 1100 am, I was signing in at the Form 700 office, attached to the side of the hangar, when I overheard two instructors talking of a Gazelle accident at Culdrose that was just being reported. One of them then mentioned that they thought a Royal Marine had been involved. I froze and told them that there was only one Royal Marine to my knowledge who was currently flying at Culdrose. I rang the Commandant's office and a few minutes later I had a call back from the Brigadier Army Air Corps Centre who confirmed that Les had been killed and asked whether Jane could accompany him down to Over Wallop where Susie was working as PA to the manager of a chicken farm in order to break the tragic news to her. I then rang Jane, gave her the sad news and the Brigadier's staff car arrived at our married quarter to pick her up about ten minutes later. Despite her nursing experience it was a tough introduction for Jane to service flying tragedies.

Les Thresh had been killed on a dual low-level navigation sortie along with his flying instructor, a lieutenant RN recently graduated from CFS (H).[4] In good weather they had strayed to the south of Liskeard, outside the designated low-flying area, and had hit the main power cables suspended from pylons over a deep wooded valley near Herodsfoot at high speed. These were not hidden wires low in a valley with the posts on each side obscured by trees but one of the largest set of pylon lines in the south west. The impact tore the main rotor head and gearbox from the Gazelle which then dived into the fir trees beyond, killing both crew instantly. It remains a sad mystery to me to this day as to how they ever came to be in that situation.

Les was buried at the Military Cemetery at Tidworth, close to the Pennings clearings in which we had practised our confined area landings on the G-4 and Sioux a few months previously. I was in charge of the pall bearers who were made up of officers and SNCOs from the Army and Royal Marines at Middle Wallop. On the day of the funeral we stood at the back of Tidworth Church with the drill instructor sergeant major from the Army Air Corps Centre, who had been drilling the pallbearers on the preceding day using an aircrew locker filled with sandbags to simulate the coffin. As the hearse arrived he produced cotton and thread and deftly sewed Les's service cap, sword and medals to the Union flag which covered the coffin. Having done this, he produced a bottle of whisky and instructed us all to take a stiff shot 'in memory of the gentleman' before the coffin was carried up the aisle. The pallbearers finished the remainder of the bottle after the burial service.

The remainder of my conversion course passed uneventfully and I finally left the Army Aviation training machine to join 3 Commando Brigade Air Squadron based in Plymouth in June 1975 with about 240 hours of flying experience. Coypool, the Squadron location near the Marsh Mills roundabout on an old military logistic site on the eastern outskirts of Plymouth, was a highly unsuitable location for an aviation unit. It was surrounded on three sides by high ground which was built-up with new housing estates. On the fourth side was a main road, a bridge over the River Plym and the A38 dual-carriageway. Getting in and out of the small concrete dispersal, bordered by workshop sheds and huts, amounted to a confined area and there were few options in the event of an engine failure. Residents in the surrounding housing estates would not have appreciated the aircraft noise especially when night flying. In the Sioux era, any sortie requiring the carriage of passengers had to pre-position at Roborough airport, a mile north, as getting safely out of Coypool required maximum performance without payload. Ever since the return from Singapore in 1971 there had been a string of various studies considering alternative locations (which included RAF Mountbatten, Exeter Airport, RAF Chivenor, RNAS Culdrose, RAF St Mawgan, RNAY Wroughton, RNAS Lee-on-Solent, RNAS Yeovilton, Netheravon and even building a new airfield on MoD land at Collaton Cross) but the Squadron was to remain at this 'temporary' site until, in 1982, a move to RNAS Yeovilton took place, forced by the impending introduction of Lynx and the construction of a new Novotel hotel on the east side of the Coypool helipad. It took some time to adjust to the new realities of Squadron life and aircraft serviceability. No longer were there lines of shiny training aircraft awaiting us each day but now aircraft undergoing scheduled maintenance, awaiting spares, having modifications incorporated and being prepared for the next deployment. The experienced CO, Major Iain Bain, summoned me in his friendly fashion and told me to plan a trip to HQ UK Land Forces at Wilton with him the next day. When I went to check the aircraft allocation I found that we were earmarked for a Scout. I explained to the CO that I was not Scout qualified (hardly even Gazelle qualified) but he cheerfully replied with words to the effect of 'That doesn't matter. It will be a good experience and all helicopters are much the same'. The next day I was in the left seat and, once airborne from Coypool, he handed the Scout over to me as we flew low level parallel with the A38 main road towards Ashburton, with low stratus a few hundred feet above us. Just east of Ivybridge the road passed over the highest ground of the route near pylons, whilst the cloud base seemed to descend ahead of us. 'Climb up through the clag is the safest thing to do,' advised the major and a few minutes later we were flying in brilliant sunlight above a sea of white. As we proceeded east on my planned heading I became increasingly concerned about where we were and how we were ever going to get down, although Iain Bain continued to chat to me and seemed totally relaxed. East of Exeter, however, the cloud thinned and the green Somerset countryside showed through large breaks. We were only slightly off track and the rest of the trip was routine. Whilst the CO attended his meeting I looked over the aircraft at the Wilton helipad and reflected on this novel experience although I was sensible enough to realise that, knowing nothing of instrument flying and IFR, I would not be emulating his level of experience on my own.[5]

During a night flying session there would inevitably be telephoned complaints from the housing estates on the high ground that surrounded Coypool which the Duty Pilot in the Ops room had to field. On my first night-flying session nine days after arrival, I was nominated captain of the aircraft but crewed with a far more experienced and senior aviator to 'show me the ropes'. I was thus somewhat surprised to be summoned to the Senior Pilot's office the next morning for a bollocking about flying an approach close to houses and causing noise complaints. I took most of this on the chin but eventually pointed out that actually I was being shown the local procedures and it seemed to me that we had taken a reasonable approach path to get to the confined pad which was surrounded by housing.

GAZELLE CONVERSION

The bollocking intensified and I left the office somewhat bemused, having received a few extra duties as Duty Pilot. Perhaps Peter Cameron felt that I needed taking down a peg or two but it was certainly a good introduction to the responsibilities of aircraft captain.

Dieppe Flight under Dick Middleton was also getting accustomed to the new Gazelle and after eight weeks of tactical training in the Squadron, flying with other pilots and occasionally with air gunners, I had nearly 300 hours flying time and was judged ready to take my passenger qualification check ride, or PQ check, with Captain Derek Blevins, the Squadron QHI. Derek had been the company sergeant major of M Company, 42 Commando, when I had joined in Singapore straight from officer training. He had then been commissioned and had also been one of the pilots on the Gazelle IFTU. My PQ check went well and I was ready to take my place in an operational squadron but still had a great deal to learn.

In June Sergeant John Cowie and I took a Gazelle for a static display for VIPs on the flight deck of HMS *Fearless* anchored off Greenwich. This was memorable because we were parked on the flight deck next to Harrier T. Mk 52 G-VTOL and met the legendary Hawker Siddeley test pilot John Farley.[6] A month later Dieppe Flight returned to Middle Wallop for four days to take part in the massed helicopter approach at Army Air Day. It was on one of the rehearsal days when we were parked in a grass field over the main road, opposite what is now the site of the Museum of Army Flying, which was then grass, that I witnessed the only engine failure that I ever saw in a Gazelle. Whilst flying at about 40 knots and forty feet over the main road in line astern, in order to re-position for another rehearsal demonstration (the road was not as busy as today and we waited until there was no traffic in sight), I heard a 'Pan' call on Wallop Tower UHF frequency. Sergeant John Cowie, following some distance behind me, had suffered a progressive loss of torque. He lowered the lever and gently ran the Gazelle onto the grass on the airfield side of the main road. It was found that a high-pressure air pipe had fractured at the point where it was welded to the engine casing, resulting in a loss of P2 air and a gradual rundown of the engine. The aircraft was completely undamaged and it had been a textbook engine-off landing from the high hover-taxi.

I was, however, quite wrong in my early assessment of the Gazelle being fragile for military operations. Forty years later the last few Army Gazelles were still flying with uprated engines and transmissions and a mass of extraneous add-on components and aerials. They had served throughout the Northern Ireland campaign, the recapture of the Falklands, Operation

DESERT STORM, Operation HAVEN and Operation TELIC. The glass fibre and 'nida' construction had proved to be robust and of course corrosion-proof.[7]

Just before embarking in HMS *Bulwark* for a Mediterranean deployment I received the welcome news that, on return from the deployment, I was to be posted to Salerno Flight in Malta to relieve Lieutenant Steve Bidmead whose tour was ending and who was returning to UK. I was heartily glad to leave Coypool and its totally 'non-aviation' environment and, thankfully, never served there again. Today it is the site of a large and modern retail park beside the A38 main road to the west side of the Plym Bridge. Plymouth had not been a particularly happy introduction to Royal Marines aviation for me and I looked forward to getting away to Malta. First, however, I was to experience deck operations and my first amphibious exercise as a qualified pilot.

Chapter 4

All at Sea

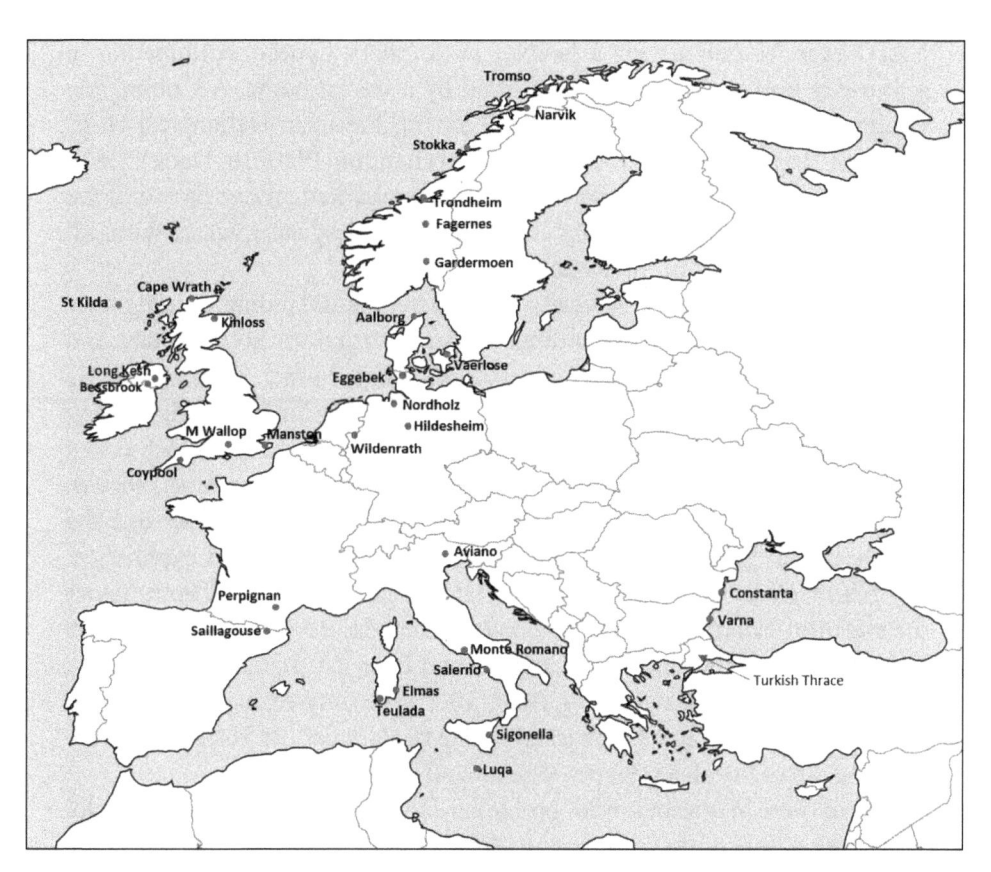

Map of Europe showing principal locations mentioned in the text. (©Author)

One of the unique facets of being a Royal Marines pilot was, and still is, the opportunity for a battlefield pilot in support of infantry to fly at sea. Two months after joining 3 Commando Brigade Air Squadron, Dieppe Flight and the HQ Scout Flight were scheduled to embark for a two-month amphibious deployment. In 1975 the Commando Brigade would deploy on shipping on average twice a year for an amphibious training package. If it were a deployment to the Southern Flank of NATO, the exercises would take place in Sardinia, Corsica, Malta, Italy, Greece, Turkey or Cyprus. If it was a Northern Flank deployment, it would be to Denmark or Norway and there were also WESTLANT deployments to the West Indies, the eastern seaboard of the USA or Canada for training. A typical seven-week Mediterranean deployment might consist of an onload in Plymouth, followed by an amphibious transit with a two-day run ashore at Gibraltar, followed by a unit work up and live firing for ten days in Sardinia, a ten-day NATO exercise comprising a landing in Southern Greece, culminating in a four-day port visit to Athens followed by a transit home. A Commando Group would be based on the LPH (Landing Platform Helicopter) HMS *Bulwark*, Brigade Headquarters on an LPD (Landing Platform Dock), HMS *Fearless* or HMS *Intrepid*, and logistic units embarked on one or two of the six Royal Fleet Auxiliary LSLs (Landing Ships, Logistic), which were all named after Knights of the Round Table.

I have always been somewhat surprised that deck-landing training only formally consisted of five landings under instruction, both by day and night, followed by a number of observed landings. In fact, deck operations encompass a wide range of factors, including operating limitations depending on the type of ship, navigation, the weather, the sea state and wind. It is a facet of flying, like so many others, which is a continual learning process, and perhaps for this reason the formal training was brief in order that the trainee could 'get on with it' and learn by valuable first-hand experience. My first deck landings took place on HMS *Fearless* off Start Point under the watchful eye of my squadron commander, Major Iain Bain. We flew to rendezvous with the ship from Coypool and I see that I obtained 'day deck qualified' on Gazelle in my log book after a seventy-eight minute sortie. Less than a month later I embarked on HMS *Bulwark* off Portland and the learning curve began to steepen dramatically.

There were numerous new problems facing the newly-qualified pilot in landing a helicopter on a moving deck at sea. First of all, the steel deck itself. This could range from the tiny deck of a frigate, with one spot, to the nine spots on the deck of a commando carrier. Surprisingly, landings on the wide expanse of an LPH deck could be some of the most testing. The clearance of rotor blade tips between the neighbouring spots, often occupied by running Wessex HU.5s, might only be nine feet and there was considerable turbulence generated by wind passing around and over the carrier's island, funnel and the high bow. Funnel fumes also caused additional turbulence and loss of lift. Operating close to obstructions called for relaxed and gentle control movements. Inevitably, inexperienced pilots tended to tense up in this new situation, used a vice-like grip on the controls and started to over-control, which was counterproductive and wasted valuable rotor thrust. Then there was the wind. At sea there is nearly always natural wind compounded by the ship's speed through the water, which might be anything up to 25 knots. What was important to flying operations was the mean wind speed over the deck. Thus a vessel steaming at 20 knots directly into a 15-knot wind would have 35 knots over the deck from 12 o'clock (the clock face being orientated on the ship's head), whilst the same vessel heading on a reciprocal course would experience a 5-knot wind from 12 o'clock. Things started to get tricky if there were strong winds from abeam and especially astern. All helicopter types had differing wind limitation charts for deck landing for each class of ship, laying down the limits of acceptable mean wind off the bow and the even more stringent limits for rotor starting and stopping when the blades were moving too slowly to have centrifugal rigidity and could 'sail' up or down. I once saw a Westland Wasp lashed on the deck of a commando carrier minus a tail boom, having neatly sliced off its own tail by 'blade sailing' during starting up in very strong gusting relative wind, which momentarily had exceeded the engagement limits.[1]

There were then the misleading visual cues of the sea racing past the hull. It was most important to ignore any peripheral cues and instead concentrate on the deck and flight deck director's hand signals. Even a glance at the sea racing past could cause an involuntary check back on the cyclic which would convert the hover alongside the deck into dangerous rearward movement relative to the ship. Superimposed on these problems were the pitch and roll of the vessel. Here again there were tables to study which gave the pitch and roll limits for each type of ship combined with each type of helicopter. How to land on a pitching deck? It was hard to explain – you just did it. By concentrating on the deck and the marshaller it was possible to judge your 'moment' and land firmly. It was important that there was no dithering about inches from the deck in order to achieve a gentle touchdown but, instead, the aim was to achieve a firm arrival in the middle of the landing spot. After landing, it was initially off-putting to feel the pitch and roll of the ship which it was important to ignore, ensuring instead that the cyclic was kept central and the helicopter's rotor disc was kept parallel to the pitching deck at all times.

FLYING LIGHT HELICOPTERS WITH THE ROYAL MARINES

Whenever an aircraft was on deck for any length of time steel chains or webbing lashings were attached to the aircraft picket points in order to secure the aircraft to the deck. This enabled the Officer of the Watch to order a turn without losing the helicopter over the side and also stabilised the aircraft for shut-down or starting up. There were moments of insecurity as I sat on deck in strong winds and a high sea state with little control over my fate until the lashings were off and I was ready to fly. In a light helicopter there can be tricky moments. Having just landed a Gazelle on HMS *Fearless* off Norway I was alarmed to have a Sea King HC.4 land on the spot next to me before I was lashed down. Even with the collective fully down, the Gazelle was blown sideways a few yards and yawed through 20 degrees across the wet steel deck. In the split second available to me to make a decision, I chose to remain on deck rather than attempt to lift off in the recirculating downwash of the Sea King and, apart from my subsequent change of underpants, all was well.

Added to all of this was the problem of navigating at sea to a landing point that is moving at up to 25 knots and regularly changes direction. Tactical considerations often dictate minimum communications at sea and the vessel was often not where the pilot had been briefed an hour earlier that it should be. This was all well and good by day but night added a further challenging dimension.

Whilst flying at sea we wore a one-man dinghy pack with a four-point quick release harness and connected by a lanyard to our Mae Wests. This we strapped on over our Mae Wests like a back-parachute. Even with the Gazelle seat cushions removed and the seat in the fully rear position the end result was that any pilot over about 5 foot 9 would end up uncomfortably hunched over the controls. There was nothing to be done about this except to get used to it and, in winter, wearing a bulky immersion suit, the situation became slightly worse. Every year we were practised in wet-dinghy drills, my first being off Plymouth Sound, and every few years we went through the underwater escape trainer at HMS *Vernon* in Portsmouth and later a more modern rig at RNAS Yeovilton nicknamed 'the dunker'. Once strapped into the dunker, resembling a helicopter cockpit and cabin, the device splashed into a tank of water and, as it quickly filled, it inverted and sank. Once all movement ceased, the occupants released their harnesses, escaped and inflated their Mae Wests when on the surface. Four run-throughs were made in the dark, with aircrew occupying different seats on each run. It replicated the disorientation and confusion of being upside down underwater whilst holding your breath and it was claimed that the experience of the dunker doubled our chances of surviving an actual ditching.

Before I started flying training in May 1973 I witnessed the effect of a momentary lapse of concentration during a deck landing. Whilst embarked on HMS *Bulwark* (RO8, the ex-Centaur-class carrier, not the modern assault ship L15) off the coast of Cyprus I was in the 'goofer's station', high up on the ship's island, taking some sun and watching deck operations. A Sioux, flown by a newly qualified Army Commando Gunner, Captain Neil Macaulay, was doing starboard circuits from the three 'Green' spots, forward of the ship's island on the starboard side, whilst the nine main spots were being used by Wessex 5s on port hand circuits.[2] The Sioux lifted into a high hover under the direction of the aircraft director and moved sideways over the starboard side of the vessel before transitioning forward. In doing so, however, it drifted rearwards. Stuck out from the starboard side of the ship was an umbrella-shaped UHF homing aerial and, in a flash, the Sioux's tail rotor impacted the edge of the aerial. There was a loud metallic 'spang' noise and the tail rotor stopped dead. What, of course, had happened was that the tail rotor drive shaft had sheared under shock loading. For a remarkable split second the Sioux appeared to remain happily hovering with a stationary tail rotor. It then began to rotate at an accelerating rate and fell away over the side of the ship and hit the deep blue Mediterranean with a heavy splash. Flight-deck personnel rushed to the side of the ship but, a moment later, when the foam and spray had cleared, there was nothing to be seen. The small helicopter had sunk like a large rock. The widening pool of foam rapidly passed down the ship's side as *Bulwark* steamed on at 20 knots. By now a group of flight-deck personnel were lining the side shouting and willing the pilot to appear. As the patch of foam passed level with the stern a small white flying helmet bobbed up supported by an orange Mae West. One of the Wessex from the port side was in the hover over him within thirty seconds and, a minute later, a shocked and bedraggled pilot was led dripping from the Wessex, trailing sodden maps and the remains of a dinghy on a lanyard which had been punctured to death by the Royal Navy crewman. He was pushed complaining into a Neil Robertson stretcher, loaded onto the bomb-lift and despatched below to the sick-bay.

Later I heard Neil's own story. When his tail rotor struck the aerial his pedals immediately went completely slack. He guessed what had happened and snapped the throttle closed to reduce the torque, at the same time trying to move the aircraft away from the carrier with cyclic. The impact with the sea was severe and knocked the breath out of him for a few seconds. When he came round he found himself underwater sinking in a rush of bubbles into a clear blue sea with the massive dark shape of the carrier's hull thundering past on the left. Because he could clearly hear the rhythmic thumping of the propellers he decided to stay in the cockpit until the dark shape of the ship had passed by. HMS *Bulwark* was a large vessel (224 metres long) and within seconds the water began to turn a darker blue as the aircraft sank. He quickly realised that his priority now was to get clear of the aircraft before he was too deep. Undoing his harness, he struggled to get through the door frame of the plexiglass bubble, not realising that the bubble had shattered on impact with the sea. His helmet kept hitting the door surround but eventually he struggled free, inflated his Mae West and found himself bobbing in the diverging bow wake of the vessel abeam of the stern with his dinghy pack attached to his back. He was actually well clear of the hull although the dark shape rushing past must have been alarming. He was picked up by Wessex and moments later he found himself back on deck and protesting as he was made to lie down in a stretcher. In fact the medics' standard procedure to lay a survivor down proved its worth because, despite Neil's protestations, he had fractured some vertebrae on impact with the sea and was in considerable pain the next morning. The will to survive is powerful and at the time he had not noticed his injuries. The Sioux had sunk in deep water and *Bulwark* continued on her way with a little more room in her crowded hangar deck and the Sioux's documentation impounded for the Board of Inquiry. Neil soon returned to flying and, years later at Middle Wallop, told me that his only hang-up concerning the event was the unforgettable noise of HMS *Bulwark*'s propellers churning past.

To return to September 1975 and HMS *Bulwark*. During the passage out to Malta for our first exercise my log book shows that I did thirty-two deck landings, all by day, as *Bulwark* steamed at speed through a deep blue sea. The initial landing of 40 Commando off Malta for Exercise DOUBLE BASE was an eye-opener. At first light I was ready on deck on the number one green spot, right up near the bow, with nine Wessex 5s turning and burning down the main port side spots. Behind me another Gazelle and an SS11 armed anti-tank Scout were positioned on Green 2 and Green 3. I had two company commanders on board with their bergen rucksacks stowed in the rear of the aircraft. As the lashings were about to be removed, a harassed staff officer, hotfoot from the amphibious operations room, rushed up with a Royal Artillery Forward Observation Officer and started to load him on board as well. I was not entirely happy about this and started doing some rapid mental mathematics concerning weight and performance but, in the extreme noise and wind on deck, my half-hearted protestations were brushed aside. The restricted rear of the aircraft was now crammed full of two bodies, each with a heavy bergen on his lap and a third in the baggage compartment. I lifted into a low hover but, as I moved starboard over the side of the deck in the prescribed manner, it was little surprise that the aircraft began to sink. Fortunately *Bulwark*'s flight deck was fifty feet above the sea but we sank below the level of the flight deck with the red torque-meter limit light blinking balefully at me before I gained translational lift and flew away towards the honey-coloured coast. This event forcefully reminded me that the decision of the aircraft captain must always prevail no matter how much pressure is exerted from above.

The major exercise on that deployment, Exercise DEEP EXPRESS, took place in Turkish Thrace. Again at H hour at first light I flew the two or three miles to the coast and by 0900 hours 40 Commando was well established ashore. Whilst on a reconnaissance task to site some 105mm artillery gun positions I received an urgent call for a casevac. On reaching the indicated grid reference I found that a lightweight Land Rover had turned over, badly injuring the driver's back. As I had been taught at Wallop, with the rotors stopped and the engine at ground idle, I quickly removed the front port seat and gave it to an NCO for safe keeping. From out of the baggage compartment we extracted the folding plywood bofors splint and trussed the driver securely into it. He was then carefully strapped onto the freight floor of the Gazelle, with his head next to the instrument console and his feet deep in the baggage compartment. It was a typically sunny but hazy Mediterranean morning as I lifted off and headed for the coast pulling power to the maximum pitch stop (approximately 140 knots) and calling the ship on UHF for homing. On reaching the coast I was surprised to hear that 'pigeons to mother' was 170 degrees at twenty-five miles range. HMS *Bulwark* was not where I had left her. All turned out well and eventually that afternoon I married up again with my front port seat. I also had another experience of the dilemmas of captaincy. I picked up the CO of 40 Commando, Lieutenant Colonel Mike Wilkins,[3] from his tac HQ and flew him to a neighbouring unit for a meeting in the evening. He told me to wait and I reminded him that we would have to depart in forty minutes in order to return before dark. The flight location had moved during the day and this part of Turkish Thrace was unknown, pitch black at night and, furthermore, I had not been authorised for night flying. After forty minutes was up there was no sign of the CO so I sent a nearby Marine with a message that I would have to leave in ten minutes. I started up the aircraft and, as the revised deadline came up, the CO appeared and strapped himself in. We landed at Commando tac HQ at last light and by the time I arrived in the vicinity of the grid reference I had been given for the new flight location it was dark. The boys had, however, thought ahead and two Land Rovers were parked with their headlights illuminating a clear landing spot. Looking back now I realise that I was single crew (before the era of two-pilot operation or even a crewman), inexperienced, with no nav aids and before the days of NVG. It was all seat of the pants stuff and my Flight Commander, Dick Middleton, must have been worried.

During this exercise in Turkish Thrace, in the early days of Gazelle operations, we experienced a couple of cases of the aircraft's nickel-cadmium battery boiling. This was due to the voltage regulator overcharging the battery in the heat and manifested itself by the appearance of bubbling alkali overflowing from the battery container and running down into the base of the canopy just in front of the yaw pedals. Since the battery was alkali based and there were no immediate support facilities available, the technicians drove into the nearest village and purchased two large glass carboys of vinegar (slightly acidic) enclosed in wicker baskets which they doused over the front primary structure in order to neutralise the alkali and prevent lasting damage to the airframe.

My first experience of night deck operations was illuminating. The flight deck was lit by red floodlights and, initially, all was pretty similar to night flying from an airfield up to the point where I transitioned away from the deck. Immediately the deck disappeared from between my pedals the world turned inky black. Suddenly we were at 60 feet above an unseen heaving sea at 30 knots airspeed and absolutely blind. The procedure was to get onto instruments and concentrate. As I levelled off 400 feet above the sea and turned crosswind, I rather looked forward to turning downwind in order to see the confidence-boosting blazing lights of *Bulwark*. It was thus the second shock of the night to look up to see – nothing! The red floods were, of course, invisible from any distance, the ship was darkened and at flying stations. Still flying on instruments at 400 feet above an invisible black sea, I eventually made out the luminescence of her massive wake and, turning finals, was relieved to see the faint red light of the angle-of-approach indicator. Maintaining height until the red turned to green, I followed a sight-picture approach down to a 60-foot hover abeam the spot. As I got closer to the ship, first the red floods became dimly apparent and then the aircraft director's lucite wands became visible. The actual landing was straightforward. It was just a matter of getting used to a new environment but it was a testing exercise to fly a low-level circuit at night as there was little time to 'settle down' on instruments and the penalty for disorientation could be severe so close to the sea.

I also had an interesting early test of captaincy. In the Squadron at that time we had a number of very experienced ex-Sioux and Scout SNCO pilots, some of them slightly eccentric and forceful characters. Most were a fount of sound knowledge and advice to an inexperienced young officer. I was authorised for an hour's DLPs with a veteran sergeant pilot in the left seat who, immediately after I transitioned away from the flight deck, unzipped the top pocket of his flying suit, extracted a packet of fags and a zippo lighter and casually lit up. This placed me in a momentarily difficult situation as a new 'sprog' pilot but I was also irritated and realised that if I did not make an issue out of this right now I could never berate him for smoking again. I thus told him never to smoke in any aircraft in which I was flying. With a loud sigh and a 'Oh for fuck's sake, sir!' he reluctantly flicked the cigarette out of the window but it never happened again.

It was not only about flying that I learned on that first deployment with the Squadron. One day whilst steaming off the Peloponnese, the Squadron QHI, Derek Blevins, quietly advised me and another young pilot to stay well clear of the Aircrew Briefing Room that night. It later transpired that one of the old and bold SNCO pilots had borrowed an adult movie and projector from the Chinese stewards on an accompanying LSL and had planned a show for a large audience. Later that evening, apparently, the movie was in full flow when the Senior Instructor Officer looked in to prepare his meteorological brief for the next morning. On opening the door, he was facing the projector and could only see rows of tiered faces reflected in the cigarette smoke and the flickering light from the projector. Hastily apologising, he backed out and, on returning to the Wardroom, mentioned to Little F that he had been unaware that a training film was being shown in the Aircrew Briefing Room. A rat was smelt and within minutes the Commander and the Master at Arms were striding down Burma Way (the main thoroughfare passageway) towards the island. It was later reported that, on opening the Aircrew Briefing Room door, they found the darkened room deserted but filled with cigarette smoke and with an unsavoury film still running. To us drinking in the wardroom there was a certain inevitability about the turn of events, and the Squadron QHI sighed in a long-suffering manner. There was a huge row and a number of the audience were rounded up and I believe later incurred the severe displeasure of the Admiralty. However, for the command chain the problem remained as what to do with the film and projector. In the LSLs Chinese stewards had secondary duties whilst at flying stations, such as crash crews and aircraft lashing hands. During these deliberations any Royal Marines' helicopter landing on the accompanying LSL was immediately assailed by shouting Chinese demanding the whereabouts of the SNCO pilot and the projector. I believe that in the interests of harmony the projector was eventually discreetly returned to the LSL without the film.

A few days later, on my same first eventful deployment, I witnessed the novel sight of my Squadron Senior Pilot being put under cabin arrest. Peter Cameron was detached to the LPD HMS *Intrepid* with a Gazelle as the task force sailed from Turkish Thrace for the Dardanelles en route to Istanbul. He had been specifically briefed by *Bulwark* to be back on deck before the ship entered Turkish airspace. However, Brigade HQ in *Intrepid* tasked Peter to check and sweep all the landing sites ashore that had been used for troop extraction at the end of the exercise[4] and, despite explaining the necessity of his return to *Bulwark*, was retained until the task was complete. When he was at last released by Brigade HQ, he found *Bulwark* was already entering the Dardanelles and, with no answer to his RT calls to the ship and short of fuel, Peter pressed on and flew a slow approach to the hover off the port quarter with his 40kg low-fuel light flashing. *Bulwark* finally transmitted 'the deck is closed' to which Peter replied that in that case they had better man the sea boats ready for a ditching. After a pregnant pause he was cleared to land on spot 3.

After shutting down Peter was immediately met on deck by 'Little F', put under 'cabin arrest' on the instructions of 'Wings' (no doubt with the Captain's sanction), and was escorted to his cabin where he was ordered to remain until further notice, despite his loud protestations at not being able to sign down his aircraft or explain the extenuating circumstances to Wings. When the CO of 40 Commando heard about the incident, matters were swiftly sorted out and he was released an hour or so later with an apology for the manner in which he had been treated by Flyco.[5] The Senior Pilot had been the proverbial 'meat in the sandwich'.

In later years the Squadron was required to operate at sea in the Arctic off Norway in winter. Despite our immersion suits and dinghy packs it was obvious that survival times in the sea would be short and the shock of immersion would be severe. There was also the problem that the survival gear itself made escape from the aircraft more difficult. Ironically, I always felt that the little single-engined Gazelle was completely reliable at sea. In the twin-engined Lynx, however, the possibility of an engine failure was considerably higher and a single-engine recovery to a small deck could be fraught with problems. The skidded Lynx was not good on deck and we often longed for the Navy wheeled variant. Unfortunately, however, the TOW anti-tank launcher hardpoints were incompatible with the wheeled version unless a prohibitively expensive airframe rebuild were to have taken place. The skids were not as tough as they looked and the aircraft had to be landed with a degree of care. The articulated skidded undercarriage caused the aircraft to rock around laterally in the wind independent of deck movement. In comparison the RN pilots could centre their Lynx HAS Mk 3 over the centre of the deck and thump it down firmly and then push Sub Min collective pitch in order to hold the aircraft firmly on the flight deck. Sub Min pitch consisted of negative pitch being applied to the blades with about 20 per cent torque downforce in order to press the aircraft into the deck and was selected by pushing the collective lever down, through a spring-loaded detent, to a bottom stop. We were instructed not to use Sub Min pitch on the Lynx Mk 7 unless it was operationally necessary as it was liable to increase rotor-head fatigue, but there were occasions when it was useful on deck.

There is no doubt that flying at sea added an extra dimension to rotary-wing aviation. It was always exciting to live in a compact mobile airfield and making an initial landfall in a different part of the world. Deck operations also increased any pilot's flying abilities and awareness. It was, and I am sure still is, a particularly hostile environment and night deck operations, such as in the Norwegian Sea in winter with often only one diversion, a deck perhaps twenty nautical miles away, were testing to say the least.

Following our NATO exercise in Turkey we sailed back to UK via Malta and Gibraltar. On 8 October 1975 the three Gazelles of Dieppe Flight flew ashore from HMS *Bulwark* in Grand Harbour to RAF Luqa for seventy-two hours in order to carry out night flying. This was to be a useful recce for me because I knew that within six weeks I would be posted with my wife to Salerno Flight, 41 Commando Group, for a two-year tour based at St Andrew's Barracks in Malta. Whilst staying in the officers' mess at RAF Luqa, we met in the bar after night flying and chatted with a visiting Avro Vulcan bomber crew on detachment from RAF Waddington. After three days ashore, we re-embarked in *Bulwark* and sailed for Gibraltar and back home to Plymouth. It was some days later whilst at sea that Sergeant John Cowie told me that there was a signal in the aircrew briefing room concerning a Vulcan crash in Malta. It turned out that it had not involved the crew that we had met, but another IX Squadron Vulcan flying from RAF Waddington five days after we sailed which had crashed at Luqa following a heavy landing. This accident would have some relevance to me a few weeks later. In late October we disembarked at Plymouth after I had completed a total of eighty-five deck landings during the deployment. Jane and I quickly packed up our married quarter in Plymouth and prepared to depart for RAF Brize Norton and the VC10 flight to Malta.

Chapter 5

Malta

On arrival in Malta I joined Salerno Flight which was based at a small helipad by the sea at St George's Barracks supporting 41 Commando Group RM. The flight's former three Sioux[1] had been returned to UK inside an RAF Belfast C.1 freighter earlier in the year and was now equipped with three brand new Gazelles which had only been issued that summer. The flight was commanded by Captain Rodney Helme, with me as second in command and Sergeants John Menghini and Barrie Shepherd as the remaining pilots. On my arrival Sergeant Ken Blain was about to depart on posting and flew with me for my initial acquaint flights around the island, pointing out the key points such as hospitals, signal centres, pumping stations and fuel farms. The helipad had landing spots on a slightly sloped pad with a small Nissen-type hangar on one side and a low limestone building containing the REME offices, ops room and Rodney's office. The perimeter was surrounded by a high wire fence and, with the sea a mere 75 metres away, salt spray from storms often lashed the base. The small REME detachment was run by a WO1 and our ground handlers, drivers and signallers were from the Royal Marines and 29 Commando Regiment Royal Artillery. Devoid of the weight, drag and limitations of the various modifications that were to be incorporated at regular intervals over the next thirty years, the aircraft were light, slick and extremely fast. Inside they smelt like new cars with US lightweight seat straps, miniaturised instruments and smart seat covers. The exteriors were finished in a matt black and green camouflage paint which had anti infra-red properties.

Because of the highly corrosive salt-laden atmosphere it was necessary to regularly carry out compressor washes. We started to use the newly laid-down procedure with a cleaning agent called Turco mixed with water, but it resulted in some very high turbine T4 temperatures on start-up after we had refuelled with AVCAT (military grade kerosene for use on aircraft carriers) at sea. So we changed the procedure to using fresh water compressor washes and then, after shutdown, sprayed the aircraft and intakes with PX-24 (very similar to WD40) from a 40-gallon drum. This produced a clean, shiny aircraft which did not please AAC UKLF who claimed that we were destroying the anti-IR properties of the matt paint finish. It seemed to us that it was simple enough to figure out that protecting the airframe and engine from corrosion was, on this occasion, the higher of the two priorities. Compressor washing became a focus in Army aviation shortly after we withdrew from Malta.[2]

Prior to the arrival of the Gazelles, Salerno Flight's three Sioux had been, in effect, restricted to the island due to their performance and range. Gazelles, however, could fly around Malta in twenty minutes and we had the advantage of range and endurance to transit to Italy without any problem. We soon established the routine of self-deploying to the US Naval Air Facility at Sigonella in Sicily once every eight weeks or so to conduct low-flying and navigation training. On a daily basis in Malta our flying training was carried out at the old Royal Naval Air Station at Hal Far which was an emergency MoD airfield, then under care and maintenance.

After being shown the island and procedures from the air, one of my first duties was to fly some members of the Board of Inquiry into the Vulcan crash with a photographer to help understand the peculiarities of the approach to runway 24 at Luqa. On 14 October, at just before 1300, Vulcan B.2 XM645 started its approach to Luqa in good weather with the co-pilot flying. The aircraft ended up with a high rate of descent, the captain took control and applied maximum power, but the aircraft touched down heavily in the undershoot with full power still coming on to the engines. It touched down again on the runway before climbing away, leaving the port undercarriage unit lying on the runway, having punched through the wing structure. The two pilots were equipped with ejection seats but the three rear-facing crew members behind them had to rely on manual bale-out with a static line through the entry hatch located just forward of the nose-wheel leg. In this case, however, there were sadly five crew members in the rear as two extra crew chiefs were on board. During climb out it was apparent to those on the ground that the aircraft was on fire but in the cockpit, as they turned downwind, they were deciding what their options were for abandoning the aircraft. With the hydraulics gone and the nose wheel stuck down, any manual abandonment was problematic due to the extended nose-wheel leg. However, without warning, the raging fire in the wing caused the aircraft to suddenly break up downwind over the town of Zabbar. The pilot and navigator ejected whilst the five rear crew members died. The wreckage of the Vulcan fluttered down onto the main street, on to the roof of the local primary school and on nearby waste ground, damaging a hundred houses and shops. One woman in Zabbar was killed.[3]

FLYING LIGHT HELICOPTERS WITH THE ROYAL MARINES

RN Sea Kings of 714 NAS from HMS *Hermes* were detached to Hal Far for training at the time of the XM645 crash. Nigel Culliford, whom I was later to work with in the avionics industry after I retired from the Royal Marines, saw the Vulcan from Hal Far airfield on fire on its downwind leg just after he had shut down after practising some SAR circuits. In the time it took for him and his crew to grab a lifejacket each, the Vulcan had exploded, leaving just a spiral of black smoke. He quickly flashed up his aircraft,[4] flew to the pall of smoke rising over Zabbar, found the two pilots, in a field, shocked and suffering from 'ejection back' but otherwise unhurt,[5] and took them to the military hospital at Mtarfa.

It transpired that optical illusions on the approach to runway 24 might have contributed to the accident and that is why I was required to fly an approach to 24, coming to the hover at various stages on the glideslope, whilst the RAF photographer took shots of the aspect of the runway threshold. The approach to runway 24 (at that time Luqa's main runway) was over the Grand Harbour and rising ground to the runway threshold at 297 feet above mean sea level. Approaching over rising ground can give the impression that the aircraft is too high, leading to reduction of power and high rate of descent on what is actually a normal descent but where the threshold is 'rising to meet you'. This in effect is what may have happened and control was taken over too late for the time required for the Olympus engines to spool up to maximum thrust. There was also the complication of wind turbulence from the large Nimrod hangar to the right of runway 24. The sad sight of the charred wreckage in the silhouette of a Vulcan was laid out on an abandoned dispersal at Hal Far airfield for the Board of Inquiry throughout most of my tour in Malta. Today parts of the Vulcan can be seen in the Zabbar Sanctuary Museum and it is widely felt within the local area to be miraculous that only one civilian was killed. Some years later, at RAF Shawbury, I met the co-pilot of the Vulcan, who had since been flying Puma helicopters, when he joined the QHI course after mine.

Our standby pilot role was a strange one. Since Malta was a tiny island surrounded by sea it was clearly evident that Search and Rescue (SAR) might be our main reason for call-out. Our Gazelles were not fitted with a winch which made any recovery of a person at sea somewhat problematic. Royal Navy Gazelle HT.2s at RNAS Culdrose were equipped with an air-powered hoist for winch training and we requested that one of these winches be issued to the Flight, together with the associated minor aircraft modification. However, we were officially informed that the HT.2 hoist was for training purposes only and was not cleared for live lifts. So, because of this bureaucracy and lack of imagination, we were left with no practical means of recovering anyone in the sea – other than perhaps an impractical knotted rope or a crewman clambering onto a skid in the hover and reaching down. Despite this 'minor' inconvenience, the SAR requirement meant that one of us four pilots had to be on one-hour standby and off booze for twenty-four hours at a time throughout our tour on Malta.

Pilots of military single-engine helicopters are bred to have the possibility of engine failure permanently in their subconscious during all phases of flight. This means that the wind direction and the choice of the best area available for a forced landing should be instinctive. Because of the carboniferous limestone out of which Malta was formed the island was composed of a craggy, rocky landform, bisected with dry wadis. Where there was agriculture the tiny fields were bounded by numerous limestone dry-stone walls. There was little opportunity over most of the island for a successful engine-off landing and a run-on into a wall, even at low speed, would have resulted in a fatal accident. Instead, whenever we had the option, we kept within autorotative range of the coastline. A ditching in the Mediterranean held no great fears for me, unless it was particularly rough, in comparison to a crash on the rocky island, and we practised our wet dinghy and winching drills regularly at Marsaxlokk.

Shortly after my arrival, I was left behind in Malta as standby pilot with one Gazelle whilst the remainder of the Flight transited to mountain flying at Saillagouse in the Pyrenees with the other two aircraft. For much of the time I was grounded as our one remaining aircraft had a hairline crack in the exhaust duct and could only be cleared for limited and necessary flying. There were only a few specialised centres in UK to carry out the specialist welding on this alloy and there was a backlog of ducts waiting to be repaired. If the crack was left, it could suddenly propagate[6] in flight and cause a problem. However on 11 December there was a call from HQ British Forces at Lascaris tasking me to Dingli where there was a report of a missing man. Dingli is the highest point in Malta and the limestone cliffs fall 830 feet sheer into deep water. Arriving overhead I could see a couple of parked police vehicles and a small crowd and I landed beside the track at the top of the cliffs. The police briefed me that a fisherman was missing. It was surprising to me that anyone could fish off 800-foot-high vertical cliffs but it was explained that there were traditional tiny ledges and cracks down which the fishermen would descend to fishing spots at the base of the cliffs, making use of 'fixed ropes' which were bleached white and frayed by sun and salt, attached to rusty iron pegs. Details of these private climbing 'routes' were handed down from family to family, so it was not just a question of sending another fisherman shinning down the cliff to see what had happened. By peering over the cliff edge the locals believed that a body, or some object, was stuck on a narrow ledge about halfway down. It gave me vertigo just to look down the cliff face routes, tackled in bare feet with a long fishing pole slung over the shoulder. I took off and approached at low speed as close to the cliff as I dared with my rotor tips, whilst a REME technician in the left seat eventually identified the dark mass as a jumper and some other items of clothing, presumably having been taken off as the day warmed up. Near the base of the cliff, hundreds of feet directly below this ledge, we found an unpleasant mark that might have been made by a body bouncing off the limestone. We transferred our search to the sea below, methodically flying a search pattern at low level out towards the island of Filfla until dusk when we gave up the search. As far as I know the fisherman's body was never recovered. A strange coincidence occurred thirty-six years later, in September 2012, whilst I was on a vacation diving trip in Malta. The Maltese father of a teenage boy who was diving with us at Ghar Lapsi lived near the brother of the missing fisherman and had often heard the story of the incident. He confirmed to me that his body was never found.

Although we were the only British helicopters permanently based in Malta, there were other helicopters on the island. A mile or so away at St Patrick's Barracks the Armed Forces of Malta (AFM) had four Bell 47G-2s (three manufactured by Agusta Bell in Italy and one by Bell Helicopters in the US)[7] and a Jet Ranger. These Bell 47s had been gifted by the West German Government in 1971, along with basic pilot training courses, and had been flown to Malta in the hold of a German C-160 Transall. The Agusta Bell 206A Jet Ranger had been a separate gift from the Libyan Government. Maintenance was a real problem in such a small and fledgling air force, then known as 'The Malta Helicopter Flight', and a Bell 47 occasionally flew in the early morning, but I never remember seeing the Jet Ranger airborne. The alleged monthly flying rate was frankly so low as to raise questions over aircrew currency and we heard that the aircraft technicians were vehicle mechanics. Although relations between the Maltese Government and the UK were somewhat strained during this period leading up to the final British withdrawal, we got to know one of the pilots well, although we were not permitted to fly him and vice versa. Co-located with the Malta Helicopter Flight at St Patrick's Barracks was an SA 321M Super Frelon of the Libyan Arab Republic Air Force. The Super Frelon was a large three-engined heavy-lift helicopter with a six-bladed main rotor, built by Sud Aviation. This was a sensitive issue as the Libyans were not on friendly terms with the UK and NATO and we had no official information on the role of the Super Frelon. The Super Frelons, which were changed over at three- or four-week intervals, were finished in either olive green or a multi-coloured chequered camouflage and one appeared to carry no national markings.[8] We learned that the crews were accommodated in the Malta Hilton and there was an apocryphal story of a bedroom suite having to be deep-cleaned after a sheep had been slaughtered, cooked and eaten on a sheet laid on the floor. This large three-engined helicopter would fly around Malta, apparently not talking to anyone including the RAF approach and Tower controllers at Luqa. We did occasionally see the Frelon in the hover over the sea just off the coast and assumed it had an SAR role although the lack of integration with RAF Luqa ATC would have greatly reduced its utility in this function. One afternoon we were unofficially invited to look around the AFM Bell 47s at St Patrick's Barracks and managed to peer in the rear ramp of the Libyan Super Frelon to see wet suits and diving gear laid out on the freight floor. Italy was also making overtures to their neighbour and on a couple of occasions an Italian Army CH-47 Chinook visited St Patrick's.[9] Towards the end of our tour incidents with the Libyans increased. A Wren was assaulted at Paceville, allegedly by Libyans, feelings ran high and for a time all shore leave at Paceville was cancelled for the unit. During the latter part of our tour, when the threat from Libya was perceived to be greater, 41 Commando regularly supplied armed guards for the sangars at RAF Luqa dominating the Nimrod dispersal and No. 3 Park for visiting NATO aircraft. On one occasion a Royal Marine on sentry duty at a sangar overlooking the 203 Squadron Nimrod dispersals had a negligent discharge with a GPMG and fired a short burst at the Nimrod Aircraft Servicing Flight Hangar, fortunately without doing any damage to either persons or aircraft. A strange incident also took place when a C-130 of the Libyan Armed Forces landed unannounced at Luqa and disgorged, not uniformed troops as had been briefly feared, but men in plain clothes.

The small size of Malta, together with the built-up areas and airspace restrictions, meant that we could not practise our primary tactical roles on the island. Fortunately the performance of the Gazelle allowed us to self-deploy north to Sicily and Italy in order to practise our tactical skills. We routed from our helipad to the north-west tip of Gozo, from there forty-four nautical miles across the Malta Channel to Capo Scaramia on the southern coast of Sicily and thence north via Comiso to the large NATO airbase at Sigonella, another forty nautical miles from the coast. A large number of US Navy aircraft were based at Sigonella including P-3 Orion maritime patrol aircraft, Grumman C-1A Traders for Carrier On-board Delivery (COD) and HH-46 Sea Knight helicopters, as well as Italian Air Force Bréguet Atlantics. We were hosted by the US Navy Air Facility, as it was then called, stayed in their transit quarters and generally got to know them well. These deployments enabled us to practise navigation and low flying over Sicily, measuring about one hundred and twenty-five miles west to Trapani and eighty miles north to south. Snowcapped Mount Etna towered to 11,000 feet just twenty miles north of the airfield.

The low flying was excellent with large tracts of wild, sparsely inhabited, country with only a few power lines and few other aircraft. We did occasionally meet Canberra PR.7 and PR.9 photo reconnaissance aircraft from 13 Squadron, based at Luqa, on similar exercises but the lower we flew the safer we were in respect to deconfliction. Due to our tactical low-level flying and the mountainous terrain, once we were over twenty miles from Sigonella we were out of radio contact until we approached our destination airfield.

Whilst refuelling at the Italian F-104 Starfighter base at Trapani I was told about a local Italian fishing boat which had recently trawled up an ejection seat and some human remains. Reportedly, the US Embassy in Rome discovered from the serial numbers on the wreckage and the type of seat that this was the remains of a pilot from a USN F-9F Panther or F-9 Cougar which had had a brake failure many years before in the 1950s whilst taxiing on a carrier and gone over the side in the Mediterranean to the west of Sicily.

There were a number of abandoned Luftwaffe airfields in the southern part of Sicily which had been used by the axis air forces for the bombing campaign on Malta in 1940-1943. Caltagirone, Comiso, Gerbini and Gela, to name a few, were used by *X Fliegerkorps* of the Luftwaffe who had been redeployed south from Norway in the winter of 1940. They had mostly returned to fields but the perimeter tracks and the old overgrown mess buildings were still visible. Located a few miles from our base at St George's in Malta was 'the ear' or 'il-widna', a fascinating relic of the era before radar. A parabolic stone wall over 200-feet long had been built in 1935 inland of the village of Baħar iċ Ċagħaq as a 'sound mirror'. The bearing of the focus on the wall aligned at 020 degrees and this was designed to allow the listening post at the apex of the convex wall to hear aircraft approaching from Sicily. Following the bearing from Malta, the coast of Sicily is reached at Grottelle sixty miles away and Syracuse at about eighty-five miles. Trials with RAF seaplanes established that 'the ear' was effective out to a range of about thirty-seven miles with a bearing accuracy of within 3 degrees. It was said that on a good day the operator could hear engines being run up sixty nautical miles away. Although there were sound mirrors built on the south coast of Britain prior to the Second World War, mostly in Kent and Sussex, this is believed to be the only sound mirror outside the UK. The ear still exists today located next to the Malta Com aerial dish with traces of red 'Malta camouflage' paint still visible.

The other resident squadron on Malta was 203 Squadron RAF flying seven or more Nimrod MR.1s in the then light grey paint scheme with white gloss fuselage upper surfaces, and was based at Park 2 at RAF Luqa. We got to know many of the crews and flew them in Gazelles on training sorties. In return we were invited to join some long Nimrod maritime patrols over the Mediterranean. I flew with Flight Lieutenant Gordon N. Millar on a patrol which monitored the Soviet anchorage off Hammamet. A couple of hours after take-off the lunchboxes were opened and the small microwave ovens in the rear cabin used to heat the contents. No sooner had we finished our meals than an HF message came through telling us not to touch the food as mouse droppings had been found in the catering spaces at Luqa. We also went to action stations when a small contact was spotted on radar; possibly the periscope of a Soviet submarine. During a tense low-level run-in, in hazy conditions of probably five kilometres visibility, we searched through the windscreen as the range counted down to see a small patch of white foam ahead. Disappointingly, it turned out to be a small isolated rock, many miles offshore, with waves breaking over it.[10]

Despite the lack of tactical tasking in Malta there was one flying skill which we could practise daily. Only the rudiments of instrument flying (IF) had been taught on the Sioux to enable the pilot to carry out a 180-degree turn to get out of trouble. A suction-powered attitude indicator, slip indicator and gyro compass had been provided, tacked on to the left side of the instrument console like the afterthought that it was. When I was awarded my wings I note that I had a total of 5.7 hours of IF of which 0.6 hour was 'actual'. Three hours of this total had been carried out on Chipmunk. With the introduction of the Gazelle with a 'proper' blind-flying panel and standby attitude indicator and compass, it was realised in 1976 that, apart from extrication from inadvertent IMC, an instrument trained pilot could position the aircraft in bad weather and have more flexibility in carrying out peacetime liaison flights. An instrument rating also improved general flying ability and airmanship. Having RAF Luqa with radar facilities on our doorstep we began to practise instrument flying. If the weather was fine we could install a black canvas and alloy screen to the panel with velcro which obscured much of the forward view through the canopy and which could be quickly torn aside for landing or in an emergency. We also had a canvas visor which attached with poppers to our helmet-mounted tinted visor and which added to the restriction of peripheral vision. Later we also used white plastic polish smeared over the lower part of the canopy, although this practice was later the subject of a flight safety warning concerning the danger of being affected by fumes in flight if the polish was used inside the transparency. So each week we conducted at least two sorties of simulated or actual instrument flying as P2 and a similar time as captain and safety pilot from the left-hand seat. The Gazelle, unlike a fixed-wing aircraft, could not be trimmed and was inherently unstable which meant that it was demanding to fly on instruments. The cyclic had to be held at all times with hydraulics running and if released it would fall over with catastrophic results. Later we would receive SAS (Stability Augmentation System) and Stick Feel for Royal Marines' Gazelles which allowed us to trim the cyclic and release it for short periods but that was in the future. Thus an hour of instrument flying was concentrated and tiring and required a constant scan and control inputs whilst trying to ignore the effects of 'the leans' caused by fluid in the semi-circular canals of the ear erroneously telling the brain that we were banked when straight and level. Most of our IF training sorties were over Gozo and the sea areas to the west of the island from flight level (FL) 35 to FL 80 (or 3,500 - 8,000 feet). We spent a great deal of time practising the five-minute exercise: from straight and level on a particular heading, two minutes in a rate one climbing turn through 360 degrees, a minute straight and level on the original heading and a two-minute descending 360-degree turn the other way to regain the original heading and level. Then limited panel work with the safety pilot placing stick-on black masks over various primary instruments. Finally, a surveillance radar approach or a precision radar approach to RAF Luqa with an overshoot for our helipad at St George's. Even in good weather IF training at Malta at night was effective because as soon as the lights of the island were left behind there was virtual IMC over the sea. In eighteen months I logged 65.8 hours of IF (of which 17.7 hours were actual) and sixty-four ground-controlled approaches to Luqa. Captain Graham Jeffs, an Instrument Rating Examiner from Plymouth, flew out to Malta to test us and the four of us were amongst the first light helicopter pilots to get our White instrument ratings in March 1976. This was to hold us in good stead in years to come in areas of less benign weather, such as in Northern Ireland.

Chapter 6

Malta – Towards Withdrawal

My first experience as a flight commander came in May 1976 when I was tasked to take two Gazelles on Exercise DISPLAY DETERMINATION at the Italian Army Training area at Monte Romano, north of Rome. The first leg was straightforward from St George's to NAF Sigonella. During flight planning, it became apparent that we needed our second refuel just short of Naples and the Italian Army Aviation base at Salerno was ideally located on our track. However, our signals requesting permission had gone unanswered. At Sigonella we were told to 'just put out a PAN call declaring a fuel shortage as you approach Salerno'. Luckily we did not have to resort to this shoddy measure and a call on the tower frequency cleared us in to the strip where a number of SIAI-Marchetti SM.109s (similar to the US Bird Dog) spotter aircraft were lined up on the grass. Whilst refuelling, there was a minor misunderstanding when the Italian Army ground crew noticed 'Salerno' stencilled on the backs of our Mae-Wests and thought that somehow we were taking the proverbial. It was a complicated explanation about 41 Commando's battle honour, and how we now supported that RM Commando unit, but eventually all were smiles. Passing overhead Naples, we reached Monte Romano after five hours of flying. We were supporting a company of 41 Commando on a NATO amphibious exercise and cross training period with a US Marine Corps Expeditionary unit. My first decision came when we were due to night fly. One look at USMC CH-53s landing in dense clouds of recirculating dust from opposing directions at the main LS, together with an Italian Agusta Bell AB-212 joining the party, indicated to me that we would be wiser to fly the next night on our own. During the exercise we took the opportunity to cross-train with USMC AH-1J Sea Cobra crews who also flew in our Gazelles. In return we were flown to the USS *Iwo Jima* and, after a briefing, each Gazelle pilot was put in the front seat of a Sea Cobra for deck landing practice, followed by a forty-minute tactical formation sortie overland. At endex we hitched a lift back to Malta aboard HMS *Fearless*, landing on whilst the ship lay alongside at the port of Civitavecchia and shooting our approaches carefully between the dockside cranes to the flight deck.

Back in Malta, having flown countless round-the-island trips for visitors and new arrivals to the unit, we felt we knew the island like the backs of our hands. A unit security exercise had been planned and the Intelligence Officer and a friend of mine, Rowan Jackson, spent a considerable amount of time planning and writing various scenarios which would occur at a given time and place all over the island. A week or so prior to the exercise it was announced that the Defence Minister, Fred Mulley, was to make an official visit to Malta and the security exercise was cancelled. Since the Minister's visit mostly concerned RAF Luqa and the Naval Headquarters at HMS *St Angelo*, Rowan went to our commanding officer to plead that the exercise should continue, albeit on a slightly amended scale. The CO reluctantly agreed on condition that the reduced exercise should in no way interfere or impact on any aspect of the Minister's programme. To cut a long story short, whilst Fred Mulley was at RAF Luqa and his official driver was waiting for him outside the headquarter building, a package containing a brick was found on the back seat of a staff car with a label attached stating 'This is a bomb'. Two and two were quickly put together and it was realised that this was a stray serial from Rowan's exercise which had slipped through the 'amendment'. As far as I know the Minister knew nothing of this but the story and associated high level hoo-ha caused us considerable amusement for days afterwards whilst Rowan looked somewhat subdued and thoughtful.

Despite the limitations of training on Malta we did exercise with 41 Commando's anti-tank troop at Hal Far airfield which had a large perimeter of rough limestone ground where an abandoned Victor tanker was waiting to be used for fire station practice. At that time the Royal Marines were using the 120mm recoilless anti-tank gun known as the L6 Wombat.[1] It was a lightweight version of the Mobat mounted on two small wheels and could be easily lifted underslung by Wessex 5. It was also light enough at 308kg to be lifted by a Gazelle, although with 250kg of fuel we were approaching our maximum all-up weight. I found the Wombat a very unstable load to fly at Hal Far, spinning and swinging in the slipstream. Entering a gentle bank turn and reducing airspeed helped to somewhat stabilise the load but the aircraft was still rolling in sympathy with the swinging gun; similar to being on the end of a pendulum. I was conscious that this was one load (one of six guns for the Commando) that I really must not jettison in flight and was as relieved as the anti-tank troop commander when the load eventually made contact with the ground, wobbled but did not turn over, and I could press the cargo release button on the collective.

There were some unique archaeological remains on Malta and on occasion we were tasked to fly museum specialists and visiting archaeologists to study the sites from the air. The 'cart-ruts' were of particular interest, being mysterious parallel ruts in the limestone which are found on a number of sites in Malta. The ruts at locations such as Ghar il-Kbir sometimes converge like railway lines at Clapham Junction and in one site, near Gnejna Bay, disappear off the end of a high cliff edge, whilst at St George's Bay a set continue underwater. They are of constant gauge of approximately 120cm width and are believed to be between 2,700 and 4,000 years old, but their purpose and formation remain a complete mystery.[2] Shortly after my arrival during a low-level sortie past the tiny island of Comino in the Gozo Channel we noticed two cannon half hidden in pits near the ruins of a small fort. Rodney Helme and I landed to inspect them and it seemed that these rusty cast iron cannon, marked on top of the breech area with the Fleur de Lys, may have been installed in the fort by the French in 1798 prior to the blockade by the Royal Navy and the eventual surrender to Rear Admiral Lord Nelson's fleet in 1800. I contacted the Malta Museum and the Director asked if he could be flown to Comino to inspect them. After getting permission from the British High Commission, there was a delay whilst the Maltese Director arranged an insurance policy to cover him for the flight. Meanwhile we calculated the approximate volume and weight of the cannon, using the specific gravity of cast iron, soon realising that it was out of the question for us to consider an underslung load. I understand that after we withdrew from the island the cannon were recovered under-slung beneath a Libyan Super Frelon and are now on display in Valetta.

Off the coast at Gnejna Bay there was evidence of more recent remains from the air. A shadow under the water 300 or 400 metres off the coast indicated the remains of an aircraft. It was rumoured that it was an Italian flying boat and one evening I snorkelled out to it. From the surface the few remains, twenty feet down, seemed rather unexciting. We were told that a patrol boat from the Malta Armed Forces had secured a line to it and attempted to pull the wreckage from the sand but it had not budged. Thirty-six years later in September 2013, whilst on a diving expedition in Malta, I asked to do two of the dives for my PADI Search and Recovery Course looking for this wreck. Although the aircraft remains were known to a few local historians, divers had showed little interest in the area as it was shallow, sandy and deemed uninteresting and thus little dived on. However, after practising our expanded 'U technique' search pattern, we found the remains at seven metres lying on a sandy bottom. It was not nearly as uninteresting as I had remembered. It turned out to be the forward fuselage section and sponson of a civil Dornier Wal-Cabina XI flying boat. Whilst flying between Tripoli and Syracuse on 16 February 1932 the aircraft landed on the sea after an engine fire and all nine occupants, including General Franco's brother, were rescued.[3] The flying boat was then towed to Malta and sank in shallow water. Much of it must have been recovered but the centre section is still there. Finding it caused some renewed interest and, as I left Malta, various dive clubs were planning to visit it.

RAF Luqa was host to a number of RAF squadrons on training camps. On 4 June 1976 a Buccaneer of 208 Squadron, one of a detachment of six from RAF Honington, landed at RAF Luqa with a hydraulic failure. When the hook missed the cable at the end of runway 24 and it was apparent that the Buccaneer would end up in the overshoot, the pilot raised the undercarriage at low speed and it gently ended up in the grass on its belly, appearing relatively undamaged. As the runway was now blocked, the remaining five aircraft diverted back to NAF Sigonella. The aircraft was raised and towed to a hangar and we were later shown a small ripple under the fuselage in line with the front of the bomb bay indicating a major structural deformation. The RAF engineering SNCO told us that the manufacturer was trying to design a repair scheme whilst the MoD was figuring out whether such a repair scheme would be cost effective. Months later it was still in the hangar with a prominent sign attached with masking-tape to the fuselage stating 'Don't ask. We don't know' in bold letters.[4]

The BAe Lightning at that time was UK's front-line interceptor and was famous for its phenomenal performance and rate of climb as well as for its short endurance and demanding pilot workload. Coincidentally, there was a Maltese officer, Flight Lieutenant Mark Micallef Eynaud, serving in the RAF at this time flying Lightnings with 92 Squadron in Germany as Malta's first fast jet pilot.[5] One morning in April 1976 we received a phone call from RAF Luqa Ops telling us that No. 5 Squadron RAF was due to detach to Luqa for armament practice camp with their Lightning F.6s. The squadron QFI was arriving with the advance party and could we fly him on a recce? This task fell to me and I met up with Flight Lieutenant Steve Horridge at Luqa who explained that he wanted to experience 'a Lightning pilot's eye view' of the approaches to Luqa and particularly to Hal Far which they were considering as an emergency crash diversion field (Sigonella being 100 miles away) if the runway at RAF Luqa became blocked. Hal Far had a barrier installed and the eleven 5 Squadron Lightning F.6s deploying were equipped with an arrestor hook without which they had no chance of stopping on the short runway. I flew a 3-degree approach to Hal Far threshold and was amused when my passenger asked me to repeat the approach but faster, arriving over the threshold at 170 knots – our VL (maximum limiting airspeed) was 168 knots in a steep dive. The sortie had unexpected benefits since I received a phone call a few weeks later asking whether I would like a right-hand seat ride in a Lightning T.5 trainer.

I leapt at the chance and found myself strapping into the right-hand seat of the 20-ton winged rocket XS452 at RAF Luqa. This aircraft was a T.5 (based on the earlier Lightning F.3, so it did not have an arrestor hook) and had been lent to 5 Squadron by the Lightning Training Flight (LTF) at Binbrook. Its other claim to fame was that it was finished in an experimental dark green matt finish on its upper surfaces with the LTF lion in dark blue on the tail together with a small white Maltese cross. A flight-refuelling probe was fitted to the port wing shoulder. I was required to prime the engines during the start sequence with Avpin, or isopropyl nitrate, an explosive chemical which ensured a rapid start of the Rolls Royce Avons. We took off in reheat, stayed low whilst the gear was rapidly retracted before reaching limiting speed and, at about 250 knots, rotated to 40 degrees or more, pointing skywards as the aircraft continued to accelerate to Mach 0.9. The sensation in the cockpit was better than any fairground ride and events happened very quickly with the outside scenery of Malta unwinding past the cockpit like a video on fast forward until we were heading straight up for the blue yonder. At above 40,000 feet reheat was again selected and, with a sudden jump on the pressure instruments, we were supersonic and accelerating in a silent cockpit except for the sound of heavy breathing synchronised with the blinking of the oxygen 'doll's eyes' indicator. I watched transfixed as the fuel indications fell in front of our eyes and, with a steer from the fighter controller at RAF Madalena, in no time we were recovering back to Luqa. I was then given the controls and talked through a max rate descent. With the throttles eased slightly back, I descended near vertically, did two rolls as we punched through layers of thin stratus at just subsonic speed, starting to pull out at 15,000 feet with the island laid out beneath us like a map to join the circuit downwind. Events in the circuit occurred faster than I could really keep up with but I remember the curving base leg onto final at about 190 knots reducing to 175 as we landed firmly followed by a pitch forward and bump as the nose wheel touched with Steve leaning forward with his left hand to reach the brake 'chute. This was of interest as I seem to remember that if the brake chute did not deploy we were to go round again for a final landing using maximum braking, during which we might burst a tyre. Our fuel reserve was about twenty minutes to NAF Sigonella, where the challenge was to get an English speaker from the US Navy detachment into the Tower in the short time available. Hence the advantage of Hal Far, a mile away from Luqa, in an emergency. This was 5 Squadron's last deployment to Malta before the airfield was handed over to the Maltese authorities.

However, the story of Lightning XS452 did not end there. When the Lightnings were finally retired from the RAF in 1988 to be replaced by the Tornado F.3, the two-seater languished at Cranfield before it was purchased in 1999 by businessman Mike Beachyhead for his Thunder City fast jet collection based at Cape Town.[6]

One of the unit deployments that we undertook in May 1976 was for the NATO amphibious Exercise DAWN PATROL which took place at Capo Teulada, the southernmost point of Sardinia. This involved an amphibious landing followed by an exercise in the training area and ranges and ending with a cross-training period with other nations. The initial plan was for the three Gazelles of Salerno Flight to self-deploy by sea via Trapani in Sicily. This was a great idea but would require an escorting aircraft with better navigation equipment than our map, compass and VHF homing aerial. It was arranged that we would meet up with a Grumman C-1A Trader from the Base Flight at US Naval Air Facility at Sigonella which would escort us across the 177-nautical-mile crossing to Decimomannu Italian Air Force base in Sardinia. Just a few days before the deployment the C-1A went unserviceable, so we re-arranged to embark the aircraft in the LSL *Sir Bedivere* and the LPD HMS *Fearless*. The exercise was good value for us in directing both live gunfire and close air support on the impact area on the headland at the far south of the ranges. During adjustment fire, using one gun of the battery of 105mm L5 pack howitzers, I was in the hover popping up from behind cover to observe the fall of shot. I could not understand why my adjustment of 'left one hundred, repeat' resulted in the next round landing even further to the right. I then realised that my gyro indicator had toppled and was indicating nearly 180 degrees from the correct reading on my standby compass. This meant that I had given a totally inaccurate 'direction' which the plotter in the battery CP was applying and which accounted for the error. We also conducted Forward Air Controller training with US Navy A-6 Intruders and A-7 Corsairs operating from a Sixth Fleet carrier dropping Mk 82 low drag bombs from a shallow dive on targets on the headland. It was often difficult to see the aircraft in the clear blue sky but it was necessary to check their heading on the attack run in order to clear them in 'hot'. Sometimes when short of fuel the pilot would pickle three or more remaining bombs in one pass before returning to the carrier. On one occasion three Mk 82s were dropped short of the headland into the sea and the concussion briefly knocked out some of the wireless communications on HMS *Fearless,* which was anchored about 1,500 metres to the north east.

Artillery support to 41 Commando was provided by 8 (Alma) Battery, who were based with us on Malta and deployed with us to Sardinia. From the ruined Torre di Porto Scudo which served as an observation post overlooking the impact area, I witnessed with interest as the visiting CO of 29 Commando Regiment tested the battery commander (BC) of 8 (Alma) Battery, Major Mike Holroyd-Smith, with drawing up a live fire plan involving artillery, naval gunfire and air support onto the headland. Having completed his fire plan against the clock, and with about twenty minutes before it commenced, Lieutenant Colonel Ron Preedy gave a change of H hour to Mike who had to rapidly re-calculate and adjust his fire plan. It was fascinating to watch and it put the BC under some pressure, but it all went off according to plan with some impressive smoke and impacts on the range headland. Early the next morning I had to take Lieutenant Colonel Preedy to Cagliari Elmas Airport to catch a flight home. There was a thick mist which covered all the hill tops at Teulada and reduced visibility to about two kilometres but I decided to follow the coastline at low level thus avoiding all high ground. Our twenty-eight-mile direct track thus became forty-five miles as we flew at about 90 knots a hundred feet above the sea following the beaches and headlands but arrived without incident and a hour later the sun had burned off the mist leaving eight/eighths bright blue.

Whilst we were in Malta, Salerno Flight, along with all other AAC units, were visited by AAC Standards Branch once a year. During my time I flew with Major Norman Overy (who five years later was to examine me on upgrade to A2 QHI) and Major John Valenzia who flew out from AAC UKLF to check us out. John Valenzia happened to be also Maltese and his visit could be combined with seeing family and friends. One very useful aptitude I found that I possessed was not being nervous of check rides. I watched many colleagues fail to produce their best and, in some cases go to bits, when being tested. Although the adrenaline flowed, I was not nervous and could produce a result to the best of my ability under test. This was a valuable attribute, especially later as QHIs were checked regularly, and I was fortunate to have it within my DNA.

FLYING LIGHT HELICOPTERS WITH THE ROYAL MARINES

Whilst living on this historic island I read about the air battle for Malta during the Second World War, including an incident at the height of the bombing, recorded by Denis Barnham, where an unfortunate Italian airman, whose bomber was shot down over the Grand Harbour, had baled out under a malfunctioning parachute and had been impaled on a fountain.

> I join a party of airmen and soldiers staring into the sky. The Italian bombers are no longer there: two have gone whilst the last one of all is dropping below a long trail of flaming debris – a huge machine, already quite low, tumbling over and over sideways in a series of convulsive jerks. Suddenly gushing with flame, it disintegrates in a shower of sparks. The blue sky is empty but for a white parachute not properly open, which, flapping and streaming behind the struggling figure, is plunging down into the harbour smoke-screen.[7]

I thought no more about this until I was sent to the residence of Commander British Forces Malta (CBFM), the Villa Portelli at Kalkara, to organise a helicopter landing site. CBFM was Rear Admiral O.N.A. Cecil CB[8] and he was to be picked up by one of our Gazelle helicopters to be flown to RAF Luqa to catch a flight back to UK.[9]

I arrived by Land Rover at the car park at the rear of the Villa about thirty minutes early together with a marine with a fire extinguisher and marshalling vest, carrying a clean flying suit and headset for the admiral. Having checked that the landing site was clear, I was waiting by the Land Rover when Admiral Cecil appeared. Having saluted and introduced myself he looked at his watch and asked me whether I had ever seen round the villa as we had twenty minutes to spare. Villa Portelli had been used by British officers since the mid-nineteenth century and by Royal Naval Flag Officers since the Second World War. During the tour we walked down the terraced garden that lies to the north-west of the villa towards Bighi hospital. Down the stone path, flanked by flower beds of red Maltese earth, was a circular fish pond in the middle of the pathway containing water lilies and goldfish. In the centre of the small pond was a stone and concrete plinth on which was mounted a short metal water spout that was dribbling water in order to aerate the pond. On the side of this rough plinth, cemented into the concrete, was a small, brightly coloured, enamel button. When I enquired about this, Admiral Cecil told me that it was the button badge of an Italian airman whose parachute had failed to open during the war and who had landed here. This story immediately rang a bell with me and I guessed that, in all likelihood, the water spout was the 'fountain' and the story had become exaggerated with the telling. The position of Villa Portelli on the edge of the heavily bombed Grand Harbour at Kalkara was also a likely location for the event.[10]

To make our night flying more interesting we planned night navigation exercises, using turning points out at sea and well out of sight of Malta. We could be monitored by Luqa Radar and at the same time use their fixes to check the accuracy of our steam navigation with chart, Dalton Computer and stopwatch. It was on one of these sorties, where we flew the route fifteen minutes behind the aircraft in front, that I had the Squadron Leader Ops of RAF Luqa, an ex-Victor tanker pilot, in the left-hand seat as a passenger. We planned to finish the navigation sortie with a PAR on Luqa's runway 24 with a planned overshoot to St George's. We were into our radar-controlled descent on the 3-degree glideslope when two things happened simultaneously. The approach controller suddenly transmitted 'Marine 489 break right off this approach' and in my peripheral vision I saw the white belly and navigation lights of a Nimrod MR.1 in a port turn onto final just ahead of us in our 11 o'clock. It was certainly close enough to make out the paint scheme in the dark. It turned out that a Nimrod in the visual circuit had been given clearance to land, unaware that there was a PAR in progress due to a momentary breakdown or interruption of the Tower's internal communication system. Although there was no immediate danger, as we had just broken out of the cloud base into VMC, it was nevertheless potentially dangerous and my passenger was certainly embarrassed. It was fortuitous to have had OC Ops at Luqa on board as he took the matter up with a certain amount of personal interest the next morning with ATC and the initial response along the lines that it had been 'no big deal' and 'the Marines are exaggerating' cut little ice with him.

Towards the end of our time we planned to navigate to the tiny island of Linosa lying eighty-two miles west of Malta, midway between Malta and Libya. We required diplomatic clearance from the Italians for this trip. Linosa is too small and rocky for any airfield and we decided not to land in case we went unserviceable and gave AAC UKLF a really testing recovery challenge. So instead we would orbit the islet and return to Malta. This was hardly in the Charles Lindbergh league but was an interesting navex before the days of GPS, when we relied on a line on our chart. Malta Radar tracked us for some of the way but the Gazelle was perhaps unintentionally one of Europe's early 'stealth aircraft'. Constructed of nida, glass fibre sandwich, plastics and perspex and with a streamlined tadpole shape, which was to later give it the nickname of 'the whistling chicken leg', the Gazelle did not give a good radar return. Whilst scientists looked for ways of developing stealthier aircraft, we were busy lining the rear baggage compartment of our aircraft with domestic baking foil in an effort to improve our radar return. Linosa is a circular-shaped black-and-rust-coloured rocky volcanic island, one and a half miles in diameter, with a single tiny fishing village whose only link to the outside world was a supply vessel to Sicily. The trip was flown as a two aircraft sortie climbing to 4000 feet under a high level layer of stratus. Visibility was good so we saw the island from twenty miles away, flew two circuits of the island taking photographs and returned to Malta after ninety uneventful minutes in the air.

We regularly practised our deck-landing skills on Royal Naval vessels calling at Malta or passing by through the Malta Channel. This also provided practice to the Flight Deck Officers and aircraft handlers on board. On one occasion, with Rodney Helme in the left seat holding his 8mm cine camera, I flew to rendezvous with the guided missile destroyer HMS *Kent*. We, and a second Gazelle, carried out a number of DLPs on the flight deck just forward of the lattice-work launcher for the Sea Slug missile system as the ship steamed westwards twenty miles north of Malta. After our last landing Rodney thanked the ship on UHF and announced that we would do one final low fly-by in formation. Lining up two miles astern of the ship, leading the second Gazelle in echelon, we descended to thirty feet, aiming to pass 100 metres down the starboard side of the ship and level with the superstructure whilst Rodney filmed. As we approached a few hundred metres astern, Rodney, looking through his viewfinder, mentioned that there seemed to be an appreciative crowd lining the rail to watch us. However, as we passed down the starboard side, I saw that the rail and flight deck were indeed lined with sailors but they were all collectively making rude gestures indicating their 'excitement' at this display. Rodney's home-movie footage did not make for suitable family viewing.

For some years we had requested refurbishment of our stone Victorian barracks at St Andrew's Barracks where the 600 men of 41 Commando were based. The officers' mess, along with much of the other accommodation, was damp in winter, the paintwork on the green wooden shutters was flaking and it generally looked 'down at heel'. As the date for our withdrawal drew closer miraculously money appeared from MoD in order to 'return the barracks in good order'. So, just prior to us moving out, the accommodation and messes were repainted. This was slightly strange thinking, especially as it was our Victorian antecedents who had built the barracks in the early 1860s in the first place. Remembering how 42 Commando had withdrawn from Singapore to return to sub-standard accommodation outside Plymouth made me realise that the diplomatic impression imparted to our former colonies appeared sometimes more important to the Government than the actual living conditions of our troops. Of course, after we left St Andrew's the Maltese Government left the barracks empty and derelict for some years, so the redecoration served little practical purpose.

In late 1976 it was decided that I should deploy with E Company to fly Sioux during jungle training in Brunei in January 1977. This involved a trip back to UK for Sioux refresher training before flying to the Far East which will be covered in the next chapter.

Our last task in Malta prior to the British withdrawal was supporting the Royal Anglians in February who were training on the island, based at Ghajn Tuffieha Camp. On 16 March 1977 the farewell parade of 41 Commando Group took place on St Andrew's Barracks square in front of a large invited crowd. The salute was taken by Earl Mountbatten of Burma. The three Gazelles of Salerno Flight performed a flypast after the general salute. After holding off Grand Harbour at the appointed moment we began our run-in from out to sea, but paralleling the coast, past Sliema and St Julian's until, with a port turn in vic formation onto 270 degrees over Paceville, we lined up with the parade ground for the overhead pass. After landing we then had a rushed change into our Blues and a Land Rover lift back to the parade square in time for the group photograph of Lord Louis with the officers of 41 Commando Group. I always remember that, just before Lord Mountbatten took his seat in the front row, he studied us all. Focusing his well-known critical eye on the Regimental Colour being carried by Lieutenant John Crosby in the second row he remarked, 'I think you might have passed an iron over it before the parade.' It would have taken a brave or foolish subaltern to have trusted his ironing skills on an invaluable silk Regimental Colour.[11] After the parade our aircraft and stores were prepared for shipment back to UK by Landing Ship Logistic (LSL) RFA *Sir Percival*.[12]

After 41 Commando Group departed, Salerno Company was left in Malta. They moved to a barrack block at RAF Luqa for security and guarding duties, and left the island when the British finally withdrew on 30 March 1979 in the RFA LSL *Sir Lancelot*, bringing 188 years of association between the Royal Marines and the island to a close.[13]

Chapter 7

Brunei – The Jungle

My experiences as a passenger in a Sioux helicopter in Singapore as a young troop commander had confirmed my wish to go flying. Each Commando unit at that time had an Air Troop of three Westland Sioux AH.1s. With doors removed, flying at low level over the Malayan jungle and along the white beaches of Pahang State seemed to me the height of fun. However, by the time I had finished my flying training those days appeared to have moved on: air troops were a thing of the past; the British had withdrawn from East of Suez and it was the age of the turbine helicopter. However, quite out of the blue, I had the opportunity to refresh back on to the Sioux and fly the Army's last two operational piston-engined helicopters over the jungle.

At the end of 1976, whilst flying Gazelles with Salerno Flight attached to 41 Commando Group in Malta, it was planned that E Company, commanded by Captain David Baldwin RM, would deploy to Brunei for jungle training on Exercise CURRY TRAIL. It so happened that helicopter support to 7th Gurkha Rifles (7GR) in Brunei was provided by C Flight of 656 Squadron Army Air Corps equipped with the last two Sioux in operational Army service. Captain Denis Lewis, 6GR, who had been on my Army flying course at Middle Wallop and nicknamed 'Big Den', commanded the Flight which had an important casevac and re-supply role for troops training in the jungle and thus Denis was required to stay in Brunei on call. After getting his wings, Denis had initially been posted to 659 Squadron AAC in Germany where, during a recce on a BAOR exercise, he had run out of power during a downwind quick-stop and ran his Sioux onto a ploughed field where it turned over. He and his passenger climbed out of the wreckage unhurt.[1] He was more than ready for some overseas leave and thus it was suggested that I deploy with E Company on Exercise CURRY TRAIL in order to relieve Denis as flight commander for a month or so. I leaped at the opportunity.

BRUNEI – THE JUNGLE

    I became a rare breed of aircrew who refreshed from Gazelle back on to the Sioux. For this I had to fly back from Malta to the UK a week after our daughter, Clare, was born by the twice-weekly RAF VC10 from Luqa in order to complete a week-long refresher course at Netheravon. I arrived on 7 December to find the UK in the throes of a bitterly cold spell and the old RFC airfield on the Wiltshire downs was bleak and windswept. I moved into a cabin in the historic black and white timbered mess with the original large wooden RFC wings mounted over the entrance. This was the setting for much of V.M. Yeats' classic book *Winged Victory* and perhaps the Sioux represented the last of operational seat-of-the-pants flying in the British Services. As I climbed shivering into bed it occurred to me that this was a novel way to prepare for hot and humid limited power flying techniques.

    My instructor was an experienced instructor of the old school, WO2 Markham. I was later to get to know him very well as Captain Tony Markham when, four years later, I became a flying instructor and served with him at Middle Wallop. However, on this cold December Wednesday morning he was faced with teaching a confident young pilot, who had been flashing around the Mediterranean skies in a Gazelle, how to coax every ounce of power out of a Sioux, without bending it, in five days. He did not seem overenthusiastic at the prospect. The cockpit drills were not difficult to recall but as I waited for the oil temperature to climb to 40 degrees C and carried out the mag drop, I became aware that the Lycoming could not be taken for granted in the same way as the reliable Astazou could be by this '800-hour veteran'. Jungle techniques were taught to me in the familiar Pennings and Linden clearings on Salisbury Plain with artificial limits put on the power available to simulate the hot and high conditions I would experience in the Far East. Thus Tony would say, 'You have only got 28 inches of manifold pressure available to get us out of here.'

    It might be appropriate at this point to mention some of the difficulties that the jungle theatre has in store for the helicopter pilot. The air is warm and thus less dense and therefore produces less lift for a given blade pitch setting. High humidity also produces less dense air and thus even more pitch on the rotor blades is required to hover. More pitch means more drag which has to be overcome with more power. Less dense air entering the carburettor also meant a reduction in power but this degradation was offset by a turbocharger on the Sioux's Avco Lycoming TVO-435-A1A engine which ensured the rated 270hp was available up to 12,400-feet pressure altitude. Power was never in abundance in the Sioux, even in temperate climes, and thus the aircraft's weight had to be carefully adjusted in order to ensure that there would be enough power available for the task in hand. This would be achieved in a number of ways: by restricting the underslung load or the load on the litters; delaying to take a passenger (or perhaps only accepting a wiry Gurkha) until fuel had been burned off or by further reducing the already meagre fuel load. The effect of running out of power was to 'overpitch' which meant the collective lever was raised in order to increase the pitch of the blades to the point where drag could no longer be countered by power from the Lycoming. The net result was that the rotor revs would start to decay out of their operating band of 280 to 320 rpm. The only way to recover the rotor revs was to lower the lever (i.e. descend). If the lever remained where it was, the revs would decay at an increasing rate to a point at which they could never be recovered. Loss of lift, loss of centrifugal rigidity of the blades and spectacular disaster were then real possibilities. Overpitching can be experienced in turbine helicopters but the modern gas turbine is so powerful that the hamfisted pilot will overtemp the turbine blades or generally reach some other limitation before overpitching occurs (hence the value of basic rotary training on piston helicopters. Valuable principles can be taught that can never be graphically demonstrated on turbine types until a limited power emergency is experienced.)

There were then the problems concerned with operating from confined areas in primary jungle. Unlike the Pennings, surrounded by thirty-foot tall trees, rainforest trees could be up to 200 feet high and the clearing from above would resemble a dark and constricted lift shaft. At the bottom of the confined area the landing point could be covered in tree stumps and overgrown with fast-growing ferns or secondary jungle growth, *belukar*, which might threaten the vulnerable tail rotor. Wind is the friend of the helicopter pilot, adding considerable performance to the aircraft by means of translational lift. Once in the confined area, there was likely to be no wind at all and the temperature would often be higher than ambient. All these factors conspired to reduce the power of the aircraft. Whilst in Europe a limited power run on or zero-speed landing might be made in a field or a clear area of grass but in the jungle theatre hover out of ground effect or HOGE performance was required in order to safely get in or out of a clearing; thus the weight of the aircraft, flying technique and smooth control movements became of paramount importance.

With a reduced fuel load, accurate navigation over the broccoli-like jungle canopy was vital. There were no navaids save for an aircrew watch, a 1:50,000 or 250,000 map and a gyro compass backed up by a small standby compass. Curiously the Sioux AH.1 was not equipped with a clock and had a small inaccurate fuel gauge graduated 'Full', '¾', '½' and 'Empty' rather as one might find on an ancient Austin Mini. There were not many options for forced landings but the technique that we talked through was to aim to achieve a zero-speed engine-off landing on top of the canopy in a tail-down attitude and hope that the engine and firewall would give some protection to the occupants during the second impact with the jungle floor 150 feet or so below. A jungle survival pack was always strapped in one of the two litters which were clipped to the top of the skids and a gollock (*gulok*, an agricultural tool and weapon) and two water bottles were stuffed between the seats in the cabin. The only usable ATC frequency for us in Brunei was Bandar seri Begawan (BSB) Airport and thus the technique on transit flights was to fly as high as was practical, 4,000 or 5,000 feet above the jungle, so that there was more chance of getting through or being heard whilst in autorotation by another helicopter or fixed wing on the BSB frequency.

Tony Markham, who had checked me out on the Sioux at Netheravon, was famous in Army Aviation for having pulled off a textbook engine-off in primary rain forest in North Borneo. Flying three passengers of the Royal Green Jackets and an RA gun position officer over the jungle in mountainous terrain in July 1965, Tony's Scout suffered a total engine failure. Entering autorotation he just cleared two ridgelines by juggling 90 knots range speed with flaring the aircraft and headed for a small patch of lower secondary forest, nearly three miles from the engine failure, only identifiable by the change of lighter colour in the 'green broccoli' of the jungle. Flaring above the canopy, he put the aircraft into the lower secondary forest tail first so that the tail boom, engine and rear bulkhead structure could absorb the inevitable impact. They all survived uninjured except for one minor back problem and, after Tony had made them all a brew of tea with his survival kit, they were winched out by a Whirlwind HAR.10 three hours later. The Scout was later recovered underslung from an RAF Belvedere and repaired by Westlands. Tony received a Green Endorsement.[2]

Allegedly a previous pilot in Brunei some years before had taken off from a landing point (LP) in the south, near the border with Sarawak, to transit back to Seria. He climbed as per the standard procedure and at about 3,000 feet the engine dramatically reduced power so that, with the maximum power available, he could not maintain straight and level. Quick as a flash he did a 180-degree turn and set up a gradual powered descent, eyeing the distant LP from which he had taken off. Would he make it? With some skill and a bit of luck he ended up in the bottom of the clearing with an intact

Sioux with a broken valve stem. This ageing experience was enough for him and he bade farewell to Brunei and jungle flying.

At the end of the five days I had completed 15.4 hours of refresher flying in Wiltshire and returned to Malta for Christmas and to become acquainted with our two-week-old daughter, Clare. On 2 January 1977 I arrived in Brunei with the rest of E Company in an RAF VC10 and was met by my old colleague Denis Lewis who flew me down to the Flight location on the beach at Seria. The plan was for me to quickly familiarise myself with the local area and procedures after which I would have a theatre qualification, or TQ check, from the Squadron QHI who was based in Hong Kong. I settled into the luxurious 7GR officers' mess, which was located on the beach a mile or so from the Flight location in the Sultan's palace or Istana. There I was immediately issued with a Land Rover which I was told was for my personal use in order to get to and from the Flight and other locations. I queried whether it could really be used to visit the Shell Panaga Club a couple of miles away, of which we were all honorary members, in the evenings and was told 'yes, of course'. A few days later I was rung up by the adjutant of 7GR who told me my Land Rover had been seen parked outside the Panaga Club. I owned up, received a hearty bollocking, and was told not to do it again. Life in the Mess was old fashioned and very comfortable with spicy mulligatawny soup for breakfast followed by fish and then eggs and bacon. Beer was served in silver tankards.

There were two Sioux in the flight, which was manned by a mixture of Gurkha soldiers and REME technicians. There was one other sergeant pilot whom I shall call Sergeant Jones* in C Flight. I began to suspect that things were a trifle strange in this far-flung outpost of the empire when Sergeant Jones took me aside on the first day and told me that he was not prepared to fly XT218, even if it was declared serviceable, and if I had any sense I wouldn't either. As a result of this prejudice all my familiarisation flights with Sergeant Jones were carried out in XT157, being the only other aircraft in theatre. Sergeant Jones was a highly experienced jungle pilot and prepared himself for each sortie as if it were to be his last, which in retrospect was not a bad policy. Most of the interesting and testing LPs were down on the border with Sarawak, which was an invisible demarcation line in the endless jungle. Our maximum allowed fuel in Brunei was thirty-six gallons of Avgas although the two flexible tanks had a total capacity of forty-eight gallons. In order to accurately measure this amount we were thoughtfully provided with an aluminium dipstick, which was stowed between the seats like everything else. The dipstick was graduated in gallons and had to be rapidly extracted from the filler cap and read before the level mark evaporated. The aircraft burned a gallon every three minutes which meant that after an hour and forty-eight minutes you could expect the engine to stop. Heading back to Seria over the jungle with the coastline clearly visible in the distance from 3,000 feet, with a fuel gauge that read 'Empty' and an aircrew watch that indicated we had been airborne for an hour and thirty minutes was a new experience for me. Sergeant Jones interrupted his tuneless whistling to remind me that the red fuel boost failure light would illuminate five or ten seconds before engine failure due to fuel starvation. After we shut down at Seria, as soon as Sergeant Jones had disappeared to sign down the aircraft, I could not resist dipsticking the tanks, discovering one gallon in each side. I soon realised that in order to provide any service to our troops near the border those were the sorts of margins that one was expected to cope with.

It was at this juncture that a signal arrived with some surprising news. A Gazelle flown by the Director of Army Aviation, Major General J.A. Ward-Booth, had crashed at Barton Stacey, a disused army camp near to Middle Wallop. It eventually transpired that the starboard front pilot's door had not been properly closed and in the cruise it opened partially. He decided to land at Barton Stacey disused parade ground to close it. At 200 feet on approach the door suddenly came free from the latch and, as he came to the hover, the airflow changed around the canopy causing the door to slam wide open and distracted him. The aircraft moved rearwards, the tail impacted the parade ground and the aircraft cartwheeled to port. The seriously injured DAAC was able to release himself from an almost inverted cockpit and stagger clear before the aircraft burned out. At that time Directors Army Air Corps were selected from the Arms and were not pilots, instead undergoing a rudimentary and shortened flying course at Middle Wallop to get their Army wings. This put them in a difficult position if they chose to fly and especially so when the Director was involved in a crash due to pilot error. He took full responsibility for the error; the accident report was published as normal and lessons learned. Major General Ward-Booth happily made a full recovery.[3]

Navigation to the LPs was simply a matter of plotting a course and sticking rigidly to heading, airspeed and time and perhaps, above all, having faith in the system. The LPs were so enclosed by tall jungle that, at 3,000 feet, they did not become visible until you were within a quarter of a mile or so of them. At low level they were very difficult to find. This basic 1914-era navigation system, however, worked time after time and it was not unusual for passengers to express surprise at how we arrived over these clearings without looking at a map. In the event of not finding a clearing, the drill was to conduct a short box search and then, always with an eye on the wrist watch, return to refuel and try again. I was shown a number of techniques to get out of clearings vertically, one of which was to allow the aircraft to gently rotate to the right as it climbed, the theory being that by applying less pitch to the anti-torque tail rotor, more power was available to the main rotor. I had one trip with Denis who demonstrated his method of getting out of a riverbed at the bottom of a deep valley. This consisted of charging at the trees 100 metres away in order to gain translational lift. As we scraped over the jungle canopy at the far end at 35 knots I was soaked in sweat and it was not only due to the humidity.

Five and a half miles down the coast to the east was the grass airfield of Anduki used by the Shell Petroleum Brunei fleet of five Sikorsky S-61s in support of the offshore rigs. It amused me that the well-equipped twin-engined S-61s were not generally permitted to fly over the jungle but I was told on the rare occasion that a C Flight Sioux had gone unserviceable in a clearing a special contract would be arranged for an S-61 to undersling our aircraft out.[4]

At the end of the first week the QHI arrived from Hong Kong to check me out. After take-off, the QHI invited me to navigate to a six-figure grid reference. With doors off, trying to fight with two large folded 1:63,600 map sheets in the cockpit was not easy. As I tried to turn over the map, which indicated uniform green jungle at every fold, without it being either sucked out of the door or plastered over our faces, the aircraft dropped like a stone. The friction on the collective lever was ineffective on this particular Sioux and the blades fined off pitch when the lever was left to its own devices. After this poor start, the rest of the trip went well although I noted that we kept to the coast and over the few tracks or roads. It transpired that the experienced QHI did not enjoy flying over the jungle. Now that I was jungle-qualified, Denis left me in charge and departed on his well-earned leave.

The scenery was spectacular. I particularly enjoyed early morning sorties with the 'jungle mist' hanging in the top of the canopy of trees in the near 100 per cent humidity. The tops of a very few of the jungle's giant trees were a blaze of colour from orchids visible from a mile or so away on the top of the canopy and, of course, invisible from the ground. I once entered autorotation at 4,000 feet, wound the engine right back, brought the airspeed back to 40 knots and, with my helmet loosened, believed that I could just hear the jungle noises above the slipstream and engine. Down in the southern border of Brunei we could look across eight miles to the east to the dramatic limestone 7,000-foot mountains of Gunung Mulu in Sarawak.[5]

However, the invisible border with Malaysia was not to be crossed and was, we were told, occasionally patrolled by armed Alouette IIIs.

During one morning start-up on the Seria pad I made a small mistake which profoundly shocked me. During my pre-take-off checks I checked 'Fuel Cock On' and felt down with my left hand that the red fuel cock was pushed firmly in as I had done countless times. As I did so I pulled it out to the 'Off' position. Quick as a flash I realised what I had done, returned it to 'On' and the engine did not falter. However, I sat there for a moment breaking into a cold sweat. Why had I done that? I could not afford to make that sort of error which could kill me and my passengers. I remembered the Scout accidents I had read of where the fuel cock had inadvertently been selected off instead of the nearby heater control.[6] No one but me saw or knew of this momentary mistake but I determined to slow my checks down and the memory of this careless slip was burned into my brain.

During the remainder of my short tour I flew on average three times a day but had two particularly alarming moments. The first was when I was tasked to collect a member of the SAS on exercise from a jungle LP in the south and take him to Tutong Camp. I found the clearing without difficulty and made radio contact with the patrol. I carried out a careful recce of the clearing, which had not been used for some time. After a power check to confirm that I had sufficient power in hand and could get max power (32.8 inches of manifold pressure corrected for temperature), I carried out a careful sight-picture approach to the top of the clearing and then a gentle vertical descent by reference to a tree trunk in front of me and to one on my left. As I got to within thirty feet of the floor of the clearing a number of uncomfortable factors became immediately apparent. The floor of the clearing was not flat but sloped uphill and the *belukar* and ferns surrounding the pad were high enough to possibly foul the tail rotor. During my vertical descent what little wind there had been had disappeared and the temperature had increased. The throttle was now fully open and I was gently descending and committed to a landing whether I liked it or not. I managed to touch down with the front of my skids balanced on the up-hill portion of the log platform which formed the LP. Landing was out of the question due to the slope and the ferns which were now out of sight but close to my tail rotor. To make matters worse, in order to cushion the touchdown I had overpitched slightly and with the throttle fully open the rotor revs were now down to 280 rpm instead of the recommended 320. The only way to restore them was to gently reduce power whilst remaining balanced on the skids and thus gradually milk the revs back to 320 rpm, after which I could consider trying to get out of the clearing. Ahead of me in the *belukar* and in the shadow of the giant rainforest the sweat-stained members of the patrol were sitting on their bergens idly watching and blissfully unaware of my predicament. They had either left their radio or could no longer hear above the noise of the Sioux because my calls to them were now unanswered. Frankly, all thoughts of picking up my passenger had evaporated and I was concentrating very hard on getting out of the clearing in one piece. You can imagine my alarm when the Sioux suddenly lurched to starboard and a heavy bergen landed with a thump in the starboard litter. This event was followed by a large soldier hauling himself bodily onto the skid post and into the cabin. My shouts to him to 'Get out, get off' or words to that effect went unheard as he knelt on the seat, fiddled with the four-point harness and pulled the lap strap straight out of the buckle, showing it to me with a grin. He was also determined not to put on his headset but eventually sat down unrestrained. We were now badly overpitched and I had visions of the aircraft settling on the rear of the skids on an out of limits slope, suffering a tail rotor strike and crashing in the clearing. Eventually, the revs slowly came back and, since I could not get the man out, I was going to have to attempt a take-off. After a long delay, where fuel burned off and we became slightly lighter, I got out with a great deal of luck and as we gained translational lift with the skids scraping the top of the jungle canopy I literally sagged with relief. At our destination I thoroughly 'debriefed' the passenger who had been totally unaware of the drama he had caused. I also refused to carry any more troops from that detachment until they had been re-briefed on Sioux drills. Probably they were more used to the twin-engined Royal Brunei Air Force Bell 212 transport helicopters, which were far more practical, tougher and utilitarian than the Sioux.

The next incident was entirely of my own making. I was due to take the Commanding Officer of 7GR to a lunch party at the British High Commission at Bandar seri Begawan. Lieutenant Colonel Miles Hunt-Davis[7] was a tall man, who could barely squeeze into the right-hand seat of the Sioux. The British High Commissioner's residence was situated beside the Brunei river. The landing pad was beside the river at the edge of a road, on the other side of which was the rear gate to the High Commission garden, which sloped gently uphill. There being little or no wind my approach therefore lay along the river. I read a book whilst sitting in the sun beside the Sioux awaiting the end of the lunch and the return of my passenger. Eventually Lieutenant Colonel Hunt-Davis appeared together with another lunch guest who was introduced to me as Brigadier Chapple,[8] Commander of the Gurkha Brigade.

Could we give him a lift back to Seria? I was down to about twenty gallons of fuel and did some rapid mathematics. It seemed that we would be OK, especially as there was a nice flat river to transition over at take-off. They squeezed into the cabin and strapped in whilst I briefed Lieutenant Colonel Hunt-Davis, cramped in the centre seat, to keep his left knee away from the cyclic stick. After lifting into the hover I did a power check and a 360-degree look-out turn. As I began the transition across the mirror smooth water of the wide river, I realised that I had made an error. With full power the rotor revs were gradually decaying. The normal recovery action, as I have mentioned before, was to lower the collective lever but this was not possible with our skids two feet above the water unless we wanted a swim. My passengers were totally oblivious to our predicament and were deeply engaged in a conversation concerning the luncheon party. Neither of them were wearing lifejackets and, in a flash, my mind envisaged the Board of Inquiry report. As the rotor revs dropped to 290 rpm a shudder ran through the airframe indicating the magic of translational lift and we slowly climbed away from the glassy surface of the river. For the second time in a week I sagged with relief whilst my passengers continued their chat in blissful ignorance of their close escape from a ducking and I slowly milked the revs back to 320.

One clear night I decided to try some dual night flying with Sergeant Jones. We did a careful daylight recce and it all seemed very straightforward, starting with a few circuits to an AAI at the pad at Seria, then flying up the coast to Tutong Camp and inland to Kampong Tanjong Maya where we intended to land on a large football pitch at the edge of the village. All went well until we left the lights of Tutong and the coast road and began to head inland over the jungle. There were no lights. There was no horizon – only pitch blackness with a faint reflection of our own instrument lighting inside the bubble canopy. We eventually saw a couple of dim lights which signified the Kampong and set up an approach to where we knew the football pitch to be. It was very disorientating with just a few dim lights to one side and instrument flying with our mickey-mouse instrument pack was not much fun. As we cautiously descended into inky black we switched on the landing light, hoping to see an early view of the surrounds of the football field. It picked up nothing until a few minutes later, struggling to maintain a gentle, low speed descent, the tops of the jungle canopy appeared in the beam. Pulling full power we established a shaky climb and headed back to the coast. No more night flying over the jungle for us.[9]

C Flight could be said to have been right at the end of the Army Aviation supply line. We were eagerly awaiting the arrival of a set of replacement main rotor blades from the UK. The standard procedure was that they would be flown out by commercial airfreight and we would be telephoned when they arrived. Having received the phone call, I detailed one of our Gurkha drivers to drive to Bandar seri Begawan Airport to collect them. By late afternoon he had not returned and we were getting concerned, so I rang the airport and asked them to page him. Yes, he had collected the blades and was awaiting further instructions. I learned that in future I must give specific and accurate instructions, including for the return portion of the journey. However, when the 4-tonner arrived back at base it was with some dismay that we saw that three new Gazelle rotor blades had been flown 8,000 miles to the Far East.

Anyone who has travelled to the East knows that an occasional runny tummy is part of the deal. Whilst ferrying stores to an LP near the border I found that I had an urgent need of a loo. This was not a great problem as we had established a forward refuelling base by delivering some forty-gallon drums and a zenith pump to a kampong about five minutes away. I landed on the kampong sports field and hastily shut down, planning to run a couple of hundred yards into the jungle. To my consternation a mass of cheering children ran from the kampong school to greet me and despite my protestations were determined to follow me. I ended up running a considerable distance in an unwelcome game of hide-and-seek before I gained a few minutes privacy hidden in secondary jungle.

Denis Lewis eventually returned from his leave in Australia so I left C Flight and flew back to Malta to re-familiarise myself with eight-week-old Clare and the Gazelle. I was certainly an older and wiser pilot for this very short experience on an underpowered piston-engined helicopter in a demanding environment. It was an experience and an end of an era that I was glad not to have missed.

Chapter 8

Northern Ireland – Trouble at t'Mill

I only undertook one brief flying tour during Operation BANNER, 'The Troubles' in Northern Ireland, which consisted of an attachment to an Army Air Corps squadron deployed from BAOR. Nevertheless, I did experience flying in the province during a time when the threat was high and during an unpleasant winter in 1977. After the UK withdrawal from Malta, Jane, I and baby Clare flew back to Brize Norton by RAF VC10. We had a few days at home together with Jane's parents in Cornwall and I then flew by BA Trident to Belfast and was driven in the dark and pouring rain from Aldergrove airport to the 655 Army Air Corps Squadron location at Long Kesh. I was only mildly surprised to be introduced to my new squadron commander wearing pyjamas at the monthly squadron disco party. Like many of the Security Force bases, Long Kesh was a portacabin camp surrounded by concertina wire co-located next to Long Kesh prison, where both loyalist and IRA prisoners were serving their time. Exhausted, I rolled into bed to be rudely awakened at dawn by deafening gunfire outside my window. No one had told me that there was a 40mm Bofors gun emplacement outside my window and that they occasionally practised with break-up shot in order, I suppose, to deter prison escape attempts by helicopter.

Unlike my infantry ground tours in Ulster, where I got to know a particular patch of ground in great detail, during a flying tour an Army pilot got to cover the whole province with a much wider perspective. It was an interesting contrast and by far the most demanding flying took place in South Armagh. The threat was so high at the time that all military movement between the security bases of Bessbrook Mill, Forkhill, Crossmaglen and Newtownhamilton was carried out by helicopter and travel by vehicle was banned. The Armagh Roulement Battalion HQ was based in the 1850 vintage Victorian spinning mill at Bessbrook, which was adjoined by the terraced cottages of the model village built for the original spinning workers. Bessbrook (known in military jargon as location R850) became famous as the busiest heliport in Europe. RAF Pumas and Wessex, together with AAC Scouts, Gazelles and RN Wessex, operated around the clock from the congested and confined concrete helicopter pads which were located in the bottom of a valley next to the mill. The helicopter pads were surrounded by corrugated iron anti-rocket fencing and a high wire fence, whilst the concrete pads were arranged stepped in a row of shallow terraces due to the slope. The rather forbidding Victorian woollen mill, complete with a 120-foot-high chimney, was the base for the South Armagh battalion. The approach and take-off path to and from the helipads, known as 'the Tube', was a restricted passage weaving between the mill chimney, high ground, wires and surrounding housing. The approach part of the tube was aligned roughly heading 250 degrees and the departure about 185 degrees, so was very much a 'tube with a bend in the middle'. Once in the tube there was not really enough room to avoid a second aircraft. A lone stunted tree on a hill 1,000 metres from the landing zone at the east end of the tube was known as 'the one K tree' and was a useful line-up marker in bad weather. A portacabin at the edge of the helipads was where the complexities of the considerable daily tasking were carried out by the aviation operations officer, callsign 'Buzzard', and his team.

It is worth remembering that the Army Air Corps and Royal Marines Scouts and Gazelles operating in the province at this time were single-engined helicopters without either auto-stabilisation or autopilot. Being required to fly at 500 feet above ground level, or lower at night and in bad weather, put a lot of strain on pilot workload and skills. The aircraft were equipped with a number of modifications such as extra radios, armour plating on the cockpit floor and armoured crew seats. Flying dress consisted of a disruptive-pattern combat flying suit, a body armour plate covering the chest and a service-issue Browning 9mm pistol in a shoulder holster. Some care had to be taken when donning the armour which slipped over your head before being adjusted. After banging the bridge of your nose painfully on the edge of the heavy breastplate a couple of times the lesson was learned the hard way. The 'NightSun' was a very powerful searchlight mounted on the Gazelle armament boom and operated by a hand-held remote-controlled joystick controlled by the observer in the front left seat. An infrared cover could be fitted over the light in order to aid illumination when passive night goggles were being used. Various other pieces of classified electronic kit were sometimes attached by specialists who operated them from the rear seats of the Gazelle and then removed them after the sortie. Technology was playing an increasingly large part in the campaign. I found that the

NORTHERN IRELAND – TROUBLE AT T'MILL

655 Squadron Gazelles were already quite different, both in modifications and basic weight to our Mediterranean runabouts in Salerno Flight.

The Squadron was required to base a Scout for the airborne quick reaction force together with a NightSun-equipped Gazelle at Bessbrook around the clock daily and before last light a second Scout arrived equipped with NightSun and passive night goggles for the extraction of covert patrols and to provide top cover overnight. A 'Bessbrook duty' for a pilot and observer lasted for twenty-four hours. During the day, in addition to the various tasks of flying individuals in and out of the company locations in South Armagh, a careful recce had to be conducted of any planned drop-off point for patrols scheduled for the night ahead. The drop-off of the troops would be achieved by RAF Puma at low level on passive night goggles (PNG) whilst the Gazelle or Scout, flying high above, illuminated the landing zone with an invisible beam of infrared NightSun. A high degree of co-ordination was required to get this right and the daylight recce had to be done with discretion in order not to compromise the landing zone. Added to the complications were the first generation of night vision equipment and appalling weather. The PNG were a boon at night although they could only be used with two crew and enabled the pilot to see the ground even if inadvertently entering the cloud base. This early version of PNG only had a 12-degree field of view which was a potential hazard and required the pilot to keep his head moving. My squadron commander lit a Wessex into a field with IR NightSun and was returning to Bessbrook when he turned his head to the right to find that he was inadvertently flying in close formation with the Wessex, who was likewise unaware of the other aircraft, both pilots being on PNG. During gaps in the flying programme accommodation for aircrew was provided in a portacabin next to 'Buzzard', surrounded by a breezeblock blast wall, which did little to improve the view. The room, however, was warm and dry and we laid out our sleeping bags on the iron bedsteads hoping for a relatively undisturbed night. I remember that an electric frying pan was provided and the Bessbrook cooks would send down sausages, chops, bread and milk. This was long before the concept of 'healthy eating' was discovered. I noticed that on each occasion after I returned to Long Kesh following my Bessbrook standbys that I suffered from a sore mouth, as if it had been burned by hot soup. Others were also affected by the same symptoms, the cause of which was eventually traced by our medics to the residual fat lying in the electric frying pan, which was of an indeterminate age.

Despite the considerable terrorist threat of anti-helicopter machine guns, mortar fire, RPGs and SAM 7s, undoubtedly the biggest danger was fatigue coupled with the weather. Naturally, in an operational environment where troops on the ground depended on the helicopter, the imperative was to get the job done and flying was conducted below the normal peacetime weather minima. Instrument flying had only recently been introduced into Army Aviation and pilots tended to be 'instrument trained' rather than 'instrument rated', partly due to the lack of qualified Instrument Rating Examiners in the AAC at this time. There were also many very experienced, and capable, pilots of the old school who were not convinced that this was the way ahead. There were instances during which I was immensely grateful for my very limited instrument flying training in Malta. It was in the early hours of the morning, when aircrew were at their lowest ebb, that was the most unpleasant call-out. A warm sleeping bag was exchanged for a metallic taste in the mouth and invariably cold drizzle under the arc lights whilst attending the brief by Buzzard in his portacabin.

Regardless of instrument flying experience, the golden rule was to '*Stay VMC and in visual contact with the ground*'. Inadvertent entry into cloud has probably been the biggest killer in Army Aviation. Groping at low level in marginal visibility and accidentally entering cloud is not the environment to calmly 'get on to instruments'. It takes a few moments to settle down, there are likely to be obstacles such as wires or high ground in the way and there is a high chance of hitting the ground before a stable instrument climb can be established. These first few seconds of unexpected stress can often lead to spatial disorientation. Then there is the problem of how to recover to a suitable airfield. To transit safely on instruments, an aircraft must be above the safety altitude. In winter this is likely to be above the freezing level and helicopters do not take kindly to the build-up of ice. Flying below safety altitude invites the possibility of collision with high ground, pylons or obstacles such as a TV mast. Once at a safe level in the cruise in cloud (Instrument Meteorological Conditions or IMC) it would be necessary to receive radar guidance for a let-down at a suitable airfield equipped with approach aids. A transit to a suitable airfield might well require considerable fuel, together with a possible hold and diversion to an alternative field if the weather was below minima. Army helicopters were not fitted with VOR navigational aids (we were told because there was no guarantee these civilian-managed beacons could be relied on in war. The fact of the matter was that Army helicopters spent 99 per cent of their time flying in peacetime.) and, in 1977, a map, a compass with a homing facility for use with military radios was all that was available. There was no radar cover below 5,000 feet over South Armagh and Belfast Aldergrove (location V813) was the only nearby airfield thirty-four miles to the north, which could provide a radar approach apart from Dublin, fifty-four miles south, with the inevitable embarrassing diplomatic consequences. The nearest military emergency diversion airfield open twenty-four hours was RAF Valley in Anglesey 100 miles south east. Because a loaded Scout could not carry sufficient fuel to divert to RAF Aldergrove from South Armagh in IMC, the AAC Scouts at Long Kesh were additionally fitted with a Decca Flight Log as a radio navigation aid. This in theory enabled a Scout in IMC to safely transit in cloud until over the Irish Sea when a descent could be made until in visual contact with the surface followed by a low level transit back to the Northern Irish coastline. Fortunately this 'Recovery of Last Resort' was not put into practice as far as I know. The message was clear therefore. Regardless of instrument flying experience, *never* go inadvertent IMC.

Eighteen months after I left the province there was a tragic accident in 669 Squadron where a very experienced Scout pilot of the 'old school' (without an instrument rating), who had given me useful help and advice, lifted from Bessbrook bound for Crossmaglen in the early hours of the morning with a low cloud base and rain. This was a classic case of a pilot with little sleep at the lowest point of the Circadian Rhythm, taking off in pitch darkness and bad weather to fly a demanding sortie on NVG. When he and his crewman became overdue there was little that could be achieved before first light. At some stage during the aerial search and a ground search by a company of the Grenadier Guards the next day, an oil slick and debris were found on the surface of Lough Ross. When the Scout was eventually recovered it was found that it had entered the water at high speed in an unusual attitude. The cause could never be categorically established.[1]

One particular Bessbrook standby on 11 April 1977 was memorable. It was my turn to fly the NightSun Gazelle (XX455) whilst the pilot of the QRF Scout happened to be my squadron commander. By 1800 the weather was so foul with heavy rain and low cloud sporadically obscuring the Mill chimney that he announced that there would be no tasking that night and that we could be stood down. This was unusual and welcome for it meant that we could go to the battalion mess in the Mill and forgo our electric frying pan. We sat down to an excellent dinner in the Mess and found to our delight that it was a mess film night so we moved to the anteroom and settled down with a drink. Ten minutes into the film, at about 2115, there was an unmistakable dull thud followed by another and then more. It was the sound of mortars being fired and as we leapt to our feet the first of the incoming rounds crashed into the concrete just outside the Mill. Above the sound of the Mill alarm and breaking glass my squadron commander shouted to me to get the NightSun airborne. We both raced to the entrance of the Mill, grabbed our pistols from the guardroom (which years later he reminded me was, for some reason, now critically unmanned) and sprinted across the public road to the helipad. It was still raining and, as we ran across the wet tarmac, shining under the arc lights, it suddenly occurred to me that it would be particularly unfortunate to be shot by one of our own adrenaline-pumped sentries from the sangars overlooking the road.

Buzzard repeated the urgent cry 'Get the NightSun airborne' from the entrance of his hut and, as I hurriedly removed the pitot cover and engine blanks from the aircraft (we had been stood down remember, so the aircraft had been covered from the elements), my aircrewman joined me and we strapped in. Whilst the Gazelle canopy gives a marvellous view in good weather, at night and in rain it tends to give off internal reflections. In addition, it is prone to misting, especially in cold weather with two sweating bodies expending heat and energy inside. There was thus not much to see externally except condensation and the reflections of arc lights on wet tarmac. These were not conditions in which one would normally night fly under visual flight rules (VFR), but there was an operational imperative, or so I had been led to believe. The heater was turned full on, blasting kerosene smelling bleed air across the top of the inside of the canopy to demist prior to take-off and in two minutes we were rotors running. As we lifted into the hover, with a blind call on the UHF to warn any unseen aircraft in 'the tube' on approach, I wondered what the height of the cloud base was. I was soon to find out. We climbed vertically clear of the pad and transitioned forward into wind. As the radalt indicated 100 feet AGL the glow from our navigation lights began to reflect back into the cockpit, a sure sign of entering the cloud base. This was not going to get us far and I visually locked onto the three red obstruction lights on the Mill chimney determined not to lose sight of them at all costs. Hopefully this would both avoid us colliding with the chimney and also prevent us from going inadvertently into IMC. With rain splattering against the canopy I flew a 60-knot orbit around the red chimney lights lowering the collective lever each time wisps of cloud whipped past us. Meanwhile my observer switched on the NightSun to illuminate the area around the mill. We were told on the FM tactical net that a foot patrol had found the mortar baseplate position, which was a flatbed lorry, parked just outside the Mill perimeter. Our job was now to illuminate the ground around the wrecked lorry in order to assist the follow up by ground forces. The million candlepower NightSun was a most effective tool but it could be dangerous to operate near cloud. The effect of entering cloud with the light on was to suddenly blind the crew with reflected light leading to loss of night vision and possible disorientation. Our workload was now very high. I concentrated solely on maintaining an orbit around the mill chimney whilst avoiding cloud and listening on the UHF aviation frequency. My observer searched the ground with the beam and monitored the FM tactical net and the Cougarnet. Mortar attacks were generally well planned and this one had been no exception. The terrorists had long since gone and, were in all probability, already south of the border. Our beam did, however, provide illumination for troops searching for unexploded mortar bombs. My logbook shows that we spent an unpleasant hour orbiting the red lights before we thankfully approached our helipad.

On returning to the Mill we found that miraculously no one had been hurt. One bomb had caused the Mill's glass roof panels to shatter uncomfortably near to a warrant officer who was sitting on the lavatory. Three other bombs landed around the yard, destroying a military van and causing fires. One had exploded on firing. If the back of the flatbed lorry had not been broken by the recoil of the first bomb firing, the others would no doubt have also landed on target.

Eighteen years later I had the opportunity to read the concise official report of this minor incident. A white flatbed Ford Transit van had been hijacked from the forecourt of a nearby garage. At 2015 a passing motorist reported a suspicious white flatbed lorry in Mill Road adjacent to the Mill. The lorry was moving very slowly and there was something bulky on the back covered with plastic sheeting. At 2115 the Mill came under attack by five Mark 8 mortar bombs. No casualties were sustained by the security forces but severe glass damage was caused to the civilian portion of the Mill. The attack lasted for less than thirty seconds and, shortly afterwards, the Ford Transit van was located at the junction of Mill Road and Bessbrook High Street and 'due to failing light ops were suspended until morning'. The Explosive Ordnance Disposal clearance action was completed by 1200 hours the next day. This short, understated report disguises the drama of the event (especially for the man on the loo) and certainly no one had bothered to tell us that ops had been suspended until the morning.

One strange daylight task was to take an officer in plain clothes (possibly Special Forces) to a military location on the outskirts of Belfast. As we approached the city from the south, he asked to have a look at the new Mary Peters running track and stadium at Malone. A group of people were gathered there near parked cars and, as we orbited, my passenger took a great interest in this meeting and asked to descend for a closer look. He then announced that there was a change of plan and he would like to be dropped off in the car park. Taken aback and loath to drop anyone from a military helicopter next to an unknown civilian crowd, I replied that I would stick to the planned drop-off destination unless it was operationally vital to land him at the stadium. He replied that it was, so I very reluctantly landed on the grass near the car park and he disembarked to join the crowd now curiously observing us. I only hoped that he knew what he was doing but I heard no more about the matter so must assume that he did.

Other regular tasks were varied and usually meant being directed anywhere in the province for any task from moving personnel to delivering service mail. Whilst flying a passenger at about 1,500 feet near Jonesborough, the local battalion radio net suddenly came alive with contact reports about a helicopter being engaged by automatic fire. It took a second or so to compute from the callsigns and locations that this was us, but we were not hit and we heard nothing untoward except the radio chatter. One inevitable frustration for any military helicopter pilot is waiting for passengers. Only a few days after the mortar incident I was collecting a brigadier at Portadown and was waiting at the appointed time, rotors stopped engine running, whilst he talked to some officers 100 metres away. I became aware that the Gazelle had a 'dragging clutch' and with the rotor brake off the blades would very slowly rotate with the engine at ground idle. There was a check to see whether this was acceptable drag which consisted of counting how many blades passed in front of the canopy in one minute with the rotor brake off. I forget the exact limiting number but it was something like six. Having done this check and finding the drag well within the limits, I re-applied the rotor brake and waited. I mentally debated about shutting down the engine but it always appeared that the brigadier, already late, was just about to approach the aircraft so I kept it running. When he eventually boarded and strapped in with his aide and a padre in the back, I released the rotor brake and gently advanced the throttle. As the clutch engaged there was an immediate loud bang, the aircraft rocked and yawed accompanied by a strong smell of burning. I rapidly shut down and we abandoned the aircraft whilst I applied the contents of the fire extinguisher over the front of the smoking engine. It was, of course, a centrifugal clutch seizure and the dragging clutch must have built up a great deal of heat during our prolonged wait despite being 'within acceptable limits'. A spectacular incident for the spectators but thankfully minor and with little damage

There was a sad sequel to the overcrowded and confined Bessbrook HLS and the dreaded 'Tube'. In November 1992 at last light a Puma on final approach to one of the lower concrete pads collided with a Gazelle just lifting off. The Gazelle's blades impacted the underneath of the Puma's cockpit. The Puma crashed into the perimeter rocket fence at the eastern end of the landing site. All four occupants of the Puma were killed and the remains of the Gazelle ended up in a drainage ditch just inside the rocket fence 100 metres away with both occupants severely injured. In twenty years of intensive helicopter operations at Bessbrook this was the only accident of its kind.[2]

Despite the operations of armed terrorists and extremists from all factions in the province the greatest danger to my mind in flying during Operation BANNER was the weather and fatigue. In order to get the job done in a hilly area subject to the moist influence of the Atlantic, often with low cloud, drizzle and mist with pylons, wires and confined sub-unit locations surrounded by rocket fences and radio aerials, there was little room for error and it was a great learning experience. It is surprising that there were so few light helicopter accidents, particularly when one considers that RAF Pumas or Wessex had two engines, were always crewed by two pilots and at least one crewman and were limited to a sixteen-hour crew duty time. It speaks volumes for the courage, professional skills and stamina of the AAC and RM light helicopter aircrew involved.[3]

After this invaluable experience with 655 Squadron, who as well as being highly professional had made me very welcome, I flew back to London for some foreign service leave after our time in Malta and then to take up a ground appointment as a Grade 3 Staff officer at HQ Commando Forces in Plymouth.

Chapter 9

Central Flying School (H) – RAF Shawbury

At the beginning of the First World War, Major Robert Smith-Barry of the Royal Flying Corps, whilst serving at Upavon in Wiltshire, decided there must be a better method of teaching people to fly than the ad hoc method of 'watch me and try and copy what I do' or the 'try and feel what I am doing on the controls' instruction of the pre-war and early war years. So, in 1916, he developed the concept of flying exercises, linked with classroom instruction, and took command of No. 1 Reserve Squadron at Gosport. His method was based on a series of individual progressive exercises which revolutionised flying training and were adopted by the Central Flying School (CFS) at Upavon. For example:

Exercise 1	Familiarisation
Exercise 2	Effect of Controls
Exercise 3	Taxiing
Exercise 4	Straight and Level Flight
Exercise 5	Climbing, Gliding and Stalling
Exercise 6	Medium Turns
Exercise 7	Taking off into wind
Exercise 8	Powered approach and landings
Exercise 9	Gliding approach and landings
Exercise 10	Spinning

and so on; a syllabus that remains much the same to this day although a number of more modern and specialist exercises have been added to the list such as Mountain Flying and Night Vision Goggle Flying etc. The list had to be adjusted for helicopter flying training, with exercises such as autorotation replacing gliding and others being introduced, such as Exercise 5 Hovering and Exercise 20 Advanced Transitions, but following exactly the same logical pattern as Robert Smith-Barry's original list. He also introduced the Gosport tube to enable two-way communication between instructor and student above the noise of the engine and slipstream. In 1917 CFS ceased to be an ab-initio flying school and instead became a school for advanced training and later, in 1920, for the training and standardisation of flying instructors. In order to be selected as a trainee instructor on the Central Flying (Helicopter) School course based at RAF Shawbury it was necessary to have completed at least one Squadron tour, be rated as above average in flying ability and to have been recommended.

As I was posted to the CFS (H) course from a ground tour at HQ Commando Forces, I was first attached to 705 Naval Air Squadron at HMS *Seahawk* at RNAS Culdrose for a flying refresher and instrument rating test on the Gazelle HT.2. The aircraft were finished in a smart gloss red and white scheme with black engine cowlings and tail with the 'Sharks' logo on the fin. They, and the RAF HT.3s, were also fitted with the Stability Augmentation System (SAS) and Stick Feel which meant there was more stability and a basic trim to the cyclic controls. It was particularly beneficial to fly with some newly-qualified RN flying instructors who could give me some useful tips on what lay in store for me. At the beginning of the second week the Commander Air's secretary rang me to book me in for a ten-minute call. On asking what the rig was, I was taken aback to be told 'Service Dress' since I had been assured that working rig and flying suits were all that was required during the course. I was told that no exceptions could be made and so the next day I drove two hours back home, collected my lovat uniform and returned to Culdrose in time for the ten-minute chat in the office next to the control tower with 'Wings'. After my Gazelle refresher I was asked whether there were any particular extra sorties I wanted to do. When I mentioned a low-level navex there was some sucking of teeth, I imagine as a fallout from Les Thresh's earlier accident, but they were good enough to agree, although I had to present my planning and marked map in Little F's office in order to get an authorisation.

Instrument flying was somewhat easier with SAS and Stick Feel than on the totally unstable AH.1. It was during my instrument rating test (IRT) that my experienced RN instructor asked me to fly a Ground Controlled Approach (GCA) to runway 30 at Culdrose. As we broke out of cloud at about 400 feet I remained on instruments as instructed and at Decision Height my instructor announced 'no visual references seen' so, calling 'overshooting' on the RT, I applied power to carry out the standard missed approach procedure by climbing straight ahead on instruments. However, the Culdrose Approach controller instantly came back with 'You are not cleared to overshoot from this approach; you were cleared to land.' This was all too late as we were already at 100 knots climbing through 350 feet above the threshold and about to re-enter cloud. Surprisingly an RN Jetstream had been cleared to take-off on the intersecting runway on the Tower's assumption that we were to land at the threshold of 30. The Jetstream passed safely 500 feet beneath us, still accelerating on the runway, but it was an off-putting experience, trying to concentrate on instruments whilst my captain was being instructed to report to the Tower on landing. He received a dressing-down after the sortie but it struck both of us as strange that the Tower could assume that any instrument approach, whether simulated or actual, would definitely end in a full-stop landing. Later I heard of a useful saying, 'A go-around should never be a surprise. A landing should be regarded as a happy conclusion to an approach.' I passed my IRT and had another valuable piece of experience to lock away after a useful and enjoyable two weeks with the Fleet Air Arm.

 The Flying Instructors' course at the Central Flying School (Helicopters), known as CFS (H), at RAF Shawbury in Shropshire was probably the most enjoyable course I underwent in the military. Our course consisted of eleven students from the RN, Army Air Corps, RAF, Royal Australian Navy and Kenyan Air Force. The first two weeks of the three-month course were dedicated to teaching us how to deliver an effective short instructional lecture and we started with practising on everyday subjects such as how to make a cup of tea. At the end of the second week we were assessed before a board of senior instructors in giving two five-minute lectures, together with visual aids and demonstration. The first lesson was to be of our own choice (and by custom light-hearted and amusing) and the second on a relevant military subject, also of our own choice. So my first was on 'firing a blowpipe', using an aboriginal blowpipe that I had been given whilst working with the Orang Asli aborigines in the Cameron Highlands of Central Malaya, aimed at a cardboard cut-out of a parrot. The lesson included smearing a 'simulated faecal poison' mixture onto the bamboo darts, simulated by folding a squashed Mars Bar in shiny MoD loo paper and keeping it inside my trouser pocket for a day or so. Other more exotic and far more hilarious presentations included 'the Australian Alarm Clock' involving a graduated candle and a hung-over sleeper (enough said) and drinking 'Peineken', whereby we were shown how to open and drink large ice-cold cans of a well-known lager, which was then re-demonstrated and re-practised until we all started to feel ill. My more serious lesson was on military map marking. Lest this be thought of as a waste of taxpayers' money, it was a remarkably enjoyable and effective way of teaching a dull subject: how to put a lesson across effectively in a short time. Having passed this phase of the course, we started a routine whereby we would fly for half the day and attend lessons in aerodynamics, engines, meteorology and airmanship for the other half. These lessons went into considerably more detail than during our flying training and we were given added motivation to learn by the realisation that in a few months we would be explaining these subjects to our students. Our instructors were outstanding in their knowledge, ability to put the subject across and sense of humour. I remember being asked to briefly explain the Astazou engine oil system and, having drawn a quick diagram on the board and given an explanation of the layout and oil flow, was congratulated as I sat down and then told that I had drawn a perfectly good system but unfortunately not the one that the designers of the Astazou had chosen. The emphasis was on quick (five-minute), relevant, accurate and convincing explanations. Within six weeks we were being invited to pick cards from a pack at random, each of which had a printed instruction such as 'explain flap back' or 'what is high density altitude?', after which we were permitted a one-minute pause to draw a diagram without recourse to any notes and then give an explanation followed by answering a question or two, all of which had to be completed in five minutes. This was an art that, once mastered, would also be a useful skill in many fields of business or education.

The flying side was even more fun. Having flown the Gazelle AH.1 for three years, I thought I knew a lot about the aircraft, whereas my other fellow students had come from Wessex, Sea King, Puma or Scout. The first surprise was that the RAF Gazelle HT.3 which CFS (H) used had a completely different checklist from the AH.1. We also learned the CFS way of flying: 800 feet meant 800 feet, not 810 feet, and 90 knots and 270 degrees meant exactly that. Flying a humble circuit thus became a highly demanding exercise if you were to strive for the perfection that CFS demanded. How else could you demonstrate a circuit to a future student who would attempt to imitate exactly what you showed him? Thereafter I learned that the best way to rapidly assess any other instructor's flying ability was to ask him to demonstrate a circuit because, in under five minutes, climbing, turning, levelling-off, descending, balance, speed control, accuracy, adjustments for wind, approach angle, transitions to and from the hover, radio calls, checks and airmanship would all be demonstrated.

After conversion to the Gazelle HT.3, we were each paired with a fellow student known as a 'stick-buddy'. In my case this was a bearded Australian Navy pilot who had flown the A-4 Skyhawk and intriguingly wore black suede flying boots, whom I shall call Sam.* Sam was a highly amusing extrovert who was never stuck for words and seemed to have limitless levels of self-confidence and bonhomie. It was he of course who had masterminded the 'Australian Alarm Clock' lesson. The form of instruction at Shawbury was that our RAF CFS (H) instructor would take us individually for a sortie to teach us an exercise. For instance Exercise 2, Effects of Controls. This would consist of a briefing, a one-hour flight, followed by a de-brief, with we students being on the receiving end of instruction acting as a pupil and thus called the 'Receive'. There was then a 'Mutual' sortie when the two students would practise teaching each other the exercise and criticising each other's technique. Then came the third element of the system, the 'Giveback', when you would be required to brief and teach Exercise 2 to your instructor who acted as a basic student. On the 'Mutual' sortie what the two students actually covered was up to them, but it can be seen that there was every incentive not to waste the flying time unless you happened to be extremely confident, skilled or stupid. Any failure in progress was noted by the instructor and three poor 'Givebacks' would result in the student being put on 'Review'. This involved a change of CFS instructor, a short revision and consolidation period and any continued lack of progress would mean a 'return to unit'. I soon found that Sam, who had previously flown anti-submarine Sea Kings, was probably happier navigating over the ocean than over land. In the north Shropshire plain, where most of our flying exercises took place, there is one striking geographical feature; the whale-back hill known as the Wrekin. In one of our early sorties in fine weather Sam saw a distant prominent hill on the borders of Wales called 'Breidden Hill' (on top of which is a feature known as Rodney's Pillar) which he immediately latched on to as 'the Wrekin', allowing him to confidently place us twenty-two miles west of our true position on that, and a couple of subsequent, occasions.

A great strength of the course was the different background and experiences of our fellow students. I got on particularly well with a tall bearded RN Lieutenant, Julian Barraclough, who was an anti-submarine warfare Sea King pilot. A man of few words but with a nice sense of humour, he and I used to run around the airfield perimeter to keep fit in the evenings. Jules had an Austin Mini and most weekends drove back to RNAS Culdrose to be with his family. On one of his early trips his Mini caught fire and burned out in minutes on a main road near Telford. When the fire brigade arrived they prised open the charred boot to find the remains of a tin petrol can with two neat holes punched in the side, where it had contacted the Mini's battery terminals and had shorted. The Mini at that time had a cardboard insulating cover covering the battery in the boot but it had shifted to one side and the can had vibrated across the boot and into contact with the battery during the drive. Julian escaped unhurt, but only in the clothes he stood up in whilst his flying gear and weekend bag had been incinerated. Since I also owned an old Mini at this time, I took a keen interest in the baggage arrangements in the boot thereafter.

Our charming Kenyan colleague was less experienced than most of us and the reason he had arrived on the course was because all the more senior pilots in his squadron had recently been killed. Whilst Sylvester was left behind at Eastleigh Airport, his Squadron boss was leading a detachment of two Pumas supporting the Kenyan Army on exercise in northern Kenya. They were flying home to Nairobi for the weekend in line astern when darkness fell and the leader led number two into the side of a tree-clad hill not far from Nairobi. Sylvester had to organise the search which found the small impact marks in the treetops the next day and thus, overnight, moved from being the most junior Puma pilot to one of the most senior and was sent to CFS (H).[1] Despite his relative lack of experience, and the total change of environment from Nairobi to the crowded airspace and changeable weather of UK, he did well on the course and was a popular and cheerful student. Our instructors also came from all three services and so there was a wealth of flying experience and stories on each CFS course.

The first flight I had at Shawbury was a one-hour dual sortie with an RAF instructor on area familiarisation. Now my grandparents had lived at nearby Market Drayton for all of their married lives and I had attended Shrewsbury School, so I knew Shropshire and the local area pretty well. No way, however, did I intend to let the CFS staff know this as I needed every advantage I could get. So, twenty minutes into the sortie, when Flight Lieutenant Al Johnson asked 'Happy where we are then? What's the name of that village in our one o'clock?' I pretended to study the 1:50,000 map for a few seconds before responding 'That must be Cheswardine'. 'Good. Absolutely right', came the reply 'although it is pronounced Cheswar*deen*'. I kept my mouth tight shut and looked the other way.

The stick-buddy system was a very good one as we learned each other's strengths and weaknesses and when to grab the controls. As student instructors we sometimes wondered how we would cope with our own engine-off autorotative landings (EOLs), let alone correcting the efforts of inexperienced students. At the base of the Gazelle's tail was a fibreglass frangible fairing, known as 'the frange', which was designed to protect the aircraft structure from a tail strike, particularly during a mishandled EOL. If the frange was damaged the aircraft could be checked and the inexpensive fairing easily replaced although it was a disciplinary event to damage a frange and something that we tried to avoid as a matter of pride. Sam had only carried out EOLs during his basic training and so our first mutual engine-off session at the satellite airfield of RAF Tern Hill was mind-focusing to put it mildly. On at least one engine-off we careered across the Tern Hill grass at 30 knots with us both on the controls with eyes wide and knuckles white.

However, during this excellent course our instructors taught us how to correct errors before they got out of hand by simulating students with abilities of good, average and often appalling. We did so many EOLs, and corrected so many of our 'students' gross mishandlings, that we grew in confidence. After our graduation we soon discovered that most students in the real world had much more common sense and sense of self-preservation than we had been trained to cope with at CFS, and this surely was a measure of an excellent course.

Given the scope for potential drama it struck me as amazing that the accident rate at CFS (H) throughout the years had been so low. I guess it was because each pair of above average pilots was concentrating one hundred per cent on what they were doing.[2] I see from my log book that we averaged between twenty-seven and thirty-five hours flying per month at Shawbury, a peacetime rate that would be envied by present-day service pilots.

The only close shave that Sam and I had was at Shawbury's other grass satellite airfield, Chetwynd, where we were practising the mutual exercise of spot turns through 360 degrees in the hover. As every helicopter pilot well knows, this is not an easy manoeuvre for the ab-initio student, especially in any sort of wind. The pilot has to anticipate the wind, differing pedal inputs during different segments of the turn, preventing the aircraft from drifting by keeping the aircraft over one spot, at a constant height and at a constant rate of turn. This involves corresponding movements of all four arms and legs on the controls throughout the manoeuvre. At some stage we were demonstrating to each other how stopping a left turn carelessly with right pedal could cause an over-torque; right pedal causing an increase in tail rotor pitch, more drag and thus more engine power to maintain governed rotor speed. Sam was demonstrating a fast spot turn which turned into a second faster turn and at a certain stage it became apparent that the situation was getting out of control as the pleasant Shropshire countryside started to become a blur. He later said that he was trying to slow the turn and with both of us now on the controls we transitioned the aircraft away from the ground with collective and with cyclic into the wind direction. As we picked up translational lift the aircraft suddenly flicked into wind and responded normally. We landed and discussed this whilst our pulse rates returned to normal. Had Sam in fact been feeding in the wrong pedal causing the turn to speed up? No, he thought not. Sometime later it occurred to me that this might have been a case of Gazelle fenestron stall; a known but rare condition where, in the event of rapid yaw to the left being countered by a rough application of corrective yaw pedal, something similar to vortex ring could occur in the fenestron 'tunnel' and effective tail rotor control might be lost.[3] This phenomenon was later put down to 'yaw divergence'; nevertheless there had been a few Gazelle accidents in the British forces connected with this which resulted in various warnings about rate of yaw, harsh application of pedal and manoeuvres such as wing-overs. Whatever the cause, we both learned a lot from this incident and I am sure that other pairs of trainee 'beefers' had similar educational experiences which they mentally filed away.

One evening in the bar I was delighted and surprised to see Derek Blevins, my ex-company sergeant major and squadron QHI, dressed as an RAF flight lieutenant. After leaving the Royal Marines he had joined the Sultan of Oman's Air Force, flying AB 205s. Reportedly, he had been involved in a crash five months earlier whilst under-slinging a load to a jebel landing site on a steep ridge.[4] A local boy, believed to be a passenger, was trapped by the fuselage and whilst Derek and his crewman tried to pull him clear, the aircraft had rolled on top of him. This naturally had a profound effect on Derek and he had left Oman, joined the RAF and was now at Shawbury to be refreshed on Gazelle. I did not see Derek during the next few days and, on asking, was told that after one sortie he had apparently decided that flying was not for him anymore and had left Shawbury. Eighteen months later at Middle Wallop I again met him as a Squadron Leader. He told me that the RAF had been very understanding, allowed him to transfer to the Supply Branch and that he was now the OC Supply at RAF Odiham.

When off duty there was also some hard partying at CFS, although most students were mindful of the fact that they would be under scrutiny the next day. Sam seemed not to worry about such trivia and could manage on little sleep. Towards the end of the course it became apparent that Sam was under particular pressure. His relaxed attitude had resulted in some less than satisfactory sorties and he was a candidate for review. His extrovert self-confidence began to slip and I found myself encouraging and supporting him during periods of despondency. Nevertheless, he went on 'review' with an instructor change in the last two weeks of the course but he got through. Lest it be thought that I sailed through the course, I should mention that I worked hard, had some moments of self-doubt but got a steady high average pass. On my final handling test with Shawbury's Deputy Chief Flying Instructor all went well until we arrived at RAF Tern Hill and he asked me to demonstrate an engine-off-landing. After this he took on the role of acting as the 'student' and I gave him control in order to practise the manoeuvre himself. Once established in autorotation, when I was sure he was going to make the grass strip of the Tern Hill engine-off area, I closed the throttle and we were committed. Shortly afterwards, at a height of about 300 feet, the 'student' suicidally heaved up hard on the collective lever. My left hand was unobtrusively resting on the lever, enabling me to detect and prevent any early input. However, his initial pull was so powerful that he pulled through my grip and our rotor RPM decayed alarmingly to just below the red minimum line. Exclaiming 'I have control', I slammed the lever fully down against his input with the strength of ten men and took over control immediately. I wondered if, on this occasion, the very experienced 'student' had over-acted his part. After flaring hard to try and recover some rotor RPM, we once again ended up careering across the grass on our flimsy skids in a very fast run-on, but no damage was done and, as I wound the throttle back up, he congratulated me and informed me that I had passed the course and was now a B2 QHI.

Chapter 10

Instructing on Gazelle – Early Days and BAOR

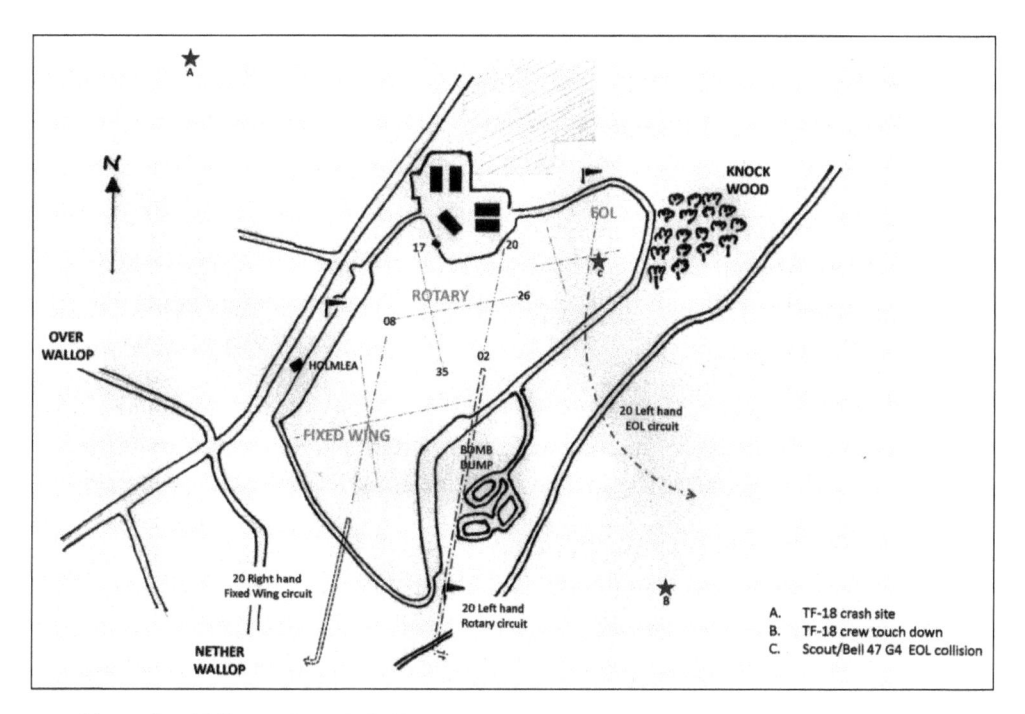

Plan of Middle Wallop airfield circa 1980. The Fixed Wing circuit was always a mirror image to the Rotary circuit with the Engine-off Landing circuit positioned inside the Rotary circuit. An approximate outline of the three circuits for Runway 20 is shown. (©Author)

From RAF Shawbury I was sent on exchange to be a flying instructor with the Army. Since 1965 Royal Marines officers and SNCOs had attended the Army Pilots Course and thus, as a quid pro quo, the Royal Marines seconded a flying instructor to Middle Wallop where I was due to relieve Lieutenant Ken Summers RM.[1] Sam, meanwhile, went to RNAS Culdrose on exchange for a two-year instructing tour with 705 NAS and, although a few months later I heard on the instructors grapevine that he had 'spread some fibreglass shards about the airfield' during a Gazelle engine-off landing, he completed a successful tour before returning to Australia.

On arrival at Middle Wallop I was assigned as an instructor to A Flight of Advanced Rotary Wing (ARW) where I would take on two students. A Flight took basic students from the Bell 47G-4A, converted them onto the Gazelle and taught them instrument flying in fifty-seven hours of flying over eight weeks before handing them on to B Flight. I had six months to consolidate before taking my QHI B1 test which would confirm me as a *bona fide* instructor. Naturally nervous about teaching my first two students on Advanced Rotary Wing, I quickly discovered what marvellous training we had received at CFS. The students were generally more skilled and had a much greater degree of self-preservation than our kamikaze role-playing 'students' at CFS and there was nothing that a student did during the next three years that CFS had not prepared me for. This included unexpected incidents such as a student removing both of his hands from the controls and folding his arms during the final stages of an engine-off landing and an occasion when a student turned off all the aircraft electrics before going into a confined area in order to 'save power'. It was living proof that fun training is nearly always good training. Even though we carried out exactly the same syllabus with each student during the two years I worked at ARW, the work was never tedious. Every human being is different and no two sorties were ever the same. In addition, weather and seasons added a different element to the same exercise. Our students were highly motivated and desperately keen to earn their wings. We had many students who had difficulties and the Army instructional method was sympathetic and designed to help them to succeed. It was an interesting contrast to call on an RAF QFI friend for a coffee during one of our regular detachments to RAF Valley for mountain flying in Snowdonia and to witness one of the Hawk fast-jet students being bawled out by his QFI for poor flight planning. This incident might not have been representative of the norm at Valley but there appeared to be a more friendly and constructive attitude at Wallop. The 'Review' period coupled with a change of instructor, was a system that worked well and usually the student pulled through. There was, of course, a danger that the pressure of a sub-standard performance on a few sorties might lead to a downward spiral of loss of confidence. However, I reflected that as military pilots they must be able to cope with pressure and, in the case of the few that did fold, it was clear that they did not have the necessary attributes required for operational flying.

INSTRUCTING ON GAZELLE – EARLY DAYS AND BAOR

I have already mentioned that, as part of the Gazelle conversion course, we demonstrated a dive to limiting speed (VL or 168 knots depending on altitude and temperature) followed by a momentary experience of jack stall. The student was also required to demonstrate the same exercise to his instructor just once to ensure he fully understood these limitations. Rather than being cavalier and dangerous I found most students apprehensive and cautious in flying this manoeuvre which often had to be repeated with a verbal running commentary from me to ensure they actually did experience jack stall. The aircraft made it very clear that it was nearing its limits and all the pilot's instincts were to relax the controls before jack stall was achieved. I was confident that they would stay clear of that part of the envelope during their flying careers.

Part of the syllabus involved instrument flying in order to ensure that each student passed his wings course with a 'White' service instrument rating. This involved many hours sitting in the left seat whilst 'blogs', the student, practised instrument flying from the right seat with canvas screens and a canvas visor on his helmet restricting his peripheral vision. Our instrument training area lay to the north of Middle Wallop as far as Newbury from FL30 to FL55 under the control of Boscombe Radar. On one memorable day, whilst flying IMC in thick stratus at about FL50, we suddenly began to ice up fast. Within moments glaze appeared on our skid posts and the 'TV-type' homing aerials mounted on the nose then started vibrating so wildly that it seemed they were about to depart the airframe. I immediately called for a descent and positioning for an SRA back to Boscombe Down to be told that we should maintain our level as we were number six in turn for a recovery. At that same moment a pair of Jaguars came on the air asking for a priority approach with Bingo fuel states. With the cloud base down to 400 feet above ground level there was nothing to be done except orbit on instruments and wait, whilst watching the torque like a hawk. The vibrating aerials, which threatened to snap off at any moment, were a considerable distraction to one's peripheral vision during the instrument scan. It was a considerable relief when eventually we were cleared to descend and the blur of our vibrating homing aerials began to calm down. It subsequently turned out that there had been a dramatic un-forecast drop in the freezing level over a large part of southern England which caught out a great many aircraft that day, including all the aircraft in the Wallop IF training area. In similar circumstances in April 1986, Jeremy Howe, who had been a fellow student on my basic flying course, and after a few years had then left the Army to become a commercial pilot, was killed flying a Eurocopter AS355 Twin

Squirrel. Tragically, he had picked up five passengers in London to take them for a day at Alton Towers when he suffered a double engine failure in cloud and the aircraft crashed, seen to be descending out of a low cloud base with low rotor rpm, near Banbury. A SIGMET (significant meteorological report) had been issued whilst he was en route warning of severe icing but Jerry would never have seen it.[2]

After six months of instructing as a probationary instructor on A Flight I was tested by Standards and upgraded to a B1, now a confirmed QHI.

During my first summer at Middle Wallop in 1980 Exercise CRUSADER was scheduled in BAOR. This was to be the largest peacetime NATO exercise conducted in Germany and involved 10,000 British regular troops and 20,000 reservists who were mobilised and moved at short notice in real time to reinforce I British Corps. Most were in their 'wartime' positions in forty-eight hours. Four armoured divisions were to take part (4th Armoured Division, 2nd Armoured Division and US 2nd Armored Division with 3rd Armoured Division acting as umpires and umpire support) with altogether 102,000 troops, 855 main battle tanks, 2,800 tracked vehicles and 350 helicopters. The manoeuvre area stretched ninety-two miles east to west between Bielefeld and the East German Border and seventy miles north to south between Hannover and Kassel, a massive amount of real estate necessary to exercise armoured formations. In the event of mobilisation Middle Wallop flying instructors would be sent as battle casualty replacements to Army Air Corps squadrons in Germany. As it would have been counter-productive to delay peacetime flying training, it was decided to send a representative section of two Gazelles from Middle Wallop to Germany. I was to lead the section with WO2 Tony Davies[3] and Captain Tony Markham, an experienced standards officer. I signed for a Gazelle from Development and Trials Squadron and it was explained to me that the rotor blades had an expensive Swedish splinter camouflage pattern applied to them and that those trial blades were now my responsibility. Our flight across the channel to RAF Wildenrath, just inside the German border, was uneventful although we saw and heard on the radio an increasing amount of air traffic. At RAF Wildenrath we were met by an extremely efficient team who issued us with 9mm pistols, rations and maps, gave us a meal and despatched us to Hildesheim with all the relevant radio frequencies. After take-off we began to see a great deal of military traffic movement as we transited east of the Ruhr and, as evening fell, we arrived at the large grass airfield at Hildesheim about fifteen miles south-east of Hanover, to see it covered with numerous helicopters from the US, UK and Germany.

INSTRUCTING ON GAZELLE – EARLY DAYS AND BAOR

We were attached to 659 Squadron AAC, which was tasked to support 3rd Armoured Division in directing and umpiring the exercise. We assembled that evening in the Squadron ready tent for a met briefing and O Group for the next day's flying. Tony Markham and I were detailed to be ready from 0500 the following morning for tasking but I was somewhat embarrassed when Tony raised his hand and stated that there was no earthly point in this as the met brief had indicated early morning fog. Nevertheless, we should be on standby was the natural response. 'What a waste of time. I am not getting up at 0500 if there is no flying.' Somehow the exchange between him and the squadron commander escalated whilst I was quietly kicking Tony and telling him to wind his neck in. He was proved correct and the fog prevented early morning flying for two days, but the outcome of this was that the squadron boss wanted Tony removed from his squadron.

To my surprise, after years of Royal Marines exercises, I found that we ate in the HQ 3rd Armoured Division mess tent, replete with tablecloths and silver. There was a mess bar and outside NAAFI arrangements, a field post office and a cinema. This was going to be fun. The next evening at supper, however, a captain arrived at our table and told Tony that he was required outside. 'Yes I'll be out in a minute when I've finished my meal.' 'No, you are required right now,' was the curt response. A few minutes later, Tony arrived back in the mess tent looking shocked. A four-ton truck full of infantry was waiting for him to get his gear together. He was being sent into the field with an infantry company (wearing full NBC gear) for the duration of the exercise. He hurriedly asked me to take care of his civilian clothes and the 'first day cover' for his stamp collection which were back in his tent beside his camp bed and that was the last we saw of him until endex.

After a full day's flying, it was refreshing to dine in the mess tent, safe in the knowledge that there would be no night flying, have a beer or two in the bar and walk over to a large open-air cinema to see the latest movie. This is where I saw the new release 'Alien', along with about 500 other servicemen and women. There was no shortage of WRAC girls and female university office cadets acting as watchkeepers and assistants and the evening social life on camp and in the various messes was hectic. Our tent was dry and comfortable and more roomy, now that Tony was absent. The only facility missing was a shower but after a few days a Mobile Bath Unit (which I knew about from my studies at the Junior Division of the Staff College but had never seen before) appeared and very efficiently we were issued with soap and towel and, as we left the long row of hot showers in a large tent with wooden duckboards, a clean combat shirt. I forget now whether the disco was every other night or just once a week, but this was like no military exercise I had participated in before or since.

On 15 July I flew all day with a streamlined trials Zeiss camera pod attached to the port side armament boom of the Gazelle. It looked at first glance like a drop-tank and was operated by a control similar to a TV remote control, held by the crewman in the left seat. When the camera was switched to 'run' it automatically took multiple overlapping images vertical and/or, oblique, until the run button was released. A 4-ton truck came as part of this kit, outfitted as a mobile photographic laboratory. On landing, the crewman unloaded the cassette from the pod and ran to the truck. About fifteen minutes later photographic prints were available from the sortie. In the late afternoon I was returning low-level to Hildesheim when my crewman began to adjust my track slightly with a 'left ten, steady, left five, maintain that heading' and a few seconds later I heard the electric hum of the camera running. After landing, I noticed an unusual crowd of REME technicians crowding around the mobile laboratory whilst the prints were being distributed. Soon I saw the results of our tactical sortie, complete with a few vertical images of a naturist campsite that we had overflown at 150 feet on our approach to Hildesheim. I still have a blown-up and grainy image of two large blonde ladies reclining in their striped canvas deck chairs, magazines on their ample laps, staring up at the belly of our aircraft. I never saw a similar camera pod either before or since the exercise.

Halfway through the exercise our Gazelle developed a slight vertical vibration and the REME technicians asked me to fly the aircraft back to the aircraft workshop at Detmold to get it fixed. At Detmold, after lunch in the mess, I was told that one blade required changing. Mindful of my responsibilities for the trial blades, I explained that the removed blade would have to be returned to D & T Squadron at Middle Wallop. Apparently there was no scope to do this within the REME repair system; the blade would just join the Army pool of blades awaiting repair or adjustment along with many others. I stood my ground as, with the high level of spares and repairs being processed in Germany, I was sure this particular blade would be lost forever in the system. After much arguing with a WO2, and then the OC LAD, the removed blade was eventually specially labelled as a trials item. I now had two camouflaged blades and one standard blade. The camouflage, although it looked sporty, was never adopted as from the air a rotor blade is a rotor blade whatever colour it is painted. A time-expired standard green military parachute thrown over the aircraft was a proven quick, lightweight and effective camouflage method which continued to be used.

INSTRUCTING ON GAZELLE – EARLY DAYS AND BAOR

On 22 July paratroopers from the US 82nd Airborne Division, based at Fort Bragg, flew non-stop from Charleston AFB, South Carolina, to their drop zone at Blomberg near Hildesheim in a formation of eight C-141 Starlifters, with in-flight refuelling from KC-135 tankers over the Atlantic. I had to fly a major of the German Military Police to secure the drop zone (from a policeman's rather than a military point of view). When we landed, the area was already filling up with German families arriving in their cars with picnics. Somehow the word had got out about the drop, the timing and the location. The German major produced an electronic loud-hailer and bellowed 'Achtung. Achtung. Hier ist der Bundeswehr. Gehen sie weg' – or words to that effect. Immediately the obedient civilians packed up their gear and, hurrying to their cars, departed. I doubted that this approach would have worked in the UK. I walked over to where a US airborne major was supervising his radioman in setting up a UHF manpack radio at the edge of the DZ. I stood behind him as he chewed on a cigar, helmet strap undone, straight out of a grainy Second World War newsreel film. Out of the haze came an amazing sight of the C-141s in staggered trail formation, approaching, flaps down, at about 1,500 feet. 'Smoke, you sucker, smoke,' growled the major out of the side of his mouth as he conned the lead aircraft a few degrees left or right to line up with the centre of the drop zone. The radioman obediently threw two red smoke grenades into an upturned dustbin lid (to prevent the grass from catching fire) and a minute later the first sticks were jumping from the side doors. The drop was apparently six minutes late and the whole jump of more than 800 paratroopers was completed in less than four minutes. The first man on the ground was the formation brigadier general. The major shook his hand with a 'Welcome to Germany Sir' as the general bundled up his chute and lit up a celebratory cigar. It was the first time the 82nd Airborne had jumped into Europe since Operation MARKET GARDEN at Nijmegen.

At some stage in the exercise I was asked to fly as part of a stream of three aircraft flying General Sir Edwin Bramall,[4] the Chief of the General Staff (CGS), on a visit to the exercise. I was tasked at very short notice as the number three aircraft behind two Scouts to carry any extra baggage or aides. The brief was simple: just follow the lead and the number 2 aircraft visiting a number of tactical locations during the morning. However, as we waited, rotors running in line astern, and I saw the staff cars draw up, General Bramall got out and unerringly headed for my aircraft, the rearmost of the three. Although various aides were flapping their arms and trying ineffectively to divert him towards the lead Scout, it was immediately obvious to me that I was about to become the lead aircraft without any detailed briefing. Perhaps he disliked flying in the Scout.[5] Thank God, we had spare headsets in the back and, quick as a flash, my crewman opened the rear doors and strapped the CGS into the back alongside his ADC. Out of the corner of my eye I could see mayhem as baggage, security details and various hangers-on clambered into the VIP Scouts in front of us whilst the gesticulations continued. Quickly and discreetly asking for the first grid reference from the aide in the rear we set off in the lead for a very demanding low-level navigation test. At the first stop I sent my crewman to get the remaining locations we were due to visit from the 'lead Scout', piloted by a major, and now reduced to the role of a lowly baggage aircraft. It was en route to the second or third grid reference that we saw a troop of Scimitar tracked reconnaissance vehicles beside a minor road, relaxing and brewing up and CGS indicated that he would like to land and talk to them. The closest we could land was in an adjoining field separated from the elevated road embankment by a wire fence. Having landed, our distinguished passengers started across the grass to the fence. But the horrified Scimitar crews, seeing helicopters land and then a bevy of brass approaching them, hurriedly chucked away their 'wets' of tea, threw their large packs onto their vehicles and started their engines to make a quick getaway out of 'the line of fire'. The aides started shouting and running forward to stop them. The first two reached the groin-high wire fence at the base of the embankment. From their sudden jerky reactions whilst astride the fence and their contorted facial expressions it was obvious that it was an electrified cattle fence. Meanwhile, the three Scimitars accelerated away down the road in a cloud of exhaust fumes. As the group turned back to the helicopters, I hurriedly lowered my tinted visor and looked away to hide my tears of laughter. However, the visit was an overall success; CGS was happy with his Gazelle tour and, once again, the lesson was learned to be prepared for the unexpected.

It was a unique sight to see two armoured divisions moving across the German countryside. One early morning I flew a passenger to witness an armoured regiment, 4th Royal Tanks, dismounting from their tank transporters, having been driven from their base at Sennelager to the west. The first of fifty-five Chieftain main battle tanks (MBT) rolled off the Thorneycroft Mighty Antar transporter onto the minor country road and effortlessly drove into the neighbouring cabbage field. The next transporter drove into the same position and the second MBT dismounted. By the time the fifth tank was off the transporter, the road surface was broken and chunks of tarmac were crumbling under the tracks. Another few tanks dismounted and the culverts began collapsing. As each troop drove across the field a shower of cabbages and mud flew high into the air behind their tracks, mixing with the throaty exhaust fumes. By the time the last tank was deployed the whole area was churned up resembling a building site. It had been an impressive spectacle and an example of sheer power. As we were starting rotors to depart a squadron of Royal Engineers arrived to rebuild the road and culverts. When required to adopt a defensive position the specially-equipped dozer tanks in each regiment bulldozed hull-down positions in the fields for the main battle tanks. Each hole was the size of a small swimming pool and one of our tasks was to fly DAMCON (Damage Control) teams around to assess the damage in order to settle claims. I recall that damage payments formed a significant proportion of the exercise costs and I remember a figure of £8 million which was then a huge sum of money.

We heard a widely circulated story of an Army pilot flying his Scout back to his squadron location from the field at endex and, seeing an agricultural rotary spraying machine watering crops, decided that it would be a neat way to save his technicians valuable time in washing-down his aircraft. Having established a hover in the field he waited for the spray head to rotate around to clean his aircraft. When eventually engulfed in the spray the Nimbus flamed out and he was forced to perform an 'engine-off in the hover' into the crops from where the clean aircraft had to be recovered.

This was not the only strange story that emanated from AAC BAOR at that time. We heard of the air trooper who was refuelling a Scout at his base airfield, I believe Detmold, together with a newly-qualified ground handler who was watching and learning. On removing the bowser's gravity refuelling nozzle from the aircraft, a quantity of fuel spilt onto the concrete beneath the Scout. The new boy was understandably concerned about getting this spill cleaned up and suggested they called the airfield fire service to hose it away but the old hand re-assured him not to worry and that Avtur was not flammable. He had apparently been shown a questionable demonstration on his refuellers' course of how a lighted match could be extinguished by Avtur and proceeded to demonstrate this by flicking his cigarette lighter over the pool of fuel. However the spill promptly ignited and the aircraft was badly damaged in the ensuing fire. A court martial followed and, after a spell inside, the discharged miscreant reportedly joined the fire service.

Tony appeared on the final day of the exercise, cheerful and much fitter after his two weeks with the infantry. We retraced our track back across northern Europe to Middle Wallop.

FLYING LIGHT HELICOPTERS WITH THE ROYAL MARINES

1980 was a bad year for 3 Commando Brigade Air Squadron. In June a Gazelle hit the surface of the sea at Lough Foyle off Ballykelly, Northern Ireland. The wreckage ended up lying in about twelve inches of sea water on the mudflats but thankfully no one was badly hurt.[6] Three months later Exercise TEAMWORK 80 was taking place off Cape Wrath on the north-western tip of Scotland. Lieutenant David Dunn was operating from HMS *Intrepid* in a Gazelle with two passengers, Lieutenant Paul Farley from 45 Commando and Lieutenant Andy MacDonald, a friend and batch-mate of mine, who was a forward air controller. Shortly after departing the ship and whilst low flying over the Falklands-like landscape of the coastal strip near Balnakiel, the rotor blades hit the turf whilst banking at low level, the aircraft cartwheeled and all three were killed.[7]

Chapter 11

Instructing on Gazelle – Flight Commander

Having experienced A Flight of Advanced Rotary Wing Squadron for six months, I moved to B Flight which dealt with the tactical use of the aircraft and field exercises during a further fifty-eight flying hours over eight weeks. B Flight was commanded by a US Army Artillery exchange IP (Instructor Pilot), Captain Ed Den Beste, who to his surprise had to complete the CFS (H) course at the beginning of his tour. Ed was a great guy and we had a lot of fun together. As a newly-qualified pilot he had been sent to a Chinook squadron in Vietnam and I remember his stories of having to fly the rest of the inebriated squadron personnel to and from Saigon crammed into a CH-47 for a few days R&R. Ed incurred the wrath of our Squadron boss by teaching some of his students to land at his own 'inverted Y' landing aid at night, a particular US technique that was not approved for our students, who were taught to approach the 'T' arrangement of tactical lights.[1]

Much of the tactical skill an Army pilot needed to master involved accurate interpretation of the ground. Reading contour lines, inter-visibility and dead ground had to become second nature. The aircraft moved forward in tactical bounds, from cover to cover, exactly the same way as an infantryman would but with events speeded up by a factor of 100. The work load for the student was high, working at ultra-low level (often less than twenty feet), low speed and in the hover, with a 1:50,000 scale map clutched in the same hand as the cyclic, taking into account wind, power margins, trees, wires, roads, livestock and other obstacles and the Forward Edge of the Battle Area (FEBA) whilst talking on a tactical radio; it seems amazing to me now that so many made the grade. It was often said that any student on the Army Pilots Course could be taught to fly but we were looking for pilots who could fly at low level, read the ground, navigate, operate ATC and tactical radios, make decisions, deal with a passenger, and carry out all the tasks of Army Aviation at the same time as safely flying the helicopter. This was still the day of single-pilot operation in Army Aviation so every pilot was being taught to be a solo aircraft captain.

FLYING LIGHT HELICOPTERS WITH THE ROYAL MARINES

There had been various attempts to try and improve the pass rate for the Army Pilot's Course over the years which had included deleting the fixed-wing Chipmunk phase and even extending it. However, although there were occasional courses in which only two or three pilots graduated and other excellent courses where only one was chopped, the overall average pass rate remained roughly at about 70 per cent. Reasons ranged from lack of aptitude or flying skills which could be assessed early on in Chipmunks or G-4s, to lack of captaincy or division of attention which sometimes did not manifest themselves until the student was loaded with tactical decision making later on in the course.

At that time the Warsaw Pact were operating the ZSU-23-4, nicknamed *Shilka*, a particularly effective tracked anti-aircraft and anti-helicopter weapon found with all Soviet motorised and tank regiments. Each *Shilka* had four 23mm automatic guns laid by a turret-mounted *Tobol* radar with a combined rate of fire of over fifty-eight rounds per second. The danger was that, once exposed within about 3,000 metres of the *Shilka*, the radar would pick up rotor blade movement and we would be quickly engaged. However, it might take five to ten seconds for the radar to acquire us, the operator to track us and to open fire. Our tactics instructor Captain Mike Hewetson (who coincidentally had been at Shrewsbury School with me and one of the very few old Salopian servicemen of our era) who acted as 'enemy' on our exercises, used ground observers with binoculars and a video camera to try and find our Gazelles on observation and Air OP tasks. Thus, if we were seen, pointed out and then filmed it was reckoned to be a reasonable simulation of a successful *Shilka* engagement. The trick was to unmask and then disappear back behind cover before the observer could see or point out the Gazelle to the camera operator. If you appeared on the video footage at debrief for more than a few seconds you had probably been shot down. It was simple, effective and fun training.

One of the skills we taught our students was flight under wires. This was a much-misunderstood term to the layman. It was definitely not a stunt and if carried out properly was a very safe manoeuvre. Flying tactically or in marginal weather there were many circumstances in which it was necessary to cross pylons at low level. Flight over pylons could either expose you to the enemy or lead to inadvertent entry into low cloud. The area we used for practice was a large line of pylons about two miles west of Amesbury surrounded by fields and with no nearby habitation. Approaching to the hover we would conduct a careful recce to check that there were no feeder cables or other obstacles and then hover-taxi at three feet slowly under the wires adjacent to a pylon, whilst looking at the ground ahead and not up at the wires. Once on the other side we could transition back to normal flight. Not only was this safe but we had a generous clearance between the top of the rotors and the lowest power cable. I cannot recall a single accident or incident whilst practising this manoeuvre. Sadly wire strikes or disorientation at low level after entering cloud killed many people.

An interesting regular exercise was also carried out with the Basingstoke Police called EAGLE EYE. This involved having radio contact with a police motorcyclist whilst flying at about 2,500 feet over the town equipped with a detailed street map. The second pilot, using stabilised binoculars, gave directions to the motorcycle in order to intercept and stop an unmarked police car. We were given the vehicle's description and initial location, and when we gave the word 'go' the police car would drive at normal speed on a random route through Basingstoke whilst the student gave directions to the motorcyclist, and then, on later serials, the student flew the aircraft whilst the instructor gave directions. This was good practice for one of the roles required in Northern Ireland. On one occasion we were asked to break off the exercise in order to follow a genuine stolen car, which we soon found leaving Basingstoke at speed on the Alton Road. It eventually stopped in woodland south of Winslade where the occupants abandoned the vehicle and hid in the nearby undergrowth whilst we directed a patrol car onto their location.

Various enhancements had been made to the Gazelle since Malta days, one of which was the Doppler 80 navigation system, known as Mini TANS (Tactical Air Navigation System), a smaller version of the TANS on the Lynx. Once the crew had got used to operating the small and somewhat fiddly LCD display and scroll switches it became a useful navaid (well before the days of GPS). Someone in MoD had also procured a portable moving map display about the size and weight of a heavy first-generation laptop PC which worked on the principle of cross-hairs moving mechanically over a paper map. It was fed from the Mini TANS via a flexible cable which plugged into the instrument console. We soon found that this was a totally impractical piece of kit. If held by the non-flying pilot it could easily foul the cyclic and if dropped was heavy enough to damage the bottom of the canopy. Very soon regulations decreed it could only be used from the rear seats and this concept of an aircraft navigation aid was ludicrous, especially when passenger space was limited. I flew one sortie through the London heli-lanes with an aircrewman operating it from the rear and with an empty left seat. After two or three sorties they disappeared and were not seen again.

FLYING LIGHT HELICOPTERS WITH THE ROYAL MARINES

During my time at Wallop there were a couple of tragedies and, as bad luck would have it, they both occurred in Beaver conversion flight, a small team who converted and refreshed pilots onto the de Havilland Beaver AL Mk 1 for liaison work in Germany and for surveillance work in Northern Ireland. Early on in my tour, during a gloomy January afternoon in two kilometres visibility and with the temperature below freezing, we heard a mayday call being transmitted by another aircraft which had seen burning wreckage. This turned out to be a Beaver practising field landings in a 425-metre-long field near the A30 main road at Popham which had crashed into a newly-constructed motorway embankment after a touch-and-go landing. The retired RAF instructor, Squadron Leader Peter Mackenzie, had over 4,000 hours on type.[2] It was subsequently found that they had touched down long into the field and, for reasons unknown, it was believed that the go-around was delayed until less than 150 metres of the field remained. The tail hit a wooden fence forming the northern boundary of the field which broke off the Beaver's elevator. The aircraft staggered on for another 70 metres over the slip road until it struck the steep embankment beside the M3 motorway and both were killed. Every time I drive to and from London on the A303 I mentally salute them both as I pass the spot. Three and a half years later, in July 1983, his successor, Major (Retired) Bill Smithson AAC, was demonstrating a Beaver at RNAS Culdrose Airday in high gusting winds. After take-off he turned downwind at low level and his wingtip hit the ground.[3] This was another sad fatal accident to a further highly experienced and competent pilot, demonstrating once again that gravity is unforgiving.

After six months with B Flight, I was told that I would take over command of A Flight of Advanced Rotary Wing. I had an excellent team of experienced Senior NCOs and Warrant Officer instructors in the Flight who taught me a great deal about student management. They also had a marvellous sense of humour which involved many pranks including a grey wooden aircrew locker standing against the briefing room wall, behind which was a hidden, disused, door into the hangar. During my introductory talk to the new course, when I introduced the instructors to the bemused students, all eight instructors appeared one by one magically from out of the locker, which had a removable panel at the rear.

One of the emergency actions in the Gazelle Flight Reference Cards was 'engine restart in flight'. This always intrigued my instructors for a number of reasons. Firstly, the Astazou engine was extremely reliable and in the rare event that it might stop in flight there would be a very good reason;

INSTRUCTING ON GAZELLE – FLIGHT COMMANDER

either a catastrophic failure or lack of fuel and, in either case, attempting a restart would be a waste of precious time. Secondly, the process of engine re-start took some time and, unless the failure occurred at medium or high altitude, there would be little time in autorotation to go through the process before *terra firma* reared its ugly head. Finally, trying to re-start would be a dangerous distraction when the pilot's concentration should be upon selecting a safe area for an engine-off landing, manoeuvring, making sure passengers and crew were tightly strapped-in and sending out a Mayday call. After some discussion my Squadron boss, Major Louis Parsons requested permission for the two of us to try this out as part of our staff continuation flying training. The plan was to take a Gazelle to over 10,000 feet above Greenham Common airfield, then MoD owned but disused, which provided a large clear area for an engine-off landing if things did not go according to plan. We would enter autorotation, retard the throttle to ground idle and then shutdown the engine. We would then go through the restart procedure, accelerate the engine to flight idle and complete a power-on recovery from autorotation. In order to comply with regulations we would both wear parachutes, not because of any danger in what we were doing but purely because we were so high that if we had an inflight fire the aircraft might suffer a structural failure whilst in autorotation before we reached the ground. Authorisation was granted specially for us to each conduct one restart. We briefed the sortie carefully together and asked the REME to select an aircraft which had a completely clear history of starting problems. On the day, with clear blue skies, we started up the aircraft on the pan at Advanced Rotary Wing and, as we had planned, carried out a simulated full rehearsal on the ground. All went well until we stopped the engine and went through the re-start drills but there was no ignition. A microswitch in the starter circuit had failed. Was someone trying to tell us something? I am afraid that we returned to the 700 Office to report the failure in fits of laughter and signed out another aircraft, realising that its maintenance history was irrelevant to the outcome of this trial. Overhead Greenham Common everything went according to plan. The only unusual occurrences were that the engine windmilled at surprisingly high RPM in the autorotative slipstream, the exhaust gas temperature (T4) cooled very rapidly due to the airflow through the engine and when 'Run' was selected the familiar starter motor whine could not be heard above the slipstream and rotor noise which gave us a momentary minor concern until a look at the engine gauges told us all was well. I forget exactly how much height we lost in re-starting but it was between 1,500 and 2,000 feet, bearing in mind that this was after rehearsal and careful briefing. However, we confirmed that the procedure worked but that our gut instincts to concentrate on a successful forced landing in the event of engine failure were sound.

During my time as OC of A Flight on Advanced Rotary Wing Squadron I applied to be upgraded to an A2 category QHI. This involved giving a briefing, a dual flight with one of the Standards officers and a de-briefing. A further requirement was a detailed lecture on one aspect of the aircraft in front of an invited audience followed by questions. I chose as a subject the Gazelle's unique (at that time) fenestron tail-rotor system. The lecture went well and after the question period, Major Norman Overy, the Standards Officer, said 'let's go into the hangar and look at one shall we?' We walked into the adjoining hangar to one of the spare Gazelles and discussed the 13-bladed fan arrangement in the tail. Marked with a red decal on the bottom of the fenestron tunnel was a diagonal red line annotated 'left pedal fwd' as a rigging mark. Norman then said, 'But look, you said that with right pedal applied the thrust would be directed that way through the fan.' I stared at the tail in silence for a moment, my mind in turmoil. Had I got the whole principle of the flow through the fan arse-about-face which would mean the whole lecture had been one big cock-up? Luckily, my brief silence whilst I thought paid off and I was able to point out that the rigging mark decal had been applied the wrong way around. I passed the test and this had not been a deliberate ploy by Norman to catch me out. We had indeed stumbled across a cock-up.

Whilst instructing on Gazelle I thought it a good opportunity to take the CAA exams to obtain my civil Airline Pilot's Licence (Helicopters). As an A2 instructor I was exempted some of the exams but I was still required to sit the Air Law, Performance, Loading and SA-341 technical papers. The SA-341 was the civilian version of the Gazelle and I had never seen one. There were various technical variances to the military AH.1 but I obtained a civilian technical manual and read up carefully on the differences. I also required a separate HF radio licence and went down to Shoreham to take the practical test in a simulator with an instructor who entertainingly adopted four or five distinctly different voices as I 'flew' across the UK. I took the written exams in a large hall at the City University of London College in Clerkenwell, sitting amongst perhaps seventy other hopefuls, many of whom were young aspiring pilots who had paid thousands of pounds for their training. I was in the happy position of sitting the exams as a useful bonus whilst for many of the others their future livelihoods depended on the results. The loading and performance papers were really aimed at public

INSTRUCTING ON GAZELLE – FLIGHT COMMANDER

transport aircraft on long-distance flights but the principles for rotary were the same. I can remember one of the examinees at a neighbouring desk collapsing in despair just before time was up as his calculations had gone awry. I failed SA-341 technical but passed the other papers so I had to return four months later to re-sit the technical. Because it was multi-choice paper I found some of the questions confusing with questions similar to this example: 'The fuel cap is found on: A. The top of the port fuselage; B. The top of the starboard fuselage; C. The rear of the starboard fuselage?' Well the answer was definitely B or C but as far as I was concerned it was on the top, rear of the starboard fuselage. But there was only one correct answer. The second time around I passed and received my precious white CAA licence and later an instructor's rating, both of which I never used but which were a useful insurance policy and undoubtedly helped my overall aviation knowledge.

WO1 Geoff Palmer was a larger than life caricature of an Army sergeant major. Tall, physically impressive, with a face which showed a lifetime of military experience and a quick turn of phrase which could instantly put down a cocky young officer or reduce us all to laughter with a ribald comment. A QHI with a wealth of experience, he was a doer rather than a talker. He ran C Flight of Advanced Rotary Wing responsible for Gazelle conversion and refresher courses for qualified pilots returning from ground tours and was particularly good at handling senior officers who clearly enjoyed his instructional techniques. As a member of our Sparrowhawks display team, he used to refer to it as 'Wilsey's Big Wing' after AVM Leigh-Mallory's Wing during the Battle of Britain. On a couple of occasions he and I would fly to Netheravon together for Staff Continuation training with a Gazelle. He always made me work hard with his habit of unexpectedly pulling the throttle back to ground idle in flight from a position where it was going to be difficult to make the field. On a couple of occasions I had to go for a max range autorotation and barely scraped in to North Field with Geoff laughing as he advanced the throttle when we were safely (just) on the ground. He was an excellent judge of character and if I had doubts about a student I very much valued his second opinion. The SNCO aircrew were much of the strength of Army (and Royal Marines) Aviation and also the source of many of the older commissioned pilots. As much as I enjoyed flying with the RAF and Fleet Air Arm I felt that they were missing out on this aspect of ethos and influence in their Squadrons.

At Wallop there were some opportunities to inspect some historic aircraft. A REME major, Roger Hannington, had purchased a Stampe SV4C biplane from Belgium which he hangared at Wallop and had spent considerable time in rebuilding. It was a lovely aircraft, built in 1946 and re-registered as G-BIMO with a Renault engine with inverted fuel system in beautiful condition after his hard work, and I often chatted to him as he worked on it in the evenings or weekends. It was the open-cockpit version and finished in silver overall and I well remember the care with which he replaced the padded brown leather trim around the cockpits. I had a memorable flight with him one summer afternoon with some gentle aerobatics and with the Hampshire countryside and unspoilt grass airfield far below us it felt as if we had been transported back to pre-war flying days.[4] John Fairey also kept his replica Fairey Flycatcher S1287 in a one of the hangars. He had supervised the rebuild himself and, occasionally at weekends, I assisted in pushing it in and out of the hangar. It was a surprisingly big and heavy biplane with a substantial tail skid and it now resides in the Fleet Air Arm Museum at Yeovilton.[5]

During my three years instructing at Wallop only one of my personal students was suspended. Although a pleasant officer and a proficient 'rudder-and-stick' aviator, it became increasingly clear in the later stages of the course that he was unsuited to be an Army pilot for lack of both division of attention and captaincy. This showed itself as an inability to prioritise what was important when the workload was high. Thus, for example, faced with navigating at low level in bad weather, whilst listening to two different radio nets, he did not aviate, navigate and communicate but instead endangered himself by studying the map and changing frequencies instead of flying the aircraft safely clear of the ground and bad weather. I was relieved when, after the standard Review procedure of a change of instructor, he flew with Standards and was 'chopped' and I suspect that, deep down, so was he.

My instructor, Charlie Cuthill, with Chipmunk T.10 of Basic Fixed Wing Flight at Middle Wallop 1974. (©Author)

The author preparing for solo sortie in Chipmunk T.10 at Middle Wallop 1974. (©Author)

Bristow Helicopters Bell 47 G-4s of Basic Rotary Wing at Middle Wallop 1975. (©Author)

Sioux of Advanced Rotary Wing at Battersea Heliport with instructor Staff Sergeant Brian Backhouse. (©Author)

How not to do a quickstop. Sioux XT225 crash Chilbolton, March 1975. Note how the fuel tanks have detached as designed. (©Author)

Casualty's view from a Sioux litter at low level over north Devon. The author's right boot being cooked by the exhaust. (©Author)

Part of 238 Army Pilots Course Wings Parade 1975. Before presentation of Army wings from the left: Capt Denis Lewis 6GR, Maj Simon Salter RCT (qualified and experienced fixed wing pilot undergoing rotary conversion), 2Lt Jeremy Howe AAC, Lt Les Thresh RM, Sgt MS Taylor RA, Author, Sgt GRM Clement RA.

HMS *Bulwark's* flight deck at first light in September 1975 off Turkey. Gazelles are on spots Green 1 and 2 with sticks of Marines from 40 Commando waiting to embark in Wessex 5s for the assault. The author is flying the nearest Gazelle and the lashings have just been removed from the aircraft on Green 1. Six 120 mm Wombat anti-tank guns are in the foreground ready for under-slinging and two anti-submarine homing torpedoes on the right. Note the UHF 'umbrella' homing aerial on the extreme right with which Neil Macaulay's Sioux collided two years earlier. (©Crown copyright, Open Government Licence v3.0)

Salerno Flight aircrew on the helipad. From left Sgt Barrie Shepherd, Capt Rodney Helme, Sgt John Menghini, Author.

Salerno Flight Gazelle over the dome at Mosta, Malta.

Gazelle XX377 of Salerno Flight on the helipad at St George's, Malta. (©Author)

Above: Author flying C Flight Sioux at landing point in the Tutong jungle, Brunei. (©Author)

Left: Approaching an LP (in centre of image) in the jungle near the Sarawak border. (©Author)

Author on the pad at Bessbrook, March 1978. Note the armoured seat and the body armour chest plate worn with a 9mm Browning in a shoulder holster. The file beside the rear seat holds detailed map coverage of the Province. (©Author)

The top end of the helipad at Bessbrook in Northern Ireland in the 1970s. At least a further six landing spots are behind the photographer. The mill is in the background together with the famous chimney. (©Crown copyright, Open Government Licence v3.0)

Freydis Sharland ex-ATA pilot on left, author centre and Capt Ed Den Beste US Army on the right at Booker Airfield in June 1980. (©Author)

The second prototype TF-18A Hornet BU No 160784 seen at Farnborough in September 1980, a few days before it crashed at Middle Wallop. (©Tony Hancke)

The results of the engine-off collision at Middle Wallop on 6 October 1981 taken that evening with the foam used on the Bell 47 G-4 still evident. The G4's skids have disappeared … chopped into short lengths by the Scout's main rotor blades.

Airfix 1:72 scale model kit of Westland Scout first issued in 1966. The box art by Roy Cross shows XP885 and Centurion tanks. The kit also included the decals for XP890. (©Author)

Cockpit of TOW-equipped Lynx AH.1 during Silver Eagles training. No 6, Capt Jim Browne in the right seat with SSgt Clint Stimson in the left seat. Note the flight reference cards under Clint's right hand which is resting on the TOW controller. (©Jerry Young)

Silver Eagles 1982 Team members. Back row from the left: Lt Geoff Young no 5, SSgt Tony Merrick no 4, SSgt Dave Stewart no 2, Author leader, Capt Jim Browne deputy leader and no 6. Front row; WO2 Mal Thwaites no 3, WO2 Ken Jackson crewman leader, SSgt Clint Stimson crewman. Note the logo designed by Wilf Hardy on the avionics bay door of the aircraft. (©Jerry Young)

Above left: The Silver Eagles with the Red Arrows at RAF Kemble, photographed from a Gazelle by Arthur Gibson on 3 June 1982. (©Arthur Gibson)

Above right: The Silver Eagles training in echelon starboard. (©Jerry Young)

The Silver Eagles overhead HMS *Hermes* on return to Portsmouth on 21 July 1982 after the Falklands War.

Lynx AH.1 at Lyngenfjord in Arctic Norway. The red cross indicates it was acting as enemy forces. (©D Irving)

Conditions above the tree line. The Rondane Mountains in central Norway. (©Author)

Norway. Lynx AH.7 in whiteout conditions. Sgt Damian Irving is equipped with RM arctic flying gear of ski march boots, cold weather flying trousers, windproof smock and two-layer flying gloves. (©D Irving)

Lynx AH.7 mountain flying at CVM Saillagouse, Pyrenees. (©Crown copyright, Open Government Licence v3.0)

Gazelle XW849 over HMS *Intrepid* in 1990, fitted with flotation gear, HF and GOA sight.

ACM Training over the Somerset Levels in a Lynx AH.7. Note the extreme attitude at 65 knots, 300 feet and 90% torque. In the left seat WO2 Pete Beeston and in the right seat Helicopter Weapons Instructor CSgt Al Blowers.

Op HAVEN. Two Lynx AH.7 armed with live TOW about to lift from Silopi on 2 May 1991, the day of 3 Commando Brigade's advance into Northern Iraq. (©Author)

FOB 1 'Capbadge' at Shirati. Note the two liberated ZU-23-2s in foreground, an armed Lynx in the background with a Gazelle undergoing engine change in the rear. Group includes, front row from left: Capt Ron Crawford Senior Pilot, WO2 Eddy Candlish the Sqn SM, Capt Jerry Burnell Adjt, Maj Rob Wilsey CO. Back Row from left: Sgt Bill Parker, Capt Derek Pulford, Capt Andy Williams, Lt Paul Denning together with members of A Flight and REME LAD detachment.

The reason why we were there. Lt Peter Norman and Sgt Eric Conway with Kurdish refugee families from the mountains at Shirati. (©Author)

REME carrying out a Lynx gearbox change at Silopi in over 35 degrees C. (©Author)

Bulgarian Navy Mi-14 Haze amongst the cranes at Varna docks, Bulgaria.

Robert Atac's T-28C after the forced landing near Aurora, Illinois. Note the wires in the background under which he flew prior to touchdown. (©R Atac)

Chapter 12

Crash, Bang, Wallop

On 8 September 1980 a two-seat McDonnell Douglas TF-18A Hornet, Bureau no. 160784, took off from RAE Farnborough en route to Torrejon in Spain for a promotional visit. This was the second of two development Hornet two-seaters and, in the climb above cloud over Basingstoke, it experienced serious engine problems and attempted to divert to RAE Boscombe Down.[1]

We never saw the Hornet impact the ground. WO2 Tony Davies and I were carrying out some dual staff continuation training at Middle Wallop and I was just advancing the throttle after completing a practice engine-off landing in Gazelle AH.1 XZ341 when we saw a large black mushroom cloud, with a fireball at its base, rise from behind the hangars, 600 metres away, and climb rapidly towards the low undercast. A few expletives bounced around the cockpit as we tried to digest this new turn of events. Something interesting had clearly happened as figures were running aimlessly to and fro in front of the distant hangars. The column of smoke emanated from the approximate area of my married quarter but I recalled that my family were driving back from Devon that morning, so they in no way could be endangered. Whilst these thoughts flashed through my mind I took off and flew to the area in front of the Control Tower as the airfield emergency brief (folded in my left lower flying suit pocket) instructed me to do in such circumstances. There had been an eerie silence from ATC on Wallop Tower UHF frequency since the incident and, as I told them what I was doing, there was no acknowledgement. During the few seconds we took to hover taxi to the tower the sergeant major and I discussed the possibilities. Neither a Gazelle nor a Lynx would produce a blaze like that, and we had not seen or heard any aircraft airborne at the time. In fact the circuit was almost deserted.

Having landed next to the tower we kept the rotors running, expecting at any instant to see a red-faced doctor arrive in his black mini, but no one appeared. At this juncture there was another exclamation from the sergeant major, and we suddenly noticed two gaudily coloured parachutes emerge from the cloud base over our left shoulders. I replied that there had been no NOTAM about parachuting at Middle Wallop that day. The truth of the matter was that it took a few seconds for us to connect the multi-coloured parachutes with the now oily column of smoke rising the far side of the playing-fields. When the penny dropped we ran through the possibilities. It must be a Chipmunk. No. A look at their dispersal showed that it was deserted. The basic students were at ground school. A Beaver? We had seen one taxi out ten minutes earlier but they did not usually carry parachutes. We were still under the assumption that the cause of the conflagration was a Middle Wallop based aircraft. Still there was no word from the tower, nor indeed from anyone else, on UHF.

We seemed to have been waiting an age and still no doctor had appeared (but it can only have been two minutes or so from the time of impact). The parachutes appeared as if they would land on the far side of the airfield or in the disused bomb dump. A large member of the crash crew then ran towards us clutching a fire axe; he was a determined man and clearly had his mind set upon sitting in the back of our Gazelle. 'Watch out! Mind the cabin roof. Careful with that axe. Watch the floor structure. Look out for the door.' It was no good; he had no headset and the sergeant major and I engaged in gesticulating and mouthing until he was safely strapped in, cradling his battle axe. Still no doctor had appeared, and now we were faced with a dilemma. Should we fly to the burning wreckage or to the parachutes? We asked the tower. 'Wait out,' was their curt reply.

Another oath from the patient sergeant major and he pointed to a Land Rover ambulance tearing across the airfield behind us towards the parachutes, one of which was now gently settling by the CADF whilst the other drifted out of sight uncomfortably close to where the camp sewage farm lay. Our Gazelle seemed to have been by-passed in the rush and we decided to fly over to help the parachutists. We assumed that the crash tender must by now have reached the wreckage as the volume of smoke was beginning to diminish. We took off and flew at about fifty feet towards the survivors. The first was lying near the CADF, clad in an orange flying suit. The Land Rover ambulance had just stopped beside him and so we flew over the airfield boundary hedge to where the second pilot was lying in a grass meadow. We touched down about 50 metres from him and the sergeant major leaped out, followed by the fireman as if he was determined to finish off any survivor with his axe. I stopped the rotors with the engine at ground idle and wondered momentarily whether it was 'operationally necessary' to leave the aircraft with engine running, rotor stopped. It was, and having applied the frictions and checked that the clutch was not dragging, I also unstrapped and ran across to where the group was now kneeling.

The scene was as follows: a middle-aged man with a crewcut was lying on his back, helmetless in a bright orange flying suit. His parachute, still attached to him, was draped on the grass above his head and, fortunately, there was no wind. He was festooned with survival equipment and plenty of unfamiliar straps. Kneeling next to him was the sergeant major who had not taken his own helmet off and an attractive nurse who was unsuitably attired for first aid in the field – she appeared to have stepped straight out of a hospital ward. The other member of the group was a tall Australian Army Aviation captain on exchange who was on his first familiarisation flight in UK airspace and found it most instructive, as he told me later over a cup of coffee.

Seeing the orange flying suit, I immediately assumed that the pilot must be from the German air force as I had seen the Luftwaffe similarly clad. This theory was immediately dispelled when he groaned and said, 'Jeez, my leg hurts.' He was cut about the face, appeared shocked, clearly had a leg injury and was unable to move. 'Where am I? What happened?' he moaned. The sergeant major, at the head end, re-assured him and muttered something about him being next to runway 26 at Middle Wallop. We straightened him out and attempted to disentangle the survival packs. Thanks to my parachute course, I could undo the Koch fasteners and thus separate survivor from his parachute, which I automatically rolled up as I had been taught on the DZ at Weston on the Green. The doctor at long last materialised and indeed the sky was now full of aircraft. The noise from so many Astazou turbines made normal conversation impossible and we tried to wave them away. I ran back to my aircraft, which was still buzzing gently next to the hedgerow, and suggested to Wallop Tower that we took our survivor to the RAF hospital at Wroughton. 'No,' I was told. 'Wait for the Boscombe Down Sea King.' Meanwhile, the doctor was giving the pilot some morphine and getting him ready for airlift. We proceeded to lift the groaning patient into a Bofors splint (kept in the baggage compartment of each Gazelle) and secured the fastenings.

At this point it became apparent that some of the helping group were unaware of how to operate this splint, a lightweight piece of hardboard with a myriad of cords and jamming cleats. The sergeant major and I, however, came into our own as the operation of this bit of kit was taught to all our students and was kept in the rear compartment of all our Gazelles. Whilst I was tightening the cords in the region of the pilot's knees, I noticed a strange expression coming over the sergeant major's face. He was not watching what he was doing and he was tightening the top cord tightly under our survivor's nostrils. The noise from nearby helicopters made conversation impossible, so I turned to see what had caught his attention. I saw that he was looking at the nurse's legs as she knelt in her short skirt by the pilot's feet. Dazed, the crewcut pilot seemed not to notice the discomfort to his nostrils, nor the nurse's thighs, and the moment passed. I wondered whether, even in his dazed state, our survivor was surprised at the speed and the magnitude of the helicopter response in the area. Had he realised that he had plunged between an active rotary- and fixed-wing circuit and through a radar approach centreline? I doubted it.

A red, white and blue Sea King from the Royal Aircraft Establishment had collected the first survivor from the area of the CADF and now approached to pick up our man. I ran across the field and marshalled it to touchdown whereupon a man in dark naval trousers and pullover, with white shirt and black tie and wearing a bone dome, jumped out of the cabin door and ran purposefully towards our survivor. When I returned to the group our doctor appeared to be giving the newcomer, who I assumed to be an RN doctor from Boscombe Down, a medical handover. The naval person nodded intently as the medical information was passed to him. When the medical brief was complete he suddenly shouted over the roar of rotors and turbines that he had not understood a word of what the doctor had said. It later transpired that he was not a doctor but merely an RN passenger in the Sea King who appeared thoroughly confused.

We carried the Bofors splint containing our survivor to the Sea King and, with some difficulty, slid him into the cabin where his fellow pilot lay. All that remained was for the doctor and nurse to get into the helicopter. The nurse was propelled in solicitously from the rear by the enterprising Aussie but the doctor was too short and tried to do a chin up on the edge of the cabin floor. With a couple of heaves both doctor and Sea King were away. Walking back to where the bundled parachute lay, I was surprised to meet a storeman from the Quartermaster's department who was completing some paperwork (in triplicate) before taking the survival gear onto his charge for storage.

As we flew back to dispersal the RT at last seemed to have come alive and the Tower was turning away aircraft from neighbouring airfields all of whom seemed determined to offer assistance. It was only when I cycled home and saw the burnt-out wreckage under guard in the field adjacent to my quarter that an onlooker explained to me that it had been an F-18 that had crashed.

There had also sadly been an associated road traffic accident as a serviceman passing by in a Mini had stopped on the nearby main road on witnessing the crash. A fire engine responding to the emergency had accelerated into the back of his vehicle. I also learned that my squadron commander, Louis Parsons, had been in a meeting in the Chief Flying Instructor's office when the jet appeared in the window behind the CFI's desk descending vertically in a nose high attitude. 'Look!' Louis cried, but when Lieutenant Colonel John Drew turned around in his chair the jet had just disappeared from view behind a hangar roof and so the CFI turned back impatiently to continue the meeting as the fireball and column of smoke developed behind him.

It also happened that a visiting officer from MoD Operational Requirements, Colonel S.M.W. Hickey late AAC, was giving a presentation on financial cuts to the Director AAC in the DAAC Headquarters block of portacabins near the Officers' Mess. Mike Hickey's presentation was interrupted by a noise of jet engines, two sharp explosions and the distinctive heavy thud of an aircraft crash. The presentation continued until someone opened the door to the briefing room and breathlessly pronounced that 'an aircraft had crashed behind the Officers' Mess'. When Mike turned to resume his presentation it was to an emptying room and was never completed.[2]

Later we learned that the crew of the aircraft were Mr Jack E. Krings, Director of Flight Operations for McDonnell Douglas, and Lieutenant Colonel Gary Post USMC, the US Navy's Test and Evaluation Centre F-18 Deputy Programme Manager. Fortunately no one was seriously injured in this aircraft accident (although the road traffic accident had caused more serious injuries), which was due to the catastrophic failure of the pre-production low-pressure turbine disc in the right-hand engine during the climb.[3] This had caused an in-flight fire and subsequent loss of control. Two days later, on 10 September 1980, the US Navy grounded their fleet of twelve Hornets whilst the accident investigation was under way. Parts of the turbine disc were discovered in fields near Basingstoke, nineteen miles from the crash site, and a reward was offered to anyone finding the missing segments which, despite an extensive search, were never located. The charred wreckage of the aircraft lay 150 metres from our married quarter which was undamaged with not a single window broken. A few days later, the wreckage and many tons of fuel-contaminated earth were removed and the field returned to its former state. Perhaps the lesson of this tale is that there is a real possibility of one accident snowballing into another due to the ensuing confusion and eagerness to assist. It pays to pause in such circumstances and think carefully what you are doing.

Chapter 13

You Need Eyes in the Back of Your Head

In early 1981 I was informed by Lieutenant Colonel John Drew, the Chief Flying Instructor, that I was to undergo a Lynx conversion course and then take over command of Lynx Conversion Flight at Middle Wallop. The Lynx AH Mk 1 was at that stage a relatively new aircraft and the first twin-engined helicopter to be operated by the Army. The role of Lynx Conversion Flight was to convert, squadron by squadron, Scout and Gazelle pilots to the new TOW-missile-equipped anti-tank helicopter. The course was eight weeks long and consisted of technical ground school and flying. A brand new Lynx Redifon simulator was being installed at Middle Wallop but was at that time not yet operational. My conversion course went according to plan and a week or so after completion I had a further Standards check ride to clear me to instruct (C to I) on Lynx.

However, one aspect worried me. Much time was spent on practising single-engine operations on the Lynx in the event of an engine failure. A double-engine failure was highly unlikely, unless fuel was contaminated or mismanaged, and thus autorotations were practised with a recovery to a hover, but no engine-off landing exercises were permitted. This was eminently sensible as the Lynx was a heavy aircraft with a small diameter rotor, high centre of gravity and the autorotative rate of descent was high. It would have been an unnecessary training risk therefore to practise an extremely unlikely emergency and to risk damage to a particularly expensive aircraft, but I felt uneasy about instructing the exercise if I had not experienced or simulated a Lynx engine-off landing. In the meantime, in the absence of a simulator, I was told that the closest replication would be to conduct some engine-off landings in a heavy Scout on a calm day. Thus the afternoon of 6 October 1981 found me strapping into the right-hand seat of the tough and somewhat agricultural cockpit of Westland Scout AH.1 XP890. Staff Sergeant Séan Bonner was the left-hand seat captain for an hour of engine-off landing practice. I was to be particularly grateful for the Scout's reputation for strength and ruggedness by the end of that afternoon.

YOU NEED EYES IN THE BACK OF YOUR HEAD

The weather that day was grey and dreary with drizzle and about seven kilometres visibility. We were clear of the base of eight/eighths stratus at 700 feet on the Middle Wallop QFE and the wind was light and variable. Middle Wallop was using runway 20, which permitted aircraft to conduct engine-off landings into the engine-off area next to a small copse known to many generations of Wallop aircrew as Knock Wood. Aircraft conducting these exercises flew a tight oblong circuit inside the conventional 700-foot AGL rotary circuit (see Map 02). Up to a hundred helicopters were based at Middle Wallop and the tempo and volume of instruction was such that it was necessary for at least two or three aircraft (and a maximum of six aircraft) to be in the engine-off circuit at any one time, whilst three or four other aircraft might be in the standard circuit. Hundreds of thousands of engine-off landings had been carried out in this 'see and be seen' environment safely over many years and this busy military air traffic zone underlined the importance of airmanship to students at an early stage in their flying training.

We carried out five engine-off landings (EOLs) without incident. Staff Sergeant Bonner demonstrated the first standard 60 knot variable flare technique from 700 feet. Since completing the instructor's course at the Central Flying School, I had always found EOLs a particularly enjoyable flying exercise. Once in autorotation into wind the airspeed was reduced to 60 knots and, when absolutely sure that the helicopter was able to reach the required touchdown area, the instructor closed the throttle. From that moment you were committed to an EOL and there could be no change of mind or overshoot. Whilst not a difficult exercise, there was little room for error in the final stages and the concentration factor for both student and instructor was high. Events in the final 200 feet of an engine-off happened quite quickly. The aircraft was flared from 60 knots at a variable rate in order to achieve about 20 knots at fifteen to twenty feet above the touchdown area. The rate of descent was then checked with an upward movement of the collective, the aircraft levelled with a small forward movement of cyclic and gently cushioned onto the ground with the remaining collective as the rotor revs decayed. Throughout the exercise it was important to keep the aircraft absolutely straight with the yaw pedals. These evolutions were only permitted to be carried out with a QHI as captain of the aircraft and were an important part of flying training.

The Scout had a higher disc loading than a Gazelle and our full fuel load and the calm conditions gave us a high rate of descent and a fast run-on of about 30 knots. After years of engine-offs in the rather thoroughbred but well-behaved Gazelle, the relatively high rate of descent and firm touchdown of the robust Scout was interesting and was a reasonable simulation of what might have been expected with a Lynx. Following Séan's demonstration I carried out a further three engine-off landings from 700 feet onto the wet grass without difficulty. After a low level EOL from 100 feet we decided that I would carry out one final standard variable flare EOL from 700 feet.

Staff Sergeant Bonner took off and flew the Scout in a left-hand climbing turn, levelling out at 700 feet downwind. During the climb we both pointed out a Gazelle and a light blue Bristow Bell 47G-4A on the crosswind leg of the conventional circuit. At the end of our short downwind leg we checked that the base leg and extended base leg were clear. At this point we noticed another Bristow G-4 joining the circuit from what we considered to be a non-standard converging long final. With the G-4 in sight we continued our left turn onto base leg and then to final. As we rolled out onto final and made our radio call, it was apparent that the G-4 intended to also carry out an EOL. At this stage the G-4 was in our 2 o'clock and the horizontal separation between the aircraft was quite normal and safe to continue with us on the left. Two aircraft were stationary on the ground in the engine-off area, to the centre and right of the touchdown area, winding up their engines from ground idle. With both of us having the G-4 in sight, I took control as Séan called 'Practice engine failure'. I entered autorotation and brought the airspeed back to 60 knots, aiming for the grass alongside Knock Wood, instinctively edging away from the G-4 which was still in view and was now in our 2.30 o'clock as we overhauled and descended below him with our much higher rate of descent. It was clear that we were going to safely make the engine-off area and Séan rotated the twist-grip throttle on the collective out of the governed range and into ground idle. As the whine of the Nimbus wound down I glanced again at the G-4, which was still safely separated from us horizontally, and at about 200 feet above ground level I looked ahead to concentrate on the flare. The flare, check and level went according to plan and within a few seconds the Scout touched down on the wet grass at about 30 knots groundspeed. On touchdown I immediately fully lowered the collective lever, which was a Scout technique to shorten the ground run, and looked well ahead at the horizon in order to keep the ground run straight with the tail rotor pedals. After less than a second, and whilst travelling at about 25 knots, there was an almighty bang from behind and the Scout started to shake violently from side to side. At the same time the rotor disk visibly distorted in front of the aircraft and debris began to fly overhead in every direction. Time slowed to many hundreds of frames per second and I well remember the feeling of utter amazement at this unexpected turn of events. What on earth was happening? My first thought was that I must have jerked the cyclic stick rearwards and had chopped off our tail boom, but I confirmed that I was holding the cyclic firmly central, although by now there were considerable feedback forces. The blades started to hit the grass in front of us and the bucking became so severe that I became acutely aware that it was only my five-point harness that was preventing me from being catapulted through the windscreen. During the final stages of our ground run there was a thump like a gas cooker being ignited and a vivid orange glow lit up over my left shoulder. Séan Bonner also came out to the controls with the famous words 'Don't worry', a statement that did little to re-assure me or indeed him.

As our wild ride came to an end the bright orange glow, which I could only assume emanated from our Nimbus engine, appeared to sail over my left shoulder. I remember thinking what a beautiful intense, incandescent colour the orange was. On looking up and to my left I was astounded to see a G-4, inverted, on fire and with its main rotor blades slowed almost stationary, crash upside down in slow-motion 15 metres from us in our 10 o'clock position. I waited until the remains of our rotor blades had thrashed themselves to a stop, released myself from my harness as Séan turned off switches, and ran around the front of the Scout towards the crumpled remains of the G-4, which was burning like a campfire, expecting to have to pull out some bodies. To the relief of both of us, two figures in flying suits rather theatrically crawled out from under the wreckage and brushed themselves down. The taller of the two I immediately recognised as a senior instructor from another service on exchange at Wallop. Pulling off his helmet Matt* exclaimed, 'What a way to end a flying tour!' Further conversation was terminated by the arrival of a fire engine whose crew started shouting at us to get away from the merry blaze from the G-4, which they quickly covered in foam. In our dazed but euphoric state we thought this was all a bit of an overreaction and a senior technician who appeared on the scene, who had little imagination or realisation of the immediate psychological effects of a crash, remarked to the growing crowd of helpers that he thought it was inappropriate for aircrew who had been involved in such a serious incident to be in such a jocular mood.

After a check-up in the Middle Wallop sickbay I was allowed home for a stiff drink and, after a further medical check the next morning, I was back on the flying programme without a scratch. Staff Sergeant Séan Bonner was similarly unscathed whilst the G-4 crew were bruised and stiff for a few days. There had been many witnesses to the crash, most of whom had stopped running towards the wreckage on seeing the fireball. It transpired that our friendly G-4, G-AXKT, was being flown by a Middle Eastern student who was being given an intermediate handling check ride by a staff instructor after only six weeks or so of basic helicopter training. During his autorotation he had drifted towards us and, in the course of the Board of Inquiry interview, the student apparently stated that he had seen the Scout, which was obscured from his instructor's seat, but said nothing as 'what will be, will be'.[1] It was Matt who saved us all. He suddenly saw the flicker of the Scout blade tips appearing from under his yaw pedals during the flare into our rotor head and pulled his collective violently right up to the top stop. Nevertheless our Scout main rotor blades had already chopped the G-4's tubular steel landing skids into neat six-inch sections, hurled them round the engine-off area, chopped into the carburettor of the Lycoming engine, causing the fire, and sliced off the anti-collision light a few inches under the cockpit floor and the crew's feet, before the input from that last heave on the collective lifted the G-4 a few feet off the Scout. With the rotor revs rapidly decaying, the G-4 was then out of control, crashing alongside us almost inverted a few seconds later. It says much for the robustness of the Scout that the four blades absorbed this treatment without breaking the droop stops, which would have allowed our blade roots to enter the cabin and decapitate us both although I doubt we would have known much about it. The remains of our blades chopped partially through our tail, ploughed up some of Wallop's lush grass and severed the main Nimbus drive shaft, whilst the impact and vibration cracked the robust skid posts. Thankfully I have always strapped in tightly and this experience graphically illustrated to me how G forces in an accident can throw the occupants around like rag dolls. I was acutely aware of the immense pressure on my five-point harness for those few seconds. After the student had crawled out of the G-4 he had allegedly been overheard asking his instructor, 'I suppose this means I fail my IHT, yes?' Aircraft accidents always have a cause and clearly this was a case of aircrew error. Aviation Standards Branch apparently referred to this accident as a 'Tri-National, Quadri-Service, Mid-Air, On-the-Ground, Collision'. Reportedly 60 per cent blame was eventually attached to the G-4 captain and 40 per cent to Séan and both of them were to be interviewed by the CFI.[2]

As a result of this accident, the maximum number of aircraft in the engine-off circuit was reduced to four. We had been incredibly lucky. It seems that there have been two other UK service helicopter collisions in autorotation and both of them resulted in fatalities.[3] Ironically, we were

YOU NEED EYES IN THE BACK OF YOUR HEAD

displaying a good lookout prior to this incident but the moral of this story is that the unexpected occurs very quickly in aviation. You must have eyes in the back of your head.

And what of the aircraft? Following the inevitable Board of Inquiry, the wreckage of G-4 G-AXKT was sold as scrap to a local dealer. Scout XP890 had been the twenty-eighth Scout to be built and was delivered in 1963. She appeared in the pages of *Flight* magazine[4] in a pencil drawing by the artist Gordon Horner featuring Army Air Corps training. After the collision Bristow technicians stated that XP890 could be repaired by cannibalising it with components from a time-expired Scout from Northern Ireland which was due to be scrapped. In effect, everything except the main cabin structure was replaced with cannibalised or new parts and a re-born XP890 was test flown by Séan Bonner a few months after the accident. XP890 was then placed in light care and preservation in a storage hangar at RNAY Wroughton until the Falklands conflict when she was readied and sent south as a battle casualty replacement. After the conflict, XP890 was returned to RNAY Wroughton for storage and, as the Scout fleet wore out, became one of various aircraft used to keep the remainder of the fleet going until she was eventually disposed of in Suffolk.[5]

There was a strange afternote to this story. In 1994 Séan Bonner, by then a captain in the Army Air Corps, told me that there had been a number of superstitious stories circulating about XP890. I repeat the story as he passed it on to me.

Apparently the old 1:72nd-scale Airfix plastic model kit of the Scout had included a set of decals for XP890, together with options for XP885 and a Royal Jordanian Air Force Scout. The Scout Flight technicians at Wallop naturally built one of these Airfix models as XP890 and suspended it from the ceiling in their form 700 office. One day, whilst XP890 was out flying, the string broke and the model fell to the floor. Within an hour XP890 had suffered an engine failure and force-landed south of Pepperbox Hill, a few miles south of Salisbury. This in itself was not remarkable but a year later the same thing happened; XP890 in 1:72 scale fell to the floor of the office and within the hour XP890 had an engine failure to the west of Chilbolton. All this happened a long time before our incident but the technicians had long memories. When Bristow helicopters took over the maintenance contract at Middle Wallop many of the same technicians removed their green Army overalls and replaced them with white coats. On the day of our accident, the much-repaired model of XP890 detached from its rotor head and fell to the floor where it smashed. The supervisor told

Séan that his immediate reaction was, 'Whoops, where is XP890?' Within twenty minutes of the model detaching itself from the ceiling, XP890 and G-AXKT were conjoined on the far side of the airfield. I leave you to form your own judgement over this strange tale.

Eighteen years later, in February 1998, during planning for Exercise DESTINED GLORY in Spain, I happened to be passing a shop in El Puerto de Santa Maria where curiously in the window was a pile of dusty old boxes containing plastic model kits. Amongst these were two Airfix 1:72nd-scale Westland Scout kits which I bought on impulse (along with a Fairey Rotodyne – remember Farnborough 1958). On returning home I was disappointed to see that Roy Cross's painting on the front of the model box portrayed Scout XP885 flying over Centurion tanks, spoiling a good story. On closer inspection though I discovered that there were three suggested 1965-era paint schemes printed on the back of the box, two camouflaged Army Air Corps' Scouts and a Royal Jordanian Air Force example. One of the Army Scouts was indeed XP890 with the appropriate decals supplied in the box. The story was still good for the telling.

Chapter 14

Instructing on Lynx

The Lynx was equipped with two Rolls Royce Gem gas-turbine engines and was a far more complex machine with many more emergency actions to learn and some quite complicated potential hydraulic or electrical malfunctions of the Automatic Flight Control System to get to grips with. The target for the servicing rate anticipated in 1976 was about 11.3 to 12.5 man hours per flying hour. By 1985 the figure was seventeen man hours and eventually dropped to fifteen by 1989.[1] In the early days of the Lynx AH.1 there were also reliability problems with the engine oil-pressure transmitters. Because it could not be assumed that it was the transmitter which was faulty, each incident of low or fluctuating oil pressure indication had to be thus treated 'for real' and the engine shut down. This action immediately turned the event into a real, albeit unremarkable, emergency. A single-engine landing was a routine that was taught during the Lynx conversion course, in the simulator and during squadron checks. It was of no great problem when at light weight in a utility-roled aircraft but in 1981, whilst I was OC of Lynx Conversion Flight, the TOW anti-tank-missile system was fitted. This, after all, was the raison d'être of the Army and Royal Marines variant of the aircraft but the UK procurement system had ensured that the aircraft had arrived prior to the weapon system and too late for the Falklands Campaign (where the Scout armed with the elderly but trusted SS.11 wire-guided missile did good service). The TOW launchers and roof-mounted sight, together with eight missile tubes, added about 452 kilogrammes to the aircraft. A single-engine landing in a heavy Lynx AH.1 on a hot day could be eyewatering if the single-engine torque limits were adhered to (I recall single-engine limits of 115 per cent max contingency torque and 166 per cent transient torque). A number of interesting scenarios could be considered; what would the action be like operating from a small deck at sea (the AH.1 did not have a fuel jettison capability)? What to do in the Arctic when deep snow would only permit a gentle run-on landing and, without a good linear reference, re-circulating snow could cause white-out? The eventual introduction of the much more powerful Lynx AH.7 with uprated Gems would do much to alleviate the situation and increased the maximum all up weight of the aircraft from 4,355kg to 4,875kg, but that was still eight years away.

One of the features of the Lynx was the accessory drive, or the ability for number one engine to power the alternators and hydraulics accessories without turning the main rotor. This was achieved by a small actuator on number one engine input freewheel unit which in effect acted as a clutch to the main rotor gearbox. The aircraft was generally started with number one in accessory drive followed by the number two engine (which was always in main drive) which started the rotors. When the rotor RPM was in the flight range number one engine would be brought into main drive also, so that both engines were powering the main rotor. In accessory drive number one engine drove only the accessory gearbox, attached to the main rotor gearbox which powered two alternators and both hydraulic pumps as well as the main gearbox oil pump. There were significant advantages to this; the aircraft systems, flying controls and AFCS could all be checked with the rotors stationary and radios, heating, TANS etc. could be run economically from a single engine without turning the rotors. It was also possible in a hurry to carry out a main drive start with number one engine selected in main drive. There was, however, a necessity for a very careful drill before selecting the small innocent-looking switch in the overhead panel from 'Acc' to 'Main' or vice versa. The check was that both engines were running or both stopped, No. 2 ECL forward and No. 1 ECL back to ground idle (ECLs were Engine Condition Levers, the new term for throttles). Selecting this small switch with the incorrect settings could lead to a very expensive noise and mechanical mess with a million-pound bill. A household equivalent might be driving your new rotary mower over a tree stump. Although there was a series of microswitches incorporated into the ECL quadrant to help prevent an incorrect selection we thankfully never put this to the test. On one occasion flying with an experienced and older flying instructor he reached up to make a 'Main' selection without thinking with No. 1 ECL still forward. Luckily, always nervous of this switch, my hand was there in an instant to stop him. We paused and, embarrassed, he thanked me. There but for the grace of God ….

One of the early Lynx AH.1s issued to BAOR crashed at Hildesheim airfield due to a technical error following maintenance.[2] There was a circular multi-pin plug, with about 76 pins, which connected with the AFCS computer, similar to the multi-pin connector you probably used on your old video recorder but scaled up with many more pins. Reportedly one of the pins had been damaged and distorted so that it made intermittent contact within the plug. The result was that, immediately after take-off, the AFCS pitch channel cut in and out in cycles faster than any pilot could react to. The aircraft hit a nearby hangar and crashed, killing both crew. This was an accident we were all fully aware of in Lynx Conversion Flight and since then I have always been very cautious about multi-pin connectors of any kind and align them with great care when attaching or detaching the plugs.

Just after completing Lynx conversion training (and the collision between the Scout and Bell 47) I began instructing on Lynx Conversion Flight and was due to instruct on one full course before I took over as OC of the flight. Having not, at that stage, flown the Lynx operationally I was well aware of my lack of experience. The Lynx AH Mk 1 was brand new in service and there were still things to learn about some of the more unusual servicing and maintenance procedures. On my fifth instructional sortie, with an experienced student in the right-hand seat, as we hover taxied back over the grass from the touch down point to Lynx dispersal, I pulled back one of the roof-mounted ECLs to simulate a single engine failure. The immediate action was to lower the lever gently and run the aircraft on to the grass keeping within single-engine torque limits, a gentle and undramatic manoeuvre. This is exactly what happened except that, as we gently slid to a halt on the grass, the aircraft started a violent vertical bounce similar to ground resonance. With the controls centred and the aircraft stationary, the bounce died away. Reporting this as I signed in at the '700 office' it was suggested that I had run on too fast on bumpy grass or I had allowed the student to lower the lever too rapidly and suffered a heavy touchdown. It was quite clear that my story was not believed. Two weeks later I was flying the same aircraft, XZ205, at Everleigh Down on Salisbury Plain Training Area, practising single-engine landings with the same student and an experienced air crewman occupying the centre cabin seat. Whilst running the skids onto smoothly mown grass at about 5 knots the same thing happened only more violently. In the front we were both slammed up against our shoulder harness whilst the crewman in the rear hit his helmet hard against the cabin roof. This time I immediately shut the aircraft down. There was no external damage and we waited whilst the REME arrived and recovered the aircraft to Middle Wallop by road. Again, as I walked into the instructors' crew room, I was met by a similar air of disbelief except that in this instance a senior crewman was able to corroborate my story and was insistent that something was awry with the aircraft. Nothing amiss was found. A week or so later a

FLYING LIGHT HELICOPTERS WITH THE ROYAL MARINES

fellow instructor walked into the crewroom, white-faced, after this same aircraft had gone into severe vibrations whilst running-on after he gave his student an engine failure whilst hover taxiing. The aircraft was now partially stripped down and it was eventually discovered that the bar alt collective hold (a height hold on the collective lever which utilised barometric altitude data) had been disabled on this aircraft and a small disconnected servo link was free-cycling, causing independent collective inputs to the rotor head during bumpy run-on landings. The disabled servo link was removed and the problem was solved. I felt relieved and my credibility was restored.

I also gave myself a scare on one of the very first instructional sorties of the conversion course which involved a brief demonstration to the student of the incredible cyclic power of the Lynx semi-rigid rotor head and the importance of monitoring the controls carefully when on the ground. With the collective lever fully down, the cyclic was displaced laterally more than usual and the aircraft was felt to lift one skid before the cyclic was returned to the neutral position. On this occasion I did it too vigorously and the aircraft tipped so far that for a split second I thought it might roll over on dispersal. Thankfully it didn't, I kept my thoughts to myself, and it probably felt worse than it really was, but my student was highly impressed by this demonstration as we clanged back upright on the concrete.

Instructors were required to have a thorough understanding of the aircraft systems and the various potential emergencies which were practised in the air, with the more dramatic events being practised in the simulator. By far the most alarming type of incident was the very rare occasion when one did not understand what was happening. Although I completed many single-engine recoveries in Lynx (most of which were precautionary) only one really shook me. As part of the Lynx conversion course a number of night sorties were conducted, including a night Navex using TANS, the Doppler Tactical Air Navigation System (no NVG was available at that time, except in Northern Ireland). The straightforward route on the night of 16 June 1981 was from Middle Wallop to a turning point near Marlborough to Chew Mendip, Blandford Forum and back to Wallop.

My student had been a fellow flying instructor on Gazelle who was being converted to the new aircraft before being sent to BAOR as a Squadron QHI. It was a clear but utterly black night and we departed Wallop in Lynx AH Mk 1 XZ221 and climbed to 2,000 feet on the QNH. All went well until we were approaching our first turning point at Marlborough when number two engine oil-pressure gauge dropped slightly out of the normal range. It was still within the permitted scale, so I pointed it out to my student. No sooner had I done so than before our eyes the indicator smoothly reduced to a zero reading. The implications were clear; we would have to shut down the engine and conduct a single-engine recovery back to Middle Wallop. Out came the Flight Reference Cards and without further ado I identified the number two engine condition lever, confirmed again that it was number two engine that was the problem, and pulled it back to ground idle before retarding it to 'HP Cock Off'. As I pulled it back there was a muffled bang from behind us as the engine seized. It clearly was a genuine oil pressure failure. I completed the shutdown checks on number two whilst my companion turned through 180 degrees for a direct heading back for Middle Wallop, which was our nearest diversion. In order to keep number one engine torque within limits on a single engine we had reduced our airspeed to 60 knots, our minimum power speed. We could now gently accelerate to about 85 knots and our TANS told us that we would arrive home in twenty minutes time.

No sooner had I put out a PAN call to Middle Wallop and told them of our intentions than I noticed that the level of vibration was increasing markedly in cycles. I looked around the cockpit for any abnormal readings but, except for number two engine readings, which were all indicating zero or dying, everything was normal. Within the space of two or three minutes the vibration level had increased to the point that my student asked me whether this was normal during Lynx single-engine operations. I assured him that it was not normal and began to wonder whether we had two engines in failure. A few minutes later and the instruments were now becoming difficult to read. What I did find alarming was that I really had no idea what was causing this vibration and I began to get a gut feeling that if we did not get the aircraft on the ground quickly this incident might turn into a disaster. Vibration is often associated with tail rotor problems and I next began to rapidly consider whether debris from our seized engine had exited the exhaust duct and struck the tail rotor. Lowering the collective lever or reducing power did not seem to make any difference. The possibility of a worsening tail rotor problem added urgency to our decision. With this in mind I switched on the landing light and started a gradual descent whilst considering a suitable area in which to land. It was still pitch dark but ahead I saw a blacker patch than the surrounding country, devoid of any lights, and I realised we were nearing Salisbury Plain training area. Fortunately, this was home territory to me and I swung gently towards a portion of the black abyss, which I knew was Netheravon Airfield, closed at this time of night. There was going to be no chance of a circuit or low recce with this level of vibration; it was a question of putting the aircraft onto the ground as soon as possible. Fortunately the wind was south-westerly and we were well set up for an approach into the sizeable engine-off area of North Field. A minute later and the landing light picked up newly-mown grass, torque was increased on number one to a momentary peak of about 130 per cent as I raised the collective in order to arrest the rate of descent and we were running along the gently undulating grass surface at 20 knots. As we shut down the number one engine we told Middle Wallop Approach that we were down safely and, as the rotors stopped, we were aware of a dead silence, save for the creaking and cracking of the cooling engine, and a profound sense of relief. We checked the outside of the aircraft with an aircrew torch and found that the starboard side of the aircraft and the tail boom were completely covered and dripping in warm oil. Eventually a Land Rover approached across the dark expanse of grass towards our navigation lights and out stepped an irritated Netheravon Duty Officer who insisted on telling us that the airfield was closed.

The next day XZ221 was recovered to Middle Wallop by road using a 70 Aircraft Workshop's low-loader. Investigation showed that a technician had failed to ensure that the oil dipstick in number two engine had been secured by its ball bearing clip. The pressure of the oil in the engine in flight had thus caused the dipstick to be ejected and had then vented the oil contents overboard through the dipstick pipe. It took twenty minutes flying for the engine oil contents to empty, resulting in engine seizure as I retarded the engine condition lever to ground idle. Oil pressure and temperature indications in the cockpit would remain normal under these circumstances until the point where the oil level was insufficient to serve the oil pumps when suddenly they would react just prior to failure. The subsequent vibration was from another source altogether. There had been a history of a few isolated cases of severe vibration following single-engine shut-down in Lynx. The cause was traced to the two-pinion design of the main rotor gearbox of the initial variants of the Lynx AH.1 but information about these unusual incidents had not been widely distributed and Lynx Conversion Flight was unaware of this possibility. Nine hundred horsepower was suddenly being transmitted through one pinion at one side of the large diameter conformal main gearwheel and, under a combination of circumstances, this uneven loading could occasionally cause distortion and vibration. The teeth loading at the mesh point could also near limits. This rare problem was to be solved by the introduction of a three-pinion main rotor gearbox (MOD 391) throughout the Lynx fleet in which a freewheeling load-sharing gear was added just below the main conformal gear which allowed all three pinions to mesh and which helped to spread any asymmetric loading evenly around the circumference of the conformal gearwheel. My student took this unpleasant experience early on in his conversion course in his stride and the new Lynx simulator, which had just entered service at Middle Wallop, was programmed to simulate this condition in order that we could be better prepared for all eventualities. I never heard of a further occurrence of this symptom.

As part of the deck-landing trials of the Army version of the Lynx on 18 November 1981 I was tasked to fly an AH Mk 1 to RNAS Yeovilton with an Army Test Pilot to pick up a Royal Navy Lynx HAS Mk 2 instructor and fly out to the LPD HMS *Fearless* for deck landings in the Channel. At Yeovilton we had briefings from the Test Pilot and Yeovilton Ops on details for joining the ship then, with me as captain, departed for the Portland sea areas with Lieutenant Andy Ragget RN in the right-hand seat. The Army Lynx skids looked substantial but were manufactured from light tubular alloy and the undercarriage was not as strong as it might have appeared. The Lynx HAS.2 differed markedly from the Army version in that it had a tricycle-wheeled undercarriage designed to absorb the descent rates of flying at sea from a moving deck, together with toed-out and lockable sponson wheels. Having joined the port circuit to the LPD's flight deck, we set up an approach to the number 2 spot on the port side. The conditions were benign and all went well, although I had to check the final collective movement as Navy operators were used to positioning the aircraft over the spot, waiting for the right moment and landing decisively and firmly, allowing the oleos to absorb the impact of up to 2.29 metres/second. However, it was not possible to 'dump' the lever in the AH Mk 1 and the aircraft had to be felt onto the deck, albeit with a firm touchdown, without the benefit of any oleos. Skids are not comfortable on a steel deck and can slide in heavy sea states although we had the option to use 'sub min' or negative pitch to force the aircraft into the deck at up to 20 per cent torque. Later it was realised that sub min pitch fatigued the rotor head, so that its use was restricted to necessary operational reasons. The skidded undercarriage at sea also gave the aircraft handlers a considerable problem in moving five tons of aircraft around a slippery, pitching steel deck. Each squadron was equipped with ML Handlers, battery-powered, hydraulically-operated, motorised jacking trolleys, which were designed to slide under the Lynx, raise it and then move it. The system was designed for moving the aircraft to and from a hangar to dispersal on an airfield. In the Royal Marines we had to adapt them for shipboard use and they would arrive as an underslung load under a Wessex or Sea King or be craned aboard. On deck they took up space, required constant maintenance and anti-corrosion treatment and were difficult to operate in a high sea state. After carrying out five landings we flew back to Yeovilton.

The Lynx had two hydraulic systems, number 1 of which worked all the flying controls and number 2, which worked cyclic and collective pitch but not the yaw pedals. A failure of number 1 system therefore meant that the tail rotor was in manual and quite hard work to move. The cyclic and collective controls had no manual link as the forces would have been too great to move and thus a hydraulic failure required a precautionary landing as soon as possible. There were two bayonet couplings above the cabin roof to enable technicians to connect either hydraulic system to a test rig for maintenance if necessary. On one famous occasion a Lynx based elsewhere flew for about five hours with the number 2 hydraulic system completely disconnected as the bayonet coupling had been left undone after the test rig was removed. The hydraulic system was working fine but not connected to anything. How this was not noticed became a source of much discussion as start-up checks included a physical check of each hydraulic system and the associated control response. It seemed that for a number of sorties either the checks had been omitted or aircrew were seeing what they expected to see. If the number 1 hydraulics had failed in flight during this event there would have been a disaster and possibly also if number 1 system been de-selected on the collective lever for training purposes.

The Lynx simulator, when it was finally up and running at Middle Wallop at a cost of £1.35m, was a huge boon. It was located in a series of three large green steel containers placed between the hangars and although it had first-generation computer visuals showing a night-only view, meant that we could practise all the emergencies, such as AFCS runaways, engine fire and double engine failures that we could not carry out in the real aircraft. All Lynx instructors quickly went through the complete emergency training syllabus in the simulator and from then on every student spent twenty hours of their conversion syllabus in the simulator together with thirty-five hours of flying. Just prior to Christmas 1981, a pair of Lynx-qualified pilots were undergoing an emergency refresher when the voice from the instructor in the outside console came through on the intercom: 'Fire, fire, fire'. The crew quickly did a cockpit check and reported no sign of fire and continued. 'Fire, fire, fire', again from the instructor. 'Confirmed no indications of fire,' from the cockpit. Eventually the penny dropped – it was the simulator that was on fire and not the simulated Lynx aircraft. The green containers were abandoned whilst the fire section put out an electrical fire which placed the simulator out of service for a couple of months. There were a few emergencies that could be selected on the simulator which you would not wish to give to your worst enemy. Main rotor gearbox seizure was one in which the rotors slowed, alternators failed, the aircraft stopped flying and fell out of the sky. Naturally these few terminal events were never shown to the students but occasionally an instructor would ask to experience them. The 'MRGB oil pressure low' caption was of course practised by all students and a safe precautionary landing could be made well before any danger of seizure occurred. Main spool seizure was an interesting emergency which could turn the aircraft upside down if the pilot was not quick enough in de-selecting the correct hydraulic system for the faulty jack.

When practising single-engine work I always kept a close eye on the engine instruments and generally alternated the engine on which I retarded the ECL. In April 1982 I was instructing a student on single-engine failures on Salisbury Plain when I noticed that no. 2 engine oil pressure was occasionally flickering, although safely in the green. I decided to retard that engine and carry out all our single-engine work on no. 1. On the way back at low level I gave the student a simulated single engine failure by again retarding no. 2. Immediately I did so there was a bang and it seized. Without any more ado we carried out a single-engine run-on landing on to a smooth grass field just south of Bulford Camp. Getting out of the aircraft I saw an impressive trail of black smoke still visible behind us marking our low level passage across the Plain where oil ejected from a failed rear bearing had burned in the exhaust section. Back at Wallop for interest I put myself at low level in the simulator and recreated the incident but with the 'good' engine suddenly failing. I seem to remember that if the retarded ECL was slammed forward without delay the situation could just be recovered, but the slightest delay would prove fatal. I was very glad I had not retarded no. 1 for this exercise.

Apart from teaching the TOW (Tube-launched, Optically-tracked, Wire-guided) anti-tank-missile procedures and tactics we were also required to give HELARM (anti-tank helicopter attack engagement) demonstrations to various service visitors. We had a prepared scenario which we briefed and flew as a three-ship tactical formation to creep up to fire positions behind trees near Longbridge Deverill where we could observe and 'engage' targets on a road 3,000 metres to our front. The Hughes TOW missile was then a technological wonder, although now surpassed by superior technology. It might lie inert in its fibre-glass tube for years in storage, apart from occasional electrical built-in test checks, until the firing trigger was pressed and within one and half seconds it came alive. Thermal batteries fired up and produced power, tiny pyrotechnics spun the gyros from a standstill to high speed, compressed gas was readied to actuate the fins and an infrared lamp in the missile's tail was activated. The one-and-a-half-second delay appeared to the Lynx crew to last for an eternity and then the launch motor fired and the missile burst from its tube, the fins unfolded and a four-kilometre thin copper wire, as thick as a human hair, started to unwind from a bobbin, along which guidance signals from the sight were transmitted to the fins. When the missile was about twenty-five feet in front of the launcher, the flight motor ignited propelling the missile to 600mph. The Lynx could then manoeuvre within certain constraints whilst the missile was being guided. After impact with the target the crew operated a wire cutter to sever up to 3,750 metres of copper wire attached to the aircraft. On firing ranges we naturally picked up the wire after our practice was complete as it could pose a danger to wildlife or humans.[3] This could be an interesting exercise especially in deep winter snow in the mountains of Norway.

Probably my least enjoyable time at Middle Wallop was during the Falklands Campaign after I had just taken over Lynx Conversion Flight. The Lynx AH Mk 1 was too new to be deployed, the initial man-hour servicing rate was poor and the TOW anti-tank system, which would have been useful against bunkers, patrol boats and even helicopters, had not yet been fully integrated and delivered. It was therefore natural that the well-proven Scout with its elderly SS.11 wire-guided missile system should have been deployed instead. Nevertheless I was stood-by as a battle casualty replacement for 3 Commando Brigade Air Squadron to fly Gazelle. I packed my kit and, with half the Royal Marines Corps already deployed to the South Atlantic, was desperately keen to join them. The next day, however, I was told to stand down. The Army had apparently told the Department of CGRM in London that I had been trained up to be OC of Lynx Conversion Flight and that there were plenty of other Gazelle pilots available who could deploy south. True this may have been, but it was no consolation to me at the time. The RM Assistant Military Secretary in London, no doubt overworked and harassed, told me to completely forget about the Falklands. Under no circumstances would I be going. I assumed that it would be expected that most RM young officers would be keen to get to the scene of action and thought that his response was unnecessarily negative, but perhaps he was disappointed himself.

INSTRUCTING ON LYNX

A few weeks later I was to hear that, firstly, two RM Gazelles had been shot down by small-arms fire near Port San Carlos, killing Sergeant Andy Evans, Lieutenant Ken Francis and Lance Corporal Brett Giffin. Seven days later the news came that Lieutenant Richard (Dick) Nunn, one of my Gazelle students and the younger brother of Chris Nunn, a former YO batch mate at Lympstone, had been killed when his Scout was shot down by an Argentinian IA-58 Pucará near Darwin on 28 May 1982.[4] I had made it an unwritten rule not to adopt RM students as my own, as I felt it was good for them to be instructed by another arm of the services in order to increase their breadth of experience. However, I did ensure that I flew with all RM students, including Dick, at least once during the course. I wondered at the time whether Dick's relative lack of experience had put him at a disadvantage but when the facts of the engagement became known it seemed that he had done everything right and just happened to be in the wrong place at the wrong time. Nevertheless I found it particularly galling for my ex-students to be fighting a war whilst I instructed and flew close formation in peaceful springtime Hampshire. Another of my personal ex-students, Captain Robin Makeig-Jones RA, whom I had taught throughout Basic Rotary Wing had been attached to 3 Commando Brigade Air Squadron and was awarded a Mention in Despatches. No doubt Jane must have found me pretty difficult to live with during the campaign.

One of the occasional tasks we were given was to convert senior officers onto Lynx in addition to our usual students. As they were not going to be required to fly the aircraft operationally, this consisted of a slightly abbreviated course. As OC I took Brigadier Michael Volkers, an experienced ex-Sioux and Scout pilot, as my student. It was a pleasant six weeks of instructing and one of our final dual trips was mountain flying in Snowdonia. Our usual refuelling stop prior to, and after, the mountain flying sortie was RAE Llanbedr, purely because it was closer to Wallop and less crowded than RAF Valley. Llanbedr at that time operated Jindivik target drones and the occasional radio-controlled Meteor. The en route supplement contained the cryptic note 'pilotless aircraft may be operating in the circuit'. As the Brigadier hover-taxied into the usually empty Llanbedr dispersal in front of the Jindivik hangars we noticed two AAC Scouts shut down with the crews standing by the aircraft. They were not Middle Wallop based aircraft and, as we drew closer, I recognised them as from Netheravon. As we shut down the engines, an officer, whom I vaguely recalled, approached our aircraft shouting 'Fook off you noisy bastards' whilst his fellow crew members looked on, laughing, from a distance. This not very amusing or witty repartee had me in fits of laughter as he clearly had not recognised his AAC Brigadier BAOR at the controls. To my surprise he continued to walk towards us, shouting other engaging expletives such as 'Get back to Wallop, you oily tossers' (the Lynx at that time used to drip quantities of hot oil from the exhaust pipes after shutdown as the scavenge oil drained from the Gem engines. We were issued with red-painted tin cans equipped with wire hooks to secure under the jet pipes to catch it). The Brigadier finished his shut-down checks without saying anything, opened his door, clambered out of the right-hand seat and, turning around, removed his helmet. The captain stopped in his stride mid-sentence and came up to attention mouth agape as the Brigadier calmly said 'Good morning David.*' The captain turned and fled and the Scout crews suddenly became busily occupied, speeded up their turnaround and departed Llanbedr judiciously.

In 1981 a plan was formulated to fly an AAC Lynx around the world in the Silver Jubilee year of the Army Air Corps. A team was set up to do the planning but there were serious complications concerning the leg from Japan to Kamchatka due to political sensitivities about the Kuril Islands. Even if the route was sanctioned, it was understood that there would have to be a minimum requirement of a Russian military observer on board the aircraft. An alternative idea was then proposed that a suitable ship with a flight deck be positioned in the North Pacific for refuelling. This was difficult to guarantee for an unknown date in the future which would anyway depend on progress and weather. Eventually the plan was changed to a more modest but practical flight from UK to New Zealand which would still have represented a 'first'. I was co-opted onto the planning team for the leg from Singapore to Brisbane, Australia. The exciting news was that the planners of each sector were likely to be the crews considered to fly the respective sector. We had access to a planning room with half-million scale tactical pilotage charts covering the Far East. We flight planned each leg with marked track, distances, latitude and longitudes of turning points, safety altitudes and frequencies with the care and motivation natural to those who might be in the cockpit and, as I pored over the charts, I could picture the terrain in my mind's eye. The marked maps were then cut into manageable strips and placed into folders together with the navigation details, TANS cards and frequencies. As far as I can remember our planned route was from Singapore, Jakarta, Surabaya, Bali, Ende, Kupang, Dili, Darwin, Tindal, Tennant Creek, Mount Isa, Winton, Rockhampton, Brisbane. Although the Lynx was to be fitted with long-range tanks, I remember that the leg from Dili to Darwin was the most interesting with little room for error (although a far cry from the margins of the ill-fated New Guinea to Howland Island leg that Amelia Earhart had taken forty-five years earlier). I can remember that we were advised by an Australian Army aviator on no account to overnight at Mount Isa and be sucked in to 'partying' with the miners but instead to refuel, depart the airfield and camp beside the aircraft in the desert en route.

The neat piles of detailed planning information grew like a mountain in the locked room until we heard the disappointing news that the Army Board had allegedly turned down the record flight attempt. We heard that it was considered that there was more to lose than to gain in terms of public relations, especially with the revised and reduced itinerary. It is quite true that with the, then, poor Lynx serviceability rates the expedition would have no doubt been a spares and logistics marathon but 'nothing ventured, nothing gained'. I have since wondered what happened to this large pile of planning material which would have represented months of preparatory work and a valuable asset to anyone planning a similar flight. In August 1982 Australian Dick Smith started out from Texas eastbound on a round the world flight in his Bell 206B Jet Ranger III. He was refused overflying rights by Russia but he solved the Pacific conundrum by using a pre-arranged vessel for refuelling and successfully completed the record-breaking trip in July 1983. It was a great effort and a very well-deserved record.

3 Commando Brigade Air Squadron, back from the Falklands, was at long last moving from the dreadful Coypool to RNAS Yeovilton. Apart from being a major Royal Naval Air Station with over 100 based aircraft including Sea Harriers, Lynx HAS.2, Jetstreams and FRADU Hunters, Yeovilton was also the home of the Sea King Commando Support Helicopter Squadrons, 845 NAS, 846 NAS and their training squadron, 848 NAS. Centred between Plymouth and Portsmouth it was thus an excellent choice for the Squadron.

The Squadron was also handing back their Scouts and re-equipping with Lynx AH.1 and so the Scout aircrew and command team came up to Wallop for Lynx conversion in September 1982. David Minords had just taken over as CO (eighteen months later I was to be his Senior Pilot) and Paul Bancroft, who had been an instructor at Wallop when I went through training, was the Senior Pilot and became my student.

In the early stages of the course, in company with another Lynx, we took the course down to the Commando Training Centre at Lympstone to attend the memorial service for Lieutenant Ken Francis, shot down in the Falklands. After the service we changed out of our blues back into flying kit. Just after taking off from the sports field at CTCRM there was a muffled bang in the roof, the HYD caption illuminated and, to the concern of my passengers, the rear cabin started to fill with pink mist. We quickly did a 180-degree turn and carried out a precautionary running landing on a sports pitch at Lympstone on the no. 2 hydraulic system. A loose hydraulic union was the cause and we were all concerned about our best blue uniforms which were happily protected by plastic covers. It was probably not the best advert for the Lynx so early in their conversion course.

Paul Bancroft, being an experienced Sioux man, had a slight initial difficulty with the 'modern' Lynx heading hold. This required the pilot to take his feet off the pedals in order to engage it and turn a heading knob to adjust the heading by a few degrees. Tail rotor pitch would then yaw the heading slightly to the desired course. Paul would put his feet on the pedals whilst doing this in order to keep the ball in the middle, the micro-switches in the pedals would then disconnect the heading hold and thus render the whole exercise void. When I explained this he said 'but the aircraft will be out of balance in the turn'. True momentarily, but this is how the system worked. Perhaps my magneto embarrassment with him during training had now been laid to rest.

My last seven months of instructing before I went to Staff College were taken up with the additional role of Leader of the Silver Eagles Army display team, which is covered separately, but came on top of the day-to-day instructing role. When I returned to flying in both my future flying appointments as Senior Pilot and then as Commanding Officer of 3 Commando Brigade Air Squadron, I regained my instructor rating as part of my refresher courses and greatly enjoyed the experience of flying with, and checking out, different pilots on both Gazelle and Lynx. There were those who claimed that I would be much too busy to retain competence and currency as an instructor in the Squadron but I never found it difficult and passed my regular standards checks without any problems. I guess if you enjoy instructing, you make time for it and I don't believe that the paperwork suffered – it still got done.

Chapter 15

Display Flying

If flying helicopters seems like a strange disease, helicopter display flying is an even stranger infection. I had two unique opportunities to experience this at first hand during my three-year tour at Middle Wallop. In the spring of 1981, during my second year as an instructor whilst commanding A Flight of the Advanced Rotary Wing, I was asked to be the standby Army solo display pilot on the Gazelle for any air shows or displays that conflicted with any event in which the primary solo pilot was performing. In addition I was tasked to lead the Sparrowhawks, a part-time Gazelle team of ARW instructors who performed at Middle Wallop Army Air Days after the demise of the Blue Eagles. We flew standard ARW Gazelles fitted with cable-operated smoke modifications temporarily attached to the rear port skid post. A team of six aircraft was formed at the beginning of May and after twenty-two training sorties we were ready for our short display on 30 June. This turned out to be an invaluable experience for my task the following year.[1]

To fly a solo display involved learning a routine of one's own design, which lasted about four minutes. Major Louis Parsons of the Scots Dragoon Guards, my squadron commander, was an experienced display pilot having led the Blue Eagles team of six Sioux some years before. After normal flying finished in the evening we would request a fifteen-minute extension to airfield opening hours in order to practise a routine with Louis watching critically from the ground and sometimes flying with me. Display flying requires plain hard work and endless practice, concentrating continuously on accuracy and timings. The aircraft must be positioned in front of the crowd line to show itself off to best advantage throughout the display. It must not be flown too low or it will disappear out of sight of all but the front row of the crowd; the position of the aircraft to the display line must not be affected by the wind and each manoeuvre should flow smoothly into the next. Under no circumstances must the fly line be crossed or the crowd endangered in any way by a manoeuvre. There will be an 'On display' time and an 'Off display' time and timings must be absolutely accurate. What might appear dramatic from the cockpit will appear to be far less dramatic from the ground. A fast jet such as a Lightning or a Phantom, though no doubt difficult to display well, has the ability to impress with sheer speed, power and noise. A light helicopter, however, cannot make a dramatic entrance and must impress by grace, manoeuvrability and the ability to dramatically change speed. By keeping the speed slow the rate of turn can be kept tight and the aircraft display kept right in front of the spectators. Once a helicopter disappears into the distance the crowd will quickly lose interest. The workload during display flying is high as the pilot is operating near to the limitations of the aircraft, sometimes at extreme attitudes, whilst keeping the display centred on the datum. Display flying is no excuse for over-torqueing or exceeding any other aircraft limitation and nor would the Services accept any such deviation.

Many evenings were spent practising under Louis's guidance. One ridiculous incident occurred when I was practising dual with him over an empty Andover airfield. He pointed out as a reference marker some white sheep grazing 1,000 feet below. I, for the life of me, couldn't see any sheep. 'Are you talking about the seagulls?' I eventually asked. 'No, the sheep,' he replied and indicated we might as well call it a day if I couldn't tell the difference. I now can't remember if they really were sheep or seagulls but we laughed about it for years.[2] The Gazelle had a fully articulated rotor head and, although an extremely agile and manoeuvrable helicopter, was not aerobatic. Nevertheless, there were advanced handling manoeuvres which, when well flown, could look impressive. The 'Elphinstone Loop' was such a manoeuvre, perfected earlier by an Army Air Corps sergeant pilot, in which the Gazelle carried out a very steep wingover-type manoeuvre, with bank applied, and which gave the impression to spectators on the ground of a loop. For a few moments the aircraft was partially inverted, but with positive G, so that if correctly flown the pilot did not come up against the straps and his bum remained firmly in his seat. I have memories of mishandling an Elphinstone Loop during early training and becoming suddenly aware of being upside down, the green expanse of Middle Wallop's grass filling the top of the canopy whilst my backside came off the seat pan. I held the controls absolutely central as dust particles fell to the top of the canopy, my shoulders came up against the straps, adrenaline surged and the aircraft recovered itself. Despite Louis saying that it looked good from the ground I never let my speed decay over the top again. I used the same aircraft each time, XZ349, and we checked with our REME Aircraft Workshop as to whether the aircraft's fatigue life was being significantly reduced by the repetition of extreme manoeuvres. The answer was that so long as I flew within the flight envelope it would make a negligible difference. After many weeks of practice I was watched by the Chief Flying Instructor, Lieutenant Colonel Paul Walters, who gave me his authorisation for the solo display routine.

One particular solo display sticks in my mind. On 6 June 1981 I was scheduled to fill a slot in the British Aerospace Open Day at Hawarden in Cheshire. I started off early on a sunny Saturday morning, together with two technicians, a box of tools in the back and six smoke grenades. Flying at the weekends was always a pleasant experience with most military air traffic zones inactive and both the sky and ATC frequencies relatively empty. We flew up to Hawarden via Gloucester and Shrewsbury, arriving at the British Aerospace airfield seventy-five minutes later, just after the Battle of Britain Memorial Flight Hurricane and Spitfire had landed. An airshow briefing then took place, which for all service pilots was a mandatory requirement before display flying, and at which all the participating pilots were present. A 25-knot wind was blowing down the runway, which would not make matters easy. I should explain for the layman that this would mean that while carrying out a 100-knot level turn through 360 degrees, whilst downwind the helicopter's speed over the ground would be 125 knots and at the next moment, whilst turning into wind, the ground speed would be 75 knots. At the same time the central datum of the aircraft's uncorrected turn would be moving downwind over the ground at 25 knots. Thus, if no allowance was made for wind, within a few minutes a display would be taking place outside the airfield. The trick, which took some practice and skill to perfect, was to tighten the angle of bank downwind and use increased power and less bank with manoeuvres into wind in order to remain centred over the same geographic point regardless of the wind velocity.

Whilst the airshow briefing took place the technicians had fitted the smoke grenades, which were initiated by cables leading into the cabin behind the collective pitch lever. When pulled sharply, coloured smoke was initiated from the freefall parachutist's smoke grenades attached to a cradle bolted on the port rear skid post. We watched the Vulcan and the BAe-owned Mosquito perform[3] and then, fifteen minutes before the 'On display' time, the aircraft was manned, a radio check carried out and the aircraft was started up. My short display consisted of a vertical, climbing, take-off whilst spot turning through 180 degrees until I reached 200 feet facing into wind. After transitioning away I climbed to 500 feet and the first smoke was pulled. A wingover was performed to the right followed by a downwind dive to 130 knots (and about 155 knots groundspeed), pulling up at the display datum into an Elphinstone Loop. At the top of the loop the airspeed had decayed to 50 knots whilst the height was about 600 feet above the runway. Diving out of the loop on the original heading, the aircraft was pulled up into a wingover to the right, diving on a reverse heading to an into-wind quick-stop and coming to the hover at 100 feet. After holding the hover for a few seconds the second smoke was pulled and a backwards take-off initiated, climbing to 300 feet and achieving 60 knots rearwards. The aircraft was then pitched vertically nose down and dived to 100 feet above the runway in order to recover the airspeed, followed by a 60-knot, 70-degree, banked turn through 360 degrees. This small display took about four minutes to perform.

Performing after a Vulcan or a Mosquito was a hard act to follow in a light helicopter and any display pilot must show a certain amount of strength of character and be prepared to accept criticism from onlookers. He or she must not be a 'show off' and have the determination to stick to the planned display routine, despite all manner of external pressures. At one particular well-attended display the weather was poor with a low cloud base and drizzle and thus many of the fast jets were unable to display. The organisers pleaded with me to extend the Army display timings by an extra 'five or ten minutes' in order to fill some of the gaps in the programme. Not only would an ad hoc display have looked poorly executed to a critical onlooker but it could have been thoroughly dangerous. This is the point at which the display pilot must have the character to ignore being thought of as a killjoy and stick rigidly to the rehearsed programme. Indeed Service pilots are authorised only to carry out their cleared display format and any extension would have been unauthorised. So I stuck firmly to my four-minute routine whilst the commentator filled in the gaps in the programme as best he could.

A year later I was faced with a very different task. 1982 was the Silver Jubilee of the formation of the Army Air Corps and it was felt that one of the ways in which the year should be marked was to form a special display team. The TOW-armed Lynx AH Mk 1 had only recently entered squadron service and was the natural choice for a display aircraft. It was a very agile aircraft with a semi-rigid rotor head. Twenty years later you could have seen Lynx carrying out aerobatic manoeuvres at air displays but in the early years the aircraft was not cleared for any negative G. The initial Rolls Royce Gem engines, the core of which rotated at about 43,000rpm, were fitted with a number of white-metal bearings and there was a danger that negative G would momentarily interrupt the oil supply to the bearings, which could then fail. All advance handling manoeuvres therefore had to be flown accurately under positive G. It was decided to form a team of six Lynx to be known as 'The Silver Eagles'. Who should lead it? The obvious choice was the OC of Lynx Conversion Flight who at that time was me, the only problem being that I was a Royal Marine and not a member of the British Army. The Army Air Corps, no doubt whilst swallowing hard, 'invited' me to form and lead a team in early March in order to display that summer and particularly at the three days of the Army Air 82 International Airshow at Middle Wallop. This was a fascinating task which we started from scratch. I found four willing volunteers from my instructors but the final man was not so enthusiastic about the commitment. The eventual team was myself as leader, Staff Sergeant Dave Stewart No. 2, Warrant Officer 2 Mal Thwaites No. 3, Staff Sergeant Tony Merrick No. 4, Lieutenant Geoff Young No. 5 and Captain Jim Browne from the simulator as No. 6 and deputy leader. The crewman leader was Warrant Officer 2 Ken Jackson with Staff Sergeant Clint Stimson as his deputy. In order to provide six guaranteed serviceable aircraft at any time I estimated that we would have to have nine airframes available.

It was also desirable for a display aircraft to be able to emit coloured smoke in order to enhance the display. At this stage in the development of the Lynx AH Mk 1 there was no smoke fit. It was, of course, a complicated business to design, test and clear even a simple modification for an aircraft and it was not just a matter of bolting on some Heath-Robinson device. The REME Aircraft Workshop at Middle Wallop designed and manufactured a smoke-holder in record time which attached to the port skid. After a few modifications, it was cleared for use and was initiated by the co-pilot in the left seat leaning back to pull toggles taped to the rear of the centre console. It was vital for safety that there were no loose articles such as grenade pins which might fall from the grenade and foul the tail rotor, let alone hit people on the ground, so we used free-fall parachutists' smoke canisters. Anticipation was required in calling for smoke as there was a delay in the initiation of the canister and a further delay as a volume of smoke built up, thus the call 'Smoke Go' was given twenty seconds before it was required. An early decision was made not to give the aircraft a special paint scheme because, not only would it be expensive, but it would limit the number of aircraft that would be available to us in the event of unserviceability. It was also part of the team ethos that we would be working flying instructors using working instructional aircraft. For this reason we also decided to fly two of the aircraft fitted with TOW missile booms and dummy missiles. The only decorative addition was that the well-known aviation artist Wilf Hardy, whose detailed cutaway diagrams I well-remembered in the centre of my *Eagle* comics at school, was asked to design a logo for the aircraft.[4] He produced a very striking circular Silver Eagles sticker and had a number of giant versions manufactured which were positioned on each side of the nose on the avionic bay access doors and varnished over. If we were required to do a rapid aircraft change and use a spare Middle Wallop airframe, this arrangement enabled us to change the avionic bay doors around to ensure that we always fielded six aircraft carrying the appropriate nose art.

We started training on 18 March by flying in close formation in pairs and then graduated to threes and, eventually, in late April, to a six-ship formation. Our authorised separation was one and a half rotor spans and soon it became second nature to sense exactly that distance. It was important of course that all six pilots had exactly the same opinion of that distance and many more hours were spent in briefing and debriefing than were spent actually flying. We were naturally mindful of the disastrous collision that had occurred to the Royal Navy Sharks display team in Cornwall in 1977 when two aircraft collided in close formation and three crew members were killed.[5]

During these weeks of basic formation practice I was racking my brains to produce a choreography for an original display lasting for between ten and fifteen minutes. There are only so many things that you can do with a helicopter and the display would have to concentrate on the flexibility of speed and manoeuvrability of the Lynx which would call for a mixture of high-speed manoeuvres, hover and low-speed formation flying. The problem with high-speed work was, that in order to gain energy, the aircraft would have to leave the crowd centreline. It was thus necessary to introduce a solo aircraft, which would perform during the gaps whilst the other five were repositioning, to ensure that the display was continuous. The solo aircraft was to be flown by Captain Jim Browne, a highly experienced instructor who would be No. 6 in the formation, performing wing overs, torque turns and Elphinstone Loops. We also did a couple of rehearsals using the Westland Lynx demonstrator G-LYNX as the solo number, flown by Westland's senior test pilot Derek Marpole, an ex-AAC major.[6] It then struck me that it would be novel to have the option of introducing a fixed-wing aircraft as the solo performer and so a de Havilland Canada Beaver was added to the Team. This would be particularly useful if we were an aircraft down due to unserviceability or that Jim Browne was unavailable or

DISPLAY FLYING

unfit to fly. Captain John Ball was co-opted to fly the Beaver, demonstrating short take-offs and landings and its impressive slow-speed manoeuvrability.

Captain John Ball, or 'JB', was an extremely experienced QFI and QHI and commanded the de Havilland Canada Beaver Conversion Flight. His solo slot on the Beaver AL Mk 1 was a masterpiece of short take-offs with high climb-out angle, steep turns at low altitude and slow speed and impossibly short-looking landings. I flew with him during his display routine on two occasions and, like a few very skilful pilots, he handled the aircraft in such a way that as a passenger I found his whole short display comfortable, unhurried and relaxed, whilst from the outside it appeared quite dramatic. The ball was always in the middle, the airspeed nailed to the peg and my bum firmly attached to the centre of the seat pan. John had a story which caused me much amusement. He was tasked to fly an Army General and his wife who lived near Tidworth to some function. Half way through the Beaver take-off run at Middle Wallop he heard a mumbling from just behind him. Glancing rearwards he saw that the General's wife had unclipped the flexible urination tube from the stowage at the side of the pilot's seat, had removed the hinged top cover and, with the device pressed close to her lips, was trying to talk into the stainless-steel cup. John told me he had problems momentarily controlling both his mirth and the aircraft.

Step by step the individual items of the display were practised and then put together. The not so enthusiastic, but utterly reliable and competent, Team member became fully immersed. Each Team member was given a secondary task, such as publicity or liaison with the aircraft technicians. The novelty for our families soon wore off as most summertime evenings and many weekends became committed to either training or displays. My two-year old son became a critical observer of our progress from our garden. My greatest worry was fatigue or carelessness on the part of the aircrew because our practice sessions often began after a hard day of instructing. We tried training in the early morning, but this was unsatisfactory as it involved pre-flighting and spotting the aircraft very early and disrupted many more supporting staff. So long as the sorties were kept short and well-briefed I found that the Team members remained switched-on.

Jim Browne and I took a Lynx to Yarnbury Castle on Salisbury Plain, where there was a grass C-130 strip, to practise our wing-overs and torque turns for our opposition pair manoeuvres. I remember the occasion well because on one of my pull-ups I let the indicated airspeed drop to under 30 knots before applying power, pedal and cyclic to turn to the right. Because of the position of the pitot tube, combined with our extreme attitude of 70-degrees nose up, the airspeed indications at low speed were unreliable. Before I had the opportunity to apply any input, the aircraft whipped violently to the right though 180 or more degrees and the sky in the windscreen was replaced by the green grass of Yarnbury airstrip. I recovered from the manoeuvre and landed, allowing our heartbeats to return to normal and noticed that the AFCS trim indicators were in unusual extreme positions due to the gyros having toppled. From then on I never let the speed drop below an indicated 40 knots before I initiated the wing over/pedal turn manoeuvre.

As we became more involved in the display routine there were many extra 'what if' factors which had to be taken into account. What would happen if an aircraft went unserviceable or had an emergency during the display? What if two aircraft were to go unserviceable during the display? What if the leader's aircraft were to go unserviceable during the display? What if the solo pilot was ill? What if an aircraft suffered radio failure? What if the leader suffered from radio failure? All these circumstances had to be talked through and briefed and some of these circumstances actually occurred at some stage during the season – and one which we had not anticipated.

Publicity for any display team is important and in our case most of the arrangements were handled by Director Army Air Corps Headquarters staff. The team was sponsored by the *Daily Telegraph* and we had a press launch in London at the Honourable Artillery Company cricket pitch off City Road. The National Air Traffic Control Services would not permit us to fly in formation down the Thames helicopter low-level route, so we therefore arrived over the City at one-minute intervals and shut down together as the last aircraft joined the formation on the ground. The noise was impressive, echoing off the high-rise office blocks surrounding the cricket pitch. The *Daily Telegraph* also wanted an article written for their Sunday colour supplement and sent a freelance journalist and writer, Diana Winsor, together with a photographer, Jerry Young, to spend a day with us. I was sceptical about how much a non-aviation journalist could hoist in about a complicated subject over a twelve-hour period. Diana, however, was a most astute observer and noted the answers to all her questions in a little black notebook. We took her formation flying, but did not subject her to the full display routine due to the fact that she was obviously pregnant. The resulting article, entitled 'The Way We Whirr', was entertaining, accurate and reckoned to be good publicity, although we took a measure of stick from our instructor colleagues for being referred to as 'the masters of ice-cold nerve'![7]

DISPLAY FLYING

It was also arranged that the famous air-to-air photographer Arthur Gibson should photograph us both from his special camera-equipped Piper Aztec and from a Gazelle. The Aztec was flown by an ex-RAF friend of his, Harry Lea, and had a special camera position installed in the belly of the aircraft.[8] The two of them knew exactly what the other was thinking and they made a formidable team. Arthur also organised a memorable photographic session with the Red Arrows at RAF Kemble. He had worked with the Red Arrows before and was trusted by them as a professional who knew exactly the image he wanted to capture and thus wasted little time. We flew up to Kemble in the early morning for a briefing with the Reds at which Arthur Gibson produced a small watercolour painting showing the exact photograph he wanted. This was vital because formations of Hawks and Lynx could not fly around at the beck and call of cameramen whilst various ideas were tried out. We took off, followed a few moments later by the Red Arrows, and flew an approach along the Kemble runway extended centreline in Concorde Formation at about seventy-five feet. The Red Arrows planned to overfly us, two hundred feet above us, at 360 knots in Vic trailing smoke, whilst Arthur Gibson photographed the two formations from a hovering Gazelle in front of both formations. After two passes, lasting perhaps ten minutes in all, it was completed and the Red Arrows continued with their display rehearsal and Arthur had another memorable photograph in the bag.[9]

At last, after eight weeks training, the choreography began to come together and I decided on a fourteen-and-a-half-minute display. The final version of the display was as follows:

H - 30 minutes	Start Engines
H - 15 minutes	Take-off
H Hour	On Display
H Hour to H + 02.20	Crossover
H + 02.20 to H + 02.40	Forming
H + 02.40 to H + 05.10	Rotor
H + 05.10 to H + 08.10	Solo slot 1
H + 08.10 to H + 10.20	Formation and 360-degree turn
H + 10.20 to H + 13.20	Solo slot 2
H + 13.20 to H + 14.30	Bomb burst/Elphinstone loop

After take-off, and well away from the display area, the formation split into two sections of three aircraft and positioned about four miles apart on opposite sides of the display datum. With two minutes to 'On Display', the aircraft started running in, each section one and a half miles from the datum, in line astern at 90 knots groundspeed. This start point was both established on the 1:50,000-scale map of the area and programmed in to our Doppler based Tactical Air Navigation System. TANS would also conveniently give us an accurate reading of our ground speed and drift and enabled us to run in at exactly 90 knots groundspeed by referring to the groundspeed and drift indicator (GSDI). At H hour exactly, the leaders of the two sections crossed starboard to starboard approximately 20 metres apart opposite the centre of the crowd line. This gave the impression of a close shave from the crowd's point of view. We then flew a figure-of-eight manoeuvre with each section in tail chase crossing over at the intersection of the eight, much in the way that motorcycle display teams do. The aircraft next formed up in the hover in line abreast facing the crowd. The inside four Lynx formed a square, facing each other, and began to rotate about an imaginary central point and at the same time climbing vertically trailing orange smoke. This was known as 'The Rotor.'[10] Simultaneously, Leader and No. 6 at each end of the line, faced each other and performed climbing backwards take-offs. When 60 knots groundspeed registered on my Doppler groundspeed and drift indicator, I called 'pitch down' and the cyclic was eased forward resulting in a 90-degree vertical pitch down from 400 feet. Jim and I then dived under the four aircraft performing the Rotor manoeuvre, crossed and circled at 120 knots well behind the Rotor to perform opposition wing overs. The Leader, followed by five aircraft, then disappeared off to a flank, joined up in close formation and climbed to 600 feet in a lazy orbit whilst transiting a mile or so behind the display line. This was the period of the first solo slot where Jim Browne would carry out advanced manoeuvres in front of the crowd or, if it was a Beaver display, John Ball would demonstrate ultra-short take-offs and landings. After two minutes, the five-ship formation would appear from the right of the crowd line in Vic formation at 60 knots. Flying in front of the crowd the formation would carry out a 360-degree descending turn whilst changing from Vic to Concorde formation. The slow air speed and the turn kept all five aircraft in front of the crowd whilst at the same time they changed both height and formation. As the formation cleared to the left of the display line it was the cue for the second two-minute solo display slot. I led the five aircraft at low level and accelerating to 120 knots to a point two miles from the front of the crowd-line datum where we ran in towards the crowd in Vic formation at 100 feet. At this point we could see the second solo slot taking place in front of us. At fifteen seconds before pull up, just as either Jim Browne

DISPLAY FLYING

was completing his Elphinstone Loop in front of Leader, or John Ball was climbing away after a steep take-off in the Beaver, smoke was initiated and the formation pulled up in a bomb-burst manoeuvre right in front of the crowd. After the manoeuvre the formation descended in loose formation on the reciprocal heading and cleared the display for the next item on the flying programme.

Whilst we were busy practising, the Falklands War had been fought and won and the troops were on their way home. On 11 July the P&O liner SS *Canberra* was due to arrive in Southampton loaded with returning troops from 3 Commando Brigade Royal Marines. We were asked to fly formation over her at the precise moment she docked. As we ran in, in Concorde formation trailing orange smoke, it was an unforgettable sight to see this beautiful white liner, now streaked with rust stains, her decks crowded with troops and the massive crowds on the dockside. The thirty feet or so between the ship and the dock was festooned with coloured streamers. I must have glanced down for a second but that momentary snapshot is burned into my subconscious. On 21 July we did exactly the same for HMS *Hermes* but out in the Solent as she approached Portsmouth. A Jet Ranger flying above us snapped a picture of us overflying *Hermes*, which was published in the press the next day.

The unexpected did happen. During Middle Wallop Air Day, about a minute after we were cleared to run in, it seemed that a vintage Max Holste Broussard was determined to prolong his display in front of the crowd. The controller asked us to delay for one minute – an impossibility as the two sections of three aircraft approached the datum head-on at a closing speed of 180 knots. There was no alternative but to break off, return to the TANS start point and begin the run in again. Fortunately, very few spectators noticed anything amiss and we arrived on display about three minutes late. At the end of the Air Day the Managing Director of the *Daily Telegraph* and the *Sunday Telegraph*, Mr H.M. Stephen CBE DSO DFC* (1916-2001), came to the flight line and presented each of us with an inscribed tankard. This meant a lot to us as Mr Stephen had been a Battle of Britain fighter ace with twenty-three victories, including eight on one day, with No. 74 (Tiger) Squadron.

On another occasion approaching the hover after the Cross-Over manoeuvre, No. 4 did not flare but continued to fly past the remainder of the formation, wobbling somewhat, and disappeared off display to the left. He had suffered a runaway oscillatory AFCS malfunction and had carried out the correct and safe procedure. At RAF Odiham one aircraft went unserviceable with an engine oil pressure problem as we taxied out for take-off and we slipped into a well-rehearsed five-aircraft formation display routine. At Yeovilton Airdays a local controller, who obviously had not paid attention to the brief, nor to our rehearsal the day before, queried on RT who had cleared a Beaver to take-off in the middle of our display. A few minutes later he asked me whether he could release a Folland Gnat for take-off on the non-active runway during the formation descent. This was a good test of 'Division of Attention' for a formation leader in the middle of a display routine.

We ended on a good note at RAF Finningley where we produced our best display of the season from our point of view; a good time to finish. But there was one postscript. Ever since the SS *Canberra* had arrived back in UK in July she had been undergoing an extensive refit in order to be ready to embark passengers for her next cruise. We were asked to do one final flypast as she left Southampton after her refit on 11 September. It was our very last sortie as the Silver Eagles and, as we ran up Southampton Water, I was formating below and behind Arthur Gibson's Piper Aztec. He pictured the formation from the ventral camera position as we overflew the liner in her brand new paint finish and with her temporary helicopter decks removed. It was an appropriate moment to disband the team.

There is no short cut to producing a display team and it took about forty-five hours of dedicated formation flying per pilot to reach, and then to maintain, an acceptable and safe standard. During the 1982 season we flew a total of forty-one formation sorties. At about £3,000 per hour per aircraft (in 1982 prices) such a display team did not come cheap and this was the only time that the Army Air Corps ever fielded a six-aircraft Lynx display team. It was a tremendous experience but at the end of the season I was relieved that we had achieved an accident- and incident-free season. So I tried to nod and smile when I heard gratuitous but well-meaning advice for the umpteenth time: 'If I had been you I would have introduced a close formation wingover with ... .' Two years was quite enough. In future I would happily be a spectator at air shows with perhaps a little more respect and sympathy for the hard work of the performers.

Chapter 16

Senior Pilot – Arctic Training

After eighteen months at Shrivenham and the Army Staff College at Camberley, I was appointed as Senior Pilot to 3 Commando Brigade Air Squadron RM based at RNAS Yeovilton (HMS *Heron*). At long last, just before the Lynx had entered service with the Royal Marines and after years of studies and options, the Squadron had moved from its entirely inappropriate location at Coypool to a suitable airfield where we were 'lodgers' under the Fleet Air Arm. So I returned to Middle Wallop for Gazelle and Lynx refresher courses and to get a clearance to instruct (C to I) on both aircraft types. Senior Pilot is a purely Naval term for Squadron 2i/c and caused some confusion in the Army where it was thought that it might just refer to the senior of all the pilots. Another common misunderstanding concerned the size of 3 Commando Brigade Air Squadron which, consisting of eighteen aircraft (six Lynx and twelve Gazelles) and 300 personnel, was nearly the size of an Army Air Corps Regiment. This made sense as the RM Squadron was commanded by an RM major (then David Minords) who at that time corresponded to an Army lieutenant colonel. The role of Senior Pilot therefore involved quite a bit of detailed administrative staff work, something not always understood by the Army. On my refresher course, I was somewhat abashed when a one-star AAC officer whom I knew quite well, after enquiring what I was up to, loudly exclaimed to his colleagues in the Officers' Mess ante-room 'Look what the bloody Marines have done – appointed a Camberley graduate to be a senior pilot!' After my enjoyable six weeks refresher training, I flew by RAF C-130 out to Gardermoen in Norway to join the Squadron winter deployment and take over from my predecessor, Paul Bancroft.

During my ground tour a few fundamental changes had taken place. The two-pilot system had been introduced within Army Aviation which meant that the Army Pilots Course now produced P2s, or co-pilots, who did not require the previous level of captaincy and division of attention qualities. After a year or more as a P2, pilots could then attend a separate Aircraft Commander's Course which could qualify them to be captain of an aircraft (P1). It was now unusual for an Army pilot to fly alone and he would be accompanied by a P2, an air gunner or an aircrewman. The Lynx required a minimum of two crew for lookout, torque-matching and to cater for many of the emergencies (although surprisingly single-crew operation was permitted and, on one occasion, I repositioned a Lynx at Middle Wallop solo). The second change was that the Gazelle was being equipped with the Ferranti/Avimo AF532 stabilised observation sight, also called the Gazelle Observation Aid (GOA), which was installed in the roof above the left-hand seat and which precluded passengers sitting in the front.

Each year 3 Commando Brigade Air Squadron were required to fly their Lynx from RNAS Yeovilton to Norway for the annual three-month winter Arctic training period. The smaller Gazelles were usually either flown to Norway in the back of RAF C-130s or freighted by sea. Although the range of the Lynx would just allow a crossing of the North Sea from Scotland to Norway *in extremis*, in peacetime it was not an acceptable option and thus the routeing was from Yeovilton to Manston, across the Channel to the RNLN base at Valkenburg, across Holland to Groningen Eelde, to Nordholz in north-west Germany, to Aalborg in Denmark and across the Skagerrak to landfall in Norway at Skien and thence to our destination at Gardermoen. The outward leg had to be conducted in early January when the weather factor was often atrocious and it was not unusual to be delayed at Valkenburg or Nordholz for a number of days due to freezing fog or icing conditions. Helicopters like to be used and the longer the Lynx were left in the open on dispersal in bad weather, the greater was the likelihood that the aircraft would be unserviceable when eventually started up, leading to even further delays. For this reason we ground-ran the aircraft daily for twenty minutes whilst weathered-in whenever possible. Sometimes minor electrical faults appeared after start-up but as the aircraft warmed up and condensation evaporated the minor glitches usually sorted themselves out.

It was vital on such trips that we travelled light. With five persons up, immersion suits, dinghy, aircraft tool kit, oil, hydraulic fluid, spares back-up and full fuel, there was neither the space nor the payload for anything larger than one grip per person (although in time the Lynx Mk 7 would give us a much improved performance and payload). We were thus ill-equipped to spend much more than a couple of nights in a hotel in the event of being weathered-in without running out of clean clothes. Some crew members became confined to their rooms whilst waiting for laundry to be returned

SENIOR PILOT – ARCTIC TRAINING

or for their hand-washed flying suits to dry. On one occasion in Holland, the hotel in which we were stuck had a very nice indoor swimming pool. On the third day of freezing fog, one of our SNCO pilots offered to go into the nearby town of Leiden to buy us all swimming costumes in order that we might take advantage of the facilities. To my horror he returned with eleven pairs of matching luminous briefs that bordered on being described as thongs. I prefer not to dwell on what the other hotel residents at the poolside must have thought as we all suddenly appeared from the changing rooms similarly attired like something out of the famous scene in 'Village People'.

The crossing of the Skagerrak could be particularly unpleasant as there was usually a marked contrast in the weather between the Danish and Norwegian coasts. Because of the payloads we were flying in the Lynx AH.1 the fuel load did not allow a return to Aalborg from Norway in the event of the Norwegian coastal airfield of Skien being closed in, and thus an important 'go/no-go' decision point was reached about two-thirds of the way across.

Arctic flying was, and is, a specialised skill and each year we put novice pilots through the Arctic theatre qualification, or TQ, whilst the previously qualified pilots did a two-sortie dual Arctic refresher with the QHIs. On my arrival the squadron QHI, Captain Jeff Niblett,[1] took me through a thorough Arctic TQ course at Gardermoen with his usual professionalism. All aircrew also had to undergo annual Arctic survival training (AST) which included an important but uncomfortable night equipped with only what you flew in and the personal survival items in your pockets and survival go-pack. Building a wind-break under a tree, lighting a fire and building a heat reflector from brushwood sounds relatively civilised but no matter how good the fire, it was a cold and sleepless night and the time was best employed by cutting firewood whilst waiting for dawn. It certainly focused the mind on what items to take in your Arctic smock pockets when going flying. We, of course, had a survival pack in the back of each aircraft but it was good training to assume that you might lose it all in a post-crash fire.

There was no radar coverage over central and northern Norway and, as the safety altitude was very high and all cloud was above the freezing level, the first lesson to drive home to new aircrew was to never enter cloud (Instrument Meteorological Conditions or IMC). A Norwegian Air Force Bell UH1 pilot sometimes visited us at Gardermoen to give the aircrew a lecture on Arctic flying. This included a description of an incident where one of his colleagues flying a Norwegian general in winter around the fjords of the Norwegian coast went IMC and started to climb. Well below his safety altitude he found himself climbing on instruments in dense cloud, with no one to talk to on the radio and icing-up fast. The vibration levels built up dramatically and the torque increased to a point at which, even pulling maximum permitted torque, the aircraft started to descend whilst vibrating severely. With his radalt needle flickering between readings differing by thousands of feet as he passed over unseen peaks and valleys in the mountainous terrain, he reduced his airspeed back to the minimum instrument flying speed and prayed. After many long minutes in an enforced descent on instruments he eventually broke out of the low cloud base to find himself 200 feet above a grey sea with the sides of a fjord towering into the clouds on either side of him; a very lucky man and a frightening salutary story which we all absorbed.

Re-circulating snow was also a danger for, as the aircraft approached the hover, especially after recent snow, it would be enveloped by a large cloud of blowing snow, which would cut visibility to zero. During landing and take-off it was imperative to have a good visual reference a few feet from the aircraft, which would show up through the self-induced blizzard. This could be a small fir tree, a rock, a kneeling soldier or a smoke grenade but, if ever the reference disappeared or was lost from view, the pilot would instantly be engulfed by the unpleasant sensation of not knowing whether he was moving forward, sideways or backwards. It is hard to explain the level of disorientation, and the speed with which it can strike, to someone who has not experienced it. The only remedy when enveloped by whiteout during landing was to pull maximum power, to go onto instruments and overshoot, but close to the ground with little or no airspeed was not the best time to start trying to settle down into instrument flying. Loss of visual references at low speed or in the hover would invariably lead to a crash or, at very best, a hard landing.

A similar phenomenon of total disorientation, known as whiteout, could be encountered when flying in a snow-covered bowl in the mountains or when the grey sky merged with a featureless snowfield above the tree line. Again we learned not to enter a bowl without a minimum of two visual references, be they rocks, or people or coloured smoke. Every pilot was shown incipient whiteout on his Arctic conversion course by the instructor retaining a couple of visual cues from the left-hand seat whilst ensuring that the student lost all his cues in the right-hand seat. For someone who has not experienced whiteout it is hard to understand the rapid transition from normal comfortable visual flight to sudden desperate unease.

SENIOR PILOT – ARCTIC TRAINING

In February 1982 the RAF and British Army damaged three helicopters in the space of a few hours at the same location near Voss. One of my fellow students on my Army Pilots course was the last to crash and told me his chilling (in both senses of the word) story. An RAF Puma HC1 of 33 Squadron, had entered a bowl in the mountains to conduct training, experienced sudden whiteout and suffered a heavy landing at low speed causing minor damage. A Gazelle from 2 Flight AAC flew to the site and, having found the Puma and the crew beside it, entered the bowl and managed a challenging landing using smoke. The Gazelle then left to pick up three engineers and, on return, encountered cloud and whiteout conditions on approach and crashed. One of the passengers broke his back and the other occupants were shocked with minor injuries. My colleague flew the last Gazelle, also from 2 Flight, which went to find the two previous missing aircraft.[2] He saw both crews and the wreckage and, fully realising the potential danger involved, carefully planned his approach into the bowl. As he neared the wreckage he must have inadvertently slightly climbed, as the rocks and the damaged aircraft, which he was using as his references, disappeared and he found himself instantly inside a white goldfish bowl. Locking on to his instruments, he commenced a 180-degree turn in order to fly out of the bowl but, when established on the reciprocal heading, was still in IMC knowing that high ground was all around his aircraft. At this stage he had a crewman and passenger who were both convinced that they were about to die which did not help his vital concentration on scan or his morale. Deciding that a crash was probably inevitable, he reduced his speed to minimum on instruments, about 40 knots, ensured the aircraft was level on the attitude indicator, set up a gentle rate of descent and waited for the impact. When it came it was sudden and severe and the aircraft ended up on its side on a slope a few miles from the Puma in deep snow but with the occupants unhurt. A rescue team eventually reached the site on skis. Two of the aircraft were subsequently repaired but Gazelle XW905 was declared a write-off. In February 1990, 2 Flight were to have another multi-aircraft accident when a formation of five aircraft was landing on an icy dispersal at Florø airfield in order to refuel during a transit. The main rotor blades of one Gazelle touched another Gazelle's disc whilst in the hover. XZ348 and XW843 both ended up as Category 5 and flying debris damaged two of the remaining three Gazelles which were close by. Fortunately, no one was hurt. Lest any reader thinks that the above tales are examples of carelessness, the truth is that the Arctic is a very demanding theatre for low-flying helicopters and many of us, however experienced, had unpleasant moments.

FLYING LIGHT HELICOPTERS WITH THE ROYAL MARINES

We flew wearing Arctic military clothing, very similar to that of the Royal Marine rifle companies that we were supporting, but with the addition of cold-weather flying trousers and gloves. The main reason for this was survival. At any time a precautionary landing before last light at temperatures of as low as minus 30 degrees C plunged the crew into an immediate survival situation. We were also soldiers first and aviators second, and were expected to live, operate and fight in the field. The sheer bulk of the Arctic windproof with survival gear in the pockets, snow gaiters and ski-march boots with a Mae West over the top took some getting used to and it was a joy to change into a standard flying suit on return to UK at the end of a deployment.

Everything in the extreme cold became more difficult and more time consuming. Our REME maintainers had a particularly challenging job in the field and aircraft maintenance in these conditions was conducted under a parachute with warm air being blown underneath from a Herman-Nelson heater. This partially inflated the canopy and raised the temperature enough for a technician to take his gloves off and work for perhaps five minutes before warming up. Metals, rubber and plastics become brittle in the cold and great care had to be taken with seals and in avoiding knocking components and fracturing them when working on the engine or gearbox. There was a limitation on both the Lynx and Gazelle of a maximum of minus 30 degrees C cold-soak. We interpreted the cold-soak as when the oil temperature in the main rotor gearbox, at the core of the aircraft, reached minus 30 C. In order to reach this limit the temperature would have to have been either considerably colder than minus 30 or the aircraft would have to be outside for a sustained period at that temperature. This could be avoided by ground-running the aircraft periodically when the temperature was really low, but there was always the danger of a situation in which an aircraft was unserviceable in the field under extreme conditions. During my time in Norway we never had a cold-soaked aircraft but the concern was that the strength and flexibility of the metallic structure that the designers had calculated for the aircraft would have changed and the whole aircraft would have to be slowly warmed before it could be used. Whenever we shut down an aircraft in the field we lost no time in throwing heavy, oil-stained, quilted covers over the engines and gearbox, fleece covers over the forward fuselage and cockpit, and sleeves over each main rotor blade, which we secured with straps to prevent any build-up of snow and ice.

The cold dense air and the stiffening of rubber seals also meant that manual control forces increased in low temperatures. In the Gazelle, where manual flying was a requirement in the event of hydraulic failure, the feedback forces in manual were carefully checked as part of the post start-up checks. The significant increase in force required to move the cyclic and pedals was clearly evident, especially between minus 10 and minus 30 degrees C, and this became a limiting factor in extreme temperatures which might require both crew on the controls in order to reach a safe landing site with a hydraulic failure. Single-engine operations on Lynx also posed difficulties in the field as a linear reference, such as a line of fence posts or a runway, was required in order to achieve a safe run-on landing in re-circulating snow and the collective lever had to be handled with care to prevent the skid-mounted snowshoes digging in during the run-on. In the likely event of there being only solitary random reference points available in the field, I decided that the best course of action would be a zero-speed landing accepting that an over-torque might be necessary on the good engine to cushion the touchdown.

The discomfort of Arctic flying was compensated by some wonderful scenery and phenomena. On some days the air was full of frozen ice particles, a million gleaming diamonds suspended in the clear air. In certain atmospheric conditions the low pressure induced above the main rotor blades caused ice fog to form round the rotor blades when hovering and the aircraft began to produce its own little cloud. On the rare instances this occurred it was a tactical dead give-away for reconnaissance or anti-tank helicopters trying to occupy a covert recce position. When landing in the snowfields above the tree line the wind caused fresh snow to blow along the frozen surface so that, when approaching the hover, the whole terrain appeared to be on the move. In the Rondane Mountains, where most of the peaks were rounded and gave the appearance of an undulating white iced Christmas cake, this effect was particularly pronounced. Once firmly landed on the snow it was a strange experience to see the whole surface apparently blowing past the aircraft at 30 knots. This could be disorientating when landing and taking off and a smoke grenade or rock was sometimes required to provide a visual reference and to anchor one's orientation. At night the ambient light levels could be so good that, with experience, snow landings could be made without landing lights or NVG and trees and rocks produced their own 'moonshadow'.[3]

Frozen lakes provided excellent landing points because they were flat and free from obstructions, so long as you landed close to the edge or used smoke, so as to retain a visual reference. Away from the edges all references were lost on the flat snow-covered ice and spatial disorientation would occur very rapidly. The lakes were usually well frozen but occasionally there could be an air gap under the ice or thinner ice caused by running water, especially if the far end of the lake was dammed for hydro-electric power. On one occasion I gave myself a fright when I landed a Lynx on a small lake surrounded by pine trees near Steinsjoen in southern Norway. I fully lowered the lever and tramped the pedals, yawing the aircraft slightly to allow the snowshoes attached to the skids to bed properly into the deep snow prior to shutting down. However, as I climbed out of the aircraft, belly-deep in the snow, it gave a sudden lurch, groaned and started to settle tail down. I had visions of achieving unwanted fame as a £6 million aircraft disappeared backwards into the lake, so I scrambled back into the cockpit and started up the aircraft in record time as the aircraft continued to slowly tilt backwards and the tail rotor got ever closer to the snow. I lifted into the hover just before the attitude indicator showed that the nose-up slope limits were reached, with the tail rotor tips inches from the surface of the snow, and moved to another location on firmer dry land as my heart rate returned to normal.

The standard issue smoke grenade, when dropped from a helicopter, was apt to disappear under the surface of the snow leaving only a momentary thin trail of smoke and a tiny stain on the surface crust which was barely sufficient for a reference. In 1984 we asked HQ Army Air Corps for an improved Arctic smoke grenade. To my surprise the response was rapid and we were called to a meeting at Middle Wallop just prior to Winter Deployment 1985 to be shown a larger smoke grenade, similar to those used by free-fall parachute display teams, with a set of folded cardboard vanes strapped to the grenade body by means of a heavy-duty plastic cable-tie. When thrown from the aircraft the red-and-white candy-striped vanes deployed in the slipstream, allowing the grenade to rotate down at a reduced rate of descent in the manner of a sycamore leaf. The smoke also burned for longer, and was ejected more fiercely and densely than the standard grenade. Industry really performed well on our behalf and a few weeks later we received 400 of these grenades for trials during the Winter Deployment. Like any good idea it was very simple, with the grenade lever being attached to the grenade body by a short length of nylon fishing line so that there were no loose articles that could fly off into the tail rotor. During the deployment we trialled the grenades on every training sortie, filling in a report form which I devised for each drop and found that they performed excellently. The deployed cardboard vanes and the reduced impact velocity meant that the grenade stayed on the surface crust of the snow, supported by the candy-striped vanes, and produced a distinct stain on the surface in addition to the smoke. If dropped at altitude, they produced a sky trail of smoke, ideal as a marker for fixed-wing close air support. There was an added survival benefit as it was coincidently discovered that, if the grenade was initiated and a lighter applied to where the smoke emitted from the base of the grenade, an effect similar to that of a small blowtorch was produced for a minute with very little smoke which was an ideal fire-lighter in an emergency situation. On the final amphibious exercise up north, as an unofficial adjunct to the trial, I dropped a grenade in the cold, grey, choppy ocean off Harstad and found the stain on the surface could be used as a marker for a short period or even as a hover reference over the sea. On return to UK we forwarded the completed grenade reports to HQ Army Air Corps with a covering letter stating that in our view it was an excellent piece of kit and recommending further production. In line with the convoluted and strange procedures with which UK military equipment was procured, we heard nothing more and this model of grenade was, to my knowledge, never again produced. It was simple, cheap and effective but maybe some staff officer wanted to improve the specification or design in some way, thus inadvertently delaying the process which eventually died, thus ensuring that the guys at the front line were stuck in the Arctic with the ineffective 83 Grenade; 'the perfect is the enemy of the good'.

In much of Norway the only air traffic communication we had at low level was by relaying through SAS and Braathens SAFE airliners as they passed overhead at high altitude. This provided an invaluable service, especially if one of our aircraft was overdue or was required to make a precautionary landing due to bad weather or unserviceability. A routine landing in the wilderness just before dark after, for example, a fuel filter warning caption, plunged the crew into an immediate survival situation. With the Arctic survival and infantry training all our crews had undergone and the survival equipment always carried in the aircraft, a night or two in the field was not a problem so long as there were no injuries but it was imperative to pass word to Oslo Centre before a major search and rescue operation was launched, which was the immediate action when an aircraft had not been heard from for over an hour. A high-flying DC-9 would relay the message from the downed aircraft to Oslo Control who would in turn ring up our Squadron operations room and pass on the message. This allayed our fears and enabled planning for a replacement part and technicians to be flown out the next day, whilst the crew set up their two-man tent, sleeping bags with Gore-Tex liners, started their naphtha burners and tucked into a 5,000-calorie twenty-four-hour Arctic ration pack.

Mike Gaines, the then Defence Editor of *Flight International* magazine, had expressed a wish to write an article on RM Arctic flying and it was arranged that he and *Flight* photographer and ex-Wren, Janice Lowe, would join us for a week during the 1986 winter deployment. The plan was that they should spend four days with us at Gardermoen and then fly by RAF C-130 with me to visit the three Gazelle strong detachment of A Flight at Evenes, well above the Arctic Circle. All went well at Gardermoen with Mike and Janice experiencing snow landings, night flying and a Lynx Helarm sortie in temperatures of minus 15 degrees C. They both spent a night in the field with our aircrew on survival training and joined in the skiing and a degree of discomfort with good humour. When we arrived at Evenes the weather was much colder; my log book shows minus 28 degrees C. Up at Evenes on the edge of Narvik Fjord, the sun does not appear at all until 7 January. On 20 January sunrise is at 1010 and sunset at 1354 so the location was particularly suitable for plenty of night flying. We enjoyed flying them up Narvik Fjord pointing out the remains of three German destroyers sunk by the Royal Navy in 1940.[4] The wrecked *Z2 Georg Thiele* and *Z19 Hermann Künne* lay alongside the shoreline on the north of the Ofotfjorden. Farther east and near to the Swedish border in Rombaksfjord the *Z11 Bernd von Arnim* lay with her sharp bow angled impressively skywards.

On 23 January Captain Mark Noble and I flew the *Flight* team up to Bardufoss on a clear, cold, day and, en route, a strange incident occurred. There was a danger area between Evenes and Bardufoss, Vågsfjorden D462, which was a military firing range extending from ground level to Flight Level 210, which we planned to pass clear to the east at 3,000 feet. Passing about seven miles to the east we suddenly saw a light twin aircraft against the blue sky on an opposing heading, about 500 or 600 feet above us and it passed safely overhead. Apart from pointing the aircraft out in our twelve o'clock, this was unremarkable but, about forty seconds, later a rapidly approaching moving object ahead and below us caught my eye against the snow. A streamlined dark rocket shape was approaching us at what appeared to be at high closing speed but would clearly pass well beneath us. All this occurred in a flash and, as I opened my mouth, Mike Gaines called over the intercom from the back 'missile!' That was certainly what it looked like and in an instant it had passed beneath us and slightly to our port. It took another second or so before the penny finally dropped and we realised that the Cessna must have been towing a target for anti-aircraft guns or missiles on the range. We quickly double-checked our position and confirmed we were outside the range boundary. A Rushton-type target might be towed 5,000 to 6,000 metres behind the aircraft on a thin steel cable and would inevitably be much lower than the tug. We filed an air-miss on the radio as soon as we were in contact with Bardufoss Approach and on landing we discovered that a civil Cessna 310R was indeed on contract to the Norwegian Ministry of Defence to act as a target tug for the range.[5] Presumably the Cessna never saw us or he would not have flown over the top of our Gazelle. I filled in the appropriate paperwork in the Tower after landing but it was not straightforward as we had not had an air miss with the Cessna but possibly with an unidentified object some distance behind it and it was difficult to judge distance and speed as we were uncertain as to the size of the target. What shook me somewhat after the event was how close we must have come to having a steel cable dragged through our rotor disc which would have had instantaneous and catastrophic results. I kept this uncomfortable thought to myself. Our refuelling stop at Bardufoss was a good illustration for Mike and Janice of really low Arctic temperatures with a breeze taking the wind chill well below minus 35 degrees C. Even losing a glove at those temperatures becomes a serious matter. The squadron had enjoyed Mike's dry sense of humour and his article, 'Royal Marines' Arctic Machines', was published in *Flight International* in March 1986.[6]

About twenty-four miles north-east of Bardufoss there was an unusual valley, Markenesdalen, nicknamed 'Death Valley', through which it was interesting for an experienced crew to fly on a good clear winter night. Entering the straight, wide, U-shaped valley from Balsfjord you flew for five miles over gently rising ground with what looked like a white wall of snow-covered mountain blocking the path ahead. In fact the valley made an 80-degree turn to the right at about 1,200 feet above mean sea level and then gently fell away. The valley was just under a mile wide but, as the white wall approached, a feeling of extreme unease crept over one. It was difficult to judge how far away it was and incipient whiteout began to raise its ugly head, so it was important to keep two or more visual references in sight and also to fly on instruments. Just as the impulse to turn away from the solid white wall became overwhelming, suddenly the valley opened out to the right and turning and flying down the slowly descending terrain the mind returned instantly to normal, wondering what all the fuss had been about.

Major Richard Balkwill RA and his wife Liz had been good friends of ours at Staff College and Richard and I were in the same syndicate for one term. After graduation Richard went to a staff job in Hong Kong whilst I went to be Senior Pilot. During the Winter Deployment of 1985 I was shocked to hear that Richard had been killed whilst a passenger in a Scout. The aircraft had lifted off from a hilltop pad at Crest Hill, Sheung Shui, with three passengers, sank after take-off, crashed and rolled over on the slope. Richard was thrown out but ended up under the Scout. The other three were injured.[7]

Chapter 17

Senior Pilot – The Mountains

I have already described an experience in Snowdonia, during my advanced rotary-wing training on the Sioux, that impressed on me the importance of leaving a good escape route for the aircraft in mountains in case of running out of power or of being trapped by deteriorating weather. Mountain flying in helicopters has its own dangers and peculiarities which must be carefully practised if disaster is to be averted. As we gain altitude the air thins and thus provides less lift. The collective pitch angle has to be increased slightly with each gain of altitude in order to maintain straight and level flight. As the pitch increases the engine torque must increase to maintain rotor revs. Eventually we reach a stage where either the angle of attack of the retreating blade is so great that it stalls (retreating blade stall) or we reach the engine torque limits in order to maintain the rotor rpm. If we ignore these limits the rotor revs will start to decay (overpitching) with potentially disastrous results unless the lever is quickly lowered (causing loss of altitude) in order to regain rpm.

If the pilot took no action, the revs could decay beyond a certain point where the drag is so great that they cannot be recovered, the rate of descent would become uncontrollable, the rotor blades would lose their centrifugal rigidity and eventually fail. However, helicopter training is such that a military pilot would be as likely to sit back and allow this to happen as to place his hand in a fire. Torque and airspeed limits were treated with great respect.

Additionally, there are the erratic winds that are normally present when air is squeezed between mountains and troposphere. Winds increase, gust and decrease in seconds and reverse direction within a few metres. Slopes and ridges produce up-drafting and down-drafting air currents that can exceed the maximum rate of climb of the aircraft and turbulence in this environment can be severe. Cloud can form quickly in these conditions, suddenly closing off what was a clear valley or reducing the cloud base in a narrow valley. Hand-in-hand with a change in cloud base a change in the freezing level can occur, suddenly producing dangerous freezing rain which destroys the aerodynamic profile of the blades and coats the windscreen. Psychological effects of slope play tricks on the mind. Flying low level up a valley in what appears to be level flight, it can be disconcerting to glance inside the cockpit to see the rate of climb indicator showing perhaps 700 feet per minute and the airspeed gradually decaying. It is extremely testing to fly at 60 knots around a bowl at a constant altitude above sea level. Without careful reference to the instruments the aircraft's altitude would vary crazily as the eyes and brain try to translate the contours of the slopes into a horizon line. All these effects can lead to tension and over-controlling with a vice-like grip on the controls, yet another way to diminish valuable rotor thrust. In summary, the mountain environment does everything it can to degrade the helicopter's performance.

Like everything else good training can diminish these risks, teach the pilot how to respond to different challenges and how to escape potential traps. This leads to greater confidence but it must be said that a degree of trepidation and adrenaline is healthy in mountain flying. Overconfidence in this environment is a real danger. Since one of 3 Commando Brigade Air Squadron's key operational roles was support of the UK Mountain and Arctic Warfare Brigade earmarked for Northern Norway, this was something we clearly needed to practise regularly. Thus in November each year the Squadron deployed to the *Aviation légère de l'armée de terre* (ALAT, or French Army Air Corps) *Centre de vol en Montagne* in the Pyrenees near Saillagouse in south-western France. This small grass airfield was situated right on the border with Spain and 200 metres from the northern airfield perimeter was a tiny island of Spanish territory, three-and-a-half by one-and-a-half miles, named Llívia, a strange hangover from the 1659 Treaty of the Pyrenees, which was Spanish territory and airspace which had to be avoided. The advantage of using Saillagouse was that it offered 'high density altitude', that is a combination of high altitude mountains up to 9,600 feet (less dense air) and unusually high temperatures (less dense than cold air). The combination of the two made the 'density altitude' artificially even higher than 9,600 feet depending on the actual temperature. In the term 'High Density Altitude', the word 'high' refers to the density-altitude, not to the density (which is low). The logic of this training was 'train hard; fight easy' in that when we deployed to the mountains of Norway every winter for three months, the extreme low temperatures meant denser air and thus the mountain flying would be theoretically easier (although there were separate Arctic-related problems to be tackled).

FLYING LIGHT HELICOPTERS WITH THE ROYAL MARINES

The aircraft self-deployed to Saillagouse from RNAS Yeovilton in what was usually a 600nm one-day trip via Cherbourg, Nantes, la Rochelle, Toulouse to Saillagouse. Once at Saillagouse, every pilot went through a mountain flying course, starting with a briefing on density altitude, the use of performance graphs and techniques followed by a number of dual sorties with an instructor, succeeded by solo trips practising skills and confidence building. Next to the hangar were a few single-storey buildings consisting of briefing rooms, offices, galley and two accommodation blocks. The food was very rustic French, delicious to some of us, but we had to request no horse steaks and tripe and that the *vin ordinaire* be delayed until suppertime and after night flying. Outside the hangar was a tarmac dispersal, leading through security gates to the grass airfield and a small control tower on stilts.

Flying a helicopter at high altitude felt slightly like balancing a bicycle whilst pedalling through an obstacle course at a progressively slower speed. As altitude increased the flight envelope became smaller, reducing both the maximum speed of the aircraft and the angle of bank due to the dangers of retreating blade stall on the retreating blade and compressibility at the tip of the advancing blade. The 'bug' on the torque meter had to be adjusted for both altitude and temperature, giving a corrected and more restrictive torque limit. But it was when flying into a valley in high mountains that the crew truly appreciated the strength of nature. The helicopter became a mere toy which could be tossed about at whim. It was not unusual to be in autorotation but still climbing in up-drafting air and, conversely, at 100 per cent torque and descending in a down-draft. The trick was to use the air currents to the pilot's advantage and to always have a clear escape route. This meant never crossing a ridge at right angles but obliquely, so that it was possible to turn away to the valley floor in severe down-drafts. Transits down valleys were flown half-way up one shoulder, leaving room for a 180-degree turn if necessary. Approaches to landing sites were normally flown in gradually descending orbits whilst checking the surface, the slope and the surrounds of the intended touchdown point as well as the wind and turbulence. The altitude and outside air temperature were noted and entered against the current weight of the aircraft on the performance graph on the pilot's kneepad. This gave the crew the correct 'density altitude' and calculation as to whether the aircraft had 'hover out of ground effect' (HOGE) capability. For mountain operations HOGE plus 10 per cent was required, the extra 10 per cent being required to give a reasonable rate of climb in the event of an abandoned landing or for take-off. Turbulence, over-controlling or down-drafts would eat into the available performance, leaving an aircraft without the power to maintain a hover or to land safely if not carefully flown. In the event that the performance calculation did not permit landing, the options were to wait until more fuel had been burned off, return to lower ground and drop off a passenger or stores, or choose a landing point at a lower altitude. After the initial landing reconnaissance had been made a smoke grenade was dropped by the non-handling pilot in order to assess wind direction and speed. The approach was made with an eye to an escape route and ensuring that the angle of approach was above the 'demarcation line', the invisible interface between smooth up-drafting air and the turbulent eddies and downdrafts created by the ridge.

Landings in bowls were also made cautiously, only entering when an acceptable wind was blowing into the bowl (also called cirque, corrie or cwm). The initial flight into the bowl was thus made downwind, hugging one side of the valley, knowing that a 180-degree turn across the valley would put the aircraft back into wind. It went without saying that the pilot would continually assess whether the valley was wide enough for this turn and avoided entering a blind alley with no room to turn around. By flying orbits, a little lower each time, the pilot could decide whether it was safe to land and, after dropping smoke, touch down facing downhill and out of the bowl. Whilst flying in Snowdonia on a wet and blustery day in a Gazelle at CFS (H) we flew downwind into a turbulent bowl near Carnedd Llewelyn at very low level, passing a group of wet, bedraggled hikers who waved. My RAF instructor, Greg Potter, remarked 'they must be mad', to which I replied 'not as mad as us' which seemed to amuse him.

Pinnacles were approached carefully in the same cautious manner, keeping above the demarcation line and planning where to place the skids, whilst ensuring that the tail rotor would be well clear of any rocks and that the rotor disc would be clear of any rising ground.

The commandant at *Centre de vol en montagne* was a major of the French Army Air Corps (ALAT) who was in charge of a small staff to administer the squadrons who rotated through his airfield for training. He was an experienced instructor pilot on Alouette and Puma and asked whether I would take him for a sortie in a Lynx. He could not speak English and I had schoolboy French, but we could easily make ourselves understood. It was agreed that I would put him in the right seat and we would start the sortie with some hovering, take-offs and landings followed by circuits at Ste Léocadie. If all went well the second half of the sortie would be a few gentle ridge landings on the nearest and least demanding of the various local training areas, all of which he knew like the back of his hand. He proved to be, as expected, competent in the circuit on the Lynx and so, in gentle wind conditions, I showed him a landing on a ridge line at about 7,000 feet. He then came on to the controls and set himself up for an approach at the correct oblique angle to the ridgeline. As we descended to the critical area, approaching the touch-down point, losing translational lift and beginning to need increasing power, we came into an area of moderate turbulence. The aircraft suddenly pitched nose up and yawed to the right. At the same time the major yelled, or should I say uttered a strangled scream, and I, discreetly following through on cyclic, collective and pedals, instantly took control. In a split second we had flicked through 180 degrees to the right and, as ever concerned about the tail rotor, I pitched the nose down, pointing towards the 4,000-foot abyss below us and away from the ridge now behind us. We dived away to gain airspeed but the aircraft responded clumsily. A further second and, as we recovered to a wallowing 60 knots straight and level and reduced the torque, I realised instantly what had happened. Tense and over-controlling when we hit turbulence, the major had inadvertently disconnected the AFCS (automatic flight control system) on his cyclic grip with his third finger. At low airspeed, high altitude, in turbulence and with a high torque setting, now without stabilisation, the aircraft took the bit between its teeth. It took a few seconds to re-engage the AFCS and I then flew a second approach and landing, so as not to end the sortie on a bad note, then let him fly the descent and landing back at Ste Léocadie. Throughout our experienced crewman in the back acted as if nothing untoward had happened. An over-torque check back at base confirmed that there was no damage (except to my professional pride and the embarrassment of the major) and it was a good lesson that, regardless of experience, the mountains are not an environment to give a flying lesson to someone who is not qualified on type. Had I not been closely monitoring the controls the sortie might have ended disastrously.

A few miles from Saillagouse was the French base known as CNEC (*Centre national d'entraînement commando*) located at Mont-Louis in an impressive old Vauban fortress at the top of the mountain pass. Troops from *les paras* and the French Marines attended a commando course there with an amphibious phase at the nearby coastal fortress of Collioure. On each deployment, we were invited to visit Mont-Louis to try out their assault course arranged around the medieval castle walls. There were four or five levels of expertise and the highest levels, which I think were red and black for instructors, involved some seriously high obstacles with small footholds and jumping points cemented in to the outside of the walls. One of the most interesting of the hurdles was a large telegraph pole standing seven or eight feet away from the castle wall with its base in the moat below. The aim was to run and jump from the ramparts onto the telegraph pole and then slide down gripping with hands and knees. Because it was a long drop and the telegraph pole looked smooth and slippery this all looked highly dodgy. In fact we all jumped outwards with so much determination that we banged hard against the pole and stuck there, hanging like leeches, until knees and arms were relaxed slightly, allowing a gentle slide down sixty feet to the bottom of the castle moat. It was said that the students on these courses were never given a training programme but paraded early each day prepared for whatever fate might decree. It might be a 'left-turn double-march' for an hour at the gym or a 'right-turn double-march' for a five-day field exercise living in the mountains.

Naturally French was the language at CVM and it was important that we made an effort to converse in the host nation's language. Our Franglais did occasionally lead to some famous brief misunderstandings. During lunch with the Commandant and his staff our CO, David Minords, in his fluent French, recently honed by some home tuition and a short exchange in Verdun, mentioned that he considered that Perpignan was the 'salad bowl' of France. There was a sudden stony silence and knives and forks froze in mid-air. It turned out that he had used the pronunciation *'salaud'* and his comment had been received as 'Perpignan was the bastard of France'.

The plump horses grazing in the nearby fields were eaten locally and if you preferred not to eat a horse steak it was important to ask for *'le bifteck'* rather than just steak in a local restaurant. There happened to be a few rare wild European brown bears (l'ourse) in this area of the Pyrenees and we were asked to fill in a special report form if we sighted one. At dinner someone, making a brave attempt with his poor French, mentioned that he preferred not to eat the local *'ourse'*, instead of using the word *'cheval'*. His statement caused some perplexed glances to be exchanged between our French Army colleagues.

A one-star officer, at the end of his visit with us, paid a call to the Commandant of CVM and signed the visitors' book with a small French flourish. The Commandant glanced at the entry, snorted and, with a 'Non, non, non', corrected, in red pen, the words the Brigadier had just written attempting to say how much he appreciated his visit. For a moment it looked as if the Brigadier would flatten him.

In the evening I often used to run at Saillagouse and on one occasion opted to run up a lane leading into the southern mountains. The run started at 4,300 feet above sea level and stretched uphill through a tiny village into fields, then scrub and, eventually, the tree line before petering out in the woods at 5,000 feet after about two miles of steady climb. I sat down amongst bushes at the edge of the woods to take a breather before starting the descent, taking in the marvellous view of the Cerdagne valley stretching away to Andorra before me. I suddenly became aware of the sound of breaking branches and twigs from something approaching fast through the undergrowth behind me, coupled with a heavy panting sound. Remaining absolutely still and partially hidden, I saw two large Alsatian-like dogs burst out of the woods about 30 metres to my left without noticing me and run downhill across the fields. It was decidedly creepy as they were not meandering and sniffing as dogs do but racing purposefully downhill in a straight line. I watched them until they disappeared from sight. Back at CVM I mentioned this to the Commandant over supper. 'Ah oui,' he said, 'never run alone and always carry "le grand couteau".'[1] I understand they were feral dogs which lead a wolf-like existence in the mountains.

On one occasion the magnetic plug on a Lynx main rotor gearbox showed tiny metal flakes which, when analysed back in UK, indicated abnormal wear and required a gearbox change. A large crate containing a replacement gearbox (worth many hundreds of thousands of pounds) was airfreighted out to Perpignan Airport where it was collected by one of our REME trucks with a hydraulic crane. After the complex procedure of removing the hydraulic connections, alternators, flying controls, engine and tail rotor inputs and fuselage attachment points, the faulty gearbox (maybe weighing 300-400 kg) was carefully lifted clear of the aircraft with a crane. When the new gearbox was in place the technicians began to re-assemble all the connections. One technician, working eight feet up on the gearbox decking, dropped his spanner which 'tinged' against the side of the gearbox as it fell onto the tarmac. Unfortunately the spanner, during its fall, had struck a tiny bracket casting on the side of the gearbox, which was damaged. This meant another replacement gearbox was required from the UK whilst the unfortunate technician, who had made a minor human error with expensive consequences, was close to tears.

The Army Air Corps had also started to use Saillagouse as a break between courses for instructors from Middle Wallop combined with some useful training. In the summer of 1986 a Lynx AH1, with the Army Air Corps Centre RSM as a passenger, on a mountain flying sortie shot an approach to the highest peak of the Eastern Pyrenees, Pic Carlit.[2] The touchdown on the pinnacle at 9,583 feet went badly wrong, the tail rotor struck a rock and the aircraft crashed down the side of the rock face, the largest part of the burning wreckage ending up jammed in a gully. We were told that a Lieutenant Colonel of the French Foreign Legion was out with a patrol training on a neighbouring peak, saw the crash in the distance and raised the alarm. He moved rapidly to Pic Carlit and carried out a tricky climb to the wreckage and confirmed that there were no survivors. Following this tragic accident the French MoD was less keen to host British detachments to CVM but they recognised that our annual detachments had approached mountain flying in a prepared and serious manner and permitted us to return the following November. The remains of the Lynx lying in the near vertical gulley acted as a timely reminder to our pilots transiting past Pic Carlit from one training area to another; one pilot recalled that the titanium rotor head jammed in the rocks resembled a memorial cross.

At the edge of the small parade ground at CVM, in front of the flagstaff on which the *Tricolore* flew, was a small memorial to the pilots of a number of nations who had died in the mountains. Sadly this included the three occupants, one RM and two AAC, of the Army Air Corps Lynx accident in 1986. Each year we held a parade together with the French staff with a two-minute silence to remember them all. I think most pilots, if they were truthful, frightened themselves at some stage at Saillagouse, but that was not a bad thing and, if the lesson was learned, without passengers on board and without damage, it alone made the training exercise worthwhile.

We also regularly deployed as separate flights up to RAF Kinloss or Lossiemouth for mountain flying training in the Cairngorms. During one of our detachments to Scotland, I was given a typed list of the grid references of some aircraft wrecks in the mountains by the RAF Kinloss Mountain Rescue team. Using this list as a base I collected further locations from other publications and various sightings and, over the years, built up a fairly comprehensive list of over 130 wrecks, mostly dating from the Second World War.[3] I used this guide as a useful means of giving Squadron crewmen, air gunners and pilots map-reading exercises in the mountains when we detached to Scotland. Not only was very precise map reading required to find the correct location but in many cases the corroded metallic remains were moss-covered and half-submerged in peat. To successfully find the target, whilst knowing the aircraft type, date and often the cause of the crash, was an interesting exercise for most of us and there were some on my list which we never found. Soon I had some aircrew coming to me with additional sites that they had heard of, or discovered, to add to the list. Since then a number of authoritative books and guides on high ground wrecks have been published but, at that time, photocopied lists were generally the only references available.

There was a curious sequel to this tale because later, in 1996, whilst in a staff job at HQ Commando Forces at Whale Island, I had a phone call from a friend in the Royal Navy informing me that 819 Naval Air Squadron based at HMS *Gannet*, Prestwick, were looking for a Fairey Swordfish engine to complete a display for their Wardroom and could I help? I was able to give Prestwick grid references for two separate Swordfish wrecks in the Highlands and at the second they found what they were looking for.[4] A Sea King lifted the remains of a Bristol Pegasus engine back to base and, after restoration, the engine and propeller were mounted on the dining room wall, powered by an electric motor so that it could sedately rotate at special events such as Taranto Night. It so happened that the Captain of HMS *Gannet* was Commander Nigel Culliford AFC (see Vulcan XM645 Malta), a Royal Navy test pilot whom at the time I had never met but, after I had retired from the Royal Marines, I was to recruit him into the US avionics business and we worked closely together in our office at Stoke-sub-Hamdon and on a number of trips to Chicago and Canada

Although we had given up our specialist hand-held and heavy Vinten F95 70mm reconnaissance cameras after the Malta era, we still used occasionally to practise aerial photography with modern SLR cameras. I was flying an RN photographer in a Gazelle to a number of targets in Cornwall near Fowey. He was sitting in the left-hand seat with the front doors removed and my crewman, Corporal Hancock, was sitting in the left rear passenger seat. Whilst in the orbit over one of the targets, without any warning the photographer put down his camera and was violently sick all over his lap. He was holding a substantial proportion of his large breakfast in his cupped hands and between his forearms and, without thinking, heaved this unpleasant load out of the open left door. There was an immediate cry over the intercom from Graham Hancock 'You dirty bugger'. Glancing over my left shoulder I saw that the slipstream had splattered the vomit all over him and the rear bulkhead of the aircraft. I could not help laughing – but the laughter was short-lived. Within a minute the overpowering smell began to nauseate us and, with traces of vomit on the centre console, my left arm and the collective, I too began to feel sick. I realised that it would be sensible to land and the nearest airfield was the small civilian grass strip at Bodmin. Calling them up on the radio they were helpful and enthusiastic about a visit from a military Gazelle. What the gathered club members must have thought when, as soon as the rotors stopped, Hancock and I baled out of the soiled aircraft and the RN photographer staggered out covered in sick, I don't know. The approaching sightseers backed off and suddenly no one wanted to give the aircraft a closer inspection. We invited our photographer to clean out the aircraft and the club kindly provided a bucket and hot soapy water whilst Graham Hancock tried to sponge the worst from his flying suit.

I found it was no problem to remain current and instruct on two types, but as I strapped into a Gazelle I would remind myself 'right pedal'. Indeed I found it a relief to get away from staff work and concentrate on something entirely different. It also meant that I could assess new pilots and help the Squadron QHIs, Jeff Niblett followed by Hugh Northam and Sergeant John Menghini, in carrying out six-monthly checks and instrument rating tests. When the Squadron disembarked off Copenhagen to Værløse Air Base in Denmark for a week's training, I assisted Jeff in taking every Squadron Gazelle pilot through engine-off landings (hover, variable flare, constant attitude, range and low level) on the grass perimeter of the airfield over a two-day period. It was glorious weather and the waiting pilots lay on the grass watching the efforts of their colleagues whilst awaiting their turn for a running change.

Chapter 18

Senior Pilot – St Kilda

Helicopters are noisy, oily, made up of thousands of moving parts and all of them vibrate to a greater or lesser extent, but I have always considered them inherently safe machines. All aircrew from time to time experience an incident, or occasionally an emergency, but by following the excellent military training, the flight reference cards and by displaying good airmanship and captaincy, the problem can usually be dealt with without drama or fuss.

Long distance transits through Europe were a particularly enjoyable aspect of flying Lynx. Because of the limitations of our military instrument fit, transits had to be conducted under VFR on the Continent, and thus we usually flew at 2,000 feet or below with a map on our knee in a similar fashion to aviators of bygone years with TANS as a useful back-up. This was fine in good weather but sometimes quite testing in marginal visibility or in winter snow.

Summer on the Continent often brought a haze, which in north-western Germany was aggravated by industrial smoke from the Ruhr. In such conditions horizontal visibility reduced considerably and a particularly sharp lookout was required in the high-density low-level airspace of the Cold War era where VFR 'see and be seen' flight was the norm. It was particularly perturbing to see a high-speed shadow racing across the countryside below you; the shadows always seemed more easily visible than the actual aircraft and were usually a pair. German F-104 Starfighters were particularly hard to see with their small cross-section and I recall staring at a white-helmeted *Marineflieger* pilot as he flashed in front of us at 450 knots over Schleswig-Holstein trailing a haze of black exhaust, followed a few seconds later by his wingman scorching behind us. During a refuelling stop at Eggebek, the home of German Navy Wing 2 (MFG2), we witnessed the extraordinary spectacle of a stream take-off of about twenty-five of the Wing's F-104Gs, each one trailing black smoke as it streaked off into the smog. Forty minutes later, our Lynx refuelling and turnaround complete, the first Starfighter was just beginning its recovery.

Occasionally precautionary landings brought their own distractions. Whilst transiting to the south of Kiel in July 1984 there came a bang and a shudder from the gearbox area of Lynx AH.1 XZ614. It was a sufficiently unusual and alarming noise to put the aircraft down at once in a meadow to the north of Lübeck. After negotiating two barbed-wire fences, we reached the nearby farmhouse where an elderly German couple invited us inside. In schoolboy German and with the aid of drawings and a navigation chart we explained the position to them and rang the German Naval Air Arm base at Kiel Holtenau to summon help from our technicians. It took about two hours for them to arrive in a second Lynx, during which time the German farmer hospitably produced bread, salami and his middle-aged and noticeably amorous daughter. It was with some relief that we welcomed the party of technicians who announced that the required checks of the transmission would probably mean an overnight stay. At this the daughter's eyes lit-up and it was not long before the technicians realised that their fate lay in their own hands. Needless to say, the checks were completed before dusk and the Lynx cleared for one flight only to Kiel for further investigation, leaving one lonely lady waving her handkerchief sadly from the farmhouse. The story has a sequel because, after a day of checks at the MFG5 German Sea King base at Kiel, our technicians pronounced that the aircraft had a clean bill of health and that it 'must have been a small bird strike or your imagination'. The next morning we departed for UK armed with enormous German naval bag rations which, amongst other goodies, contained a supermarket family-sized bag of crisps for each individual. No sooner had we crossed the Kiel Canal at 1,000 feet than a similar thump and shudder ran through the airframe. As I scanned the panel for any abnormalities and began a 180-degree turn back to Kiel I was banged on the shoulder by a white-faced REME technician in the back gesticulating that the aircraft should be put down *immediately*. It is amazing what a little bit of first-hand experience can achieve. We returned to the German Navy at Kiel Holtenau, only two kilometres away, and the Lynx continued its journey on the back of a low-loader by road to the BAOR Aircraft Workshops at Detmold. The fault was eventually traced to a faulty freewheel unit. This was yet another reminder that it is the unknown or the unrecognisable that is potentially alarming in an emergency. Knowledge is re-assuring.

The ability of the Lynx to carry a reasonable payload inside the cabin or as an underslung load meant that we could be deployed on more interesting tasks. In May 1985 the Squadron was asked to support the Royal Artillery range at Benbecula in the Outer Hebrides for a week which would enable key range personnel to visit the tracking station on St Kilda without having to catch the re-supply landing craft from Glasgow and being absent for many days. It would also allow the movement of some urgent stores out to the island. St Kilda is an island, or rather a mountain, sticking out of the Atlantic forty-one miles west of the Outer Hebrides. A small bay with a jetty served as the only landing place, weather permitting, and the wind and waves around this pinnacle arising out of an otherwise empty ocean result in some fierce and unpredictable winds and orographic cloud on the mountain.

The inhabitants of St Kilda used to live at Village Bay, a row of crofts below the mountain in the horseshoe-shaped bay. Amongst their traditions was collecting gannets from the cliffs and storing them in stone cleits, stone cairn-like storage structures, as a staple part of their diet. Victorian tourists used to come and visit St Kilda and the islanders out of curiosity. As the population declined, however, life for the remainder became increasingly hard. Eventually, after the First World War, when the local population dropped to thirty-six, they were finally evacuated by the Royal Navy in 1930. St Kilda statistics are full of superlatives: the largest colony of fulmars in the UK and biggest colony of gannets in the world; the highest cliffs in the UK (1,400 feet), the tallest stacs in the UK and unique sheep (Soay sheep).

The leg from Benbecula to St Kilda was only fifty-one miles, passing over the Monach Islands shortly after take-off. Twenty miles from our destination, St Kilda was already an impressive sight as we approached: a conical mountain rising out of a dark blue windswept ocean with its summit cloaked in orographic cloud looking like something out of *The Lord of the Rings*. To the north was the imposing rock of Boreray, accompanied by two great stacs.

The approach to the small concrete helicopter landing pad on the beach in the enclosed bowl at Village Bay was tricky. Allegedly, the first helicopter to land there, a Royal Navy Dragonfly, had crashed on take-off (although I can find no record of this). There was usually a wind blowing around this large obstruction in an otherwise flat ocean. Normally quite benign wind speeds of 20 knots can do strange things around mountains and bowls but the wind velocity could be assessed by the white horses and streaks on the sea inside the bay. Having established a shallow into-wind approach diagonally into the bay with low torque in the up-drafting breeze, during the final stages the wind died, the aircraft started pitching in turbulence and the wind started gusting from aft. The torque increased from 60 to 100 per cent and with a tailwind and 1,000 feet of steeply-sloping rock directly ahead, an overshoot was not a practical option. I was relieved to touch down with only a transient over-torque. Over the next days we tried to refine a safer way to approach and take-off but every approach was hard work. I eventually favoured the vertical take-off, climbing to a sufficient height to dive in order to attain a safe airspeed before turning out of the bowl. The flight I least enjoyed was when I went out as a passenger in order to be dropped off for an afternoon of exploration on the island. I felt much happier at the controls rather than sitting strapped in the rear cabin listening to the high frequency transmission noises just above my head fluctuating between 50 and 110 per cent on the approach through my headset.

Having looked at the remains of the village, where some of the houses still had the names of the original owners painted on a stone left in the fireplace, I started the climb up the mountain, passing numerous cleits on the way up. After a stiff walk I reached the sharp ridgeline just below the cloud base and suddenly could see the ocean on the far side way below. Heading now steeply downhill following a re-entrant, I came across aircraft wreckage amongst the grass. Recognisable items included a radial engine and a throttle quadrant and, as I approached the items, I began to be dive-bombed by skuas, pulling out of their dive centimetres from my head and causing me to involuntarily duck and place my map over my head. Other skuas approached at low level, camouflaged against the rocks and pulled up to attack. St Kilda has had its fair share of aircraft accidents over the years and I had found the remains of a wartime RAF Sunderland flying boat which had crashed at night in June 1944. St Kilda was allegedly one of their turning points during a night navigation exercise. I could well imagine the navigator on a dark night staring at his chart under a red filtered lamp, with the dot and spot height of the island barely visible. Anyway, what were the chances of actually hitting this dot in the ocean? The flying boat flew straight into the 40-degree steep re-entrant about 600 feet above sea level with all on board being killed.[1] The wreckage was buried after the crash but large items have come to the surface over the years. Farther down the slope I approached the 'Amazon's House', previously visited by an old family friend, a doctor, climber and archaeologist,[2] who had told me that nothing would have persuaded him to spend a night amongst what he had sensed was a threatening atmosphere of 'early man'. I felt no such aura but, nevertheless, was glad to climb back up the slope and away from the skuas.

Other aircraft that came to grief on St Kilda included a Beaufighter, within feet of the summit of the mountain, Conachair, the front half of the wreckage falling over the steep slope a thousand feet into the sea. A weathered three-bladed propeller stood on the crest of the ridge as a monument to this little tragedy.[3] Another 100 feet or so higher and they would have made it, returning to their mess for tea and toast. An unidentified Wellington bomber also crashed into the near vertical grass and rock cliff of Soay, 500 metres from the north-western point of St Kilda. In 1978 this had been the subject of an interesting operation when the RAF Kinloss Mountain Rescue Team was winched down by a Sea King to search for and recover any evidence. They found some human remains, an RCAF cap badge and RAF-pattern black shoes, which seemed to have been a strange choice of footwear for a cold and draughty flight over the North Atlantic whatever the time of year. However, following lengthy investigations, as no ID discs or serial numbers had been found and the aircraft and remains could not be positively identified, the Procurator Fiscal ordered that they should be returned to the site.[4]

A civilian helicopter company at that time was contracted to re-supply St Kilda from Scotland using an SA 365 Dauphin, but it was restricted to winds of 25 knots or less on St Kilda for reasons which have already been explained. Just prior to our visit there had been an extended period of bad weather and, beginning to run short of supplies, the St Kilda detachment were to receive an airdrop from a chartered twin-engined light aircraft which would make a low pass over Village Bay whilst stores were pushed out of the open door. During this evolution a frozen chicken in free-fall hit an officer on the ground injuring him. Although this might sound amusing, a frozen chicken might just as well have been a lump of granite at that speed and height and he was fortunate not to have been killed. A casevac was called for, but the irony was that a helicopter now had to try and land at Village Bay, regardless of wind speed, in order to casevac him to the mainland, which it did successfully.

Back at Benbecula there was an underslung load task for the RA Ranges which involved taking adventure training stores up to a mountain hut thirteen miles to the south west at about 1,900 feet on the side of Hecla. The stores arrived at the airfield and it was clear that it was not going to be a standard underslung load. We eventually netted up the load as follows: a grey steel 6-foot service locker was packed with two full gas liquid bottles and a collection of saucepans and cooking utensils alongside a wooden box full of hexamine cooking fuel tablets. Underneath were two 10-inch-thick mattresses which were secured together and on the bottom was a large table with steel folding legs. The whole netted load weighted 280 kilogrammes and was to be attached to the aircraft via an eight-foot strop. Concerned about the potential aerodynamic properties of the mattresses, but re-assured by the considerable weight stacked above them, I asked the Tower to visually check the stability of the load as we transitioned away. After take-off the Tower informed me that everything looked normal and I accelerated gently to 50 knots and started a gentle climbing turn to starboard onto track. As we reached about 300 feet the aircraft started to oscillate both in pitch and roll. Checking that we were in balance I reduced the speed slightly but the oscillations became worse. At that moment I received a punch on my left arm and my crewman reported that the load was touching our left skid. He was making dramatic cut motions with his gloved hand. Superimposed on this interchange, the Tower was now reporting that our load was behaving abnormally. Checking that the area of moorland below was clear, I jettisoned the load and orbited to see that it had splashed in on the edge of a small lochan. A lone fly fisherman on a promontory about a quarter of a mile away had his peaceful reverie shattered as he watched entranced. The steel locker had disassembled into four sides, a top and a bottom like a squashed cereal packet whilst saucepans and cooking pots littered the side of the loch. The two mattresses were sailing across the surface propelled by a stiff breeze. Having ascertained that the load was destroyed, we flew on to the mountain hut at Hecla where a marshaller and team from the QM's department waited to receive our load. After landing, the QM ran over to my crewman who had opened his left cockpit door and a shouted conversation ensured. When the crewman explained that the load had been jettisoned, the QM affably responded that it was a pity but not to worry; he would make alternative arrangements to collect the load by Land Rover and have it man-packed up the mountain. To which my crewman, rather tactlessly, shouted back above the rotor and engine noise, 'No, no, no, you don't understand. It's all completely fooked.'

That afternoon a flight Land Rover and trailer reached the lochan and recovered the net, strop, and assorted bent and dented utensils. I remember particularly that all the saucepans had lost their insulated bakelite handles and were now equipped with only steel prongs. The sodden mattresses were found beached on the far side of the loch. I later wondered if a whole generation of soldiers based at Benbecula were subjected to cooking with too-hot-to-handle and dented saucepans during their days-off on adventure training.

In the summer of 1985 HRH Prince Edward was at Cambridge University and was intending to join the Royal Marines. As part of his pre-entry training he, along with other RM potential officers at university, spent a few weeks of his July vacation with Royal Marines units. He had specifically requested to spend some of this time with the Air Squadron. It was decreed that he would spend a week at the AAC Centre at Middle Wallop, receiving some introductory basic flying training on the Gazelle before spending a week with us deployed in the field. It was decided that I would give him some flying familiarisation and instruction on the Gazelle on tactical tasks whilst Sergeant John Menghini would give him a few familiarisation flights on the Lynx. Rather than stay at RNAS Yeovilton, we thought it appropriate for him to live with a flight in the field so that he could experience RM Aviation working in a more typical and realistic environment. His flying could therefore be interwoven with living in the field, night navigation (on foot) and some other basic infantry training skills. Six weeks before his attachment Sergeant John Menghini and I were summoned to the Royal Flight at RAF Benson. We flew up by Gazelle and had a pleasant interview with the Captain of the Queen's Flight, Air Vice Marshal John Severne OBE AFC.[5] Afterwards, his staff discussed our proposed flying programme and syllabus with us and, with a few minor changes, approved it. I suspect this was the Royal Flight sensibly 'sussing us out'. The selected aircraft, plus a spare, were then brought up to Royal Flight servicing standards by having their deferred defects cleared. Our week's training went just as planned and I flew ten hours of dual instruction with HRH, including an introduction to general handling, low-level navigation, observation and controlling live artillery from the air, provided by 105mm light guns on the Salisbury Plain Training Area. It was interesting that, as we flew around south-west England and changed from one VHF air traffic control frequency to another, the frequencies were completely silent. All other aircraft were correctly obeying the strict rules of 'purple airspace' and had vacated the vicinity of a moving sterile 'bubble' around our track fifteen minutes before and thirty minutes after our ETA.

A month later C Flight under Captain Colin Baulf RCT deployed for two months with three Gazelles to Wainwright, Alberta, to support the Coldstream Guards Battle Group whilst live firing on the Canadian ranges. I flew out to visit them for a week in August. After my flight out by BA and Air Canada to Calgary, Colin met me with a Gazelle and, after a night's sleep, I read through the Canadian Air Traffic regulations at Calgary Airport before flying the 180 miles directly north-east to Wainwright. The terrain en route was virtually flat and, at about the one-third point, we passed the little township of Three Hills, aptly named after three hummocks rising 100 feet above the plain to the north of the town. The prairie was criss-crossed with tracks every twelve miles or so, mostly running in a north-south and east-west grid. Canadian Forces Base Wainwright was a large area of 600 square kilometres of empty flat grassland and trees used for live firing and exercises. It had been a bison reserve until taken over by the military in 1940. The small township of Wainwright, about a mile from the camp, was established in 1908 alongside the new Grand Trunk Pacific Railway which was being extended across Canada. Before the railway there had been nothing and I admired the early trappers and fur traders who had first explored the area in the 1750s, a long, long 1,800 miles from the St Lawrence River.[6]

On my third day after flying, I was dropped off by Land Rover at the beginning of a dusty track to run the seven miles back to base via Crossing Lake. I had a map and compass with me and set off running down a long abandoned sandy track in the bush. The countryside was similar to East African grassland. After about twenty minutes I had the strangest feeling that someone might be following me. This was ridiculous as the area was deserted but, looking back along the sandy track, I could clearly see my footprints in the sand. I therefore decided to break track and moved at right angles off the trail into the trees and resumed my route about 400 metres further on. Arriving back at Camp forty minutes or so later I was about to have a shower when I noticed Colin Baulf looking strangely at me. He asked if I had received any news. I looked blank and he then handed me a signal which informed me that my father had suddenly died earlier that day in Shropshire. It turned out that the message had been received whilst I was being driven to my drop-off point. When the Land Rover returned, Sergeant Eddy Candlish had volunteered to run after me with the message. He was dropped off at the same spot and followed my tracks without difficulty until he reached a point at which they disappeared, finally returning the way he had come. There was no flight available home to UK for forty-eight hours and, the next day, whilst flying a sortie with Sergeant Geoff Carvell with Eddy Candlish in the back, I asked him to show me the route he had taken. Sure enough he had followed me as far as the point at which I had broken track. I can offer no explanation for this and can assure the reader I am not in the habit of breaking track when out for a run or a walk. I flew back from Calgary two days later by Air Canada Tristar arriving at my parents' house within fifteen minutes of my brother who had flown back from Luanda. The value of helicopter support was again proven when, a few days after I left, a Gazelle picked up a guardsman who had been accidently shot by a GPMG during field firing and delivered him back to the medical centre in Wainwright in fifteen minutes.

FLYING LIGHT HELICOPTERS WITH THE ROYAL MARINES

Exercise ROLLING DEEP 1985 took place in the North of Scotland at the Kyle of Lochalsh and then Cape Wrath. Scotland in September should be pleasant – not a bit of it. It was cold, windy and wet, so much so that a company of Portuguese Marines attached to the Brigade for the exercise were withdrawn suffering from potential hypothermia. The second phase near Cape Wrath remains etched in my memory for a very close call we had. During the incident in question our Squadron FOB was located on gently rising ground at the top of Loch Eriboll facing north towards a bleak North Atlantic. The amphibious shipping, including the Headquarters LPD HMS *Intrepid,* was about two miles offshore amongst the whitecaps visible between breaks in the heavy showers. During a particularly dark night, at about midnight, we received an urgent helquest in the CP for a medevac of a marine from 45 Commando from a mountain top near Beinn Spionnaidh, 2,536 feet, on the western side of Loch Eriboll. Most medevacs are not life or death but this one was unusual in that the marine had been injured in the face by a Schermuly flare and, in the unit doctor's opinion, his eyesight was in danger. After consulting the CO, Major Ady Wray, we decided that Captain Peter Taylor RA, the OC of A Flight and a contemporary of mine during training at Wallop, should fly the sortie. We did a careful map recce with him and decided that he should slowly ascend the final stage to the top of the peak in a high hover-taxi, using his landing light and keeping clear of any cloud or mist, until he picked up the torches of the rudimentary tactical landing site that the rifle company had laid out. Peter set off with us following events on the Squadron radio net from the CP and after an hour we were mightily relieved to hear that Pete had picked up the casualty and was taking him back to HMS *Intrepid* lying offshore. Another thirty minutes or so and Peter was back at the FOB drinking a wet of tea we had made for him before turning in (in the standard metal mug with old black 'maskers' taped round the rim to prevent lips being burned on the metal). Pete, however, looked shaken and, taking me aside, told me what had happened. After a tense hour and having left his casualty on the LPD he had taken off for the simple four-mile transit back to the FOB which was within line of sight. At about a mile away he picked up the location where he knew the FOB to be. The angle-of-approach indicator had been set out at the FOB on a safe heading facing north. He realised that he would pick up the red 'low' light first and planned to continue, maintaining his height, to the 'green' to start his descent. Knowing the FOB was on rising ground when he saw the AAI he knew that there were no intervening obstacles. He suddenly felt that all was not well and, on impulse, switched on the landing light at about half a mile. His beam picked up heather and rocks racing past at 70 knots twelve feet or so just under the aircraft's nose. It turned out that there was an intervening hillock between him and the landing site which he only just cleared. This illustrated the danger of relaxing after a tense mission and was exactly the same lesson drummed in to our infantry fighting patrols; that the return to friendly lines was always a danger period when human nature encouraged relaxation and inattentiveness. I was glad to remove my boots and turn in at about 0300 exhausted for a few hours' kip in my green sleeping bag alongside the snoring Squadron QHI, CO and Ops Officer in a 9x9 tent. It seemed only a few minutes later that I was rudely awakened by a shout from Ady Wray, 'Senior Pilot, Senior Pilot! Look at the time.' Looking at my watch, the luminous hands read 0400 and wondered what all this was about. 'Oh sorry, I've misread my watch,' muttered the adjoining green slug and, nerves jangling, I fell back into a deep sleep.

In May 1986 I was appointed to an SO2 staff job at HQ Commando Forces in Plymouth. The role of Senior Pilot had been challenging and there had been a few occasions when the staff work had not been as complaisant and enjoyable as I had anticipated. Although the flying was as much fun as ever, the staff work and interaction with the Royal Navy at Yeovilton had not been easy. It was hard for them to understand that we were part of Army Aviation with differing rules and a quite different role to that of the RN Commando Support helicopter squadrons. It was no doubt equally difficult for them to have a lodger unit on their airbase operating Army-owned aircraft, maintained by the REME and manned by officers and SNCOs from the Royal Marines, part of their own Naval Service. The Navy was also not used to SNCO pilots, who to my mind were one of the strengths of Royal Marines and Army Aviation. A particular difficulty was tasking outside normal airfield hours. At an Army airbase an aircraft could depart for a task over the weekend with just the station fire section warned and stood-to. At Yeovilton, in order for even a light helicopter to move out of hours, the airfield would have to formally be 'open' with many duty personnel (ATC, medics, fire, met etc.) turning to. We even toyed with the concept of operating out of hours from an adjoining farmer's field but this idea did not go down well. However, it was a significant advantage to operate from a busy and professionally run airfield, equipped with radar, especially after the eleven years of Squadron experience at Coypool.

The unique and complex situation the Squadron operated under is explained thus. Our manning and complement of REME maintainers and attached Army pilots was organised by AAC UKLF at Netheravon, who also oversaw our maintenance standards, flight safety and our flying assessments through UKLF Standards branch. Our annual aviation inspection was carried out by Brigadier AAC UKLF from Netheravon. Operationally we were under the command of the Brigadier at HQ 3 Commando Brigade at Plymouth and, of course, the CO of RNAS Yeovilton for our hangarage, lodging and our airfield flying administration. Amongst the staff work I dealt with was a detailed explanation to the Department of CGRM in London of why we wore Army wings rather than 'proper Naval Wings'. This nugatory exercise was as a result of a series of letters received in London from a long-retired and distinguished Naval-trained RM aviator who held some disparaging and outdated views about Army flying. This difficult balancing act was a strange anomaly and it became increasingly evident that, in the existing financial climate, 3 Commando Brigade Air Squadron should logically become part of either the Army Air Corps or the Fleet Air Arm.

Chapter 19

Squadron Command

In October 1989, following three and a half years of ground tours and courses, I was appointed as CO of 3 Commando Brigade Air Squadron to relieve Major John Meardon. After two months of Gazelle and Lynx refreshers at Middle Wallop, I regained my instrument ratings and Clearance to Instruct before joining the Squadron at RNAS Yeovilton. There was one new critical check we had to carry out on the Lynx as part of pre-flight walk-round which was to inspect the ball-bearing races supporting the sliding cabin doors. A tragic accident had occurred to a Royal Naval Lynx near Mombasa when the port cabin door detached in flight and struck the main rotor blades, sending debris into the tail rotor and causing the tail boom to detach. All nine occupants were killed.[1] Some of these ball bearings habitually escaped from the door's runners during operation, so there was a limit on the number of permitted missing bearings and the spacing between any gaps.

Earlier that year I had heard the sad news that my old chum from CFS (H) Julian Barraclough, whose Mini had burned out near Shawbury, had been killed together with his co-pilot when his Jetstream T.2 of 750 Naval Air Squadron had crashed in Portland Bay.[2]

When I took over, the Squadron had just received its first two Lynx AH.7s (XZ180 and XZ182). The Lynx AH.7 had Gem 41-1 engines, the three-pinion main rotor gearbox, a gearbox oil cooler, a larger improved tail rotor with a spring bias unit which rotated in the opposite sense to the Mk 1 and a main rotor head vibration absorber (MRHVA).[3] These major modifications were carried out by RNAY Fleetlands by converting 107 Lynx AH.1 airframes between March 1988 and 1994, whilst an additional twelve AH.7s were new-builds by Westlands. We also received the first Lynx AH.1s with uprated engines (Gem 41-1 instead of the Gem 2) three-pinion gearbox and a new tail rotor. This was an intermediate mod state (MOD 391 - 205GTI) and the aircraft was nicknamed the AH Mk 1 GT. These aircraft, although looking identical to the standard AH.1, had different engine-torque limitations which allowed more power to be pulled, especially useful when on one engine. It was important to know the aircraft MOD state and refer to the correct flight reference cards to avoid any confusion about performance.[4] For instance, according to my old knee-pad, the Lynx AH Mk 1 GT max continuous torque limit was 86.5 per cent with a transient of 103.8 per cent, whilst for the Lynx AH.7 the figures were 100 per cent and 116 per cent. So for the next six months or so we had three different Lynx variants in the Squadron, each with their own differing flight reference cards, torque and weight limitations. Gradually the AH.1s disappeared to be replaced by the interim AH Mk 1 GT and eventually the whole Squadron was equipped with AH.7s.

Our first annual training deployment was back to the *Centre de vol en montagne* near Saillagouse on Exercise GADFLY in November. We hosted a number of RM and AAC visitors to witness our mountain-flying training. I flew down to Perpignan Airport to collect Brigadier Andrew Whitehead[5] from his flight from Paris but, by the time we had collected his suitcase, all the doors out to the dispersal where our Lynx was standing had been locked and no one could find the keyholder. We resorted to climbing onto the baggage belt and, sitting behind each other, were transported through the plastic strip curtains back out to 'airside' to reach our aircraft to the amusement of the airport staff and waiting passengers. This would no doubt be a serious security offence today and no one should try to emulate our example.

Immediately after Christmas 1989 most of 3 Commando Brigade deployed for their annual winter warfare training in Norway. Since I had last served with the Squadron our location had moved from the airfield at Gardermoen to a small civil airport at Fagernes in the Valdres valley about ninety miles north-west of Oslo. The airport, which at 2,700 feet above sea level was the highest in northern Europe, was closed for most of the winter except for a single charter Caravelle that landed once per week in March to take tourists to the Mediterranean. Otherwise we had the airfield to ourselves. Whilst the Gazelles were transported to Norway by sea, the Lynx self-deployed out via Manston and Denmark. I have already mentioned that the crossing of the Skagerrak in early winter could be particularly unpleasant as there was usually a marked contrast in the weather between the Danish and Norwegian coasts. Even with the increased fuel load of the Lynx AH.7, our fuel was tight and a decision had to be made two-thirds of the way across whether to continue or return to Aalborg. On the trip in January 1991 I was leading the formation in a Lynx AH.7 flying from the right-hand seat. A newly-qualified Lynx pilot, who had never flown in the Norwegian winter theatre before, was acting as my P2 from the left-hand seat. We were at about 700 feet above the grey waves and warily watching the patchy snow showers ahead, having just passed the halfway point, when the audio warning sounded, accompanied by numerous amber captions on the central warning panel. I cancelled the noise immediately in accordance with the drills in order that we could think and communicate and saw that the primary caption was 'ALT 1' (number one alternator failure). My left-seater should have by now got out his flight reference cards and be referring to the drills in the emergency section; however he appeared to be showing little reaction to this minor emergency and seemed to be transmitting on the HF radio, which I had deselected on my station box as I was monitoring UHF and VHF. I told him to get the flight reference cards out but, to my surprise, he asked me whether this meant I wished him to cancel his phone call. I was so astonished by this response that there was a pause whilst it sunk in that he was busily arranging a GPO phone call home via HF and the RAF Flight Watch Centre (call sign 'Architect') at Upavon on HF. No purpose could be achieved by displaying a loss of sense of humour in the cockpit and it also took some self-control to refrain from laughter on this particular occasion as I invited him to terminate the call. We carried out the vital actions and continued the transit on one alternator. This was no big deal but a second alternator failure in this condition would have been eye-watering. Having made a landfall in Norway and whilst transiting over the Christmas-card landscape of Southern Norway, I pointed out a mink fur farm. These long low buildings had to be avoided by a healthy margin at low level by aircraft otherwise the animals might go berserk and hefty claims for compensation would subsequently be submitted to UK MoD. My co-pilot, who subsequently had a long and impressive flying career, cheerily replied that he would have no trouble in avoiding similar farms because of their obvious long white roofs. Bootneck humour!

Following our nine weeks of cold-weather training at Fagernes in Southern Norway, the Squadron was required to self-deploy 360 miles north to join the rest of 3 Commando Brigade afloat off Bodø for the Norwegian national Exercise COLD WINTER 90. On 8 March we set off in three loose formations in appalling freezing/wet, mild weather – the very worst combination. The aircrews had been deliberately mixed with at least one Arctic veteran crewed with any newly-qualified Arctic pilot. Despite anti-icing on the Lynx, flight in freezing rain was prohibited on both types as the droplets could instantly form clear ice on contact with the rotor blades and fuselage. The 360-mile straight-line track to where the shipping was supposed to be loitering was entirely theoretical as, in this land of mountains and steep valleys with icing cloud covering most of the high ground, our track northwards, following the valleys and fjords could easily double that distance. Mindful of the fact that there was no radar coverage in that part of Norway, the safety altitude was some 9,000 feet and to achieve that by flying into IMC in plus 1 to minus 10 degrees C was inviting death, and that aviation re-fuelling facilities were confined to a few regional airfields, we planned our route with the utmost care. Our first day took us north to the bleak Hjerkinn ranges,[6] which we used for our annual TOW live-firing, and on to the small civil airfield at Røros for fuel. There one of the Lynx went unserviceable. This posed a problem. The aircraft had to be left with a crew and a couple of technicians to repair the aircraft and to sign for the repair. The aircraft commander would have to be self-authorising and be capable of making decisions as to routeing and weather once the fault was fixed. The shipping by then would no longer be off Bodø and would be likely further north towards Tromsø. Since spares might have to be collected from a major airfield such as Vaernes, it also made sense to leave a second aircraft with the disabled Lynx. We set off for the next leg to Vaernes with me leading in gradually deteriorating cloud base and visibility. We had planned for a number of dog-legs in order to follow low ground and lakes and, as we approached Trondheim Fjord, flying at 150 feet in 1,500 to 1,000 metres visibility in snow, we reduced speed to 70 knots. The real concern was now the outside air temperature which was unusually warm at about minus 1 or 2 degrees C, a dangerously high temperature which could lead to the dreaded freezing rain. I was mindful of the aircraft in line astern behind me but was aware that they at least had my aircraft and strobe lights as a solid reference whilst in the lead we had to rely on continuously picking a chain of visual references in the incipient white-out conditions. The worst few moments were near Hommelvik where the low cloud base, wet snow piling on the windscreen and poor visibility all combined to make the conditions marginal and there were few options for a precautionary landing. My experienced co-pilot, Sergeant Kevin Butler, assisted by TANS, did a magnificent job of talking me through the terrain and around obstacles until we broke out over the cold, grey sea of Trondheim Fjord covered with white horses. As dusk fell the approach lights of Vaernes Airport sticking out on posts into the fjord were a welcome sight. During the last few minutes the wipers were smearing a combination of wet snow and freezing rain at the edges of the windscreen, through which very little could be seen apart from dirty white sky and ground. It was only after we had signed in the aircraft and secured the covers that I noticed the strain and responsibility of the day's flying lift from my shoulders.

The next day the weather was a little better and the Royal Norwegian Air Force Met staff indicated that there was no scheduled improvement over the next five days. However, a Gazelle was now unserviceable and so another self-authorising flight commander had to be left with two technicians and a second Gazelle. At least the spare part could be air-freighted directly from UK to Vaernes airfield. We therefore planned a leg to Namsos to get to the western coast and where there was a chain of outlying islands, a few of which had small airstrips serviced by Widerøe Dash-7 aircraft. After fuelling at Namsos we intended to join HMS *Intrepid* and the LSLs, which we believed were just south of Bodø but as we tracked north the visibility and cloud base reduced and we crept into Stokka airfield, overlooked by the dramatic peak of Kvasstind hidden by the low cloud base, as the light faded. We were going nowhere until daylight and a weather improvement and we put on the cold weather aircraft covers in heavy snow. As we were doing so landing lights suddenly appeared out of the blizzard and a Dash-7 landed. The local pilots were very skilled and flew in what appeared to be almost impossible conditions.[7] There were no buildings or facilities at the airfield so that we had no option but to book into a small hotel at the small fishing town of Sandnessjøen six miles north of the airfield. I guess that our cold weather combat flying clothing was probably beginning to smell. That day we had covered a distance of 155 nautical miles in an hour and fifty-five minutes flying time, giving a mean groundspeed of 81 knots.

On arrival at the airfield early the next morning there was cumulus nimbi about with strong winds and heavy snow interspersed with 'sucker's gaps'. However, in the early afternoon, an appreciable gap appeared and I got airborne in company with a second Lynx and flew north over the sea on a weather check. Fifteen miles north we suddenly found the task force sheltering in the inner leads and with no more ado we radioed their position back to Stokka with a warning to wait until a suitable gap between the heavy snow showers occurred and to keep a visual reference on a suitable landing place ashore. Dodging around the edge of a heavy snowstorm, we started our approach to HMS *Intrepid*. I can well remember shutting down as large slabs of wet snow and melting ice slid off the windscreen, cabin roof and tail boom onto the flight deck. I remained in Flyco until the last Gazelle had landed on the nearby LSLs and, with huge relief, headed below to find my cabin. Within a few minutes I received a summons to the

Brigadier's cabin where he wanted to know why we had arrived forty-eight hours later than planned and where the other four aircraft were. I explained that the relatively warmer temperatures were far more demanding than the usual cold and drier temperatures of minus 10 to minus 30 degrees. I also mentioned that I was greatly relieved that we had arrived without a serious accident and that I remained concerned about the safety of the remaining four aircraft and their crews. We had operated to the very limits of peacetime flight safety to marry up with the task force for what, after all, was just an exercise and I would probably have been justified in opting to stay at Røros. Leading this transit with all the varying decisions on weather, unserviceabilities, authorisation, technical support and the location of the task force shipping was certainly the most demanding navex of my flying career and illustrated clearly the reasons for our extensive training and the Arctic TQ syllabus. It was two days prior to the end of the exercise that the final two aircraft at last caught up with us.

As part of Army Aviation we regularly assisted on roulement tours and in 1989 one of our Gazelle Flights was detached to help out in Belize. I flew out by RAF VC10 with Lieutenant Paul Morris, who was joining the Flight, from Brize Norton. About an hour and twenty minutes after take-off for Washington we had a problem which resulted in no. 3 engine being shut down and, after jettisoning fuel off the north-west coast of Scotland, we returned to Brize. That afternoon Paul and I went to see *The Hunt for Red October* in Oxford before a night in Gateway House and continuing our journey the next day. On arrival in Belize, before we left the airfield, I went through an unusual process of queuing up to be interviewed by Commander British Forces Belize, Brigadier R.M. Lambe. He wanted to know why each visitor was there and, without a satisfactory explanation some were reportedly put back on the same VC10 to UK. Although I fully agreed with the concept of only bona fide visitors arriving in theatre, this is what the staff approval process was meant to ensure before issuing a service flight authorisation. When my turn came my response was clearly acceptable, as with a smile, I was passed into arrivals.

In Belize the full-time detachment commander was Major David Woods AAC, who had been one of my team of instructors on ARW at Middle Wallop and a fellow member of the Sparrowhawks. Lieutenant Paul Denning was the Flight Commander and I spent an interesting week flying with him and his pilots throughout the country on tasking. Jungle flying in Belize in the Gazelle was not as demanding as the Sioux in Brunei but the margin for any error was still reduced. By coincidence I had the happy task of flying

SQUADRON COMMAND

AVM R.J.M. Alcock[8] and the Station Commander of the RAF in Belize, Wing Commander Richard Thomas, in a Gazelle, to HMS *Newcastle,* the West Indies guardship off the coast. Richard had flown me in a Harrier T.4 on a three-ship tactical sortie from RAF Wittering when I was attending the Joint Services Defence Course, so I was able to return the favour, although not in quite such a dramatic way.

In September 1990 we had the pleasure of exercising in central Norway in the summer months during Exercise TEAMWORK and were able to enjoy lengthy warm daylight hours amongst an endless vista of wooded hills, lakes and mountains near Namsos. I was despatched from HMS *Intrepid* to pick up our new Commandant General, Lieutenant General Henry Beverley,[9] who was visiting the exercise, from Vaernes Airport. During the seventy-five-mile trip back to Brigade HQ onboard *Intrepid* we made a small track adjustment to fly over Fættenfjorden where *Tirpitz* had been moored between January 1942 and October 1943 alongside the steep side of the fjord covered with camouflage netting. We could still see the two concrete mooring jetties jutting out from the cliff face and the remains of various buildings and anti-aircraft sites in the woods above the anchorage. The RAF unsuccessfully attempted to bomb Tirpitz on five occasions at this location[10] and she was eventually sunk off Tromsø.

Another reminder of the Second World War occurred a few days later when locals told us of a wartime crashed German aircraft in the mountains to the north of our Squadron HQ. During a gap in our tasking one afternoon a Gazelle dropped the OC REME LAD, Captain Adrian Went, and myself in a clearing about 2,000m from the approximate grid reference we had marked on our maps. Adrian was a keen mountain runner and a regular competitor in the Karrimor Mountain Marathon so I found it extremely testing to keep up with him as we orienteered steeply uphill in the woods. After about 40 minutes we found the scattered wreckage covered in ferns and moss. It was a Ju-188 operating out of Vaernes which had failed to find its convoy target in the Atlantic at night and had returned short of fuel and in bad weather.[11] A body of a torpedo, with the warhead removed, originally carried under the inboard wing of the aircraft, was immediately apparent lying amongst the undergrowth. By the time we reached the clearing below us for the Gazelle pickup I was knackered.

A highlight in November 1990 was the news that the Squadron had won the Rolls Royce Trophy, an annual award for the most efficient and effective Squadron in Army Aviation. The cup was presented at Yeovilton by Chris Fairhead, the Director of Customer Support for Rolls Royce Military

FLYING LIGHT HELICOPTERS WITH THE ROYAL MARINES

Engines, with Brigadier Andy Keeling also attending. We had ten of our eighteen aircraft lined up with personnel paraded in front of them. This was the closest I ever got to having the whole Squadron on parade, as there was always at least one Flight detached in Northern Ireland, Belize, Canada or supporting a Commando exercise elsewhere.

During the run up to Operation DESERT STORM in the autumn of 1990 training intensified as the involvement of 3 Commando Brigade fluctuated between an 'on' and 'off' likelihood. Because of the predicted chemical threat it made good sense to practise tactical flying in full NBC gear wearing aircrew respirators. This was hot and uncomfortable with narrowed peripheral vision, so we always flew with a normally-clad safety pilot. We talked through rules of engagement scenarios and casualty procedures and made sure that every pilot was in date for his instrument rating, six-monthly checks and aircrew medicals. We received a number of inoculations but, as Christmas approached, it seemed less likely that the Brigade would be involved in the Middle East and we turned our minds to our annual winter deployment at Fagernes on CLOCKWORK 1991. It was somewhat unreal to watch Operation DESERT STORM unfold on Sky News whilst we were in Norway between training serials. As we transited back through Northern Germany to UK the ceasefire was announced and, as far as we were concerned, the affair was over. Little did we know that we would unexpectedly deploy to the Middle East ten days after our return from Norway. It might sound totally inappropriate to have spent three months in the Arctic before deployment to the Middle East but the training was ideal both for ground troops and for aviation. The discipline and fitness required for Arctic operations are such that military operations in temperate or hot climates are relatively straightforward by comparison. We were also well-trained in mountainous operations.

Chapter 20

Air Combat Manoeuvring – Tally One, Visual One, Fight's On

'Tally one, visual one, fight's on.' With these clipped UHF transmissions, the leader of a pair of Lynx over the Somerset Levels indicated that they were about to engage an aggressor helicopter rapidly approaching head-on at five kilometres range. This was a typical serial in the many hours of Air Combat Manoeuvre (ACM) training that the Squadron carried out in 1990. It was 3 Commando Brigade Air Squadron Royal Marines who first introduced the US Marine Corps ACM training syllabus for helicopters in the United Kingdom and it was not a straightforward process.

In answering the question why it was felt necessary to introduce this training after forty years of helicopter operations, we need to consider some aviation history. In the period between the Vietnam War and 1990, rotary-wing aviation experienced a rate of technological advance equivalent to the fixed-wing transition from the biplane of 1918 to the first jet of 1945. In 1970 we were operating the Sioux, cruising at 70 knots, powered by a single piston engine, without any form of instrument flying capability and with a maximum all-up weight of 1,340 kilogrammes. Twenty years later we were operating the Lynx Mk 7 with a maximum cruise of 140 knots, twin turbine engines, an anti-icing capability, near aerobatic manoeuvrability and the option of carrying eight TOW missiles, seven troops or a 1,360kg underslung load.

We were also mindful that the Lynx was due to be replaced by the WAH-64 Westland Apache attack helicopter by 2000. With a millimetric Fire Control Radar, forward-looking infra-red, thermal imaging coupled with a helmet-mounted sight and flight display, the WAH-64 would provide a twenty-four-hour attack capability for the first time. The weapon load had developed from a single 7.62mm GPMG occasionally fitted to the Sioux to the Apache's load of eight Hellfire laser-guided missiles, a fully articulated 30mm chain gun for ground suppression and 2.75-inch free-flight rocket pods. Weighing approximately 9,000kg, the Apache represented a quantum leap in technology and capability since the 'clockwork mouse' of 1970 – and all over the span of thirty years.

In parallel with these developments were those of Russia who manufactured on a prolific, more affordable, scale than the West. In the 1980s many third-world nations were equipped with Mil Mi-17 Hip transport helicopters, often equipped with machine guns and rocket pods. Russia operated the Mil Mi-24 Hind and later developed the Mil Mi-28 Havoc and Kamov Ka-50 Hokum attack helicopters which had the armament, range and survivability to operate beyond the forward edge of the battle area (FEBA) as the US Apaches were to prove during Operation DESERT STORM. Thus in the fluid and fast moving actions that we might have been called upon to fight there was an increased possibility of chance helicopter-versus-helicopter engagements.

It was against this background that, in 1988, we started training in helicopter Air Combat Manoeuvring (ACM). We adopted and modified the United States Marine Corps Tactical Formation and ACM syllabus that was being used by the Marine Air Weapons and Tactics Squadron 1 (MAWTS 1) at Yuma, Arizona. This excellent course, developed as a result of years of experience in Southeast Asia, was attended not only by USMC Sea Cobra attack helicopter pilots but also by CH-53, CH-46 and UH-1N utility transport pilots. In adopting this programme, we were greatly assisted by the aircrew exchange scheme that our squadron was running with the USMC. A Royal Marine, Captain Mark Noble, was flying AH-1W Cobras at Camp Pendleton on the West Coast of the USA and, in return, a USMC weapons and tactics instructor, Captain Steve Heywood, was at Yeovilton flying Lynx Mk 7.

The syllabus we adopted and which was eventually approved by the Army Air Corps consisted of:

- 13 hours of classroom instruction
- 6 hours of tactical formation flying
- 7 hours of air combat operations covering one versus one and two versus one simulated air combat.

In order to give some idea of the training load involved in covering this syllabus it required some 288 flying hours to train all eighteen aircrew of our Lynx anti-tank flight. This had to be achieved in addition to the existing mandatory night flying, instrument flying and tactical flying training currency, which were laid down by Army Aviation Standards Branch. Clearly something had to give and we reduced the amount of day-to-day passenger liaison flying that we carried out at Yeovilton in order to accommodate this extra flying load.

We gained a number of benefits from being ACM qualified. Primarily, the ability to conduct tactical formation flying or 'Tac Form'. This was a flexible method of moving two or more aircraft tactically at low level whilst covering each other visually and at the same time retaining the ability to change direction, formation or spacing. This was very similar to the way riflemen in an infantry platoon moved when in close proximity to the enemy. Tac Form was used by all NATO fixed-wing fighters as well as by USMC and US Army helicopters and thus increased mutual confidence and inter-operability during multi-national operations. As chance would have it, within months of formally adopting this training our TOW-armed Lynx were using Tac Form on reconnaissance sorties over Iraqi positions in Northern Iraq during joint patrols with USMC AH-1T Sea Cobras and US Army AH-64 Apaches. The mutual support, which was a foundation of Tac Form, also acted as an effective deterrent to ground fire.

We practised Tac Form against Fleet Air Arm Hunters of the Fleet Requirements and Air Direction Unit (FRADU) in a series of fighter evasion exercises, which took place in South Wales. Tac Form helped to confuse fixed-wing aggressors who found difficulty in establishing which direction the helicopter formation was tracking due to the regular formation changes. All of our instructors also had the opportunity to fly in the right seat of a two-seat Hunter T.7 as one of a fighter pair searching for the low-flying Gazelles over Carmarthenshire. Interception was assisted by the Squadron informing the Hunter leader that the pair of Gazelles would be in a certain ten-kilometre grid square at a particular time slot. We could then experience the difficulties of tracking the target each time the Hunter made a gut-wrenching turn to attempt another gun attack. This was a confidence building measure for a rotary-wing pilot with a strong stomach.

Fighter evasion was a demanding exercise with a high workload at low level and it was whilst I was leading a pair of Gazelles near Castlemartin in an identical exercise that my wingman, Sergeant Alan Barnwell, had a close shave with a wire strike. As the lead Hunter turned in for a gun attack behind us I called 'break' and turned hard right at low-level. Barney Barnwell, 1,000 yards to my left, broke left and disappeared out of my sight into a narrow valley. Almost immediately we heard on UHF 'Mayday, Mayday. Wire strike.' Calling 'Knock it off' to the fighters, I was intensely relieved to find the Gazelle safely on the ground in a cow pasture 300 metres beyond a broken high-tension line slung between two poles, partly hidden in the trees on the shoulders of the valley. The Gazelle had blade damage to all three blades and arcing damage to the main rotor gearbox cowling but the crew were unhurt.[1] A nice lady from the nearby farmhouse offered us a cup of tea whilst Colour Sergeant Al Blowers and I were phoning Yeovilton. However, she appeared a few minutes later to ask whether lemonade would do instead as unexpectedly there had been a power cut. After a night of guarding the aircraft with the co-operation of the local police, the Gazelle was recovered the next morning, underslung by Sea King to a convenient hardstanding where a low-loader had been positioned. There was no excuse of course: aircraft hit wires, wires do not hit aircraft. However, this wire was not marked on the map and had not been spotted during the wire reconnaissance, which had taken place before the low-flying tactical exercises began. Green with verdigris, the single-strand copper wire was very hard to see against a dark background.

The ACM syllabus also taught our crews how to react when surprised by an armed enemy helicopter. In the event of sighting an aggressor helicopter, our first reaction would be to hide behind cover. With the Lynx we also had the option of engaging the aggressor from an ambush position with our TOW anti-tank missiles. However, we could be faced with a problem if we were surprised by an aggressor within a range of about five kilometres. Merely running away might not be possible due to the effectiveness of enemy air-to-air missiles such as AT6 Spiral.[2] The aim of our ACM training therefore, was to close the range with him as quickly as possible so that he could not use his missiles. By gaining maximum energy it might be possible to evade his guns and get into his 6 o'clock, thus turning the tables on the aggressor. This, of course, was nothing new and was what young RAF pilots were learning at similar closing rates in the early 1920s.

However we required a suitable weapon in order to achieve a kill. Our TOW missiles had a minimum range of 500 metres and were not designed for tracking hard-manoeuvring targets. The answer lay in a short-range air-to-air missile but in 1990 an affordable system was not available to us. In the interim we believed the solution was an accurate fixed-forward-firing gun with a good reflector sight. After much research, we decided that the gun we needed was the FN .5 inch Heavy Machine-Gun Pod (HMP) manufactured in Belgium, which was capable of firing explosive ammunition. The gun was aimed with the Ferranti Isis reflector sight, which was a standard fit in the RAF Hawk T.1 trainer. This complete gun package was in use at the time with Royal Navy Lynx HAS.3 and had been used operationally during

AIR COMBAT MANOEUVRING

Operation ARMILLA and Operation GRANBY in the Gulf. Nothing in aviation is straightforward and, unfortunately, the Lynx HAS.3 had entirely different weapon pick-up points to the Lynx AH.7. A special Westland-designed weapons carrier was required as the interface between the TOW pick-up points on the airframe and the HMP. As only a small number of weapon carriers would be required, this was likely to be an expensive item; otherwise the project was relatively simple and low-cost, utilising well-tried and tested in-service items. We therefore submitted a detailed procurement paper for the HMP.

During training the aggressor aircraft was usually a Gazelle and was flown to pre-determined angle of bank and airspeed limits, which simulated the performance profiles of potential enemy helicopters. Having experienced sorties of one versus one, the student would act as wingman and, eventually, as the leader of a pair conducting two-versus-one profiles. Evading attacks were practised from head-on, abeam and then astern from initially outside enemy weapon parameters and then inside them.

The workload during ACM training was high and it was necessary for pre-sortie briefings to be detailed and clearly understood as helicopters would get close to each other in extreme attitudes and any misunderstandings could easily lead to disaster. Most Lynx pilots readily took to this sort of exercise but we soon discovered that ACM did not suit all aircrew. A few did not have the aptitude to think tactically in three dimensions whilst at the same time manoeuvring the aircraft to the limits of its operating envelope and it was no reflection on their abilities as anti-tank pilots.

In order to test the effectiveness of our existing anti-tank missiles against helicopters we requested to conduct a trial to test TOW in the air-to-air role. In the months leading up to the first Gulf War, Operation DESERT STORM, the trial was approved by the authorities, who allocated us some practice missiles, and thus Exercise HIGHLAND DRONE was born. Although some computer simulations had been done on this subject, we could find no evidence that live air-to-air firings had taken place either in the US or in the UK. We wanted our target to manoeuvre at helicopter speeds at a range of about 2,000 metres. After considerable research we found that an FR Aviation Cessna Conquest towing a sleeve at about 150 knots was the slowest aerial target that we could obtain, other than a balloon. We could also use a Dassault Falcon 20 twinjet, also operated by Flight Refuelling Ltd, which towed a Rushton target equipped with flares, but its minimum practical airspeed was approximately 190 knots. The Ministry of Defence designed the TOW missile air-to-air danger area templates for us and we found that, for range safety reasons, we would be limited to engaging the target at a 90-degree angle at a range of about three kilometres. The RA Range Hebrides in the Outer Hebrides was chosen as the most suitable range and in December 1990, on the eve of Operation DESERT STORM, we deployed to the Western Isles in order to fire six missiles in the air-to-air mode. The effectiveness of the trial was to be monitored by the RA range staff at Benbecula using their radars and weapon analysts, most of whom were WRAC girls who wore a locally-designed tartan kilt (an attractive but apparently unofficial item of 'uniform').

For the trial both the Conquest[3] and the Falcon deployed to Stornoway airfield on the island of Lewis. We spent the first day tracking the pencil-thin trail of orange smoke which emanated from the sleeve towed some 5,000 metres behind the Cessna. Our two Lynx were established in a fifty-foot hover over one of the firing points on the beach looking out over a cold grey Atlantic towards St Kilda. The sleeve itself appeared as a speck but, once the smoke trail was picked up, could be tracked by our air gunners looking through their gyro-stabilised magnifying sights. Having armed the Lynx, we were ready for our first live engagement on the second day. After a telephone brief the Cessna took off from Stornoway, some fifty miles to the north, and checked in with the range on VHF. Whilst streaming the target over the sea in the north of the range area the Cessna flew through some cumulus cloud at Flight Level 60, icing rapidly built up on the sleeve, which became unstable and the pilot was forced to operate his cable-cutter in order to jettison it. Apart from losing much of the cable and the target sleeve, there was some tangled wire and whiplash damage to the aircraft winch and the glum pilot announced that his part in the trial was concluded. This was frustrating and there was no option but to move immediately to the Dassault Falcon towing at much higher airspeeds. During the afternoon of the same day, we engaged six targets. Although we could track the Rushton target with the sight, it was apparent that the missile could not manoeuvre sufficiently to engage a crossing target at that speed and ran out of control authority before it managed to intercept the flare. The missile's response became increasingly sluggish as the range increased and they ended up eventually diving into the Atlantic with a spectacular splash. Nevertheless a couple of our missiles were judged close enough to the flare to count as hits. After all, the TOW missile was designed to take on tanks grinding along at 30mph and not aerial targets travelling at 210mph. We learned some useful lessons and felt that we might be able to register some success against a helicopter target approaching us obliquely at a relative slow crossing rate.

AIR COMBAT MANOEUVRING

ACM was not something that we could demonstrate to the uninitiated as, quite rightly, we were not permitted to carry passengers on ACM training sorties. I did receive clearance to fly a number of influential senior officers, some of them sceptical, as passengers in a Gazelle which trailed the engaged pair and gave a feel for what was involved. After seeing it for themselves, most agreed that it was worthwhile training and were supportive of our efforts to procure a forward-firing gun.

The initial enthusiasm of the Royal Marines staffs proved to be no match for inter-service rivalries and endless staff work concerning who might pay for the development and procurement of the HMP. Eventually we were told that we needed a suitable operation in order to acquire HMP as a urgent operational requirement (UOR). When we later deployed to Northern Iraq we accordingly requested a UOR but were then asked for a detailed procurement case (formally submitted a year previously). Shades of 'Catch 22' and, sad to say, nothing ever came of it.

In summary the introduction of Air Combat Manoeuvring improved our overall flying skills and standards and improved the survivability of our aircraft on future operations. The Squadron used ACM tactics during our armed patrols during Operation HAVEN in Kurdistan and on one occasion our TAC-Form manoeuvres helped identify our aircraft as friendly to a pair of USAF A-10s who were uncertain whether we were Iraqi attack helicopters. What we were not to know in 1991 was that later financial pressures on the UK Defence Budget would dictate a significant reduction in the purchase of Apache attack helicopters from over a hundred to an eventual total of sixty-four in 2000. This reduction meant that the Royal Marines were not to receive their own attack helicopters and, instead, would be supported by an Army Air Corps Apache squadron. This was a bitter disappointment to Royal Marines aviation at the time.

Chapter 21

Op HAVEN – Deployment

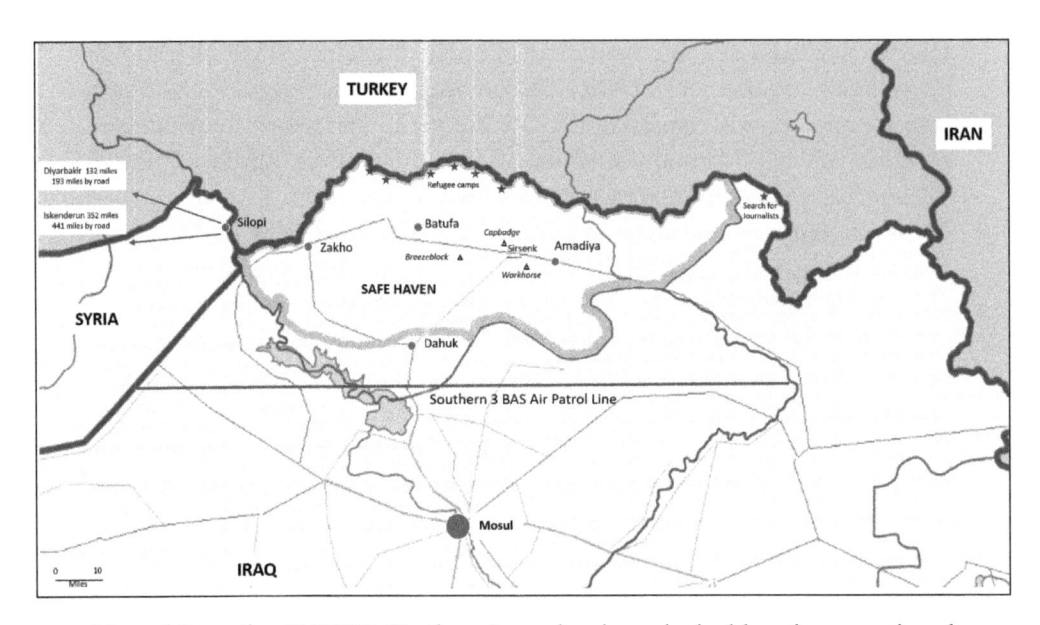

Map of Operation HAVEN, Northern Iraq, showing principal locations mentioned in the text. (©Author)

For centuries the Kurdish people have fought for their own nation in the vast mountainous area which is now divided between Turkey, Syria, Iraq and Iran. Twenty million Kurds now form the largest ethnic minority without their own homeland. In April 1991 President Saddam Hussein launched yet another of his brutal repressions of the Kurdish people, which had been a feature of his dictatorship since 1975. As a result, between 500,000 and 600,000 Kurds fled from their homes all over Iraq into the mountains in the far north of their country on the Turkish border. It is difficult for us to understand the degree of intimidation which motivated so many people from all walks of life to leave everything they owned and take refuge in such an inhospitable area. It is also difficult for most of us to comprehend the extraordinary scale of this exodus.

The area into which the Kurds fled was largely inaccessible except by mountain track, and one of the many extraordinary scenes was the assortment of vehicles of all descriptions which had been abandoned where the few tracks that existed petered out 8,000 feet up in the mountains. Northern Iraq was, in effect, a total vacuum, with no provincial or local government, no judiciary, no police, no hospitals or emergency services, no agriculture, no economy, no communications and no civic amenities.

Conditions in the mountains were appalling. Winter temperatures still prevailed, there was no natural cover or clean running water, and the only available food and shelter was that which the families could carry on foot into the mountains. The great majority of displaced Kurds, who included peasant farmers, shopkeepers, lawyers, professors and officers who had deserted from the Iraqi army, had little or no experience of living in such conditions. The crowding and ignorance of field hygiene led to the onset of disease which took its toll on the very young and the very old who were already weakened by the cold and lack of food and water. There was no topsoil in which to bury the bodies and so conditions deteriorated. Anti-personnel minefields on the Turkish border added to the misery.

On this occasion, however, the plight of the Kurds was not ignored by the rest of the world. Following initiatives by Prime Minister John Major, the United States and European Community decided to intervene. So it was that a unique humanitarian operation was launched at extremely short notice. It was unique in a number of respects. It was the first occasion on which Western military forces had conducted operations on humanitarian grounds in another state, Iraq, uninvited by Iraq, albeit in response to the UN Security Council resolutions. It was the first occasion on which a large multi-national coalition force, consisting of 23,000 troops from thirteen different nations, had worked together for humanitarian purposes. It was the first occasion on which large-scale humanitarian operations had been conducted alongside governmental and non-governmental aid agencies.

The UK military force selected for Operation HAVEN was 3 Commando Brigade Royal Marines, the UK's mountain and arctic warfare amphibious force, commanded by Brigadier Andy Keeling.[1] From January to March 1991 the Air Squadron had been conducting annual Arctic and mountain training in Norway and watching the progress of the Gulf War on Sky TV. On 17 April 1991, two days after returning from Easter leave, I was catching up on the inevitable paper war in my office at RNAS Yeovilton. Having been on tenterhooks since the Iraqis invaded Kuwait the previous summer, we had long since reconciled ourselves to the fact that the Commando Brigade was unlikely to be involved in events in the Middle East. It was a total surprise, therefore, when I received a phone call at 1600 that evening from Colonel Ady Wray, Chief of Staff at HQ Commando Forces, who told me that I should join the Brigade recce team at RAF Brize Norton at 0600 the next morning to fly to Northern Iraq.

After a quick orders group, or 'O Group', to the Squadron key personnel, I hurried home to pack a few items in my bergen, telling my wife, Jane, that I would be back home in three or four days. At RAF Brize Norton the next morning I met the other members of the Brigade recce team and we were inoculated against meningitis and cholera, issued with US dollars and briefed by the Chief of Staff of HQ Strike Command. We learned that we were to work as part of a multi-national coalition under the leadership of the United States who already had troops and a command staff in theatre. The Combined Task Force of Operation PROVIDE COMFORT, as the overall operation was to be named, was to be under command of Lieutenant General John M. Shalikashvili, the Deputy Commander of USEUCOM, who was destined to become Chairman of the Joint Chiefs of Staff a few years later.[2] He was already in theatre with his HQ set up at the NATO airbase of Incerlik in Southern Turkey. We also were told that the potential military threat that the allies faced was three Iraqi infantry divisions from 5 Corps based at Mosul. Our recce team was to be led by Air Vice Marshal R.E. Johns and a planning cell from the Joint Force HQ.[3]

At 1145 we took off in an RAF VC10 for Incirlik air base where we arrived that evening to plunge straight into briefings from General Shalikashvili's staff until sleep became a necessity. All day and night, as a background to our planning, a steady procession of C-5 Galaxies, C-141 Starlifters and C-130 Hercules droned in and out of the air base with cargo and troops in an impressive demonstration of what a major power can do when it has determined a course of action. General Shalikashvili, or Shali as he was known, was a short bespectacled and industrious American of Georgian descent who always had a ready word for any troops whom he passed and very quickly earned widespread respect. We learned that Operation PROVIDE COMFORT was further divided into two joint task forces, JTF Alfa (initially known as EXPRESS CARE) under the command of Brigadier General Richard W. Potter and JTF Bravo (formerly ENCOURAGE HOPE) under the command of Major General Jay M. Garner.[4]

OP HAVEN – DEPLOYMENT

JTF A was to be deployed to the North, on the border with Turkey, with the task of supplying aid to the refugees in the mountains whilst JTF B was to evict the Iraqi Army and establish a Safe Haven to which the Kurds could be persuaded to return. It was decided that 40 Commando would be initially detached to JTF A, whilst 45 Commando and the rest of 3 Commando Brigade would be deployed to JTF B. To their intense disappointment, 42 Commando were told that they would not be required to deploy from UK. After a further twenty-four hours of planning we were told that three of our recce party, Lieutenant Colonel Graham Kerr, the Commanding Officer of 29 Commando Regiment Royal Artillery, myself and Captain Jon Spencer, the Brigade Quartermaster of 3 Commando Brigade RM, would now become the advance party as 45 Commando would shortly be arriving from UK by VC10. I was thus not to return home for thirteen weeks and quickly grabbed ten minutes on the RAF C-130 detachment satellite telephone link in order to pass a long kit list of items for my wife, Jane, to pack for me.

The next day, 20 April, I hitched a lift with Captain Jon Spencer in an RAF Chinook for a two-and-a-half-hour flight to Diyarbakir and from there on for another hour by US Army Chinook to Silopi on the border with Iraq. It was hot and noisy in the Chinook and I had difficulty reading my 1:500,000-scale air chart whilst looking backwards through the open ramp as we thudded at low level along the course of the River Tigris. It was the first of many heavily-laden Chinook rides that we were to make over the next three months, surrounded by piles of bergens, jerrycans, spare engines and rations. On arrival at Silopi, we found ourselves on a large plateau surrounded by spectacular snowcapped mountains. The plateau was totally devoid of trees but surprisingly green under large areas of young cereal crops. The US Marines had just arrived at Silopi and were setting up a large forward operating base (FOB). We borrowed a USMC Hummer, which drove us down the dusty road towards the Iraqi border in order to look for a suitable site for a Brigade concentration area. It was a unique experience to be in this relatively remote area at very short notice as the advance of what was to be a considerable UK military effort. The dusty area which had been indicated to us as a probable location we found covered in rubbish and excrement. A mile farther south we found a vast flat field covered in young green wheat shoots bounded on one side by a small river flowing in a deep ravine. This, we decided, should be the concentration area and we roughly marked out unit areas. I chose a spot next to the river for the Squadron because I wanted to operate as far away as possible from the dust and vehicular activity of the Brigade units and also to minimise the nuisance of helicopter noise to the HQ. Jon Spencer drove off to negotiate the compensation for the farmer's crop whilst I went to liaise over airspace co-ordination and communications with the USMC Aviation Combat Element, based on HMM-264 Reinforced, who were setting up LZ Leatherneck a mile away beside the Silopi road. That night the two of us laid out our sleeping bags next to our bergens in the empty wheat field and tucked into a ration pack whilst far off in UK the machinery of operational deployment moved into high gear. This field, at various stages, became the staging post for Commando units, the base for my Squadron, the Brigade Headquarters and, once the Commando Logistic Regiment Royal Marines arrived in theatre, the Brigade Maintenance Area. Throughout the next few months a nomadic shepherd grazed his goats amongst the military equipment on the steadily diminishing fodder that was growing.

Three days later the Squadron advance party departed from RAF Lyneham in two RAF C-130 Hercules transports with a Gazelle folded into the cargo hold of each. I hitched another lift from Silopi back to Diyarbakir by USMC CH-53 Sea Stallion and, lulled by the heat and noise, promptly fell asleep. I awoke to unusual vibration and the sound of major power fluctuations. Going forward to the cockpit I found that the aircraft was at 6,000 feet, IMC in dust at 120 knots, in-flight refuelling from a USMC KC-130 tanker which was trailing a hose and basket from a pod under the port wing. In the afternoon convection turbulence at one moment we were above the KC-130's horizontal stabiliser, within a rotor span of separation, and the next below it and our refuelling probe in front of the nose flexed alarmingly. The vibration came from the CH-53's tail rotor, the top of which was intermittently entering the KC-130's prop wash in the turbulence. We were refuelling in a racetrack pattern and at the end of each leg we banked into a 180-degree rate-one turn behind the tanker and I was impressed at the skill involved in this uncomfortable, very close, formation. With a brief spray of fuel on our windscreen we eventually disengaged from the drogue and descended again to relatively comfortable low level. I arrived at Diyarbakir to find Ron Crawford, my Senior Pilot, busy assisting our REME technicians in assembling the two Gazelles. The air base was now a hive of activity as the allied effort moved into top gear. VC10s, C-130s, French C-160 Transalls, C-141 Starlifters and C-5 Galaxies were landing in stream. A mass of Chinooks and Blackhawks were being readied on the grass adjacent to the taxiways. We had an interesting evening as Turkish Air Force F-104S Starfighters were determined to continue to use their air-to-ground gunnery range on the airfield perimeter, some 400 metres from the forward mounting base accommodation area, with their M61A1 Vulcan cannon. It was an impressive floor show for the troops who sat down to watch whilst they ate their first of many US 'meals ready to eat' or MREs, enlivened by the growl of the Gatling guns and the occasional 20mm ricochet overhead.

We were to operate in an area that was largely unknown to Western military since the British Army and RAF had operated against the Kurds in the 1920s.[5] Mapping was therefore a problem. US satellite photography came to the rescue and the 1920-era UK-surveyed 1:100,000 maps were rapidly overprinted with up-to-date satellite information in purple. Much of the overprint consisted of marking villages as 'destroyed'. Other than the destruction of countless villages and a couple of recent roads, the ground had not changed during the intervening years. It was a thrilling moment to fly the Gazelles forward the next day to Silopi, along the impressive course of the River Tigris. The great river ran through deep ravines and past countless antiquities ranging from ancient bridges to ruins and mounds. There was no one to speak to on the radio other than 'Cougar', the NATO AWACS aircraft on task at high altitude in a racetrack pattern over Northern Iraq and South-Eastern Turkey. On arrival at Silopi, no sooner had we refuelled than we were immediately tasked to recce the main road heading east into Northern Iraq. Again it was a strange moment as the pair of aircraft in tactical formation crossed the trench works which designated the border, without permission, at low level. Once in Iraq, we flew over extensive First World War-style defensive positions. Doubts about the value of our years of vehicle recognition training were dispelled as we came across a wide range of Soviet bloc equipment including T-62 tanks, IMR combat engineer vehicles, BRDM armoured scout cars and D-20 field guns. It was a unique experience for us to fly over manned Iraqi positions but no fire was directed at us. Contour flying at fifty feet, we penetrated as far as Saddam Hussein's summer palaces and the adjoining airfield under construction at Sirsenk some sixty miles to the east. The airfield had been designed to specifically serve the palace complexes but the completion date had been delayed considerably by allied bombing during Operation DESERT STORM NORTH and a number of 1,000lb bomb craters were spaced diagonally across the runway and surrounding terrain.

On our return to Silopi we refuelled at the USMC forward arming and refuelling point (FARP). This was a quick and efficient system, with aircraft queuing up in the hover to use four or five adjacent refuelling hoses, which snaked out from large black rubber pillow tanks (known as HERS or Helicopter Expeditionary Refuelling System). The considerable danger to our small Gazelles from the 100-knot rotor downwash of Chinooks and CH-53s meant that we were glad of our ability to use zenith pump refuelling from 40-gallon AVTUR drums, something we had hitherto believed was long since redundant. So, on the second day, we moved away to our quiet greenfield site and refuelled our aircraft in the time-honoured fashion of the First World War era, much to the amusement of the Americans.

Further to the north, where the mountains increased to between 8,000 and 12,000 feet near the Turkish border, we began to fly to Kurdish refugee camps in order to drop off troops to man drop zones for air re-supply. This was part of Phase 1 of the operation which had been conducted by US and RAF C-130s since the plight of the Kurds had been brought to our TV screens. Flying in these high altitude, narrow, valleys was not without risk as, without warning, C-130s would appear in stream running in low level to air drop supplies. There was no room for manoeuvre for either the C-130s or us and our aircraft were particularly effectively camouflaged at low level. The Coalition was fortunate not to lose a helicopter from aerial-delivered stores in the first few days before a system of LZ control on manned frequencies was introduced. However, during these early days the imperative was to save life and thus short cuts were fully justified. On the ground conditions were appalling, with death amongst the refugees due to starvation, exposure and disease. Every bush or piece of scrub had been used as fuel for fires. The dead could not be properly buried in the stony ground and were put in scrapes and covered with rocks. Airdrop parachutes and packing materials were littered everywhere and were put to use as shelters. Remarkably, even at these high altitudes, anti-personnel minefields had been randomly laid and many of the Kurds scrambled into minefields in their efforts to recover airdropped supplies. This did not seem to deter onlookers and this acceptance of the risk of mines was a Kurdish characteristic with which we were to become familiar.

On 30 April the rest of the Squadron arrived at the Turkish port of Iskenderun with the remaining ten helicopters on the RFA *Argus*, together with the balance of 3 Commando Brigade. It was to be a long flight of approximately 350 nautical miles for the aircraft over unfamiliar ground and we arranged for a Turkish refuelling bowser to be pre-positioned at Gaziantep, at roughly the halfway point (this was some years before Gaziantep Oğuzeli International Airport was constructed). I flew to Diyarbakir to meet them and was relieved to hear the familiar tones of callsign 'Magpie' on the Squadron UHF frequency when they were about fifteen minutes out to the west. They eventually arrived with minutes of fuel remaining in the middle of a totally uncharacteristic rainstorm. They were not to see rain for the next three months.

After a wet night at Diyarbakir (at least there were no air to ground firings by the F-104s) and multiple requests from the Turks to move aircraft from one parking spot to another, we set off the next morning in two formations, ten minutes apart, for Silopi, where we arrived at 1100 to find our wheat field a mudbath. However, there was little time to spare as the O Group for the Brigade advance into Iraq was to be held at 1500 and, as the mud dried, the remainder of the day was spent fitting TOW booms and loading live warshot missiles to the aircraft.

In order to save life the operation was mounted at very short notice with little or no time for combined planning. The aim was to provide security and humanitarian assistance in order to expedite the movement of Kurds from refugee camps to their homes. The operation fell into three phases. Phase 1, already underway, consisted of immediate lifesaving support by air drop which continued to be an ongoing process by the C-130s, augmented by the recently arrived helicopter lift. Phase 2 was to move refugees down from mountains. In order to achieve this, the CTF would have to push back an Iraqi division so as to establish a 'Safe Haven' for the Kurds. The Iraqi I Corps was responsible for Northern Kurdistan and it was reported that two of their infantry divisions plus two independent tank units were occupying, or positioned nearby the Kurdish area with two Republican Guard armoured brigades on standby near Mosul.[6] The third and final phase was to assist in starting to re-establish the Kurds' livelihoods. This as yet tenuous task was to be achieved by supplying food and medical treatment to the refugees whilst they re-settled, but this was to be in the future. We were about to embark on Phase 2 at the rush.

Chapter 22

Op HAVEN – Establishing the Safe Haven

Half an hour before first light on 2 May the air was filled with the sound of aircraft running up. Our six Lynx Mk 7s were given the task of armed escort for the RN Sea King HC.4s lifting 45 Commando into the Zhaku area, and then for subsequent armed reconnaissance. At H Hour the sky was filled with USMC CH-46s, CH-53s, UH-1Ns, AH-1Ts, US Army CH-47s, Blackhawks, Lynx, French Pumas, Gazelles and RN Sea Kings, not to mention USAF and USN fixed-wing support at higher level. We spent most of that day in the air but it was soon apparent that our rate of advance was much quicker than expected and the point troop of 45 Commando had to halt in order to give the Iraqis time to withdraw. At mid-morning I flew the Brigadier to Batufa, twenty-two miles inside Iraq, for an O Group with Major General Robin Ross,[1] the commander of JFHQ at Incirlik. It was at Batufa (also called Batifa) police station that I saw the first of many scenes which indicated the level of persecution of the Kurds. The ground floor of the police station was covered in abandoned Kurdish belongings – clothes, children's shoes, sleeping mats, cooking utensils, pots and a cradle. It was immediately obvious that these precious belongings would not have been abandoned without good reason and the impression was that the Kurds must have fled hurriedly in fear. There were no signs of Kurds, bodies or graves, and one of the riddles of Kurdistan was the absence of bodies, although the evidence of flight and fear was commonplace.

The next day, 3 May, the advance had progressed so far that it was time to move half the aircraft to the first of our forward operating bases, or FOBs, forty miles into Iraq. We called this FOB 'Capbadge' and it was situated in the most beautiful mountainous country next to a destroyed village called Shirati. The rocky ground was sparsely covered with carob and olive trees, thyme and spice bushes, and the surrounding terrain was riven with deep gullies and rocky outcrops. On all sides jagged ochre-coloured mountains thrust up against a clear blue sky. Above all, the country was completely devoid of human beings, villages, livestock, paved roads and any form of infrastructure. In our area of operations there were some 2,000 destroyed villages which had been completely bulldozed and only overgrown foundations and piles of stones indicated where Saddam Hussein's forces had carried out their policy of ethnic cleansing over the previous fifteen years. In one particular valley, at Kani Masi, there was a large area of what, from the air, looked like rows of burnt matchsticks. I was later told that this was all that remained of once lush orchards which had been defoliated in order to deter any future resettlement.

Our FOB was remarkably simple. A number of dispersed helicopter landing sites were cleared of rocks and a refuelling point set up 300 metres away, which consisted of a bowser with a hose running out from each side. The Flight technicians worked from a tent alongside their trailers fitted with tool bins. A larger tent was erected for aircrew briefing and planning next to the radio-equipped Land Rover which the duty pilot and signaller occupied as the nerve centre of the Flight. The rest of the Flight personnel quickly settled into twelve-man tents whilst the Senior Pilot and I pitched two small 9 by 9 tents beside my Land Rover, weighted down with rocks. Two Elsans were positioned discreetly in a small re-entrant a few minutes' walk away (although when time permitted I preferred to take a long walk with a spade). Washing facilities initially consisted of pouring half a jerrycan of water over myself whilst standing on a convenient flat rock outside the 9 by 9, although later a homemade shower was constructed for the FOB. Nine days after we had settled into Capbadge, the remaining half of the Squadron moved to a second FOB in Iraq known as 'Breezeblock' some seven kilometres west of FOB 1, whilst the supporting elements, or Echelon, moved to a third site known as 'Workhorse'. I decided to remain based at FOB 1, which was only a ten-minute drive from Brigade HQ, although of course I visited the other locations almost every day. We quickly settled into a busy but satisfying routine of flying from half an hour before dawn until dark. After flying came a daily 2100 briefing. Then, after cooking a boil-in-the-bag ration on a 'Peak' cooker, it was time for six hours of deep sleep until 0500. It was a simple and pleasant way of life.

It was clear that the Iraqi Army was literally falling over itself in its efforts to withdraw in response to General Shalikashvili's advance warning to General Nashwan Dahnoun of the Iraqi Army as to Coalition objectives. Any vehicle that was unserviceable was abandoned and we came across large quantities of 152mm artillery ammunition and even T-62 tanks. The Iraqis were short of transport and anything that could not be trucked out was abandoned, although they did deliberately leave over 300 'armed policemen' behind, believed to be from the Iraqi 66 Special Assault Brigade.[2] As we flew over the recently vacated areas, I spotted a twin-barrelled anti-aircraft gun that appeared to have been left behind on a hillock near Swartuka. Two days later we briefed our MT troop to recover it with a patrol including a 4-ton Atlas vehicle equipped with a hydraulic crane. Because of the real possibility that it had been booby-trapped they were accompanied by an RE search team. We found the ZU-23-2 intact with live rounds in the chamber and with spare barrels and a tool kit lying beside it.[3] In a gully behind the weapon were 10,000 rounds of Soviet ammunition efficiently packed in olive-painted greased cans, like giant sardine tins. The only item which was missing was the optical sight but this weapon *in extremis* can be used by adjusting the fall of shot of the tracer. We lifted the weapon just as a group of *Peshmerga*, or armed Kurds, tried to claim it and took it back to FOB 1 where it was cleaned and set up to defend the landing site. Soon it was joined by a second weapon which we recovered from elsewhere and utilised in a similar fashion. There was a sequel to this tale at the end of the operation.

Within days Coalition forces had pushed the Iraqis back to the boundaries of what became known as the 'Safe Haven'. As far as I am aware, this was not a pre-designated boundary: it was the point at which political clearance for further advance was no longer forthcoming. The geographic limits of the Safe Haven seemed to be satisfactory with the exception of the town of Dahuk, a prominent and intact town in a land of otherwise destruction and the Kurds' provincial capital. Despite US Secretary of State James A. Baker instructing the Iraqis to withdraw thirty kilometres south of Zakho to the 37th Parallel, the Iraqi 44th Infantry Division continued to occupy the town of Dahuk in some strength[4] and it appeared that this was the point at which the Iraqis might choose to stand and fight. We conducted recces and O Groups for the occupation of Dahuk, with or without opposition. D Day was delayed by twenty-four hours and then delayed yet again but the political go-ahead for the advance on Dahuk never came.

As soon as the advance was over the Brigade embarked on the next stage of Phase Two, moving the refugees down from the mountains. Our sorties were a mixture of humanitarian tasking and tactical armed patrols against the Iraqi Army. Each day at least one pair of TOW-equipped Lynx would fly along the forward Iraqi positions to check whether there was any build-up of troops or encroachment, often covered by a pair of often invisible USAF A-10s high above us at medium level in the heat haze. On one occasion an armed pair of Lynx, callsign 'Spartan', captained by Colour Sergeant Kevin Butler and Sergeant Damian Irving, on patrol at low level about twenty-five miles north of Mosul, noticed that two A-10s had descended and were rolling in on them in an aggressive manner. Using their Air Combat Manoeuvring training, a 'tac right' was immediately called turning towards the closing A-10s, followed by 'dig, dig' whilst Sergeant Irving tried to contact the AWACS on the radio. As Colour Sergeant Butler called 'Radar Section pinch, pinch', the A-10s on Cougar's frequency were heard to identify the Lynx as friendly by the Union flags on the aft fuselage and by their familiar ACM manoeuvres. Apparently from altitude the Lynx pair had resembled Mil Mi-24D Hinds. Our armed patrols led to an interesting exchange of signals later in the operation when we were asked by MoD how many hours each war-shot TOW missile had been flown. Our answer led to an immediate message to change all our missiles and replace them regularly after a specified number of hours in the air. Usually UK TOW had been fitted and then shortly afterwards either fired or removed; exposure to extended periods of carriage in flight and vibration was unusual. The Gazelles were fully utilised in the liaison and communication role in the mountainous country which only had a single useable vehicle supply route.

I generally liked to fly with all the Squadron aircrewmen but during Op HAVEN my usual crewman was the quietly efficient and professional Sergeant Kevin Dale and, knowing how each other was thinking, we worked well together in the cockpit.[5] Typical of the tasks the Squadron undertook was a call on VHF FM to my Lynx as I returned after a task on 3 May informing us that a patrol near Sarsing had found a critically ill Kurdish girl. A six-figure grid was passed and, as we approached the location, blue smoke curled up from an 83 grenade. I put the Lynx into a high hover and held it there for thirty seconds whilst a maelstrom of dirt, debris and litter blew away and then descended vertically into the confined area. It was hard to believe that the pitiful bundle of rags which was placed in the rear of the aircraft was really a seventeen-year-old girl. Knowing that once we flew her away contact would be lost with her family, we helped her teenage brother into the back where he squatted on the freight floor next to the leading medical assistant who was cradling the inert bundle in his arms. Twenty minutes later we landed at Zakho in another large cloud of re-circulating dust where the hard-pressed French Army surgical team stationed there took her into their care. We were told by the medic that her forearm had been nearly severed by a bayonet some weeks before and gangrene had set in. Much later I wondered whether she survived and whether or not she or her brother met up with their family again. At the time there was no opportunity to worry about such niceties and indeed it was better not to do so.

Sadly we also had to fly US Army casualties who had unwittingly entered minefields. The Italian plastic Valsella Valmara 69 jumping mine was a particularly unpleasant weapon with a lethal radius of 25 metres, which often seemed to kill the individual who initiated it and took the legs from the next nearest person.[6] Reportedly Iraq had acquired nine million of them over the preceding years. One of our pilots, Sergeant Damian Irving, was particularly courageous in landing his Lynx in a minefield on top of a mountain in order to rescue a critically injured US soldier from 3/325th US Airborne Regiment. He had just flown Brigadier Keeling to meet with Lieutenant Colonel John Abizaid, the CO of the 3/325th[7] when they heard a distant explosion. Realising the probable cause of the blast, use of the Lynx was immediately offered to the Americans. They found a four-man recce patrol, of whom one man was critically injured with blast injuries and a missing lower leg and two others suffering less severe blast and shrapnel injuries. Thanks to the prompt casevac all survived and Sergeant Irving subsequently earned a well-deserved Mention in Despatches. On returning from dropping off the casualty the aircraft suffered a bird strike with a large vulture-sized bird which covered the front of the aircraft in gore but thankfully did no other damage.

Fortunately throughout the operation there were no British casualties through mines. Good training may have played its part but luck undoubtedly had a great deal to do with it. There were many occasions when marines saw mines and, on one memorable occasion, I found myself in an anti-personnel minefield in the company of Brigadier Keeling, the Brigade CoS, Major Rob Fry,[8] and an escort party. One of the Air Squadron clearance patrols had found the abandoned remains of the village of Zewa Piramus located in a gully up against a mountainside, rather like the 'hole in the wall' in the Wild West. There was only one pass affording entrance to the village which had once been defended by well concealed sangars. Although Saddam Hussein's forces had made their customary thorough job of demolishing the village, they had left the well and the fruit trees intact and the ruins had a haunted air. Knowing that the Brigadier and Rob Fry welcomed the chance to get into the hills and have a break from Brigade HQ, I suggested that we might take another patrol to Zewa Piramus. A Lynx flew them to an RV a mile from the village where they both joined our foot patrol. They were fascinated by the ruins where we met a Kurdish family who had walked up from the way-station at Daudiya in order to see their former village. They were busy picking fruit when we found them and their much embarrassed son of about ten years old was having a bath in the stream. We chatted and it appeared that the father was resigned to the fact that the village was beyond rebuilding. Two Kurdish youths were with them, one of whom was mentally retarded, and they accompanied us as we moved on through the village towards the cliff face. The youths went ahead up a steep overgrown path between the boulders when we suddenly became aware of Valmara 69 mines in the long grass on either side of us. They had been surface-laid for a long time and were weathered, with their rusting sand-coloured spike-like probes sticking up amongst the dry grass. The boys thought nothing of this and, before any of us could stop him, the leader picked one up to show to us. It was pointless shouting at him – he might have dropped it, so we quietly and firmly told him to put it down and retraced our steps to the ruins, carefully stepping on rocks where possible. The danger from mines will remain an Iraqi legacy in these hills for many years to come, until they eventually rust away.

In early May the BBC Chief News Correspondent, Kate Adie, and her cameraman, Nigel Bateson, spent time with us, flying on some of our Lynx patrols and reporting on the operation. This led to a strange and sad supplementary task which involved the Squadron. She asked us to keep our eyes and ears open for any word on the fate of three British journalists, Nick de la Casa aged thirty, his wife Rosanna and his brother-in-law Charles Maxwell who had been missing since 23 March when they had left the Turkish border town of Yuksecova on foot with a Kurdish guide for the Iraqi border. On 5 May Kate arrived at FOB 1 to say that she had received reports of their bodies being beside a tributary of the Tigris on the Iraqi/Syrian border. We received clearance to check this out and conducted a hover search over the minefields there, finding only a dead dog. Kate Adie was shortly afterwards taken ill and flown back to London where it was found she had contracted the rare Congo-Crimea haemorrhagic fever.[9] Two weeks later, however, a member of the PKK (Kurdistan Workers Party), Kara Saiid, sought sanctuary at Brigade HQ and offered to lead us to the bodies of two Europeans that he had seen in the mountains in totally the opposite direction to the previous tip-off. Sergeant Damian Irving and Lieutenant Steve Reynolds, accompanied by an Intelligence Corps officer, collected Saiid from the US Special Forces and decided to search him before flying, whereupon they found a grenade tucked inside his clothing. He was flown to Brigade HQ zip-tied to the floor of the cabin which made the crew feel slightly more secure. After interviewing him, it was decided that we should fly Saiid together with an armed escort, a French-speaking intelligence officer and Major Viv Rowe, the second-in-command of 40 Commando RM, to wherever he directed us the following day. Our Lynx Mk 7 lifted off from the Brigade Headquarters landing site at Sirsenk at 1430 the next day. We headed east, past the ancient hilltop town of Al Amadiyah, where the Headquarters of 45 Commando was based, and on to where the Great Zab River flows from the north through a dramatic limestone gorge, before turning east. Following the Great Zab River some thirty-two miles further east, we flew to another less impressive, gorge where the Ru e Shamdinan River joined the Great Zab from the north. From here onwards we were over totally uninhabited terrain as Saiid directed us north-north-east along the line of the Shamdinan River. We climbed steadily following the twisting river gorge, and the country became increasingly dramatic the further we flew. Around us the mountains grew more rugged and tortured as they rose from 6,000 feet above sea level to 12,500 feet on the Turkish border, where the snow-capped summit of Samdi Dagi loomed above us thirty miles ahead through the windscreen. His directions consisted of 'a gauche', 'a droit' or a hand signal indicating straight on. Eventually, after thirty-five minutes of flying, Saiid became gradually more excited and pointed to a tributary running away from the main gorge to the east as we turned to follow his directions. We soon narrowed his area of interest to a small dried-up gully on a steep mountainside. We were flying at 5,000 feet above sea level in moderate turbulence and even at that altitude the outside air temperature was 22 degrees centigrade. A glance at the aircraft performance graphs showed that in these conditions a free air hover was out of the question. I started to fly a right-hand orbit at 60 knots (the minimum power speed) in the turbulence, passing as close to the gully as I dared in the area at which he was now wildly gesticulating. It became clear that there was something out of the ordinary amongst the rocks in the steep dried-up streambed. Concentrating on the flying, I only had an impression of a piece of black cloth on the stones but Saiid in the back was highly excited and Viv Rowe agreed that there were objects there and that the site was worthy of further investigation. We finally returned to Sirsenk after eighty minutes in the air.

Brigade HQ decided to mount a company operation using B Company of 40 Commando to carry out a search and to recover any human remains. Two days later, four Sea King HC.4s, escorted by a pair of TOW-armed Lynx, dropped them on a ridge line 2,000 metres south of the site. Later that morning I flew Lieutenant Colonel Graham Dunlop, the CO of 40 Commando, together with RSM Gordon, to the scene. I found a very small confined area 500 feet below the site, amongst dwarf oak trees, to land in and we walked up to where B Company had indeed found the remains of two bodies. The company stayed overnight whilst they searched the area for the third journalist and completed their investigations. Incredibly, a marine found Rosanna's intact diary beneath the ashes of a campfire but there was no sign of the third person. This led to further investigations by Scotland Yard and it was later established that the two bodies were those of Nick de la Casa and Charles Maxwell who had been shot by their guide, probably during an argument. Rosanna's body was never found but evidence suggests that she died in the mountains. The KDP eventually found the guide and in 1993 he was tried for murder at Irbil. He was sentenced to death, later commuted to life imprisonment, and reportedly escaped from Irbil during fighting in 1997.

Although tracer was often visible at night, there was only one occasion when Iraqi forces deliberately tried to take on Royal Marines. On 13 May 1991 one of 45 Commando's OPs on a steep hillside came under fire from three or four Iraqi troops stationed at the entrance to Saddam Hussein's Summer Palace complex near Qadish. The summer palaces, together with their military guards, had been deliberately by-passed by the Coalition as a political gesture designed to show that we were not at war with the Iraqis. The fire team manning the OP took cover behind a convenient wall and the lance corporal in charge of them ordered them to hold their fire. The AK47 fire was from a range of about 500 metres and when it at last became effective the OP opened up with their Light Support Weapon (LSW) and at least two Iraqis were seen to fall.

I was called to Brigade HQ to pick up Brigadier Andrew Keeling in a Lynx and flew him to rendezvous with the CO of 45 Commando, Lieutenant Colonel Jonathan Thomson. We landed beside the main supply route about fifteen minutes after the shooting. I was keen to see what had happened and, leaving the Lynx in the capable hands of Lieutenant Steve Reynolds, joined the Brigadier and CO of 45 Commando in a Land Rover to drive up to the OP. Unfortunately, the road, which was the only route up to the OP, passed the entrance to the Summer Palace where the firefight had just originated from. As we drove past the Iraqi soldiers on the main gate in our lightweight Land Rover I half expected us to be taken out. It was a bizarre moment, seeing as we had shot two of them minutes earlier, but they merely stared in amazement at us as we sped past a few metres away. At the OP we found a very calm and collected lance corporal surrounded by empty cases. The Brigadier gave him a 'Bravo Zulu' as the section started to count and collect their expended cases. That evening, just before sunset, the OP watched the Iraqis bury their two dead in the palace gardens.

Chapter 23

Op HAVEN – Life in the Field

We also had some brushes with the wild life in Iraq. The Squadron Sergeant Major, Eddy Candlish, on entering his tent at Echelon, found a snake curled on the top of his bergen. A few days later at dusk Corporal Dusty Miller stopped his Land Rover on a dirt track in order to avoid running over a four-foot long snake. After driving on he was concerned that there was no sign of the snake in his rear-view mirror. He assumed that it might have wound itself round the front axle and would probably drop off en route. He thus continued to drive the ten miles to FOB 1 with his mind working overtime. His worries were not without foundation as, on arriving at the FOB, the snake was found to be alive, well and very angry on top of the engine rocker box cover. A crazy chase ensued by torchlight between the FOB tents until the viper was beheaded by a blow from a gollock wielded by Lieutenant Peter Norman, our OC Support Flight. Alastair Rogers, the Senior Pilot, was something of a naturalist and sent a photograph of the carcass to the Natural History Museum in Kensington who identified it as a venomous Levantine Viper. All sleeping bags were thereafter rigorously checked before entry. In my experience whilst living in the field animals and reptiles will go out of their way to avoid human beings if you, in turn, leave them alone. Kurdistan seemed to be an exception. Many of us found scorpions in, or on, our sleeping bags and a pack of wild dogs approached FOB 2 every night, becoming increasingly bold, until permission was finally given to use a 9mm pistol if necessary, whereupon the pack disappeared before a shot was fired.[1]

Throughout this period at least one armed recce was flown daily in addition to the humanitarian tasks. The recce comprised a pair of TOW-armed Lynx, sometimes additionally armed with a door-mounted GPMG. Using tactical formation flying techniques, the pair would recce the southern boundary of the Safe Haven noting Iraqi troop movements and any changes to their order of battle. The patrols were monitored by AWACS Cougar at high level and, during the last six weeks of the operation, these patrols were often conducted in conjunction with a pair of US Army AH-64 Apaches.

It was hard to imagine exactly what the Iraqis were thinking as we flew low over their positions, many of which were picturesque Beau Geste-style mud forts. Although sometimes gun barrels tracked us, we were never knowingly fired upon, as we noted a wide variety of Soviet-made vehicle and weapon types on our kneepads. The southern extremity of our patrol area was at 36 degrees 45 minutes north (approximately ten miles behind the Iraqi front line) where the hills gradually gave way to the dusty plains, covered in wheat or grassland, stretching south in the haze towards the ruins of Ninevah and the city of Mosul some thirty miles distant. We could let down to 50 feet over the wheat in this area, in combat spread formation 1,000 yards apart, and Iraqi villagers and children working in the fields would wave wildly as we flashed past them at 120 knots. I wondered at the time whether they greeted us as British/Coalition forces or whether they had waved just as readily to Iraqi Hind helicopter gunships a few months before.

Proof that our annual training in the Pyrenees had stood us in good stead became apparent in Northern Iraq. The altitude at 'ground level' in the region averaged about 3,500 feet and the temperature rose to 40 degrees C during the deployment. This high density altitude meant that a Lynx Mk 7 at a temperature of 30 degrees C in Northern Iraq could carry 520kg less payload than it could at 4,000 feet altitude at 15 degrees C in Scotland, so great care was required in calculating aircraft payload and performance. By late June the temperature at midday started to reach between 43 to 47 degrees C. This was on the operating limits of the Lynx AH Mk 7 and hydraulic and battery temperatures had to be carefully watched.

Early on in the operation a USN CH-53E had crashed, fortunately without loss of life, at one of the refugee camps after having apparently run out of yaw control whilst landing. Thankfully, no one was seriously hurt but the dark blue giant lay with its tail boom detached alongside it in the hills for some days as a visual reminder to us of the limitations of performance at high density altitude.[2] Lieutenant Paul Denning had a lucky escape when he suffered loss of yaw control whilst landing passengers at Kani Masi in Gazelle XX380. By immediately lowering the lever he stopped the yaw after two complete revolutions to port and was able to land the giddy passengers safely. Loss of fenestron control under certain circumstances was a known, albeit rare, problem with the Gazelle (in the UK military fifteen reported yaw control accidents or incidents in approximately 600,000 flying hours) and we never determined whether this incident was tail rotor breakaway due to a combination of the density altitude and weight of the aircraft or to the fenestron stall phenomenon.

Another potentially hazardous situation occurred when a Lynx returned to FOB Breezeblock just after last light. A ground handler had erroneously fitted a red and a green filter on the two right-angle torches he was using for marshalling in addition to the 'T' of white lights that had been laid on the ground. The red and green lights were initially mistaken by the pilots for an AAI, used to provide a safe glideslope to an LS at night. Luckily careful monitoring of the radalt avoided an accident and the confused crew chose to ignore the red and green indications and landed by the visual aspect of the white 'T' alone. My greatest concern, however, was that the debilitating combination of fatigue and heat might lead aircrew to make a careless mistake in this highly unforgiving environment.

Throughout, all our REME technicians worked night and day in the open to keep the aircraft serviceable. Although we were on operations it had been decided that the aircraft would be maintained to peacetime standards. They performed seven engine (ECU) changes and three main rotor gearbox changes but most remarkable of all was the first ever B5 servicing (or 800-hour deep servicing) of a Gazelle in field conditions. This procedure normally took place in a clean hangar and involved stripping the aircraft down to its component parts and re-assembling over a period of about two to three weeks. I was apprehensive when I saw Gazelle XW849 reduced to 'Airfix-kit' form lying in a myriad of parts laid out on the dust and dirt of Echelon. The technicians worked stripped to the waist whilst rotor down-wash blew grit onto their sweat, into their eyes and over their tools. Every piece, however, had been cleaned and wrapped in protective polythene and three days later the completed kit took to the air. The REME technicians, augmented by 703 AMG from 70 Aircraft Workshop, provided us with 85 per cent aircraft availability throughout the twelve weeks. I was particularly sorry that none of them received an award after the operation.

The deployment certainly proved the value of the UK ration pack. The longest period that most of us had remained on twenty-four-hour rations prior to Operation HAVEN had been about two weeks but, with no refrigeration available and no local produce, fresh rations were impractical in Northern Iraq. A few units briefly tried 'fresh food' trucked from far-off Iskenderun but suffered from 'dog' as a result. We opted therefore to stay on twenty-four-hour packs throughout the deployment, supplemented by Turkish bread every other day, oranges and apples. We had access to US MREs but, after the initial attraction of a change of diet, we continued on the British twenty-four-hour ration pack which kept us remarkably fit and well, although many of us returned home slightly slimmer. Water was collected in jerrycans daily from a Brigade waterpoint at an ancient natural spring near Sirsenk, where a detachment from 59 Commando Engineer

Squadron RE, the Brigade Royal Engineer Squadron, filtered and treated vast quantities of water daily in flexible tanks. There was an overflow from the ancient six-foot-high stone cistern downstream of the water collection point and it was an occasional real luxury to strip off and stand in the mud under the torrent of icy water clutching a bar of soap. Having pulled dusty desert DPMs back on again and walked up the hill to the Land Rover one was sweaty again within minutes and the shower just a memory.

Being interested in history I always kept an eye out for any antiquities but, apart from an ancient stone gateway at Al Amadiyah and the foundations of an ancient bridge near FOB 2, there was little obvious evidence of the past in the mountains.[3] From time to time, I used to bend the rules and go for a long walk by myself in order to think and relax in peace. On one of these walks, near FOB 2, I noticed a bank of clay and gravel which had been exposed by gully erosion. I spent a few minutes examining the exposed sub-surface for pottery and there, staring me in the face, was a large piece, which I carefully extracted from the clay. The fragment was decorated with four rows of designs. I found a few more smaller shards but no further pieces with decoration. Looking around there was no evidence of any ancient settlement although there was a stream nearby. When cleaned up the fragment looked too good to be true and I was subject to some ribbing as to whether the piece was one or two months old. Ten months later, when I was working in the Ministry of Defence in London, Professor Dominique Collon of the West Asiatic Department of the British Museum identified the piece for me. The four designs had been made with a finger pressed in the wet clay, a piece of stick and a hollow reed and it was from part of the rim of a large Hellenistic storage jar dating from between 325 BC to 30 AD, evidence of the influence of a previous military campaign in the area when the army of Alexander the Great, approximately 47,000 strong, had crossed the Tigris in the September of 331 BC prior to the battle of Gaugamela.[4]

There were times when it became very clear that we did not have a full picture of exactly what had happened, or what was happening, in the wild. This was again dramatically illustrated to me at the end of May during a flight in Gazelle XX380 from the Turkish border over the inhospitable mountains. Our track passed over a destroyed mountain village, named Hish on the map, and as we overflew what was only a pile of stones we noticed the wreck of a Soviet-built Mil Mi-8 Hip helicopter on the ground. I descended for a closer look and came to the hover beside an old Iraqi Army helicopter landing pad. The Hip had crashed beside the pad and had been there for many years. The area appeared deserted except for a number of abandoned vehicles. This was amazing because we were many miles from the nearest track and some 4,700 feet high in the mountains, yet strangely commonplace in Northern Iraq. We had seen many such sights around the mountain refugee camps and it was an indication of the level of desperation of the Kurds. As I transitioned away, we noticed two figures gesticulating at us beside an abandoned Japanese earth mover. They were pointing to their mouths and their meaning was crystal clear. It was such a remote location that I decided on return to our FOB that we would load up with rations and return to Hish. Two hours later, we were on approach to the overgrown LS with bread, water and US MREs. We were not heavy so I had put Corporal Mark Teakle as an escort in the back to show him something of the country and to assist with loading and unloading. I stopped the rotors but decided in this remote area to keep the engine running at ground idle and handed the controls to Lieutenant John Salisbury, my co-pilot. The two men approached the aircraft. One was young and bearded the other elderly, both dishevelled and dirty. Corporal Teakle and I unloaded the rations and carried them fifty yards before both men fell upon the bread and desperately stuffed it into their mouths. Leaving the two to eat, the corporal and I inspected the shell of the Hip and walked amongst the abandoned vehicles. Breasting a small rise, we realised that the ground before us was littered with clothes, children's shoes, sleeping bags, cooking pots, pans and blankets. It was like the police station at Batufa but on a much larger scale. The impression was that a large group of refugees had dropped everything in terror and fled. But where to and from whom? There were no signs of bodies (although we expected to find some at any moment) and no concrete evidence of unpleasantness. Our two strangers were watching us intently as we rummaged about and there was no mistaking the sullen hostility in their eyes. For a moment I half expected them to pull a weapon and start shooting, a sensation shared at the same instant by John Salisbury in the Gazelle 200 metres from us, as he told us later. In clear sign language we asked what had happened and where were the people. We were answered with sullen shrugs. What were they doing there on their own? Trying to repair the earth mover was the grudging answer. Not a likely tale as one of the seven-foot diameter wheels was missing and the electrics were spilling like spaghetti from the corroded engine compartment. We re-boarded the aircraft and departed, our two Kurds still munching, still watching, until they became specks in that immense mountain scenery. Although it was not our job to discriminate between the hungry, we all felt that on this occasion we might have fed the wrong people.

Chapter 24

Op HAVEN – Withdrawal

On 5 June the last refugees were lifted out of Çukurca Camp and Phase Two was complete. My field notebook showed that 466,000 refugees had been moved down to the valleys from the ten known camps in our immediate area but undoubtedly there were many more refugees. Phase Three consisted of the more nebulous task of assisting the Kurds to re-establish their livelihoods. This was achieved by setting up way-stations in order to feed and give medical treatment to the refugees on their way to resettlement. The children in particular were suffering from dehydration and lack of vitamins. It was no surprise when large encampments sprung up beside the way-stations. The Kurds seemed reluctant to start to re-build permanent houses until they were more certain of their future. There were also countless other tasks in which troops could assist during this phase, from drilling wells to erecting tents.

There was one social occasion with the Kurds that I attended during my time in Iraq. It was particularly memorable in that it took place in an abandoned and ruined hotel overlooking a deep valley with the ancient hilltop town of Al Amadiyah beyond. Brigade HQ had invited a number of COs and staff to attend and we arrived at the appointed time in our Land Rovers. We were greeted by Peshmerga who invited us to remove our weapons and leave them in the derelict foyer, much as you might leave your coat and hat. We naturally declined and gathered on what must have once been a marvellous stone terrace overlooking the valley glowing in the setting sun. A number of Peshmerga and Kurdish leaders from both the Patriotic Union of Kurdistan (PUK) and the Kurdistan Democratic Party (KDP) were there but no food or drink. The Kurdish leader Hussein Sinjari arrived in Peshmerga dress, sporting a London accent and rimless gold glasses. He was later to become the deputy representative of the Kurdish Government in London. After about two hours of polite conversation on the terrace we were led to the now dark garden where tables were laid out lit with candles. Bowls of yoghurt containing mint and raw vegetables were on the tables, bottles of Arak al Lavali from the Lebanon materialised out of the darkness, followed by slices of roast sheep. A veritable feast after weeks of ration packs. Since we were strictly dry in theatre we looked to the Brigadier for a lead before we accepted a drink. It was yet another biblical scene. We departed happily into the night but later in my tent my stomach violently rebelled against the sudden and unexpected change of diet.

The operation wound up nearly as quickly as it had started. First of all 45 Commando were thinned out back to UK. I was invited to an unforgettable farewell guest night by the unit in the hillside town of Al Amadiyah on 8 June where the menu was cleverly devised from twenty-four-hour rations washed down with lime juice. Major General Jay Garner, the US Army Divisional Commander of Joint Task Force Bravo, was guest of honour and was particularly complimentary about the patrolling skills of our marines. The next stage was for FOB 1, under command of Lieutenant Paul Denning, to move back to Silopi. The day that they were to move, on 17 June, a number of Kurds came to watch us pack up, including an old man who had once lived in the adjacent destroyed village of Shirati. He stood amongst the pile of stones that was once his house with tears streaming down his face. Once our tents and the homemade shower had been removed there was little to show that a flight of helicopters had been based there for over two months except for 'the Patio', which had been built by one of our marines whose father owned a patio-laying business in London. 'The Patio' had been beautifully constructed using abandoned marble blocks left over from Saddam's Summer Palace construction project. It was sited under an olive tree and, at the entrance, a globe and laurel RM cap badge had been cemented into the floor. Each evening members of the Flight used to gather on the Patio to chat whilst eating their ration packs. I wonder if it is still there and, if so, what future generations of Kurds will make of it. I left my bivouac site that I had occupied for the past nine weeks and moved to the Squadron echelon site near to Saddam Hussein's summer palace complex.

Earlier I mentioned how we had taken two Iraqi ZU-23-2 anti-aircraft guns into safe custody and which were subsequently added to the defences of FOB 1. At the end of the operation it seemed sensible to destroy the two weapons to prevent them being used by either side. It occurred to me that it would be nice to take them back to UK as museum pieces and signalled HQ HAVEN for permission to take them home. Knowing how tight airlift was, I expected a firm answer in the negative, but to our surprise we received an immediate signal telling us to de-activate them and deliver them to Sirsenk airfield early the next morning. De-activation in accordance with REME instructions involved two armourers working most of the night but the deadline was just achieved and the two guns departed strapped to pallets

OP HAVEN – WITHDRAWAL

in an otherwise empty C-130 bound for Cyprus. Rather disappointingly the 23mm ammunition was buried deeply in situ by the Royal Engineers, as I was looking forward to a spectacular demolition. On our return one gun was presented to the Fleet Air Arm Museum at Yeovilton whilst the other went to the Royal Marines Museum at Eastney.[1]

It was at this point that an irritating minor incident occurred which caused both myself and the Brigadier some embarrassment. Serving in the Squadron were two accomplished free-fall parachutists who, always hopeful for a jump, had brought their parachutes with them to Iraq. The Brigadier asked me if we were able to stage a farewell free-fall display in front of Major General Garner and Colonel James L. Jones Jr, the CO of 24th Marine Expeditionary Unit (SOC),[2] after which they would each be presented with a pewter statuette of a Royal Marine. We practised this evolution with the two parachutists dropping from a Lynx from 5,000 feet over Sirsenk (i.e. some 9,000 feet above mean sea level) finally touching down accurately in the patch of dusty scrub outside the Brigade HQ (known as landing site Mulberry) where the Brigadier and General Garner were due to stand. After the rehearsal I asked the very experienced sergeant leading the duo how he was going to secure the two statuettes during the jump and I was assured that they would be safe wrapped in bubble-wrap packing buttoned inside his combat jacket. At 1600 on 21 June the drop took place in front of the assembled US guests and all went exactly according to plan until the sergeant smartly saluted Brigadier Keeling who held out his hand for the statuettes. To my dismay the sergeant looked rather uncomfortable and muttered that they had fallen out of his jacket as his parachute had opened. Although the guests were amused at this turn of events, Brigadier Keeling was not and I kicked myself for not ensuring that the statuettes were hidden in the long grass on the drop zone in order to cover every eventuality. Both damaged statuettes were subsequently picked up a few hundred yards away after their free-fall by Kurds who did not seem the least bit surprised to find pewter figures lying in the grass. The battered and bent originals were presented by me to the two guests the next day with apologies, together with two new replacement figures. Once again the lesson of Murphy's Law had been re-learned.

Twelve days after FOB 1 had moved back into Turkey, FOB 2 packed up and moved both aircraft and vehicles the 500 miles back to Iskenderun for embarkation for UK. At this juncture in the allied withdrawal, a pause was ordered for political reasons. There were certainly some demonstrations from the Kurds against our withdrawal but the rumoured threat that was widely circulated that they would kill their children rather than be left to the whims of the Iraqis thankfully proved to be groundless.

Back across the Turkish border Silopi was now a far cry from the 'greenfield' site that Jon Spencer and I had chosen so many weeks before and was now a vast white plain of dust, vehicles, tents and latrines. Troops suddenly succumbed to bouts of a particularly unpleasant D and V, which prompted the Americans to analyse the dust that covered everything, that hung suspended in the air and blew about in the gusts of hot wind. They found that it contained a high proportion of animal and human faeces. Conditions at Silopi were so bad, and the transit time for supporting 40 Commando at Sirsenk was so inconvenient, that on 25 June Paul Denning's FOB moved happily back into Iraq in order to occupy a position at Sirsenk which had been just vacated by the ALAT (French Army Air Corps) Pumas and Gazelles. On 28 June the Brigade HQ staff finally left Sirsenk and flew back to Incirlik leaving the CO of 40 Commando in command in Iraq.

Three days later I reluctantly left Sirsenk airfield in an Armée de l'air C-160 Transall and two hours later was back in 'civilisation' at Incirlik. The reality of cold beer, a swimming pool and burgers were not quite as much fun as the anticipation and I admit that I was sorry to leave Kurdistan. The Kurds still required our help and protection although there were clearly sound political reasons why our assistance could not be open-ended, and it was important that they did not become dependent on us. We all realised that the future of the Kurdish people lay in their own hands. Events had overtaken us and a sortie to take Brigadier Andy Keeling to Rawanduz, eighty nautical miles to the south east of Sirsenk, for which special permission had been granted by General Shali, remained unaccomplished. I was well aware that I was unlikely to visit this amazing area again, or certainly not whilst Saddam Hussein remained in power. Paul Denning's flight stayed on at Sirsenk, providing support for 40 Commando for a further two weeks until Monday 15 July 1991, Z Day, when all allied troops were required to be clear of Iraq.

So ended Operation HAVEN, to be replaced by Operation WARDEN which was the protection of the Safe Haven by fixed-wing Combat Air Patrols flying out of Turkey and, for a few months only, the added deterrent of troops based at Silopi. When the Rainbow Battalion, as the allied ground force was known, was withdrawn, the security of the Kurds depended on the invisible trigger of allied air patrols from Incerlik. The 'no fly zone' north of the 35th Parallel was regularly patrolled by US, UK and French aircraft and continued until the Second Gulf War of March 2003 (Operation TELIC).[3] Amongst the major obstacles to any form of stability in the region were the continuing PKK attacks in Turkey which in turn resulted in punitive raids by Turkish Forces into Northern Iraq. Since Operation HAVEN, the general area of this northern zone has been regarded as the embryo Kurdish autonomous state, eventually to become the Dihok Governate in 2005 when the Iraqi Kurdistan Region was recognised in the new constitution of Iraq with Irbil as its capital.

Only history will tell how successful Operation HAVEN proved to be in the long term. General James L. Jones has described Operation PROVIDE COMFORT as 'an under-appreciated success story of geo-strategic importance'.[4] It was hoped that this successful security and humanitarian operation would prove to be the model for future similar operations. Sadly, the lessons learnt from establishing this very effective Safe Haven were not remembered. Unsupported by the necessary military and political will to ensure security, the ensuing Srebrenica massacre four years later in Bosnia and Herzegovina was the unfortunate legacy with which the term 'Safe Haven' is today more often associated.

However, in the short term, there were considerable achievements. It was a mere fifty-six days that had elapsed between the first airdrop of supplies and the last of the Kurds coming down from the mountains. The Squadron had flown 2,322 hours without accident, carrying a total of 4,213 passengers. Armed sorties by Lynx (each typically armed with four live TOW missiles and GPMGs) had amounted to a total of 180 hours of patrolling. It also proved that a properly structured, balanced and well-trained multi-national military formation can respond quickly and effectively to disaster relief and humanitarian crises. It was an operation that was tailor-made for the Commando Brigade. We were trained to operate in the mountains and to live simply with what we carried on our backs, and the decency and compassion of our marines came to the fore.[5] Operation HAVEN dramatically underlined the flexibility of the military helicopter and the years of training and professionalism invested by all members of the Squadron resulted in a very successful deployment in demanding terrain and climate, thankfully without any Squadron loss.[6]

This was the end of my flying tour as CO and thus, in the Royal Marines, the end of my active service aviation career, although I would still be involved in commanding air assets in future years. I was fortunate to have been in command during this humanitarian operation with such a large amount of varied and worthwhile flying and it was a good note to end on. The aircraft required servicing and deep cleaning back at Yeovilton with large amounts of sand and dust being removed from inside fuselage compartments and tail booms. My successor, Major Nick Pounds, enjoyed a reduced flying rate until the peacetime norms were regained.

Chapter 25

In the Back

There were a number of incidents which are firmly embedded in my memory which occurred when I was not on a flying tour, all of which contributed to my overall aviation knowledge and experience. During a staff appointment in Plymouth during 1977, I was permitted to occasionally fly Chipmunks at the Britannia Flight at Roborough Airport, Plymouth. This flight of twelve RN aircraft, commanded by Lieutenant Commander 'Sandy' Sinclair, was to provide flying grading for potential Fleet Air Arm pilots and also to give air experience to cadets at the Royal Naval College at Dartmouth. Lieutenant Commander Tim Gedge, a QFI also on a ground tour, kindly let me fly with him on a number of occasions, one of which still embarrasses me to recall.[1] Roborough airport was originally a small wartime grass field, surrounded by modern development with a single narrow 752-metre long runway 24/06. The runway was built in 1976 for the Twin Otters and Dash-7s used by Brymon Airways and lit by edge lighting on metal stalks. Later a longer runway, 31/13, was added. Whilst landing on 24 with Tim I touched down in a three-point attitude and shortly afterwards the aircraft started to swing. I applied corrective pedal and it yawed the other way. Tim called out for left or right pedal, I forget which, and with both of us now on the controls the aircraft at low speed suddenly ground-looped with a shudder, ending up in the grass facing about 150 degrees from the runway heading. Thankfully we had passed between two of the edge lights and there was no damage except to my pride and embarrassment at letting Tim down. What the passengers awaiting the arrival of the next Brymon flight thought as they watched this spectacle from the terminal windows I dare not think. Tim was good enough not to show any annoyance and it was the only time I ever lost directional control of an aircraft on landing. Since then I never relaxed my concentration on maintaining the heading of a fixed wing on landing until the aircraft has come to a complete standstill, especially with a tail dragger.

Notwithstanding my love of flying, I enjoyed infantry soldiering and commanding marines as much as a flying tour. By a twist of fate I was appointed as OC M Company of 42 Commando, in the steps of fellow QHIs Terence Murphy, David Storrie and my first CSM Derek Blevins. As a company commander, my feet were very firmly on the ground commanding three rifle troops each commanded by a lieutenant or second lieutenant and totalling 120 marines. With their average age of twenty, any worries I had of not being fit enough were soon dispelled as I found that the concerns and duty of responsibility overcame most feelings of fatigue, aches and pains. It was much more difficult for a nineteen-year-old marine GPMG gunner lying dripping wet in a hedgerow at night, with only his own discomfort to think about, than for me concerned about tactics, timings, communications and the danger of cold casualties, all of which kept my mind working overtime. But this is about flying as a passenger. For the most part I just kept quiet about being a pilot and got on with my job. The marines, especially in Northern Ireland, loved the fact that I was a pilot and used every opportunity to loudly curse 'fricking pilots' whenever weather grounded their pick-up by a support helicopter. During M Company's three-month tour in South Armagh, based at Newtownhamilton, the danger from improvised explosive devices (IEDs) on roads was severe and the only movement permitted was by helicopter or on foot. Most of our helicopter support was provided by RAF Pumas based at Bessbrook but, occasionally, by AAC Lynx from Aldergrove. Dropped at night by Puma on NVG at a certain grid in the pitch dark, our patrols would cover many miles before being picked up four or five hours later at another pre-determined grid. My memories of patrols in South Armagh are of wet nights with low cloud, although there must have been some good weather. The news that the Puma could not reach us because of early morning fog or mist was greeted by the muted cursing of 'fooking wafoos' or words to that effect. Although I personally preferred to walk rather than fly in the back of a heavily-laden Puma at night in marginal conditions, I could well understand their reactions as I shared with them the prospect of patrolling ten to fifteen kilometres back to base through muddy cow pastures and forcing our way through endless blackthorn hedges (we could not use gates or stiles for tactical reasons), laden with our bergens. After a few weeks of patrolling our two sets of well-darned combat clothing were holed and torn by barbed wire and blackthorn and we began to look like tramps until our quartermaster organised replacement trousers.

Only once as a pilot did I complain to our supporting aviation. Our daylight pick-up was by an AAC Lynx and the six of us scrambled into the back of the aircraft with our bergens piled around us on the freight floor. Usually, we might transit at low level but sometimes, in order not to set a pattern, the transit might be at medium level, following an indirect route.

FLYING LIGHT HELICOPTERS WITH THE ROYAL MARINES

On this occasion we climbed to about 4,000 feet and fifteen minutes later arrived overhead the Newtownhamilton landing site, just across the road from our base, which would be secured by the duty troop whenever it was to be used. Entering autorotation, the pilot pulled the speed back and I naturally took a close interest in proceedings, peering from the back at the panel showing the ASI flickering at about 20 knots. Vortex ring is a dangerous state whereby, if an aircraft is descending at a high rate of descent with zero or low airspeed and power is applied, the aircraft will start to vibrate heavily with no decrease in the rate of descent and unless forward airspeed is gained or autorotation is re-established quickly, disaster will occur. So I waited for the pilot to convert from 20 knots to 60 knots at about 700 feet before recovering with power. To my horror he failed to do so and instead just pulled collective pitch. The aircraft began vibrating heavily, protesting at this mishandling but, with a small forward airspeed component, we got away with it. I said nothing, de-planed anonymously with the patrol, went to our Ops Room and immediately phoned Captain Barry Board, the Army QHI at RAF Aldergrove and a fellow instructor from my days at Wallop, to inform him of this horrendous piece of airmanship. This was the only time I intervened in flying matters during a ground tour.

During the annual winter deployment M Company spent three months in the remote Jotunheimen mountains of central Norway, based at Gjendesheim. This was a summer hiking hotel in the middle of nowhere, surrounded by marvellous scenery, which in winter was completely cut off except by over-snow vehicle or skis. My notebook shows that we spent forty nights out in the mountains, so Gjendesheim was a location in which to catch up on eating, sleeping and washing between exercises. We were supported by RN Sea King HC.4 helicopters based at Bardufoss, whose crews were skilled in Arctic Commando support operations. A typical experience of a helicopter insertion was to the top of a mountain plateau for our Arctic warfare course students to carry out snow-hole survival training. On the day of the lift the sky was white and a light snow was falling in about minus 15 degrees C. As we approached the summit plateau I could see that there were potential white-out conditions with the snow surface melting into the sky, falling snow reducing visibility and devoid of obvious references. Twice we approached and entered re-circulating snow, but the surface was either sloping or unsuitable for touch-down. On the third occasion the door was slid open and we deplaned, lying on a heap next to our pile of bergens face down in deep snow, in accordance with the drill, as the icy blast of the rotor downdraught disappeared and we were eventually left in silence. I was relieved to get out of the aircraft and realised that I enjoyed flying in these conditions much more with a set of controls in front of me. However, a new challenge faced us as, meeting up with the other Sea King load of troops, we skied to the summit to find a suitable area for digging snow holes. How then a blizzard struck and the snow-hole training exercise turned to reality, as we were stuck in a howling white-out without communications for the next forty-eight hours, is another story. Good training is realistic training!

After return from Kurdistan in August 1991 I took some vacation with my family in the Outer Hebrides. We were dropped by fishing boat on the uninhabited island of Ensay where we swam and picnicked until we were picked up in the late afternoon. After lunch my fourteen-year-old daughter Clare told me that she had discovered 'a piece of crashed aircraft' behind a sand dune. Sure enough she had found a six-foot-by-two-foot section of modern fibreglass honeycomb structure edged by fourteen camlock fasteners, similar to a portion of radome. It appeared recent with little corrosion and only a few small barnacles attached. Back at our hotel that evening I passed the six-figure grid reference of the object to the Search and Rescue Co-ordination Centre at Pitreavie. Soon afterwards the Bristow S-61N duty Coastguard crew phoned me from Stornoway and told me that they planned to find the item the next day during a training sortie. The following afternoon I received a call to say that they had recovered the object and were sending it down to the Air Accident Investigation Branch (AAIB) at RAE Farnborough.[2] Some months later the AAIB told me that it was an interesting item. At first they thought that it might be connected with a Shackleton that had crashed near Northton, two and a half miles to the north-east, the previous year.[3] That was discounted and they then considered that it might have originated from the Air India Boeing 747 that was blown-up over the Atlantic.[4] After a few years with no positive identification, the part was eventually disposed of. It wasn't until about fifteen years later that it suddenly occurred to me that it might have been part of Space Shuttle Challenger.[5] It was too late to prove it one way or another but today I believe it was a reasonable theory, taking into account the Gulf Stream, the structure and images of similar recovered shuttle wreckage.

During my final tour in Naples as Assistant Chief of Staff (ACOS) for Amphibious Warfare to Commander Striking Forces Southern Europe (STRIKFORSOUTH), I was a distant witness to the fallout of a couple of sad but interesting aviation disasters. The first was when an extraordinary accident happened seventy-five miles off the Skeleton Coast of Africa. On 13 September 1997 a USAF C-141B Starlifter from McGuire AFB was flying from Windhoek to Ascension Island, having delivered mine-clearance equipment to the UN in South Africa with nine onboard. Whilst cruising at 35,000 feet just before sunset the aircraft disappeared. When, hours later, Ascension raised the fact that the aircraft was overdue, a search started and, at about the same time, it transpired that a Luftwaffe Tu-154M (from the former East German Air Force) flying from Cologne to Capetown with twenty-four on board was also missing between Niger and Windhoek. Gathering information was difficult because in large parts of Africa there was little or no air traffic control service and aircraft were assigned quadrantal cruising levels depending on their magnetic headings. In these areas HF was often the sole way to contact a Flight Information Region and verbal aircraft position reports were the only means of tracking progress. However, on this occasion, the US reported that one of their surveillance satellites had picked up a momentary bright flash off the Skeleton Coast at the time the aircraft went missing, so it was suddenly realised that a mid-air collision had taken place.[6] I know Namibia well and one of the joys of the Skeleton Coast is its absolute solitude; no people, no lights, no traffic and no vapour trails or aircraft. How could this have happened? It was comparable to two hunters firing rifles from each side of a wide valley and their bullets colliding with each other in mid-flight. When search operations were initiated, the nearest USN P-3 Orion maritime aircraft were from VP-45, stationed at NAF Sigonella in Sicily 4,000 miles to the north, and our colleagues in AIRSOUTH despatched two aircraft to Windhoek to assist with the search.

The US enquiry eventually found that the German crew were to blame for the accident which was also caused by inadequate air traffic control arrangements in west central Africa. The German crew flight planned for 35,000 feet, climbing en route to 39,900 feet, neither of which were correct quadrantal flight levels to ensure separation for their magnetic heading. In the event the collision occurred at 35,000 feet without the Namibian controllers knowing that a Tu-154 had entered their Flight Information Region. Angolan ATC authorities had apparently failed to inform Windhoek of the German aircraft, a standard ICAO procedure. Even though it was VMC, the position of the low sun in the windscreen may have prevented sight of conflicting traffic to the C-141 crew and who, anyway, would have considered a serious risk of collision in empty Namibian skies? Some wreckage and a body were initially found and eventually flight recorders and more bodies were recovered from the deep by ROVs. This sad and unlikely accident was a major impetus for the Traffic-alert Collision Alert System (TCAS) to be installed on aircraft.[7]

The second incident concerned my immediate boss, Brigadier General Guy Vander Linden USMC, who was the senior USMC officer in the region when a USMC EA-6B Prowler was involved in a tragedy in northern Italy. EA-6Bs were detached to Aviano air base in order to provide reconnaissance over Bosnia. On 3 February 1998 a Prowler of VMAQ-2 with a crew of four took off on a low-level sortie around the lakes and mountains of the Cavalese Dolomites. Their briefing stipulated a 1,000-foot minimum, although it later transpired that regulations stated that they should have been above 2,000 feet. Near Cermis the Prowler's right wing hit the two-inch steel cable of a cable car at approximately 360 feet AGL.[8] The cable snapped and the twenty occupants fell to their deaths. Astonishingly, the main spar of the Grumman Prowler remained intact and the aircraft recovered to base with a deep gouge in the leading edge of the wing. I was told that passengers waiting in the lower cable-car station heard a loud crash and felt the earth shake as the 16-ton counterweight tensioning the cable fell to the floor. By a sad coincidence, Cermis had been the scene of an earlier cable-car accident in 1976. The incident caused a lot of bad feeling and anger in Italy and Guy Vander Linden was in an unenviable situation when approached by the international press immediately after the event.[9]

My job involved planning and running NATO amphibious exercises in the Mediterranean. Particularly interesting were the CO-OPERATIVE PARTNER series which involved nations who wished to join NATO. These included Bulgaria, Georgia, Romania and Ukraine. The exercises also introduced these ex-Warsaw pact countries, who at that time still operated predominantly ex-Soviet equipment, in how to integrate with NATO procedures and practices. On a number of occasions I visited the Bulgarian Naval Aviation base Tchaika (Seagull) near Varna, an old seaplane base built by the Germans in the First World War and where the Bulgarian Navy operated eleven Russian-built Mil Mi-14PL Haze amphibious anti-submarine helicopters.[10] This was a heavy twin-engined lump of a helicopter weighing in at 26,000lb empty and 31,000lb at max take-off. It was based on the troop-carrying Mi-8 Hip but with an added boat-like hull, float sponsons including a tail float, four retractable undercarriage legs, radar, weapons bay and a towed magnetic anomaly detector. Most of the twelve helicopters based there were unserviceable, requiring, amongst other items, new rotor blades which, since the fall of the Soviet Union, had become unduly expensive. Two were serviceable, although the crews logged very few annual flying hours, and I was taken for a memorable flight in one of them. I clambered into the typically Russian turquoise-painted cockpit with a myriad of alarm-clock-sized instruments and heavy-duty switches and sat in the jump seat. The thing was built like a tank. After ten minutes of very low flying, the captain indicated that I should take his left-hand seat and the controls. I would naturally have loved to have flown the Haze but, since he did not speak English and I could not speak Bulgarian and all instrumentation was in Cyrillic markings, I felt that this was definitely not sensible and declined the offer. I had learned my lesson with the French major in the Pyrenees fourteen years earlier. This caused temporary minor offence and I had to do quite a lot of explaining afterwards to smooth ruffled feathers. After a thirty-minute low-level nav just above the tree tops to the south of Varna, we returned to the port and 'beat up' the quayside, flying between the dockyard cranes and over the Navy Headquarters building where the rest of my team were working on the forthcoming exercise. The crew decided to come around for a second 'better' pass whilst I looked out at the cranes, wires and radio masts and rather wished I was somewhere else. No doubt they thought I was a bit of a 'Western' wimp. Later, after a wealth of signal traffic, we managed to get clearance for the first deck landing of a Bulgarian helicopter on a US naval destroyer with a USN aviator advising and observing from the cockpit.

A year later Captain Bob Wilde USN, a rotary aviator and one of my planning staff, and I had an interesting flight in a Romanian IAR 330 Puma near the Danube delta. It was a licence-built aircraft manufactured by IAR Brasov and this particular one was fitted with VIP seating and tables which had been installed by local carpenters. We were at the Babadag live-firing ranges on the northern coast in bitterly cold weather, an area of wetlands and rolling grasslands overlooked by the magnificent Enisala castle ruins dramatically perched on a rocky outcrop. We embarked for a flight back to Constanta Naval Base where our exercise planning staff were located. It was interesting to see a flight engineer board the aircraft and start the engines before the two pilots took their seats ready for their pre-take-off checks. Unfortunately, this sortie involved another display of ultra-low flying, partly over an icy Black Sea without life jackets. Where the ethos comes from that the lower and faster you can fly, the better pilot you are, I don't know. It seemed to be an aerial version of 'mine is bigger than yours'. So it became another white-knuckle ride until we arrived at the helipad at Constanta which was situated on a grassy mound raised above a public footpath. I could see Bob Wilde's face registering some alarm and surprise whilst looking out of his window on the opposite side of the cabin as we landed. It transpired that an elderly man in coat and hat was walking his dog on a lead along the footpath and lay flat on his face in the snow, clutching the dog, as the helicopter transitioned to the hover just above him.

IN THE BACK

One of my responsibilities as director for Exercise CO-OPERATIVE PARTNER 1998 in Romania was to organise a public day at Constanta on the Sunday following the end of the exercise. Since it was June everyone would be on Mamaia beach, so it was convenient to plan an amphibious landing, static display and demonstration on a section of seashore. There would also be an 'air display' which was more accurately a fly-past of various aircraft of contributing nations along the beach. Captain Bob Wilde, our air-co-ordinator, did the planning which consisted of pairs of aircraft each separated by a few minutes, flying along the six miles of gently curving public beach. The idea was that the fast jets would lead at about 420 knots, followed by slower types and ending with helicopters. We carefully stipulated a height of not below 300 feet and a 'display line' not closer than 500 metres from the shoreline. We made the point that, apart from safety issues, it was much easier for spectators to view aircraft flying at a reasonable height at a reasonable distance rather than too low and too close. During the Saturday rehearsals Bob and I were positioned with a UHF radio in the centre of the beach, and all went according to plan with a few small adjustments and the fast jets being reminded to fly a little further away from the coastline. On the Sunday the initial pair of MiG-29 Fulcrums signed-in off the Port of Constanta, followed a few minutes later by a pair of MiG-21 Lancers. The third serial of two MiG-23 Floggers then checked-in and also began their run-in as the MiG-21s cleared, but for the life of me, I could not see them approaching, normally trailing black exhaust parallel to the coast. I began to curse under my breath as the two-minute separation ticked away with still no sign of the Floggers. However, I had been looking in the wrong direction! With seconds to go, to my astonishment the pair appeared above the heads of nearby sunbathers on the beach. The height of low-flying jets is often exaggerated by onlookers but experience told me that they were approximately forty feet above the sand. In a few seconds they approached soundlessly and then in a deafening blast of noise, hot kerosene fumes and wake turbulence they had gone. I was furious, as was Bob, at the flight safety implications and ill-discipline of this stunt but our reactions were in contrast to the delighted public who clapped and cheered at the best spectacle of the day.

I should add that the officers and men whom we dealt with from both the Bulgarian and Romanian armed forces were charming, hospitable and eager to learn NATO procedures. Their approach to flying at that time was no doubt born out of the many years of Soviet training and ethos that they were in the process of shaking off.[11]

Chapter 26

Private Flying

After leaving the service I quite fortuitously found myself working for a Chicago-based avionics company manufacturing Head-Up Displays. I was asked to set up a small UK office for the company, recruited a few salespeople (including Nigel Culliford, the ex-CO of HMS *Gannet* at Prestwick, to whom I had supplied the grid references for Swordfish remains) and travelled overseas extensively. The whole ethos of this small company was aviation and this spurred me to renew my private pilot's licence. I knew it would never compare with the excitement and challenges of military flying. I was right; but it was still satisfying to get back into the air. I joined Exeter Flying Club as the nearest and most convenient location and regained my licence after a few hours dual on the Cessna 150 and 172 Skyhawk. These were certainly not the most exciting aircraft to fly but, after my Chipmunk experience, familiarised me on modern tricycle undercarriages. Sadly there were no aerobatic aircraft within reasonable distance of Somerset where I lived and so I became interested in short-field operations on the smaller strips. The avionics factory near Chicago was located at Aurora municipal airport and I did a few hours dual on one of Lumanair's fuel-injected C172 SPs before being interviewed at the FSDO (Flight Standards District Office) at DuPage Airport to get issued with my FAA reciprocal licence. The chief flying instructor, Bob Eckhoff, a fellow ex-marine of the *Semper Fi* variety with spit and polished boots, became a good friend and a fount of sound advice about US airspace regulations and procedures, as well as checking me out on each visit. Despite his trim build, nothing would get in the way of a midday visit to the local diner for a coke, large omelette and fries.

Over the next fifteen years I found flying in the USA a great deal more enjoyable than in the UK. Firstly, the cost was much less. A typical hourly solo rate for the Cessna 172 in 2013 was about US$123, or approximately £78, compared to £179 plus VAT in UK. There were also no landing fees at the regional airports and smaller airfields in the US compared with the

£8 plus VAT touchdown fee at Exeter Airport. Private flyers were positively encouraged to visit and many airfields had excellent restaurants. The aircraft were immaculately clean, fully-fuelled and ready to go in comparison to many British clubs where the internal furnishings were literally falling apart and the first chore was to remove the covers, taxi to a fuel pump and refuel the aircraft. Many times in UK I would take a black bin bag and clear out oil-stained kitchen tissues, old nav cards, sweet wrappers and empty plastic oil containers from the aircraft (as I am sure some other club members did) before taking it over. I also found it galling to pay a hefty fee every time the aircraft wheels touched the grass or concrete in landing fees. I realise that this was not the fault of the struggling flying clubs but rather a generalised dismissal of General Aviation by the government in the UK, compounded by being in a small country with crowded airspace. Since I flew a low number of hours per year, I tended to treat each solo sortie as a training exercise and carried out a couple of circuits, a flapless landing, some steep turns and stalling in order to stay proficient rather than just go off sightseeing. My previous flying experience helped keep me reasonably competent, despite my low annual hours, but I would have felt happier if I had flown more regularly. Nevertheless, I had no problem with my bi-annual checks.

By contrast, in the USA I found that there was a fascinating range of aircraft at nearby fields in Illinois; T-6 Texans galore, two MiG-21s,[1] a T-28 Trojan, L-29 Delfin, L-39 Albatross, Curtis P-40 Warhawk, P-51 Mustang and B-25 Mitchell to name but a few, all within twenty minutes flying time and with enthusiastic owners keen to talk and show you around. The B-25 was of particular interest as it was the last remaining flying H-version with the solid nose.[2] Nicknamed 'Barbie III' with a 75mm cannon mounted in the nose together with four .50-calibre machine guns, two more on the port side and a two-gun turret above, it was similar to a 1943 version of the A-10 Thunderbolt. A friend of mine was then a part-owner and it was fascinating to squeeze into the oily lower belly and see the navigator/gunner's position where he hand-loaded the 15lb 75mm shells into the breech in flight.

My then boss, Robert Atac, a man in his late thirties, was a pilot, aviation enthusiast and had a razor-sharp scientific mind. He had worked at the Fermi National Accelerator Laboratory prior to starting up his own business manufacturing Head Up Displays in the corner of a hangar with a couple of friends. Fifteen years later he was supplying HUDs for US Navy F-14 Tomcats. Bob owned a North American T-28C Trojan, the US naval trainer version with a 1,425hp radial engine and tail hook.[3] I had a marvellous sortie in this aircraft which was stable in flight and, in order to preserve the valuable engine, the throttle setting was kept in the mid-range with the aircraft barrelling along at 190 knots without even trying. Bob kept this aircraft at SkyHaven, a collection of individual hangars off Aurora airport that were rented out, each hangar containing a kitchenette, running water, heating and power. Owners would spend the day with their families working on the aircraft whilst kids watched TV and played. If I had been living in Illinois, without doubt I would have purchased an aircraft and rented a hangar. It would have been a similar expenditure then to running a second mid-range car in UK. This was another contrast with general aviation in the UK where owners' valuable assets were left out in the rain or, if lucky and prepared to pay a fortune, found a cramped space in a leaky and draughty Second World War hangar crammed with other aircraft.

There was a sad sequel to the T-28 story as, a year later, in January 2002, six minutes after take-off at about 4,500 feet Bob suffered a total oil loss. The propeller increased speed, the engine backfired, started to vibrate heavily and then seized completely whilst on an emergency approach back to runway 15. The T-28 glide ratio engine-out was not great, especially with three blades frozen in coarse pitch, and it became clear they were not going to make the runway. The Illinois countryside consists of dead flat farmland and Bob set up for a wheels-up landing in one of the many large ploughed fields. As he got lower, he suddenly noticed that there were two sets of power lines across his intended approach path. The closer were high-tension pylons and the further low-tension poles. Bob had to decide whether to go over or under the high-tension set. In a quick decision, he chose to go under both sets, reasoning that it was better to be closer to the ground than to stall. He also noted that the engine had seized with one of the three prop blades in the six o'clock position which was a concern as he thought it might dig into the ground and flip the aircraft over. Bob held the aircraft airborne until it could fly no more and then executed a textbook belly landing. The downward prop blade bent as if it was made of butter, so all was well. The story did not end there. It turned out that an oil drain valve had stuck partially open and had been venting the contents of the oil tank overboard during the climb. Although the damage appeared minimal, the engine was a write-off and the undersurfaces required repair. After about eighteen months of work, the repaired Trojan was ready for an engine run. A few minutes after start-up the reconditioned engine was badly damaged. It appeared that the wax used to prevent corrosion in storage had not been totally removed and had blocked a critical oil gallery. After further insurance wrangles, and after a third engine was procured and fitted, six years after the forced landing, it was all enough hassle and Bob and his business partner sold the T-28.

Not far from Bob Atac's house in Batavia there was an unusual and historic art-deco-style factory building. Viewed across a wide expanse of lawn, it was so striking that I used to stare at it as I drove past. I discovered that it had been built in 1936 by the Campana Corporation and is on the National Register of Historic Places. As a segue, whilst reading about recent attempts to trace Amelia Earhart's disappearance in the Pacific on 2 July 1937 in her Lockheed Electra, I learned that a fragment of a glass bottle found on Nikumaroro Island in 2007 had originally contained Italian Balm, a then best-selling hand-lotion produced by Campana at this very factory in 1933. Although no conclusive evidence has yet determined where Earhart's Lockheed Electra crashed, the finding of traces from US-made cosmetic items, which Amelia was known to have used, on this otherwise remote Pacific Island 400 miles south of her planned destination at Howland Island was an extraordinary coincidence.[4]

Another of Bob's employees, Todd Ashcraft, owned a Christen Eagle II sports biplane, not unlike a two-seat Pitts Special.[5] After flying a Grumman Tiger AA-5 with Todd, he kindly offered me an aerobatic flight in his Eagle from Aurora. Normally I don't feel queasy doing aeros but this aircraft was so twitchy and the response was so rapid that, after forty minutes, I had had enough. Compared with the Chipmunk the wing drop at the stall was such that, unless you recovered correctly and accurately, you could flick straight into a spin but perhaps that was just my handling. I admired the way Todd flew a fast curving approach to the secondary narrow paved runway at Aurora, losing most of the view ahead as he straightened out and flared – I imagine similar to landing an F4U Corsair on an aircraft carrier in the Second World War.

Eight months later Todd was flying a fellow aviator in the front seat to an aerobatic competition when he had a total loss of oil pressure at 2,500 feet, ten miles north of Aurora. After making a Pan call and turning back for Aurora, smoke started to fill the cockpit, the engine vibrated severely and then seized. Whilst setting up for a forced landing, the increased smoke, smell of burning and reduction in forward visibility were such that he decided to abandon the aircraft. The bubble canopy did not jettison smoothly, needing a firm shove, and by the time it eventually departed, striking Todd a glancing blow on the head as it went, they were low. Shouting at his passenger to get out, Todd rapidly tried to abandon as soon as his front-seater had gone at about 700 feet – much too low for comfort. However, the special aerobatic harness required both hands to release and the aircraft bunted when he let go of the stick. He was very low when he jumped (estimated 200 feet), pulling the D-ring as he dived over the side with the green fields filling his peripheral vision. The canopy opened, breathed and filled and Todd found himself on his back in a soy-bean field, twelve feet from the wingtip of his wrecked aircraft. The rigging lines had witness paint marks on them from the turtle deck of the aircraft as his chute had deployed. Both occupants were fine and Todd delivered a lifetime supply of coffee to his parachute packer (who didn't drink alcohol). Todd then set to building a replacement aircraft in his hangar, incorporating, amongst other small adjustments, an improvement to canopy jettison.[6]

There was one particular evolution during my fixed-wing training that I had read about but never had the opportunity to experience – inverted spinning. This was because there were few aircraft cleared for this manoeuvre and certainly it was beyond the limitations of the Chipmunk. However, at Gauntlet Warbirds at Aurora there was a Bellanca Decathlon high-wing aerobatic monoplane, fitted with inverted fuel and oil systems and cleared for + 6G to - 5G.[7] I therefore signed up for a two-day spinning and inverted-spinning course during one of my trips to Chicago. This consisted of two ground-school sessions and two flights with civil test pilot Greg Morris. I never realised how little I knew about the aerodynamics of the spin until I sat in that classroom on a one-to-one with my instructor and whiteboard. Greg told me that very few customers had asked for this particular course and he was looking forward to it. The first sortie covered a refresher on standard erect spins and on the second day we flew to a clear area twenty miles west of Aurora to carry out inverted spinning at 12,000 feet in good VMC. It all went exactly as planned. I could not describe the inverted spins as comfortable but recovery was straightforward although the loss of altitude was impressive. I could well understand how incredibly disorientating an unexpected inverted spin would be and the difficulty in recognising it and then carrying out the correct recovery procedure in the altitude available. It was a valuable experience.

Two other aircraft of note that I flew were a 1943 North American SNJ-5 (also known as Texan in the US Army Air Corps or Harvard with the RAF) in its original Second World War US Navy yellow training colour scheme[8] and a homebuilt Zenith Zodiac. A careful briefing was required on management of the Pratt & Whitney Wasp in order to preserve the SNJ's valuable radial engine. I loved the SNJ – strong, manoeuvrable and solid, and it gave a clear understanding of the advanced training that many thousands of young men received during the Second World War before going on to front-line pistons. The Zodiac[9] had been built by a father of a diving buddy of mine living near Lansing outside Chicago. John Sherly had served as an aviator in the US Navy during the 1950s and I gained some kudos over lunch with his family by knowing the nickname of the A-4 Skyhawk – 'Ed Heinemann's Scooter' – so he kindly invited me to fly with him on my next visit. The little Rotax-powered aircraft had been beautifully built with a perfectly smooth polished finish. We just squeezed together in the side-by-side cockpit, sharing a Y-shaped stick. I thought it was a bit slippery and twitchy to fly, but perhaps that was after flying the SNJ at the other end of the single piston spectrum.

Back in UK it was useful to be flying from a busy commercial airfield which kept my RT procedures and airmanship up to date but it was expensive and time consuming. The downside of operating from a major airfield was that often light aircraft were left in the hold downwind or crosswind whilst commercial traffic arrived or departed adding to one's sortie time with little added benefit. Many times I considered whether it was really worth renewing my licence and the answer was 'yes' because of the benefits and fun of flying, especially on my visits to the US.

Chapter 27

Envoi

Thankfully, since the events I have described, the accident rate in UK military aviation has fallen to an all-time low. It is dangerous to tempt fate but it is a fact that, in the month of September 1970 alone, ten British service aircraft were lost.[1] During 1975 we lost forty-seven aircraft, in 2000 fifteen aircraft and in 2017 one. The service pilots of the 1930s would have thought the 1970s' flying era was much safer than theirs. Fortunately, despite smaller Armed Forces, delays in the training pipeline and fewer flying hours, the attraction of military flying still seems to be as strong as it ever was amongst young men and women.

The amazing advances in aircraft handling and avionics have not negated the importance of basic handling skills. Accidents such as the AF447 Airbus A330 over the Atlantic and the B737 Max accidents illustrate how important the 'stick and rudder' instincts are to a pilot when technology lets you down. Hence my old-fashioned belief in the value of engine-off landings and limited power in helicopters. (I am glad to say I didn't even damage a 'frange' during the 1,037 engine-offs I carried out with students, unless of course you count my part in destroying a Scout and a Bell 47G-4 with the assistance of two other experienced instructors.) It is interesting to read in 2019 that the US Army plans to disable some of the advanced functions in their UH-72 Lakota training helicopters at Fort Rucker to make them more unstable for basic rotary students.[2]

It was inevitable that 3 Commando Brigade Air Squadron would have to dramatically re-organise. The delicate balancing act that had gone on since the return to the UK in 1971 between Royal Marines operational command, Army Aviation administrative command, REME technical support, Royal Marines and Army aircrew whilst lodging at a Fleet Air Arm air station was becoming gradually more anomalous with the decrease in the size of the UK armed forces. The Squadron would have to become part of either

ENVOI

the Army Air Corps or the Fleet Air Arm. As part of the Naval Service the decision to reform the Squadron as 847 NAS had an inescapable logic.

For me personally there was sadness at the disbandment of 3 Commando Brigade Air Squadron at Yeovilton on 1 September 1995. One of the major strengths of the Squadron had been SNCO aircrew with their experience, first-hand knowledge of infantry soldiering and close ties to the men they supported in the field. An SNCO pilot, many of whom had been former air gunners or aircrew-men, could be an experienced guide and mentor in aviation matters for a newly-qualified officer pilot in the same way that a troop sergeant guided a newly-appointed troop commander. The loss of our SNCO aircrew was a sad blow that some senior RM aviators at the time thought was unnecessary.[3] Additionally, the ethos of being a soldier (or marine) first and a pilot second, which stemmed from the formation of the Glider Pilot Regiment, was unique to Army Aviation.

I mentioned previously that, in 1990, 3 Commando Brigade Air Squadron was nearly the size of an Army Air Corps Regiment; 847 NAS saw a significant decrease in complement of men and aircraft. When the Gazelles were retired, 847 NAS was reduced to six Lynx, later replaced by six Wildcat, in effect the size of our old B Flight. None of this, of course, is meant as any criticism of 847 NAS who have a different modern role and have performed superbly on operations in Sierra Leone, Afghanistan and Iraq.

For those who have served in it and enjoyed its unique 'esprit de corps', it is always sad to see a unit's demise. From the wider RM perspective, it meant losing their own independent 'air arm' after a productive thirty-year period. The very title '3 Commando Brigade Air Squadron' suggested a unique and special relationship whilst '847 Naval Air Squadron' offers a different sense of the unit's role. But times demand change, and with historic regimental titles falling like ninepins in wider defence reviews, RAF squadrons disbanding and the Fleet diminishing, what may once have been arguable was probably no longer justifiable.

In early 2019, as I approached my seventieth birthday, I decided not to renew my Class 2 aircrew medical and to allow my PPL Aeroplanes to lapse. This was not out of any desire to stop flying but it is an increasingly expensive hobby in the UK; it is hard to get sufficient flying time each month to remain competent by the professional standards that I was trained by the military to expect and it seemed sensible to quit whilst still on top.

Do I miss it? You bet!

* * * *

As the battery master was selected 'off', the warning lights and indications died. The harness and mic-tel lead were undone and the helmet de-tensioned and pulled off. Only the whine of gyros running down from the AIs and the tinkling and clinking of hot metal contracting in the jet pipes disturbed the sudden silence. I clambered out of the cockpit and its familiar smell of electrics, rubber, kerosene, hot oil and sweat with a hint of vomit.[4] 'Marine Air 489 is clear complete.'

Glossary

The number of abbreviations mentioned in this account is, I am afraid, a fact of aviation and military life. I have described most abbreviations the first time that they are mentioned in the text but this list might be a helpful reminder:

AAI	Angle of Approach Indicator
AAIB	Air Accidents Investigation Branch at RAE Farnborough
ACM	Air Combat Manoeuvring
Actual	Instrument flying time in cloud or IMC
AFB	Air Force Base (USAF)
AGL	Above Ground Level
AH	Attack Helicopter
Air OP	Air Observation Post (observing gunfire)
ALAT	*Aviation Légère de l'armée de terre* (French Army Air Corps)
AMG	REME Aircraft Maintenance Group
ARW	Advanced Rotary Wing
ASI	Airspeed Indicator
ATC	Air Traffic Control
AWACS	Airborne Warning and Control System
BAOR	British Army of the Rhine
Beefer	Slang for flying instructor.
Bergen	Military Rucksack
Bingo	A low-fuel critical situation
Cat	Degree of damage after aircraft accident. Cat 1 repairable to Cat 5 damaged beyond repair.
CATO	Concealed Approach and Take-off
CFIT	Controlled Flight into Terrain
CFS	Central Flying School

CFS(H)	Central Flying School (Helicopters) RAF Shawbury
CGRM	Commandant General Royal Marines
CGS	Chief of the General Staff
CNEC	*Centre National d'Entraînement Commando* (Mont-Louis & Collioure)
COD	Carrier on Board Delivery
CoS	Chief of Staff
CP	Command Post
CTCRM	Commando Training Centre Royal Marines at Lympstone
CTF	Commander of Task Force
C to I	Cleared to Instruct
CVM	Centre de Vol en Montagne, Saillagouse
DAAC	Director Army Air Corps
DLP	Deck Landing Practice
DPM	Disruptive Pattern Material camouflage
ECL	Engine Condition Lever (throttle)
ECU	Engine Change Unit
Endex	End of an Exercise
EOL	Engine Off Landing
FARP	Forward Arming and Refuelling Point
FL	Flight Level
FOB	Forward Operating Base
Form 700	British Military Aircraft Servicing Record for each aircraft
Frange	Frangible fibre glass fairing beneath the tail of Gazelle
GCA	Ground Controlled Approach
GSDI	Ground Speed and Drift Indicator (Doppler)
HF	High Frequency
HLS	Helicopter Landing Site
HMP	Heavy Machine Gun Pod
HOGE	Hover Out of Ground Effect
ICAO	International Civil Aviation Organization
IED	Improvised Explosive Device
IF	Instrument Flying
IFR	Instrument Flight Rules
IFTU	Intensive Flying Trials Unit
IHT	Intermediate Handling Test
IMC	Instrument Meteorological Conditions
IPS	Intermediate Pitch Stop
IRE	Instrument Rating Examiner
IRT	Instrument Rating Test

GLOSSARY

JTF	Joint Task Force
kt	Knot or nautical mile per hour (1.15 mph)
LP	Landing Point (often jungle clearing)
LPD	Landing Platform Dock
LPH	Landing Platform Helicopter
LS	Landing Site (a number of LPs)
LSL	Landing Ship Logistic
Mag	Magneto
MATZ	Military Air Traffic Zone
MOD	Modification state
MoD	Ministry of Defence
MPS	Maximum Pitch Stop
MRE	Meal Ready to Eat
MRGB	Main Rotor Gearbox
NAF	Naval Air Facility
NAS	Naval Air Squadron
NBC	Nuclear, Biological and Chemical
Navex	Navigation Exercise
NightSun	Powerful searchlight fitted to side of aircraft
NVG	Night Vision Goggles
O Gp	Orders Group
P2	Pressure 2 point behind gas turbine compressor
P2	Second Pilot
PAR	Precision Approach Radar
PQ	Passenger Qualification
QFE	Altimeter pressure setting which gives height above the airfield
QHI	Qualified Helicopter Instructor
QNH	Altimeter pressure setting which gives height above sea level
RA	Royal Artillery
RAOC	Royal Army Ordnance Corps
RCT	Royal Corps of Transport
REME	Royal Electrical and Mechanical Engineers
RNAS	Royal Naval Air Station
RNAW	Royal Naval Aircraft Workshop
RNAY	Royal Naval Air Yard
Submin Pitch	Negative Pitch on Lynx main rotor blades
SNCO	Senior Non-Commissioned Officer
SRA	Surveillance Radar Approach
SS.11	Wire guided anti-tank missile used by Scout

TANS	Tactical Air Navigation System (Doppler)
TI	Thermal Imaging
TOW	Tube-launched, Optically-tracked, Wire-guided, missile originally designed by Hughes Aircraft.
T4	Exhaust temperature at location no. 4 in a gas turbine engine
T6	Exhaust temperature at location no. 6 in a gas turbine engine
TQ	Theatre Qualification
UKLF	United Kingdom Land Forces
UOR	Urgent Operational Requirement
VFR	Visual Flight Rules
VHF FM	Very High Frequency, Frequency Modulated
VL	Velocity Limiting (max permitted speed)
VMC	Visual Meteorological Conditions
'700'	or Form 700. British Military Aircraft Servicing Record

Bibliography and References

Adie, Kate, *The Kindness of Strangers*, Headline, London, 2003.
Ashcraft, Todd & Helfer, Andrew, 'What we Learned about Farming from That', *Sport Aerobatics*, Vol. 32, No. 5, May 2003.
Balch, Adrian M., *Westland Scout & Wasp*, Warpaint Series No. 110 Guideline Publications, Buckinghamshire, nd.
Barker, Ralph, *That Eternal Summer*, William Collins Sons & Co., London, 1990.
Barnham, Denis, *One Man's Window*, New English Library Ltd, London, 1975.
Brown, Ronald J., *Humanitarian Operations in Northern Iraq, 1991. With Marines in Operation Provide Comfort*, History and Museums Division USMC, Government Printing Office, Washington DC, 1995.
Cerniglia, Joseph, 'Notion of a Lotion: Artifact 2-8-S-2a', *TIGHAR Earhart Research Bulletin*, 13 February 2012.
Deaton, Doug, *Bitten by a Mosquito*, Vintage Wings of Canada, nd.
Dudley, Roger & Johnson, Ted, *Weston-Super-Mare and the Aeroplane*, Amberley Publishing Ltd, 2010.
Elwood, Brasher & Croton, *Effects of Noise on Hearing*, Report APRE 39/73 MoD APRE, Farnborough, 1973.
Farara, Chris, *Happiness is Vectored Thrust*, Aviation Classics, Mortons Media, Lincolnshire, 2019.
Holland, James, *Fortress Malta: An Island under Siege 1940-1943*, Orion, London, 2003.
Holmes, Godfrey, 'Cavalese Cable-Car Disaster', *The Independent*, 3 February 2018.
Hudson, Lee, 'US Army Shakes Up Pilot Training Programmes', *AW&ST* Vol. 181 no. 10, 20 May-2 June 2019.
Hutchison, Iain, *The Flight of the Starling*, Kea Publishing, Erskine, 1992.
Jones, James L., Gen., *Operation Provide Comfort: A Forgotten Mission with Possible Lessons for Syria,* foreignpolicy.com 6 February 2017.

Kneen, J.M. and Sutton, D.J., *Craftsmen of the Army* Vol. II, Leo Cooper, London, 1996.

Lake, Jon, 'Westland Lynx Variant Briefing Part 1', *World Air Power Journal*, Vol. 39 Winter 1999.

Reece, Michael, *Flying Royal Marines*, Royal Marines Historical Society, 2012.

Ross, R.J., Maj Gen, 'Operation Haven', *The Globe and Laurel*, July/August 1991.

Weir, Graham, '633 Squadron', *Air Pictorial*, September 1963.

Winsor, Diana, 'The Way We Whirr', *Sunday Telegraph Magazine*, No. 302, 18 July 1982.

Withington, Tom, 'ALAT's Agile Afghan Antelope', *Defence Helicopter Magazine*, Vol. 29, No. 5, September/October 2010.

Woodhouse, Mark, *Aerobatics in the DHC.1 Chipmunk*, Waypoints Aviation, New Zealand, 2013.

Wootton, Frank, *50 Years of Aviation Art*, David & Charles, Newton Abbot, 1992.

Wynn, Humphrey, 'Army Aviation's New Role', *Flight International*, 24 July 1969.

AAC Journal No. 8, 1982.

Army Aviation Newsletters, various, issued by Director Army Aviation, Middle Wallop, Hampshire.

AAIB Report 7/1987 Twin Squirrel, G-BKIH, 8 April 1986, Air Accidents Investigation Branch, HMSO.

Armed Forces of Malta Air Wing website:
http://www.aeroflight.co.uk/ops/mil/armed-forces-of-malta.htm

Australian and New Zealand Military Aircraft website:
http://www.adf-serials.com.au/n8.htm

Aviafora Helicopters Website:
http://www.aviafora.com/forums/forum/helicopter-fora

Aviation in Malta website:
http://www.aviationinmalta.com/MilitaryAviation/AccidentsMilitary/19501959/tabid/651/language/en-US/Default.aspx

Aviation Safety Network website:
https://aviation-safety.net/database/

C-141 website:
https://c141heaven.info/dotcom/pic_65_9405.php

BIBLIOGRAPHY AND REFERENCES

ENR-1-1 UK MIL AIP 2 Jan 20.
Demobbed Aircraft Website:
http://www.demobbed.org.uk/aircraft.php
Helis.Com Database:
https://www.helis.com/database/
Lynx Engines and Airframes Precis S.A.E. REME Issue 02 nd.
RAF Luqa Remembered website:
https://raf-luqa.weebly.com/xm645-crash-oct-75.html
The Shackleton Association website:
https://www.thegrowler.org.uk/avroshackleton/mark-one.htm
The War Lover (1962) website:
http://www.aerovintage.com/warlover.htm
https://www.pbase.com/easystreet/notes_on_the_filming
UK Serials Resource Centre website:
http://www.ukserials.com/

Endnotes

Introduction

1. 17 May 1953. Valetta C.1 VW810 of 70 Sqn, RAF Fayid, crashed taking off from RAF Luqa. As the aircraft became airborne an aileron jammed and the pilot was forced to put the aircraft down on the grass beside the runway, retracting the undercarriage to reduce the ground slide. The aircraft's wing hit the runway control caravan, injuring the controller. It then hit the wing of Valetta VX575 and went through a drystone wall. Two Marines of 40 Cdo RM died in the post-crash fire and twenty were injured. CSgt O.B. Falconar RM received the GM for rescuing a survivor. VX575 was to crash during its post-repair test flight in December 1953, killing the navigator.
2. Gloster Meteor FR.9 208 (Reserve) Sqn RAF.
3. Mr W.H.W. Lucas AFC, an ex-flight lieutenant RAF, was awarded the Pike Trophy by the Honourable Company of Air Pilots in 1970 for outstanding contribution to civil flying instruction. Today (2019) Auster J-1N G-AGVF is reportedly being re-built in Perth, Australia as VH-UXB.
4. *The War Lover* was filmed in 1961 using three B-17s operating from RAF Bovingdon and RAF Manston. They were B-17G N9563Z found at Tucson, Arizona, and two stored ex-US Navy PB-1Ws, purchased by the film company in Dallas, which were put back into flying condition by Aero American Inc. as N5229V and N5232V. The PB-1Ws were scrapped in UK (one at Biggin Hill) after filming whilst N9563Z is today displayed at the Lyon Air Museum in Santa Ana, California (aerovintage.com).
5. *633 Squadron* was produced by The Mirisch Film Corporation in 1964 starring Cliff Robertson and George Chakiris. Six airworthy Mosquitoes and seven unflyable aircraft were used, three of which were destroyed in crash scenes (which reportedly upset Cliff Robertson). Ten of these were assembled at RAF Bovingdon. Apart from two T-3 trainers (also

ENDNOTES

used to check out the pilots) the Mosquitoes were TT-35 target tugs and so had their Perspex noses painted over and fake guns fitted for the cameras. Flying aircraft were RS709, RS712, TA639, TA719, TW117 (T.3) and RR299 (T.3) (Weir 1963 and Deaton nd).

6. G-AOSO is today believed to be in private hands in Duluth MN, USA, finished in RAF colours as WD288, and registered as N122DH.
7. The end of an era. Shackleton T.4 WB832 was withdrawn from service three months later and scrapped at RAF Cosford.
8. More than 115 Grasshopper TX1s were delivered to the RAF and were in operation between 1952 and the 1980s. The glider was based on the pre-Second World War German Lippisch Zögling SG35 (Pupil) and later DFS SG38 Schulgeiter (School Glider) designs but fitted with Slingsby T.7 Cadet type wings. The Schulgeiter was used in the 1930s to train many of the future Luftwaffe pilots, including Hannah Reitsch, at sites such as Grunau and Wasserkuppe. Alexander Lippisch went on to design the Me163 Komet.
9. Hawker Tempest FB II A129. After an hour's familiarisation on Tempest A135 at Langley, Fay departed Manston on 17 March 1949, routeing via Bordeaux, Bari, Nicosia, Baghdad, Bahrain and arriving at Karachi on 24 March after 19 hours 15 minutes of flying. The aircraft developed an oil leak in the constant-speed unit and a faulty TR1143 radio on her initial legs, which were fixed during a 2-day stopover at RAF Nicosia. Fay returned to London by Pan American World Airways Lockheed Constellation N88857 'Clipper Flying Mist'.
10. Miles Hawk Major G-ACYO race number '45'. It was fitted with a metal propeller and a high-compression Gipsy Major IC engine giving an average speed of 135 mph. After the race Fay sold 'Charlie Yoke Oboe' to Mr Howard Stirling, an air traffic controller, on 28 August 1954 and it was written off in an accident 3 months later at Elstree.
11. Then the Parliamentary Secretary to the Minister of Civil Aviation.
12. Joan Hughes MBE (1918-1993) also flew the Demoiselle replica in the film *Those Magnificent Men in their Flying Machines* because she was the only skilled pilot who was light enough to enable it to get airborne.
13. Later Air Vice-Marshal D.E. Hawkins CB DFC*(1919-2017).
14. 25 November 1952, Valetta C.1 VW203 collided with Venom FB.1 WE258. Both aircraft crashed near Great Durnford, Wilts. The test pilot of the Venom was killed.
15. The initial helicopter courses to fill the squadrons for the new commando carriers HMS *Albion* and *Bulwark* included a contract with British United Airlines (later Bristow Helicopters) at Redhill for thirty-two

RN and RM pilots to undertake basic rotary training on the Hiller 12C and advanced training on the Whirlwind S55 Mk1. This followed RAF fixed-wing training on the new Chipmunk at RAF Linton-on-Ouse and the first Redhill course included Lt David Storrie RM and Lt David Rowe RM. The courses then moved to RNAS Culdrose for Wessex HAS.1 conversion for 845 NAS or Whirlwind Mk 7 for 846 NAS. In later years helicopter training took place at Culdrose throughout, with basic rotary being conducted on the RN Hiller T.2.

16. Sgt Peter Lawrence was the first in 1965, shortly followed by Sgts Derek Blevins and John Frost.
17. 3 February 1972, Sioux XT106 'R', 3 Cdo Bde Air Sqn RM crashed at Beacon Hill, Woodhouse Eaves, near Loughborough, Leicestershire, flying into high ground in fog/low cloud.
18. The Canberra was notoriously difficult asymmetric and, until a full throttle safety speed of about 170 knots was attained, an engine failure on take-off meant ejection or a forced landing straight ahead.

Chapter 1: Basic Training

1. Sqn Ldr George Darley CO of 609 Aux Sqn RAuxAF. The pilots lived in tents on the dispersal and there was a small barrel of bitter always at hand at Holmlea Bungalow (Barker 1990: pp. 36 & 166). This was probably the basis for a similar scene in the 1969 film *Battle of Britain*.
2. C.R. (Charlie) Cuthill died in 2010 aged 87. He had joined the RAF as a Halton Apprentice in 1938. He was captain of a Lancaster of 149 Squadron as a Pilot Officer aged 21, followed by a tour as a QFI on heavy conversion. He was awarded the DFC in 1945 and the AFC for post-war instructing.
3. Our checks all had acronyms to assist the memory. For instance, the downwind checks in the Chipmunk were 'My Friend Fred Has Hairy Balls' (Mixture, Fuel, Flaps, Harness, Hood, Brakes). The system worked – I still remember!
4. The NATO Air Training Plan in Canada existed between 1952 and 1957. Tony had learned to fly the Harvard at 2FTS Gimli and then, as an experiment, was fortunate enough to briefly experience a few hours on a converted USAF two-seat P-51D Mustang (the TF-51D) and an RCAF B-25 Mitchell Mk 2 PT at Gimli in 1953, just before 2FTS moved to Moose Jaw.

ENDNOTES

5. 4 September 1970, Sioux XT502 of 17th/21st Lancers' Air Troop, Aldergrove.
6. In the Gazelle, the landing light switch on top of the collective was located next to the guarded hydraulic switch and, on occasion in later life as an instructor, we suffered an unplanned 'practice hydraulic failure' on night finals at the stage where the student would be expected to switch on the landing light.
7. To be precise in UK there was no such thing as VFR at night so we were technically flying IFR in VMC using outside references.
8. Bell MOD 6013.
9. In researching past events I was surprised how many of the traditional flying tales were either true or based on truth. This particular story seems to refer to Sioux XT544 on 27 November 1970 but belonged to the Air Troop of 15th/19th Hussars based near Tidworth. The pilot was authorised by his Air Troop commander to conduct an observation sortie with an observer near Colingbourne Ducis. Having established a downwind high hover between 50 and 100 feet behind trees, he descended in an overpitched state, hit the ground, bounced and crashed in a field near to the Pennings. The pilot and observer escaped from the aircraft which then caught fire. This is within 200 metres of the A338 road. There would have been a column of smoke and the two crew would have been given a lift back to the Air Troop location at Tidworth if the story was based on this incident. Research shows there was only one other Cat 5 accident involving a solo student in a confined area near Wallop during that era and that was Sioux XV322 on 6 May 1971. XV322 crashed when a basic student hit trees in a confined area at Harewood Forrest. The pilot extricated himself from the wreckage and extinguished a small fire with the aircraft's fire extinguisher. This could also have been the basis for this story although it is less likely that the student hitched a lift from a nearby road but the tail rotor or fin of XV322 could have ended up in the Officers' Mess bar. Interestingly, this aircraft had an RAF serial number but was clearly listed as an Army Aviation accident and was operating from Middle Wallop on a basic instructional sortie. It is likely to have been an ex-RAF Sioux HT.2 from CFS, either transferred or lent to the Army at Middle Wallop.
10. A.O. (Arthur) Sharples MBE had flown Spitfires until he was captured and spent 1941-45 as a PoW. He then flew de Havilland Hornets before converting to the first generation of helicopters and qualifying as an A1 QHI.

Chapter 2: Advanced Training

1. Fifty Sioux AH.Is were built by Agusta in Italy for the British Army (Agusta-Bell 47G-3B1) and 250 by Westland Helicopters (Westland-Agusta-Bell 47G-3B1).
2. MOD 5018 introduced a removable bolt-on/off instrument pack onto the Sioux consisting of a suction-driven slip indicator, artificial horizon and a compass repeater which attached to the top left of the instrument pedestal, just above the plastic fan.
3. 16 December 1996, Bell 206B G-BFJW crashed near Ledbury during a night take-off from a lawn with 2 passengers. The main rotor struck trees.
4. RAF Type LE/58 Portable Runway Light manufactured by Metalite Ltd.
5. Confusingly, the AAI was also known as the Glide Path Indicator (GPI), the Glide Slope Indicator (GSI) and, today, as the Helicopter Approach Path Indicator (HAPI). To minimise confusion, I will use the old term of AAI throughout.
6. 17 March 1975, Sioux XT225, ARW Middle Wallop near Chilbolton.
7. 7 May 1971, Scout XR603, Tidworth area. In 1999 XR603 was transferred to the Royal Australian Navy Historic Flight and stored at RANAS Nowra. In 2019 it was sold for A$21,209 in Victoria, Australia as VH-NVW (www.adf-serials.com.au).
8. The RAF operated 15 Sioux HT.2s at RAF Tern Hill until circa 1976 when they were replaced by the Gazelle HT.2.
9. Chipmunk T.10 WP964 was finished in a Second World War style dark earth and green camouflage at Middle Wallop until at least 1988. WP964 is now in South Africa as ZU-DXO. The beautifully camouflaged 'WP964' that can be seen at UK airshows today is actually a Mk 20 which had served with the Portuguese Air Force as '1304'.
10. Tragically on 29 May 2008 Squirrel HT.1 ZJ247 from Middle Wallop flew into a similar set of wires, crashing into the woods at the side of the estuary, killing both the AAC WO2 instructor and his student, a lieutenant AAC.
11. 8 May 1969, Alouette AH.2 XR387, 24 Flight, Herford, Germany.

Chapter 3: Gazelle Conversion

1. Russian and French designed helicopters are unique in having clockwise turning main rotors (as viewed from above). For example, the Mil Mi-8 and Mi-26, Aérospatiale SA 330 Puma and Alouette II and III. The SA-321 Super Frelon was an exception, explained by the

ENDNOTES

fact that Sikorsky designed the rotor system. Strangely, Igor Sikorsky's first helicopter, the VS-300 of 1940 was arranged clockwise but this was reversed to counter-clockwise with the first production helicopter, the Sikorsky R-4 of 1942, and all his designs thereafter.

2. In the late 1980s many Gazelle pilots were sent to RAF North Luffenham, the RAF Aviation Medical Training Centre, to be fitted for individually tailored fibreglass back supports, secured by a velcro band around the waist, to mitigate back problems.
3. 31 May 1973, Gazelle XW850, Gazelle IFTU Middle Wallop at Whitsbury, near Fordingbridge, Hants. This Gazelle had only been in service for one month.
4. 22 May 1975, Gazelle HT.2 XW867, 705 NAS, wirestrike at Herodsfoot near Liskeard, both crew killed.
5. Scout XP887 had a long and useful life and was scrapped after service with the Army at Hong Kong in 1994.
6. G-VTOL was a unique Hawker Siddeley-owned two-seat Harrier T. Mk 52 then painted in a two-tone desert camouflage. John Farley OBE AFC (1933-2018) had landed on *Fearless* the previous day, gaining the words 'NAVY' painted in white on G-VTOL's tailfin and, after we departed, took off with a near vertical climb (the 'Farley climb') over the Thames as part of the naval equipment exhibition display (Farara 2019, p. 96).
7. Indeed French Army (ALAT) Gazelles have been in operational use since 2010 on Operation SERVAL in Mali, where a pilot was killed by small-arms fire, on Operation LICORNE in Cote d'Ivoire, on EU peacekeeping missions in Darfur and at sea on Operation CORYMBE off the coast of West Africa embarked on Mistral-class LPDs as part of the *Jeanne d'Arc* Amphibious Group (Withington, 2010). In Afghanistan ALAT SA342M Gazelles armed with MBDA HOT antitank missiles and the SAGEM Viviane electro-optical sighting system, served as part of the French helicopter battalion (BATHELICO) at Kabul and were finally withdrawn in October 2012.

Chapter 4: All at Sea

1. For some years I wondered what the Wasp was doing aboard HMS *Bulwark*. I later discovered that HMS *Bulwark* was allotted a Wasp HAS.1 XT422 'Z' from 845 NAS from 1970-1973 and in 1972 it was finished in semi-gloss dark green with a white 'B' on the tail. It was used for liaison, forward air controlling and reconnaissance work

(Balch ND:22). During the same period HMS *Albion* had also been issued with a Wasp HAS.1 XS539, operated by 848 NAS which in 1970 was finished in a gloss green with high visibility roundels (Balch ND:27). It might have been one of these that I saw with the tail boom chopped off or, alternatively, a damaged Wasp from a small ship's flight of 829 NAS being transported home.
2. 5 May 1973, Sioux XT503 Z, 3 Cdo Bde Air Sqn RM, HMS *Bulwark* off Cyprus.
3. Later Lt Gen Sir Michael Wilkins KCB OBE (1933-1994).
4. He found a number of assault lifejackets (ALJs) which were routinely dumped in a pile prior to extraction. Invariably the excess ALJs were left to be picked up after the exercise. A spare GPMG barrel and a set of webbing were also recovered.
5. Later Maj Peter Cameron MC was CO of 3 Cdo Bde Air Sqn RM and was awarded the MC for his leadership of the Squadron during the hugely testing time of Operation CORPORATE in the Falklands.

Chapter 5: Malta

1. Sioux AH.1 XT168(E), XT170(P), XT514(W).
2. June 1977, Lynx AH.1 XZ172 from the Army Lynx Intensive Flying Trials Unit (IFTU) at Middle Wallop. XZ172 was delivered to the IFTU in early June 1977 and was undergoing a compressor wash on dispersal a few weeks after delivery. The number one engine ran away up with a T6 of 850 degrees noted before an over-speed led to explosive turbine failure. The aircraft rapidly caught fire and burned out completely aft of main cabin forward bulkhead with the two crew and technicians in the cabin escaping injury. Comp washing with water/kerosene mixture was then suspended. Allegedly, the technical manual contained a misprint for the water/kerosene ratio for the washing mix which caused the uncontrollable acceleration. By July 1977 the minimal surviving lower fuselage and cockpit had been transported to Westlands at Weston-Super-Mare for a complete re-build and was delivered again as a virtually new aircraft in December 1981. I never realised the history of this aircraft when I later instructed on it and flew it with the Silver Eagles in 1982 (Dudley & Johnson 2010).
3. Aviation-safety.net and RAF Luqa Remembered.
4. Sea King HAS.1 XV712, 714 NAS, HMS *Hermes*.

ENDNOTES

5. The captain was Flt Lt G.R. Alcock AFC. Five years earlier, on 7 January 1971, Flt Lt Alcock had remained at the controls of Vulcan B.2 XM610 when it caught fire near Tyneside. He had climbed to 6,000 feet to allow the rear crew to bale out and the co-pilot to eject and then pointed the aircraft out to sea before ejecting himself. Ironically, the abandoned aircraft then turned back inland and crashed at Wingate, fortunately without injuring anyone on the ground. Flt Lt Alcock received the Air Force Cross (aviation-safety.net).
6. Propagate was the engineering term for the manner in which a fatigue crack could grow.
7. The four Malta Armed Forces Flight Bell 47s were registered as 9H-AAE, 9H-AAF, 9H-AAG and the Bell-built example 9H-AAH. From 1972-1976 they were based at St Patrick's Barracks and moved to Hal Far in 1976. In 1979 they moved to Park 7 at Luqa Airport.
8. This was SA 321M LC155 which in 1975 was marked 'Civil Aviation Search and Rescue' in small arabic script. By late 1977 it was in standard markings with Libyan Arab Republic Air Force roundels as were LC151, LC153, LC154 and LC157.
9. In 1978 the Libyan Super Frelon detachment was supplemented by three SA 316B Alouette IIIs. In August 1980 the Libyan Military Mission ended after overstepping the mark with their hosts but the three, by then unserviceable, Alouette IIIs were left behind and donated to the Malta Armed Forces in 1991. The Libyan presence was replaced by a detachment of two AB.204s from the Italian Air Force.
10. Some of the parked Nimrods had a close shave on 14 November 1977 after Salerno Flight had withdrawn from Malta, when a Boeing 720 of Pakistan International Airways, who were at that time training crews for the Air Malta B720 fleet, was undergoing circuit training. It touched down heavily on its nose wheel, which detached and bounced between the parked Nimrods without doing any damage. The B720 AP-ATQ, after burning off fuel, landed successfully on a foam carpet.

Chapter 6: Malta – Towards Withdrawal

1. The Wombat was spectacular to watch firing, with a 290m back-blast danger zone behind the weapon. The Wombat and 84mm Carl Gustav were both unpleasant to fire with noise levels greater than most weapons of 187dB compared with the Chieftain gun at 174db (APRE

1973:22). The Wombat was replaced by the Milan anti-tank missile in the mid-1980s.
2. Theories include: the ruts were made by sledges which gouged the limestone; they were worn by cart wheels or they formed some type of irrigation system. It is believed that they date from about 2,000 BC although some historians postulate that they might date from the Phoenicians in 700 BC.
3. Dornier Wal-Cabina XI flying boat I-AZEA of SANA (*Società Anonima di Navigazione Aerea*) was powered by two Italian-built Jupiter radial engines. The aircraft, callsign '92', ditched with engine problems whilst flying between Tripoli and Syracuse on 16 February 1932.
4. Buccaneer S.2A XT273, 208 Sqn RAF, eventually departed from Luqa following a complex structural repair in August 1977, after Salerno Flight had left the island.
5. Ex-RAF Lightning pilot and QFI, Flt Lt Mark Micallef Eynaud returned home and was appointed Chief Officer Flight Operations for Air Malta in February 2012.
6. Thunder City eventually operated four airworthy Lightnings, two of them two-seaters, and 27 years later I was to see XS452 again finished in a gloss black paint scheme at Cape Town Airport registered as ZU-BBD. Her sister Lightning T.56 XS451, in natural metal finish, crashed during an air show at SAAF Overberg on 14 November 2009 following an inflight fire. Tragically it was a fatal crash because the canopy/ejection seat mechanism failed to operate. The South African Airworthiness Authorities conducted an investigation and allegedly found that the routine servicing of seats and canopies had been deferred. As a result a hard look was taken at the private operation of fast jets and in 2010 Thunder City put their fast jet fleet up for sale.
7. *One Man's Window*, p.131, by Denis Barnham who flew from USS *Wasp* to RAF Luqa on Operation CALENDAR on 13 April 1942. He flew Spitfire VCs with 601 Squadron RAF until 21 June 1942.
8. Later Rear Admiral Sir Nigel Cecil KBE CB (1925-2017).
9. R Adm Cecil was due to leave Malta in 1977 but, at the request of Prime Minister Dom Mintoff, was extended and eventually left Malta for the final time in HMS *London* two years later.
10. Thirty years later, whilst on a diving trip to Malta, I went to visit Villa Portelli, now used by the Malta Maritime Institute, and was allowed to look around the garden. However, although I had a distinct

memory of roughly where it was located, I could find no evidence of a fishpond. It was a year later, in 2009, that I met the Director, Captain Reuben Lanfranco, who told me that there had been a fishpond in the garden, which had been demolished when the garden fell into disrepair following the British withdrawal. I suspect that no one at the time realised the significance of the little *Reggia Aeronautica Italiana* Squadron lapel badge that was cemented alongside the water spout. I now had to find out whether I had been dreaming of this incident or not. It took some time for me to find the reference that had remained in my sub-conscious since 1976, but I eventually found it in one of my favourite books on the war in Malta, *One Man's Window* by Denis Barnham:

> 'Hullo Denis,' the happy faces smile a greeting, 'did you hear what happened to the Eyetie who baled out of the burning bomber last night?' I shake my head. I don't want to know. I can guess all too easily. The picture of the tumbling bomber and now of the poor helpless figure with streaming parachute, is starkly vivid in my mind. 'Well, he came down on top of a fountain and the spike went up through his arse hole and impaled him there'.
> I am back in the RAF, a member of a war team. (p. 141)

The incident is also reported in Holland's *Fortress Malta* with the added explanation:

> By the evening of the 11th, he'd been feeling much better and returned to the Mess just in time to hear about an Italian who had baled out, only to land on top of a fountain. 'The spike went through his arsehole and impaled him there', one of Denis's fellow pilots told him cheerfully. Denis confided to his diary that this apparent lack of respect for fellow human beings depressed him greatly. ... But this disgust was largely misplaced. The banter between pilots – soldiers or sailors for that matter – was a defence mechanism. (p. 309).

It seems that this incident took place on 10 May 1942 when a Cant Z.1007bis of 211 *Squadriglia* was shot down by Sqn Ldr John Bisdee of 601 Sqn and was very probably the event that was commemorated in the garden at Villa Portelli.

FLYING LIGHT HELICOPTERS WITH THE ROYAL MARINES

11. Email correspondence amongst ex-41 Cdo officers thirty-seven years later indicate that Lord Louis may have been referring to the US Presidential citation ribbons on the Colour rather than the Regimental Colour itself.
12. The fate of our three Salerno Flight aircraft might be of interest. Gazelle XX377, tail letter 'E', continued to serve with 3 Cdo Bde Air Sqn RM and then with the Army until 6 June 1982 when, during the Falklands War, it was hit by a Sea Dart missile fired from HMS *Cardiff* whilst operating with 656 Sqn AAC at night near Mount Pleasant with the loss of all four occupants. XX381, tail letter 'F', continued in military service with 3 Cdo Bde Air Sqn RM and 662 Sqn AAC until moving to storage at RAF Shawbury in 2005 and ending up on display at Welbeck Defence College in 2010. XX383, tail letter 'G', returned to Plymouth and then to 666 Sqn AAC and was in storage at RAF Shawbury by 2007. It was then sold on the civilian market and was located at Stapleford Tawney (possibly with MW Helicopters Ltd) in 2010.
13. I returned to the flight location once again on holiday in September 2009. St George's Barracks had long since been handed over to developers and four blocks of flats were being built next to where our flight offices and hangar had once stood. All that remained was our POL (petrol oil and lubricants) store house on the edge of the range and that, too, was about to fall victim to the JCB. The last flight of an AFM Bell 47G-2 had taken place on 30 May 2008 when AS7201 (formerly 9H-AAE) landed at Ta'Qali and was handed over to the Malta Air Museum.

Chapter 7: Brunei – The Jungle

1. 30 September 1975, Sioux XT849, 659 Sqn AAC near Kellinghausen, Germany. As he and his QOH intelligence sergeant passenger crawled out from under the wreck, Denis looked up to see a British soldier running towards him with a mug of tea. 'Fookin hell Sir, I think that you could use this!' As Denis later remarked, a typical British military 'cure-all'.
2. 4 July 1965, Scout XP905, 656 Sqn AAC near Padawan, Sarawak. Tony had three officers of the 2nd Royal Green Jackets and one Royal Artillery officer as passengers. The RA 2/Lt hurt his back on the Sunair HF radio fit on the rear bulkhead and was later to become Lt Gen Sir Michael Willcocks KCB CVO and Black Rod. The CO of

ENDNOTES

2RGJ at the time was Lt Col E. Bramall (see page 101). The cause of the accident was the incorrect fitment of a fuel pipe during night time maintenance in the jungle. The dangers of flying over the jungle were further illustrated when, on 20 September 1965, Scout XR599 of 656 Squadron disappeared with three on board during a night flight between Lundu and Kuching. Neither the aircraft nor crew were found.

3. 4 January 1977, Gazelle XX461, AACC Middle Wallop at Barton Stacey, Hants.
4. The final S-61 left Anduki in September 2007, after 40 accident-free years of operations, to be replaced by S-92s.
5. This was a few months prior to the Royal Geographical Society expedition which 'discovered' the Gunung Mulu Mountains with underground rivers and spectacular caves in the karst limestone geology. Mount Mulu is the highest of a series of mountains, rising to 7,795 feet and the area is now a national park with a resort and an airstrip.
6. In a poor example of ergonomic design the Scout AH.1 HP fuel cock was located next to the cabin-heater control. Examples of Scout accidents reportedly caused by mistakenly closing the HP cock instead of operating the cabin heater were: 3 January 1966 Scout XR638, Marlborough, 2 killed. 10 March 1966 Scout XT619, Thetford, 3 injured. 8 February 1979 Scout XR604, Hereford, 1 injured. XT619 was carrying a soldier in the external stretcher pod on exercise which must have been a particularly unpleasant experience for the simulated casualty.
7. Later Brig Sir Miles Hunt-Davis GCVO CBE (1938-2018) Private Secretary to the Duke of Edinburgh.
8. Later FM Sir John Chapple GCB CBE and CGS.
9. To my amazement I note from my log book that we were flying XT218, the aircraft Sgt Jones* did not like to fly.

Chapter 8: Northern Ireland - Trouble at t'Mill

1. 2 December 1978, Scout XW614 of 659 Sqn AAC at Lough Ross. Take-off was at 0350 in a reported 1,000 foot cloud base in rain and pitch darkness on PNG. Pilot and observer killed.
2. 27 November 1992, Puma HC.1 XV233 of 230 Sqn collided with Gazelle ZB681 of 665 Sqn, Bessbrook Mill, Northern Ireland whilst landing. All 4 passengers and crew in the Puma were killed and the 2 Gazelle crew badly injured.

3. On 12 February 1997 L/Bdr Stephen Restorick 3 Regt RHA was killed by a single shot from a PIRA 0.5 inch Barrett M82 rifle whilst checking a vehicle at a checkpoint just outside Bessbrook. He was the last of 1,441 servicemen and women who died during Op BANNER. By 2009 the Bessbrook HLS had disappeared. It was bulldozed, re-landscaped and returned to pastureland with a five-bar gate where the former busy entrance to the HLS had been.

Chapter 9: Central Flying School (H) – RAF Shawbury

1. Despite much research I have been unable to find any reference to this KAF accident. However, not all nations are open about military accidents. Two SA330H were delivered to Kenya in 1977 and a further two in 1978 (serials 403-406). There was a Kenya Air Force coup in 1982 and thereafter Super Pumas and IAR 330s are listed, so the story is credible and is unlikely to have been invented.
2. Sadly this enviable record was tragically broken on 10 January 2007 at RAF Tern Hill with a fatal mid-air collision between a DHFS Squirrel HT Mk 1, ZJ259, which was carrying out an engine-off landing and collided with CFS Squirrel ZJ263 practising a hydraulic failure run-on approach.
3. Vortex ring is a dangerous state whereby if a helicopter is descending at a high rate of descent with zero or low airspeed with power on and collective pitch is applied, all lift can be lost on the blades. There was also a possibility that the interaction of airflow round the fenestron blade tips in certain conditions might have led to turbulence in the duct. Later Aérospatiale designs such as the SA365, EC135 and EC120 had the fenestron rotating in the opposite direction and reportedly did not suffer from loss of yaw control.
4. 2 May 1979, Agusta-Bell AB 205A-1 710 (4174) SOAF, Jabal al Akhdar, Oman.

Chapter 10: Instructing on Gazelle – Early Days and BAOR

1. The first RM staff QHI at Middle Wallop in 1965 had been my ex-Company Commander Lt Terence Murphy. He was followed by Sgt Derek Blevins, Lt David Storrie, Capt Duncan MacMillan, Capt Mike Gregson, Lt Paul Bancroft and Lt Ken Summers and then myself.

ENDNOTES

In addition all RM QHIs spent an initial 6 months at Middle Wallop as B2 probationary instructors until they graduated to B1 and were then eligible to be posted to a squadron as a QHI.
2. 8 April 1986, Twin Squirrel AS 355 F1 G-BKIH, Swalcliffe near Banbury (AAIB Report 7/1987).
3. Tony Davies was an experienced and amusing QHI and a considerable asset to ARW. During his next tour in Cyprus he was injured on 11 June 1983 flying Alouette II XR380, UNFICYP flight, which crashed picking up an underslung load in the Troodos mountains.
4. Later FM Lord Bramall KG GCB OBE MC (1923-2019).
5. See note 2 of Chapter 7.
6. 10 June 1980. Gazelle XX390, 3 Cdo Bde Air Sqn RM at Lough Foyle, Ballykelly. Whilst flying in Northern Ireland I had noticed the badly corroded wreckage of a Fairey Firefly and a Vought F4U Corsair about half a mile off the coast at low tide on these same extensive mudflats. The wrecks dated from the time when the Fleet Air Arm were operating from RNAS Eglinton (HMS *Gannet*) 5 miles west of Ballykelly. Lt Cdr Sandy Sinclair RN, the OC of Britannia Flight at Roborough, later told me that he remembered a Firefly spinning in as it turned final for Eglinton. Probably either MB566 on 8 March 1954 or WB378 on 3 December 1954, both from 737 NAS.
7. 15 September 1980. Gazelle XX401, 3 Cdo Bde Air Sqn RM at Balnakiel, Sutherland. All 3 passengers and crew killed.

Chapter 11: Instructing on Gazelle – Flight Commander

1. Col Edwin J. Den Beste went on to have a distinguished career in the US Army and died in Alabama in 2015.
2. 14 January 1980, Beaver AL.1 XP819, AACC Middle Wallop at Dummer, Hants. Sqn Ldr Peter Mackenzie was awarded a DFC in 1944 flying Mosquitoes. After working in civil aviation and a second spell with the RAF, he spent 27 years instructing at Wallop, amassing 11,400 hours (*AAC Journal* 1980, p. 69).
3. 22 July 1983, Beaver AL.1 XP811, AACC Middle Wallop at RNAS Culdrose. Maj Bill Smithson AAC had started flying as a NCO in 1957 and was a civilian QFI at Wallop at the time of the accident (*AAC Journal* 1984, p. 96).
4. Stampe G-BIMO in subsequent ownership was written-off on 10 July 2010 after entering an inverted spin from 3,400 feet whilst carrying

out a rolling manoeuvre. It crashed in a wood at Rotherfield Peppard, near Henley-on-Thames, killing both occupants (AAIB Bulletin 5/2011).
5. John Fairey died when his Piston Provost G-AWVF suffered a catastrophic engine failure and fire whilst returning from an air show at RAF Waddington on 8 July 2009 (AAIB Bulletin 10/2010).

Chapter 12: Crash, Bang, Wallop

1. McDonnell Douglas TF-18A Hornet, bureau number 160781 was the first full-scale development (FSD) two-seater finished in a stylish gold-and-dark-blue scheme. 160784, the second aircraft, was finished in a low visibility blue-grey scheme. Later these FSD aircraft were designated as F/A-18B-3-MC Hornet.
2. *AAC Journal* No. 8, 1982.
3. The pre-production turbine disc had been manufactured from sintered '60 mesh' material and had flown for 275 hours. Production discs were of stronger '150 mesh' powdered grain. Despite an extensive search of farmland the two critical missing pieces of disc were never found (GAO 114371 18 Feb 1981).

Chapter 13: You Need Eyes in the Back of your Head

1. I only learned of this 38 years after the event.
2. According to Séan, some days later a somewhat chastened Matt* told him that he had never received a bollocking the like of which he had just received from John Drew. Séan waited a day and, still hearing nothing, decided to present himself in front of the CFI. When Lt Col John Drew asked what he was doing in his office, Séan replied that he had come for his interview. John said, 'What did I say to you the day after the accident?' Séan responded, 'You said eff off and go flying.' John's reply was, 'That was the interview, now bugger off', and that was the end of the story.
3. 12 November 1970, Wessex HC.2 XT679 and Wessex HC.2 XR510, both from the Helicopter Operational Conversion Flight collided at RAF Odiham with 5 fatalities. AS 350 Squirrel HT.1 ZJ263 and Squirrel HT.1 ZJ259, both from RAF Shawbury, collided at RAF Tern Hill on 10 January 2007 with one fatality.

ENDNOTES

4. *Flight* magazine, 24 July 1969 p. 147, includes a Gordon Horner drawing of Scout XP890 (the 28th Scout built and delivered in 1963). The same article contains good sketches of Lt John Meggy RA, posted to 3 Cdo Bde Air Sqn, who flew me on a number of occasions in Singapore and Maj John Valenzia AAC from Malta.
5. XP890 was eventually stored at Wroughton and stripped for spares in 1987. In 1997 the fuselage was at RNAW Almondbank, Perth, being offered for sale by tender and was purchased by Bolenda Engineering, Ipswich.

Chapter 14: Instructing on Lynx

1. Kneen & Sutton 1996, p. 106.
2. 5 July 1979, Lynx AH.1 XZ189, 1 Regt AAC, Hildesheim, both crew killed (ukserials.com/losses-1979).
3. At Suffield Ranges in Canada a Scout in the hover unknowingly became entangled with spent SS11 missile wire and, within half a minute, conducted a forced landing with control problems. It was found that the wire had wrapped around the rotor mast in the manner of a fishing reel, bending the rotor pitch change links progressively inwards as the hundreds of wire turns increased.
4. RM aircraft of 3 Cdo Bde Air Sqn lost during the Falklands conflict:

   - 21 May 1982. Gazelle XX411. San Carlos Water. Ditched after being hit by small-arms fire. Sgt A.P. Evans killed, Sgt E. Candlish swam ashore supporting his pilot.
   - 21 May 1982. Gazelle XX402. Clam Creek, San Carlos. Hit by small-arms fire. Lt K. Francis and L/Cpl B.P. Giffin killed..
   - 28 May 1982. Scout XT629. Camilla Creek House. Shot down by Pucara. Lt R.J. Nunn DFC killed. Sgt A.C. Belcher badly wounded.

Chapter 15: Display Flying

1. The 1981 Sparrowhawk team consisted of myself, Lt David Woods, WO1 Geoff Palmer, WO2 Rod Lambert, WO2 Jack Robson, WO2 Keith Willingale, S/Sgt Pete Arger and S/Sgt Jim Kirkpatrick.
2. Major Louis Parsons was also an accomplished racing driver and photographer. Despite his years of flying, he never transferred

to the AAC. He left the Army and worked for the BBC, the Parkinson's Disease Society and for the National Wage Negotiation and Arbitration Panel when we met regularly for dinner in London in the mid-1990s. He died unexpectedly in 2005. A talented and amusing man.
3. This was then the last flying Mosquito, owned by British Aerospace and the same aircraft which I had seen as a boy at Bovingdon in 1963 being used for the film *633 Squadron* (see Introduction, Note 5). This Mosquito T. 3 RR299 crashed on 21 July 1996 when the port engine lost power during an air display at Barton, Manchester, and crashed, killing both crew on board.
4. Wilfred Hardy GAvA (1938-2016).
5. Gazelle HT.2 XW859 and XS415 collided 13 June 1977, Praa Sands, 705 NAS, 3 killed.
6. On 11 August 1986, G-LYNX, fitted with Gem 60 engines, lightened and with BERP III blades, was to achieve a world speed record of 216 knots (249 mph) over a 15km course above the Somerset Levels flown by Trevor Egginton, a record which stands to this day.
7. *Sunday Telegraph Magazine* No. 302, 18 July 1982.
8. Piper PA-23-250 Aztec G-FOTO.
9. Arthur Ernest Gibson (1926-1992). Amongst his most famous photographs are those of Concorde and the Red Arrows in formation over the QE2 taken from an inverted Red 10 on 14 July 1985 and an extraordinary image of Concorde at high altitude with the sun just behind her, used on the cover of the book *Concorde, New Shape in the Sky* by Kenneth Owen, Jane's Information Group 1987.
10. The four aircraft in 'the rotor' was the subject of an oil painting by Frank Wootton OBE PPGAvA (1911-1998) titled 'Helicopters at an Air Display, Middle Wallop 1982' now in the Officers' Mess at the Army Air Corps Centre. In his book Frank Wootton was kind enough to add the note: 'The Lynx team gave a brilliant display of flying in different formations, reminiscent of the manoeuvres carried out by the Red Arrows. I chose to paint this formation as it was the one that the Red Arrows could not perform' (Wootton, 1992, p. 91).

Chapter 16: Senior Pilot – Arctic Training

1. Capt Jeff Niblett had been leading the pair of Scouts on 28 May 1982 in the Falklands when they were engaged by two Argentinian IA-58A

ENDNOTES

Pucaras near Camilla Creek. Lt Dick Nunn was shot down and killed whilst Sgt Bill Belcher was thrown clear, badly wounded. Both Jeff and Dick were awarded DFCs.

2. 24 February 1982 near Voss, Norway. The Puma HC.1 was XW234. The first Gazelle AH.1 to crash was XW905 and the second was XX378. Gazelle XW905 was the only aircraft written-off.
3. 'Moonshadow' was made famous as a hit by Cat Stevens in 1971. The moon does cast a shadow but in the Arctic it is particularly pronounced.
4. Ten German destroyers were first engaged by the 2nd Destroyer Flotilla on 10 April 1940 and later by HMS *Warspite* in company with 9 RN destroyers on 13 April 1940. The three vessels we saw were all scuttled during the fighting on 13 April, the *Z2 Georg Thiele* having blown the bows off HMS *Eskimo*.
5. Probably either LN-HAE or LN-MAJ.
6. *Flight International* magazine, 8 March 1986, No. 4001. I kept in touch with Mike Gaines afterwards and last saw him when he was working with Volga Dnieper at Farnborough. Mike died in 2011.
7. 12 March 1985, Scout XP906, 660 Sqn AAC, Sheung Shui, Hong Kong. Apparent loss of power after take-off, although the cause was never conclusively proven.

Chapter 17: Senior Pilot – The Mountains

1. *Le Grand Couteau* is also the title of a film released in 1955, starring Robert Aldrich and Jack Palance.
2. 17 September 1986, Lynx AH 1 XZ640, Lynx Conv. Flt Middle Wallop, near CVM Saillagouse, France; 3 killed. (ASN Wikibase #59978).
3. Ranging from a Hawker Fury from 8 FTS, 18 January 1938 to an F-100D Super Sabre, 7 August 1969.
4. Fairey Swordfish unidentified, possibly Mk 1 L9730 from RNAS Arbroath, HMS *Condor*, Glen Callater.

Chapter 18: Senior Pilot – St Kilda

1. 7/8 June 1944, Sunderland III ML858, 302 Flying Training Unit at Oban, crashed on Gleann Mhor during the night. The aircraft was conducting a night navex from Oban with 10 onboard.
2. Dr John Gask MA BM BCH (1914-2004).

3. 3/4 June 1943, Beaufighter TF.X LX798, 304 Ferry Training Unit at Port Ellen, Islay, crashed St Kilda. The aircraft wreckage was not found for 3 months (Hutchison 1992, p. 91).
4. The Wellington may have been Mk VIII HX448 from 7 OTU, Limavady, of which 5 of the crew of 7 were Canadian, which went missing on 28 September 1942. However, there is another possibility: Wellington Mk VIII LA995 of 303 Ferry Training Unit from Stornoway which disappeared on 23 February 1943 with one RCAF crewmember on board. The only identified body from these two aircraft wrecks was Sgt Alston, the rear gunner of Wellington LA995, who was washed up on a beach on the Isle of Lewis in March 1943.
5. Later AVM Sir John Severne KCVO OBE AFC DL.
6. Anthony Henday first visited the area in the 1750s, having journeyed from the St Lawrence River, when the area was populated only by the occasional Blackfoot Indians.

Chapter 19: Squadron Command

1. 14 May 1989, Lynx HAS.3 XZ244 of 829 NAS near Mombasa, Kenya.
2. 8 May 1989, Jetstream T.2 XX489 of 750 NAS crashed into Portland Bay during a Cadet Corps Open Day display, following a wing-over manoeuvre.
3. From 1992 onwards the Lynx AH.7 upgrade also included composite main rotor blades and a shorter-span horizontal stabiliser. The spring bias unit automatically put about 13 degrees of pitch on to the tail rotor blades in the event of a no. 1 hydraulic failure, thus reducing some of the manual control forces on the yaw pedals.
4. For those of a technical mind the following from my kneepad *aide-mémoire* may be of interest:

Gem 2		671kw (900shp)
Gem 41-1		835kw (1,135shp)
Lynx AH.1	Max AUW	4,355kg (4,425kg with MRHVA)
Lynx AH.7	Max AUW	4,875kg

5. Later Maj Gen A.F. Whitehead CB DSO.
6. Hjerkinn Range was used by the Germans during the occupation and was one of the locations selected for the film *Star Wars*. As from 2008 it is no longer a military training area; it is now a nature reserve.
7. However, two years previously a Widerøe Dash-7, Flight 710, had crashed into the mountain of Torghatten whilst attempting to land at

ENDNOTES

   Brønnøy and three years later a Twin Otter, Flight 744, was to crash whilst on approach to Namsos.
8. Later ACM Sir Michael Alcock GCB KBE FREng FIMechE FRAeS.
9. Later Lt Gen Sir Henry Beverley KCB, OBE.
10. A small monument made of anchor chain links from *Tirpitz* and an aerial mine lies just off the E6 road, commemorating the allied aircrews who died.
11. Ju-188A-3 Rächer Wnr 190330 of KG26 crashed at Høknesvatnet, 4.5 miles north east of Namsos, on 30 March 1945. It had taken off from Vaernes to attack a convoy near Iceland but failed to find the target and ran low on fuel. The crew bailed out and survived.

Chapter 20: Air Combat Manoeuvring – Tally One, Visual One, Fight's On

1. 26 July 1990, Gazelle XW851, 3 Cdo Bde Air Sqn RM, near Lampeter, South Wales.
2. Shturm or AT-6A Spiral, was a sonic Soviet anti-tank missile guided by a radio-command link and had a secondary anti-helicopter capability with a range of 5,000 metres.
3. This aircraft was probably G-FRAZ operated by Flight Refuelling Aviation out of Hurn. It had been operated as a yellow target tug by Swedair as SE-GYC. In 2002 it was sold to the USA as N441DR, later N441LC and, in 2019, was operating in Australia as VH-EQU.

Chapter 21: Op HAVEN – Deployment

1. Later Maj Gen A.M. Keeling CB CBE.
2. Gen. John Malchase David Shalikashvili died on 23 July 2011, aged 75. He had a very hard act to follow after Gen. Colin Powell as Chairman of the Joint Chiefs. I remember how he defended his father (an ex-Georgian Legion member of the Wehrmacht) in a dignified way when questioned by the US Senate. He could not have had a much better eulogy than this, delivered by ex-President Clinton: 'He never minced words, he never postured or pulled punches, he never shied away from tough issues or tough calls, and most important, he never shied away from doing what he believed was the right thing.'
3. Later ACM Sir Richard Johns GCB KCVO CBE.
4. Later Lt Gen J. Garner and Director of Reconstruction and Humanitarian Assistance in Iraq in 2003.

5. There had been a number of Kurdish revolts against British rule between 1919 and 1932, led initially by Sheikh Mahmud Barzanji who pronounced himself King of Kurdistan. One of his followers was Mustafa Barzani who led the 1931 revolt in the area we were operating in. His nephew was Massoud Barzani, the current leader of the KDP. We met a few old boys who remembered the RAF air attacks in support of the Iraqi Army as young boys and the curiously named 'English Valley' was located just north of Sirsenk. We met no residual hostility from the Kurds, however.
6. Brown 1995, p. 57.

Chapter 22: Op HAVEN – Establishing The Safe Haven

1. Later Lt Gen Sir Robert Ross KCB OBE.
2. Brown 1995, p. 62.
3. The ZU-23-2 is a Russian-built twin-barrelled towed 23mm anti-aircraft gun with a range of 2,500m. First introduced into service in 1960, its simple, rugged and effective design has meant that many hundreds of thousands are still in service with ex-Warsaw Pact countries and within Russian spheres of influence in Africa and Asia. It is also effective in the direct fire role.
4. Brown 1995, p. 54.
5. By coincidence seventeen years later my son, then a Captain in the AAC, was to be crewed with Sgt Dale AAC (no relation) in their Apache AH Mk1 during Op HERRICK.
6. The Valsella Valmara 69 was an Italian-built anti-personnel mine with a cylindrical plastic body. Initiated by either contact with the prongs sticking up from the top cover or by a trip wire attached to the prongs, a propelling charge launched the mine 18 inches into the air before the main charge detonated.
7. Later Gen John Abizaid, Commander of US CENTCOM and US Ambassador to Saudi Arabia (2019-2020).
8. Later Lt Gen Sir Robert Fry KCB CBE.
9. Adie 2003, p. 285.

Chapter 23: Op HAVEN – Life in the Field

1. The wildlife challenge was clearly not just a product of my imagination as, four years later, in June 1995, I read this paragraph in the *Daily Telegraph*: 'A plague of snakes has struck the Kurdish enclave in

ENDNOTES

Northern Iraq, with doctors reporting at least five snakebite deaths and dozens of people admitted to hospital.'

2. USN CH-53E 161539 (construction no. 65-460) of Combat Support Squadron 4, Black Stallions, based at Sigonella, Sicily. Bu. No. 161539 was partially dismantled, recovered underslung by CH-53 and reportedly repaired in Israel. In 2014 she was assigned to the USMC with VMX-22, based at New River, NC.
3. Some years later I saw a school map of Europe drawn by A. Schmidt of München, dated 1830, in the Deutsches Historisches Museum in Berlin. 'Amadia' was clearly marked on the otherwise blank expanse of what is now the Northern Iraq border area.
4. I was to recognise a similar intact decorated storage jar in 1998 at the Archaeological Museum of Olympia in the Peloponnese.

Chapter 24: Op HAVEN - Withdrawal

1. Two years later I found an abandoned pair of Soviet ZU-23-2 wheels in Luanda which the Angolan military readily gave me. They were fitted with solid, bullet-proof tyres and were extremely heavy. The British Embassy in Luanda kindly arranged for them to be shipped home in a returning container and they were presented to the Eastney Museum where they slipped smoothly onto the axles of the Iraqi gun.
2. Col James L. Jones Jr went on to be Commandant of the USMC 1999-2003 and SACEUR from 2003-2006. After retirement from the USMC he was appointed National Security Advisor 2009-2010.
3. A tragic incident occurred when, on 14 April 1994, two USAF F-15s under AWACS oversight shot down two US Army UH-60 Blackhawks inside the Northern No-Fly Zone after mis-identifying them as Mi-24 Hinds, killing the 26 coalition occupants from Op PROVIDE COMFORT.
4. Jones, 2017.
5. Ross, 1991.
6. List of 3 Cdo Bde Air Sqn RM aircraft deployed on Op HAVEN:

Gazelle AH.1

ZA776	CF	By C-130 to Diyarbakir 21 Apr 91
ZA728	CE	By C-130 to Diyarbakir 21 Apr 91
XW849	CG	RFA *Argus* arrived 30 Apr 91
XX380	CA	RFA *Argus* arrived 30 Apr 91

FLYING LIGHT HELICOPTERS WITH THE ROYAL MARINES

XX412	CB	RFA *Argus* arrived 30 Apr 91	
XX450	CD	RFA *Argus* arrived 30 Apr 91	
XW851	CH	By C-130 from Yeovilton arrived 5 May 91	
XX413	CC	By C-130 from Yeovilton arrived 5 May 91	

Lynx AH.7

XZ180	DX	RFA *Argus* arrived 30 Apr 91	
XZ182	DM	RFA *Argus* arrived 30 Apr 91	
XZ605	DY	RFA *Argus* arrived 30 Apr 91	
XZ612	DZ	RFA *Argus* arrived 30 Apr 91	IRCM
XZ644	DV	RFA *Argus* arrived 30 Apr 91	TOW TI IRCM
XZ673	DW	RFA *Argus* arrived 30 Apr 91	TOW TI IRCM

4 Gazelles remained at RNAS Yeovilton during the Operation.

Chapter 25: In the Back

1. Five years later Lt Cdr Tim Gedge AFC RN was to command the re-formed 809 NAS of Sea Harrier FRS.1 during the Falklands conflict.
2. Bristow Helicopters S-61N, probably G-BIMU, based at Stornoway. They were kind enough to compliment me on my map reading as I guess they were used to being passed incorrect grid references.
3. 30 April 1990, Shackleton AEW.2 WR965, 8 Sqn RAF, hit high ground near Northton, Isle of Harris. All 10 crew killed.
4. 23 June 1985, Air India B747 VT-EFO disintegrated south-west of Ireland, killing all 329 occupants.
5. Space Shuttle Challenger, 28 January 1986, broke up during launch off Cape Canaveral, Florida, when a seal on one of the solid rocket boosters failed, killing all 7 crew members. The wreckage fell into the sea off the Florida coast.
6. 13 September 1997, USAF C-141B 65-9405 and Luftwaffe TU-154M 11+02, collided 65nm off the coast of SW Africa at FL350. 33 killed.
7. Aviation Safety net database www.flightsafety.org.
8. 3 February 1968, EA-6B Prowler VMAQ-2 hit cable near Cermis, NE Italy. 20 cable car passengers killed.
9. BGen Guy Vander Linden USMC was a Presidential Helicopter Command pilot with HMX-1 during President Ronald Reagan's presidency. After retiring from the USMC and later Agusta-Westland helicopters, he became Republican member of the Iowa House of Representatives where he served 4 terms.

ENDNOTES

10. The Bulgarian Naval Aviation in 1998 had 9 Mil Mi-14PL ASW versions and 2 of the Mil Mi-14BT mine-countermeasures variant with towed sled. Hats off to Russian test pilot G.R. Karapetyan who, in 1973, carried out night engine-off landings with an Mi-14 into water. (Global Security.org). There was also one lonely, old and unserviceable, Ka-25Ts Hormone B, Red 821, in the corner of the hangar.
11. The Bulgarians replaced their Mi-14s with the AS565 Panther although, for financial reasons, their order for 6 aircraft was reduced to 3 (one written off in June 2018). Romania now has 59 IAR 330 helicopters.

Chapter 26: Private Flying

1. One of these, MiG-21MF N9307 from Dekalb, was badly damaged on 12 July 2012 when it overran the runway at Eden Prairie MN after the drag chute failed to deploy. The other was a two-seat MiG-21UM. Both were ex-Polish Air Force.
2. B-25H N5548N 'Barbie III' was built in August 1943 as the second B-25H and was used for test purposes at Wright Field. She was recovered from a farm in Illinois in 1981 and restored to flying condition.
3. T-28C N2215D fitted with Wright R-1820-86B Cyclone 1,425 hp 9-cylinder radial engine.
4. Cerniglia 2012.
5. Corken/Guillet Christen Eagle II N96CG with Lycoming 200hp 4-cylinder engine.
6. 10 August 2002, Christen Eagle II N96CG, Kaneville IL. The failure was due to a spun bearing on the crankshaft which blocked an oil supply feed (Ashcraft/Helfer 2003).
7. Bellanca 8KCAB Decathlon N5068G with Lycoming AEIO-320 SER 160hp 4-cylinder engine.
8. N. American SNJ-5 N11HP with Pratt & Whitney R-1340 600hp 9-cylinder radial engine.
9. Zenair CH-601-HDS Zodiac N94CS with Rotax 912 81hp 4-cylinder engine based at Lansing IL.

Chapter 27: Envoi

1. A Sioux, three Varsities, a Lightning F.6, Sea Vixen, Beaver, Jet Provost, Lightning T.4 and a Hunter GA11. (ukserials.com)

2. The US Army is downgrading technology in their Eurocopter UH-72 Lakota training fleet so that students can better master basic flying skills. The force trim will be degraded to make the aircraft less stable. (AW&ST, Vol. 181 No. 10, p. 40).
3. I caused some irritation by occasionally reminding RAF and FAA colleagues that without sergeant pilots we would never have won the Battle of Britain or sustained the bomber offensive over Germany. Some of our SNCO pilots transferred to the Army Air Corps where they were welcomed and many gained commissions. Others went into commercial aviation where they fly as captains on types ranging from Dash-8 to B747. A large number continued to fly helicopters for the police, air ambulances, charter or supporting the oil and gas industry. It is no surprise that they have all done well.
4. An abiding aeronautical puzzle is how, over the years, differing military aircraft from different manufacturers can be imbued with a similar, unique, cockpit smell.

Index

Ranks are shown as at the time of the narrative.

A-6 Intruder, Grumman, 60, 229, 270
A-7 Corsair, LTV, 60
A-10 Thunderbolt II, Fairchild Republic, 197, 208–209, 233
AACC Middle Wallop, viii, xiv, xvi, 1–31, 33, 40, 66–7, 71, 93, 95–152, 158, 168, 178, 183, 188, 246, 251–4, 259–61, 264–5
AAC UKLF, 47, 61, 63, 181–2
Aalborg, Denmark, 152–3, 184
AB-212, Agusta Bell, 55
Abizaid, Lt Col John, 210, 268
Adie, Kate, 211, 245, 268
AH-1 Sea Cobra, Bell, 55, 192–3, 206
Airfix kit, viii, 123–4, 216, image 19
ALAT, 163, 165, 222, 253
Alcock, AVM R.J.M., 189, 267
Alcock, Flt Lt G.R., 255
Alouette II, Aérospatiale, 25, 252, 261
Al Amadiyah, Iraq, 212, 217, 219–20
Ambassador, Airspeed, x
Anduki, Brunei, 72, 259
Arger, SSgt Peter, 263
Ashcraft, Todd, ix, 235, 245, 271
Atac, Robert, ix, 233, image 36

Auster, Taylorcraft, xi, 18, 248
AWACS, Boeing, 203, 209, 214, 241, 269

B-25 Mitchell, North American, 233, 250, 271
Backhouse, SSgt Brian, 15
Bain, Maj Iain, 32, 36
Baker, James A., 208
Balkwill, Maj Richard, 161
Ball, Capt John, 145, 148–9
Bancroft, Capt Paul, ix, 18, 137–8, 151, 260
Bandar Seri Begawan, Brunei, 69, 74, 76
Bardufoss, Norway, 160–1, 226
Barnham, Flt Lt Denis, 62, 245, 256–7
Barnwell, Sgt Alan, ix, 193
Barraclough, Lt Julian, 90, 183
Barzani, Massoud, 268
Basingstoke, 107, 113, 117
Bateson, Nigel, 211
Baulf, Capt Colin, ix, 178–9
Beaver, de Havilland, Canada, 108, 114, 144–5, 148–50, 261, 271
Beeston, WO2 Pete, image 30
Belize, 188–90

273

Bell 206 Jet Ranger, 14, 50, 137, 149, 252
Bell 47,
 G-2, 50, 258
 G-3B Sioux AH.1, xiv, xv, 1, 6, 10, 12–28, 31, 39–40, 43, 47, 53, 65–76, 135, 138–9, 162, 188, 191, 250–2, 254, 258, 271
 G-3B Sioux HT.2, 18, 251–2
 G-4A, 1, 5–6, 9, 11–13, 31, 96, 106, 120–2
Belvedere HC Mk1, Bristol, 69
Benbecula, 174, 176–7, 196
Bessbrook, 77, 79, 81, 83, 85, 225, 259–60
Beverley, Lt Gen Sir Henry, 189, 267
Blain, Sgt Ken, 46
Blevins, Capt Derek, xv, 33, 43, 93, 225, 250, 260
Blowers, CSgt Al, 194, image 30
Blue Eagles, 139
Board, Capt Barry, 226
Bodø, Norway, 185–7
Bonner, SSgt Séan, ix, 118–21, 123
Bramall, Gen Sir Edwin, 191, 259, 261
BRDM scout car, 203
Bristow Helicopters, xiv, 5, 11, 120, 123, 227, 249, 270
Broussard, Max Holste, 149
Browne, Capt Jim, ix, 143–5, 148, image 20, image 21
Brunei, 65–6, 69–70, 72, 74, 188
Buccaneer, Blackburn, 58, 256
Burnell, Capt Jerry, image 32
Butler, CSgt Kevin, 186, 209

Cagliari, Sardinia, 61
Calgary, Canada, 178–9

Cameron, Maj Peter, ix, xiv, 33, 44, 254
Canberra, English Electric, xvi, 52, 250
Candlish, WO1 Eddy, ix, 179, 214, 263, image 32
Capo Teulada, Sardinia, 60–1
Carvell, CSgt Geoff, ix, 179
Castlemartin, 193
Cecil, RAdm Sir Nigel, 62, 256
Cessna Conquest, 195–6
Cessna 310, 161
Chapple, Brig John, 74, 259
CH-46 Sea Knight, 192, 206
CH-47 Chinook, 51, 105, 201, 206
CH-53 Sea Stallion, 55, 192, 202, 204, 206, 215, 269
C-1A Trader, 52, 60
C-5 Galaxy, 200, 202
C-130 Hercules, 51, 145, 151–2, 160, 200–202, 204–205, 221, 269–70
C-141 Starlifter, 101, 200, 202, 227–8, 246, 270
C-160 Transall, 50, 202, 222
Chipmunk T.10, de Havilland, xi, 1, 3–7, 15, 53, 106, 114, 232, 235–6, 246, 250, 252
Chipmunk T.22, de Havilland, xi
Christen-Eagle II, 235, 271
Clement, Sgt Mark, image 7
Collins, Tony, ix, 5, 7–8
Collioure, France, 166, 242
Collon, Prof Dominique, 217
Colquhoun, Hugh, 13–14
Comino, Malta, 57
Commando Support Helicopter Sqns, 181, 226
Constanta, Romania, 230–1

INDEX

Conway, Sgt Eric, image 33
Cowie, Sgt John, 27, 33, 45
Coypool, Plymouth, 31–2, 34, 36, 137, 151, 181
Crawford, Capt Ron, 202, image 32
Crosby, Lt John, 65
CTCRM, Lympstone, 138, 242
Culdrose RNAS, xiv, 27, 30, 31, 48, 87, 90, 95, 108, 250, 261
Culliford, Capt Nigel, ix, 48, 170, 232
Cuthill, Charles, ix, 3, 250, image 1

D-20 152 mm howitzer, 203
Dahuk, Iraq, 208
Dale, Sgt Kevin, ix, 209, 268
Dash-7, de Havilland Canada, 187, 224, 266
Dauphin, Aérospatiale SA 365, 176
Davies, WO2 Tony, 98, 113, 261
De la Casa, Nicholas and Rosanna, 211, 213
Decathlon, Bellanca, 236, 271
Decimomannu, Sardinia, 60
Den Beste, Capt Ed, 105, 261, image 16
Denning, Lt Paul, 188, 215, 220, 222, image 32
Detmold, Germany, 100, 103, 173
Dieppe Flight, 33, 35, 45
Dihok, Iraq, 223
Dingli, Malta, 49
Diyarbakir, Turkey, 201–202, 204–205, 269
Donkin, Capt Tim, xiv
Dornier Wal-Cabina, 58, 256
Drew, Lt Col John, 117–18, 262
Dunlop, Lt Col Graham, 212
Dunn, Lt David, 104

EA-6B Prowler, Grumman, 229, 270
Ear, Sound Mirror, 52–3
Earhart, Amelia, 137, 235, 245
Eckhoff, Robert, ix, 232
Eggebek, Germany, 172
Evenes, Norway, 160
Ex CLOCKWORK, 190
Ex CO-OPERATIVE PARTNER, 229, 231
Ex COLD WINTER, 185
Ex CRUSADER, 98
Ex CURRY TRAIL, 66
Ex DAWN PATROL, 60
Ex DEEP EXPRESS, 41
Ex DESTINED GLORY, 124
Ex DISPLAY DETERMINATION, 55
Ex DOUBLE BASE, 40
Ex EAGLE EYE, 107
Ex GADFLY, 184
Ex HIGHLAND DRONE, 195
Ex JASON'S QUEST, 22
Ex ROLLING DEEP, 180
Ex TEAMWORK, 104, 189

F-104 Starfighter, Lockheed, 52, 172, 202, 205
F-18 Hornet, McDonnell Douglas, 113, 116–17, 262
Fagernes, Norway, 184–5, 190
Fairey, John, 112, 262
Fairhead, Chris, Rolls Royce, 189
Falcon 20, Dassault, 195–6
Falconar, CSgt O.B., 248
Falkland Islands, vii, 33, 104, 123, 125, 134, 137, 149, 254, 258, 263–4, 270
Farley, John, 33, 253
Farley, Lt Paul, 104

275

Farnborough, x, xi, 15, 113, 124, 227, 241, 265
Flight International Magazine, 123, 159, 161, 246, 263, 265
Flycatcher, Fairey, 112
Forward Operating Base (FOB)
　Breezeblock, 207, 215
　Capbadge, 206–207
　Workhorse, 207
Francis, Lt Ken, 135, 137, 263
Fraser, WO2 Don, 29
Frost, Sgt John, 250
Fry, Maj Rob, 210, 268

Gaines, Mike, 159–60, 265
Gardermoen, Norway, 151–3, 160, 184
Garner, Maj Gen Jay M., 200, 220–1, 267
Gazelle,
　Aérospatiale SA341, 111
　AH.1, 9, 27–35, 35–45, 46–65, 67, 71, 76, 78–85, 89, 95–111, 113–17, 119–20, 128, 134–5, 138–42, 147, 151–2, 155–6, 161, 165, 170–1, 178–9, 183, 187–9, 193–5, 197, 202, 215–18, 251–3, 258–9, 261, 263–5, 269
　HT.2, 27, 48, 87, 252–3, 264
　HT.3, 87, 89
Gaziantep, Turkey, 204
Gedge, Cdr Tim, ix, 224, 270
Gurkhas, 2, 66, 68, 70, 74, 76
Gibraltar, 36, 45
Gibson, Arthur, 147, 264
Gjendesheim, 226
Gnejna Bay, Malta, 57
Gozo, 51, 54, 57
Gregson, Capt Mike, 260

Hal Far, Malta, xiv, 47–8, 56, 58, 60, 255
Hancock, Cpl Graham, ix, 170–1
Hannington, Maj Roger, 111
Hardy, Wilf, 144, 264
Harrier, Hawker Siddeley, 33, 189, 253, 270
Hawarden, 141
Helme, Capt Rodney, 46, 57, 64
Hewetson, Capt Mike, 106
Hickey, Col Mike, 117
Hildesheim, Germany, 98, 100–101, 126, 263
Hiller T.2 and 12C, xiv, 250
Hjerkinn Range, Norway, 186, 266
HMS *Albion,* xiv, 249, 254
HMS *Bulwark,* 34, 36, 39–42, 44–5, 249, 253–4
HMS *Condor,* 265
HMS *Fearless,* 33, 36, 38, 56, 60–1, 131, 253
HMS *Gannet,* 170, 232, 261
HMS *Hermes,* 48, 149, 254, image 24
HMS *Heron,* 31, 38, 112, 131–2, 137, 150–2, 164, 178, 181–2, 183, 189, 192–4, 199, 221, 223, 239, 270
HMS *Intrepid,* 36, 44, 104, 180, 187, 189
HMS *Kent,* 64
HMS *London,* 256
HMS *Newcastle,* 189
HMS *Seahawk,* xiv, 27, 30–1, 48, 87, 90, 95, 108, 250, 261
HMS *St Angelo,* 56
HMS *Vernon,* 38
HMS *Warspite,* 265
Holroyd-Smith, Maj Mike, 61
Hong Kong, 12, 70, 72, 161, 253, 265

INDEX

Horner, Gordon, 123, 263
Horridge, Flt Lt Steve, 58
House, Maj Gen D.G., 26
Howe, Lt Jeremy, 97, image 7
HMM-264, 202
HMP .5 in MG, 194–5, 197, 242
HRH Prince Edward, 177–8
Hughes, Joan, xiii, 249
Hunt-Davis, Lt Col Miles, 74–5, 259
Hunter, Hawker, x, xvi, 24, 193, 271

Incerlik, Turkey, 200, 222
Irving, Sgt Damian, ix, 209–11
Iskenderun, Turkey, 204, 216, 221

Jackson, WO2 Ken, 143
Jackson, Lt Rowan, ix, 56
Javelin FAW.9, Gloster, xiii
Jeffs, Lt Graham, 54
Jetstream, Handley Page T.2, 88, 183, 266
Jindivik, GAF, 16, 135
Johns, AVM R.E., 200, 267
Johnson, Flt Lt Al, 91
Joint Task Force, (JTF) 200–201
Jones, Col James L., 221, 223, 245, 269
Ju-188, Junkers, 189, 267

Kalkara, Malta, 62, 63
Kani Masi, Iraq, 207, 215
KC-130, Lockheed, 202
Keeling, Brig Andrew, 190, 199, 210, 213, 221–2, 267
Kerr, Lt Col Graham, 201
Kiel Canal, Germany, 173
Kiel Holtenau, Germany, 173
Kirkpatrick, SSgt Jim, 263
Krings, Jack E., 117

Lambe, Brig R.M., 188
Lambert, WO2 Rod, 263
Lawrence, Sgt Peter, 250
Lewis, Capt Denis, ix, 66, 70, 76
Lightning, English Electric, xi, xv, 16, 58–60, 140, 256, 271
Linosa Island, 63–4
Long Kesh, 77, 79, 81
Lowe, Janice, 159
Lynx,
   AH.1, Westland, 118, 125–38, 142–50, 153, 173, 183–4, 254, 263, 266
   AH.1 GT, Westland, 183–4
   AH.7, Westland, 126, 183–4, 195, 266, 270
   HAS.3, Westland, 194–5, 266
   G-LYNX, Westland, 144

M Company, 42 Cdo RM, xv, 33, 225–6
MAWTS 1, Yuma, 192
Macaulay, Capt Neil, ix, 39–40
MacDonald, Lt Andy, 104
Mackenzie, Sqn Ldr Peter, 108, 261
MacMillan, Capt Duncan, 260
Makeig-Jones, Capt Robin, 135
Markenesdalen, Norway, 161
Markham, Capt Tony, ix, 67, 69, 98–9
Marpole, Derek, 144
Maxwell, Charles, 211, 213
Meardon, Maj John, 183
Meggy, Lt John, 263
Menghini, WO2 John, ix, 46, 171, 178
Merrick, SSgt Tony, 143
Meteor, Gloster, x, 29, 135, 248
MFG2, 172
MFG5, 173
Mi-8 Hip, 217, 229, 252

Mi-14 Haze, 229, 270–1
Mi-24 Hind, 192, 209, 269
MiG-21 Fishbed/Lancer, 231, 233, 271
MiG-23 Flogger, 231
MiG-29 Fulcrum, 231
Middleton, Capt Dick, 27, 33, 42
Middle Wallop, viii, xiv, xvi, 1–11, 12–26, 27–31, 33, 40, 66, 67, 71, 93, 95–112, 113–17, 118–24, 125–38, 139–52, 158, 168, 178, 183, 188, 246, 251–4, 259–61, 264–5

Millar, Flt Lt Gordon, 53
Miller, Cpl Dusty, 214
Minords, Maj David, ix, 137, 151, 167
ML Handler, 131
Mombasa, 183, 266
Mont-Louis, France, 166, 242
Monte Romano, Italy, 55
Mosquito, de Havilland, xi, xiii, 141–2, 245, 264
Morris, Lt Paul, ix, 188
Mosul, Iraq, 200, 205, 209, 215
Mountbatten, Lord Louis, 65
Mulley, Rt Hon Fred, 56
Murphy, Maj Terence, xiv, xv, 225, 260

Namsos, Norway, 187, 189, 267
Narvik, Norway, 160
Netheravon, 17, 31, 67, 69, 111, 129, 130, 135, 181–2
Newtownhamilton, 77, 225–6
Nimrod MR.1, Hawker Siddeley, 48, 51, 53, 63, 255
Noble, Capt Mark, 160, 192

Nordholz, Germany, 152
Norman, Lt Peter, 214, image 33
Northam, Capt Hugh, 171
Niblett, Capt Jeff, ix, 153, 171, 264
Nunn, Lt Richard, 135, 263, 265
Nunn, Capt Chris, 135

Op ARMILLA, 195
Op BANNER, 77, 85, 260
Op CORPORATE, 254
Op DESERT STORM, 34, 190, 192, 195–6, 203
Op GRANBY, 195
Op HAVEN, 34, 197, 198–223, 246, 267–70
Op MARKET GARDEN, 101
Op PROVIDE COMFORT, 200, 223, 245, 269
Op TELIC, 34, 222
Op WARDEN, 222
Overy, Maj Norman, 61, 110

P-3 Orion, Lockheed, 51, 228
Palmer, WO1 Geoff, 111, 263
Panaga Club, Brunei, 70
Parker, Sgt Bill, image 32
Parsons, Maj Louis, 109, 117, 139, 263
Perpignan, France, 167–8, 184
Peshmerga, 208, 219
Portadown, 84
Portland, 36, 131, 183, 266
Post, Lt Col Gary, 117
Potter, Flt Lt Greg, 165
Potter, Brig Richard W., 200
Pounds, Maj Nick, 223
Pryke, Col Wally, xiv
Pucará, FMA IA 58, 135, 263
Pullford, Capt Derek, image 32

INDEX

Puma, Aérospatiale SA330, 91, 165, 230, 252
Puma HC.1, Aérospatiale, 48, 79, 85, 89, 155, 225, 259, 265
Pyrenees, 49, 163, 167–8, 215, 230

RAE Boscombe Down, xiv, 97, 113, 115–16
RAE Llanbedr, 16–17, 135–6
RAF Aldergrove, 6, 77, 80–1, 225–6, 251
RAF Benson, 178
RAF Brize Norton, 45, 77, 188, 200
RAF Chivenor, xvi, 23–5, 31
RAF Finningley, 150
RAF Honington, 58
RAF Kemble, 147
RAF Kinloss, 169, 176
RAF Lossiemouth, xi, 169
RAF Lyneham, 202
RAF Manston, xi, xiii, 152, 184, 248–9
RAF Mountbatten, 31
RAF North Luffenham, 253
RAF Odiham, 93, 149, 262
RAF Luqa, x, 45, 47, 51–4, 56, 58–60, 62–3, 65, 67, 247–8, 254–6
RAF Shawbury, xi, xii, 48, 86–95, 183, 241, 258, 260, 262
RAF St Mawgan, xvi, 31
RAF Ta Kali (Ta' Qali), x, 258
RAF Tern Hill, 18, 92, 94, 252, 260, 262
RAF Valley, 81, 96, 135
RAF Waddington, 45, 262
RAF Wildenrath, 98
RAF Wittering, 189
RAF Hospital Wroughton, 115
RFA *Argus,* 204, 269–70

RFA *Sir Bedivere,* 60
RFA *Sir Lancelot,* 65
RNAS Culdrose, xiv, 27, 30–1, 48, 87, 90, 95, 108, 250, 261
RNAS Eglinton, 261
RNAS Hal Far, xiv, 47–8, 56, 58–60, 255
RNAS Lee-on-Solent, 31
RNAS Portland, 36, 131, 183, 266
RNAS Yeovilton, 31, 38, 112, 131–2, 137, 150–2, 164, 178, 181–3, 189, 192–4, 199, 221, 223, 239, 270
RNAW Almondbank, 263
RNAY Fleetlands, 183
RNAY Wroughton, 31, 123, 263
Ragget, Lt Andy, 131
Reynolds, Lt Steve, 211, 213
RM Eastney, 221, 269
Robson, WO2 Jack, 263
Rogers, Capt Alastair, ix, 214
ROLLING DEEP, Exercise, 180
Rondane Mountains, 157
Rotodyne, Fairey, xi, 124
Røros, Norway, 186, 188
Ross, Maj Gen Robin, 206, 246, 268, 269
Rowe, Maj Viv, 212
Rowe, Lt David, 250

S-61, Sikorski, 72, 227, 259, 270
Saillagouse, France, 49, 163–4, 166–9, 184, 242, 265
Salerno, Italy, 55
Salerno Flight, 34, 45–7, 60–1, 65–6, 79, 255–6, 258
Salisbury, Lt John, 218
Schofield, Capt Mike, 15
Scimitar F.1, Supermarine, xi

Scimitar FV107, tracked vehicle, 102
Scout AH.1, Westland, viii, xv, 15, 17, 32, 35, 40, 43, 69, 73, 79, 81, 89, 101–103, 118–25, 127, 134–6, 161, 238, 243, 245, 252–3, 258–9, 263, 265
Sea Hawk FGA.6, Hawker, xiv
Sea King, Westland, 89–90, 115–16, 170, 173, 176, 194, 254
Sea King HC.4, Westland, 38, 132, 206, 212, 226–7
Seria, Brunei, 69–71, 73, 75
Severne, AVM Sir John, 178, 266
Seymour, Lt Peter, xv
Shackleton T.4, Avro, xii, 247, 249
Shackleton AEW.2, Avro, 227, 247, 270
Shalikashvili, Gen John Malchase, 200, 207, 267
Sharland, Freydis, née Leaf, xii, xiii, 249, image 16
Sharples, Arthur, 11, 251
Shepherd, Sgt Barrie, ix, 46, image 9
Shirati, Iraq, 206, 220
Sigonella NAF, Sicily, 47, 51–2, 55, 58, 60, 228, 269
Silopi, Turkey, 201–203, 205, 220, 222
Silver Eagles, 138, 143–4, 150, 254
Sinclair, Lt Cdr Sandy, 224, 261
Sinjari, Hussein, 219
Sioux AH.1, Westland, xiv, xv, 1, 6, 10, 12–28, 31, 39–40, 43, 47, 53, 65, 66–76, 135, 138–9, 162, 188, 191, 250–2, 254, 258, 271
Sirsenk, N Iraq, 203, 212, 216, 220–2, 268
Skagerrak, 152–3, 184

Skien, Norway, 152–3
SM.109, SIAI-Marchetti, 55
Smith, RH Dick, 137
Smith-Barry, Maj Robert, 86
Smithson, Maj Bill, 108, 261
Sparrowhawks, 111, 139, 188
Spencer, Capt Jon, ix, 201–202, 222
Squirrel HT.1, Eurocopter AS350, 252, 260, 262
Squirrel, Twin, Eurocopter AS355, 98, 246, 261
Srebrenica, Bosnia & Herzegovina, 223
SS.11, Nord missile, 125, 134, 243
St Andrews, Malta, 45, 65
St George's, Malta, 46, 52, 54–5, 57, 63, 258
St Kilda, 172–6, 196, 265–6
St Patrick's, Malta, 50–1, 255
Stampe SV.4, 111, 261
Stephen, H.M., 149
Stewart, SSgt David, ix, 143, image 21
Stimson, SSgt Clint, 143, image 20, image 21
Stokka, Norway, 187
Stornoway, 196, 227, 266, 270
Storrie, Maj David, ix, xv, 225, 250, 260
Summers, Capt Ken, 95, 260
Sunderland III, Short, 175, 265
Super Frelon, Aérospatiale SA321, 50–1, 57, 252, 255
Syracuse, Sicily, 52, 58, 256

T-28 Trojan, North American, 233–4
T-62 tank, 203, 207
Tu-154, Tupolev, 228, 270
Ta'Qali, Malta, 258
Taylor, Capt Peter, 180

INDEX

Taylor, Sgt Michael, 3
Teakle, Cpl Mark, 218
TEAMWORK, Exercise, 104, 189
TELIC, Operation, 34, 222
Tempest FB II, Hawker, xiii, 249
Thomas, Wg Cdr Richard, 189
Thomson, Lt Col Jonathan, 213
Thresh, Lt Leslie, 2, 5, 27, 30, image 7
Thwaites, WO2 Mal, 143, image 21
Thunder City, Capetown, 60, 256
Tirpitz, 189, 267
TOW, Hughes missile, xv, 44, 118, 125, 133–4, 142, 144, 186, 191, 193–6, 205, 208–209, 212, 223, 244, 270
Tromsø, Norway, 186, 189
Trondheim, Norway, 186
Turkey, 36, 41–2, 44–5, 198–204, 211–12, 216–17, 221–2
Tutong, Brunei, 73, 75

UH-1N, Bell, 192, 206
USS *Iwo Jima*, 55
USS *Wasp*, 256

V-22, Bell Osprey, xi
Vaernes, Norway, 186–7, 189, 267
Værløse, Denmark, 171
Valenzia, Maj John, 61, 263
Valetta C.1, Vickers, x, xiv, 248–9
Valmara 69 mine, 210, 211, 268
Vander Linden, Brig Gen G., ix, 229, 270
Varna, Bulgaria, 229–30
VC10, Vickers, 45, 67, 70, 77, 188, 200–202
Victor, Handley Page, 56, 63
Viking, Vickers, x
Villa Portelli, Malta, 62–3, 256–7

Viscount, Vickers, x
VMAQ-2, 229, 270
Volkers, Brig Mike, 135
Voss, Norway, 155, 265
VP-45, 228
Vulcan B.2, Avro, 45, 47–8, 141–2, 170, 255

Wainwright, Alberta, 178–9
Walker, CSgt 'Hookey', 23
Walters, Lt Col Paul, 141
Ward-Booth, Maj Gen J.A., 71
WARDEN, Operation, 222
Wasp HAS.1, Westland, 37, 245, 253–4
Wawn, Maj Mike, ix, 12, 17, 23–4
Went, Capt Adrian, ix, 189
Wellington, Vickers, 176, 266
Wessex,
   HAS.1, Westland, xiv, xv, 250
   HU.5, Westland, xiv, xv, 1, 36, 39–40, 56, 78, 89, 132
   HC.2, Westland, 78–9, 85, 89, 262
Whirlwind,
   Westland S55 and Mk7, xiv, 250
   Westland HAR.10, 69
Whitehead, Brig Andrew, 184, 266
Wilde, Capt Robert USN, ix, 230–1
Williams, Capt Andy, image 32
Wilkins, Lt Col Mike, 41, 254
Willingale, WO2 Keith, 263
Wilsey, Clare, 67, 70, 76–7, 227
Wilsey, Jane, ix, 2, 30, 45, 77, 135, 200–201
Wilsey, Simon, ix, 268
Winsor, Diana, 146, 246
Wombat, L6 120mm, 56, 255–6
Woods, Maj David, ix, 188, 263
Wootton, Frank, 246, 264
Wray, Col Ady, ix, 180–1, 200

Young, Lt Geoff, 143, image 21
Young, Jerry, 146
Yuksecova, Turkey, 211

Zabbar, Malta, 47–8
Zodiac, Zenith, 236, 271
ZU-23-2 anti-aircraft gun, 208, 220, 268–9

5.5-inch field gun, 18–19
25-Pounder field gun, 18
83 Grenade, smoke, 158–9, 209
105mm field gun, 19, 41, 60, 178
705 NAS, xiv, 27, 87, 95, 253, 264
714 NAS, 48, 254
737 NAS, 261
750 NAS, 183, 266
803 NAS, xi
809 NAS, 270
829 NAS, 266
845 NAS, 137, 250, 253
846 NAS, 137, 250
847 NAS, 239
848 NAS, 137, 254

3 Cdo Bde RM, 149, 182, 184–5, 190, 199, 201, 204
40 Cdo RM, x, 40–1, 44, 201, 212, 222
41 Cdo RM, 45–6, 51, 55, 61, 64–6
42 Cdo RM, xiv, xvi, 33, 65, 201, 225
45 Cdo RM, 104, 180, 201, 206, 212–13, 220
29 Cdo Regt RA, 46, 61, 201
59 Cdo Engr Sqn RE, 216
1 Regt AAC, 263
2 Flt AAC, 155
655 Sqn AAC, 77, 79, 85
656 Sqn AAC, 66, 258–9
659 Sqn AAC, 66, 99, 258–9
70 Ac Wksp REME, 130, 216
703 AMG, 216
IX Sqn RAF, 45
13 Sqn RAF, 52
33 Sqn RAF, 155
74 Sqn RAF, xv, 149
203 Sqn RAF, xv, 51, 53
208 Sqn RAF, 58, 248, 256
601 Sqn RAF, 256–7